III II II IIIIIIII III II II IIII IIIIIIIIIIII III IIII III

⟨⟨ **W9-BAT-775**

Galatians

By closely engaging with the distinctive features of the cultural setting of Galatians, and through application of insights from social identity theory, Philip Esler sets out a new understanding of Paul's rhetorical strategies as designed to establish and maintain desirable identity for his congregations in the face of competing Israelite claims. Major issues in the letter, such as the problem in Galatia, Paul's use of rhetoric, his previous relationship with the Christ-movement in Jerusalem and Antioch, righteousness and the law and the nature of life in the Pauline congregations, emerge in a fresh light as related to the overall aim of creating and legitimating group identity.

Galatians presents a highly innovative and detailed reading of one of the most important texts in the New Testament which is significantly different from all current interpretations. At the same time, by setting his exegetical results within a framework of intercultural theory, Philip Esler demonstrates how they may be brought into provocative association with our own experience. Paul emerges, paradoxically, both as a stranger to our culture, and as the bearer of a message which makes insistent claims upon us.

Philip F. Esler is Dean of Divinity and Professor of Biblical Criticism at the University of St Andrews.

New Testament Readings
Edited by John Court
University of Kent at Canterbury

Galatians

Philip F. Esler

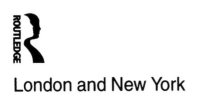

London and New York

First published 1998
by Routledge
2 Park Square, Milton Park, Abingdon, Oxon, OX14 4RN

Simultaneously published in the USA and Canada
by Routledge
270 Madison Ave, New York NY 10016

Transferred to Digital Printing 2006

© 1998 Philip F. Esler

The right of Philip F. Esler to be identified as the author of this work has been asserted by
him in accordance with the Copyright, Designs and Patents Act 1988

Typeset in Baskerville by RefineCatch Ltd, Bungay, Suffolk

All rights reserved. No part of this book may be reprinted or reproduced or utilised in any
form or by any electronic, mechanical, or other means, now known or hereafter invented,
including photocopying and recording, or in any information storage or retrieval system,
without permission in writing from the publishers.

British Library Cataloguing in Publication Data
A catalogue record for this book is available from the British Library

Library of Congress Cataloguing in Publication Data
A catalogue record for this book has been requested

ISBN 0–415–11036–X (hbk)
ISBN 0–415–11037–8 (pbk)

Publisher's Note
The publisher has gone to great lengths to ensure the quality of this reprint
but points out that some imperfections in the original may be apparent

Printed and bound by CPI Antony Rowe, Eastbourne

To Dominic, Thomas and Sinéad

'I greatly enjoyed Philip Esler's attempt to fill with life the difficult reasoning of *Galatians* in a way which would have made sense in Paul's mundane Mediterranean context. Esler combines discerning exegesis in the traditional style with fresh insights from cultural anthropology. Thereby he, in effect, demonstrates the fruitfulness of the historical approach – here enriched by social-scientific theory – to biblical texts against its vociferous recent critics. No scholar of *Galatians* can afford to neglect this book.'

Professor Heikki Räisänen, Professor of New Testament Exegesis
University of Helsinki

'Esler's reading of *Galatians* is fresh and highly stimulating. Through judicious deployment of social-scientific theory, he deftly illuminates the social strategies of this deeply significant letter.'

Dr John Barclay, Senior Lecturer in Biblical Studies
University of Glasgow

'Philip Esler has presented a social-scientific reading of Paul's letter to the Galatians that is consistent, clear and inventive. By reading through lenses provided by Mediterranean social anthropology and social identity theory, the author's every chapter offers a fresh perspective, new sets of ideas and lucid, readily comprehensible scenarios for understanding this most debated of authentic Pauline documents. Readers will come away with unexpected insights into the social identity of Paul's Galatian Christians, the focal quality of table fellowships in early Christianity and an appreciation of what righteousness, law and freedom meant to Paul's first-century audience.'

Professor Bruce J. Malina, Professor in the Department of Theology
Creighton University, Nebraska

'Philip Esler uses his extensive knowledge of the social sciences to offer numerous fresh insights into Paul's most polemical letter. This fine book is so lucid that it is accessible to students. The author cannot write a dull paragraph: every page sparkles as the reader is encouraged to consider the text from new perspectives. His reading of *Galatians* will stimulate and sometimes provoke scholars for a long time to come. This book is a major contribution to New Testament scholarship.'

Professor Graham Stanton, Lady Margaret's Professor of Divinity
University of Cambridge

Contents

Illustrations

Series editor's preface

This volume has every right to stand on its own, as a significant contribution to the study of the book of the New Testament with which it is concerned. But equally it is a volume in a series entitled *New Testament Readings*. Each volume in this series deals with an individual book among the early Christian writings within, or close to the borders of, the New Testament. The series is not another set of traditional commentaries, but is designed as a group of individual interpretations or 'readings' of the texts, offering fresh and stimulating methods of approach. While the contributors may be provocative in their choice of a certain perspective, they also seek to do justice to a range of modern methods and provide a context for the study of each particular text.

The collective object of the series is to share with the widest readership the extensive range of recent approaches to Scripture. There is no doubt that literary methods have presented what amounts to a 'new look' to the Bible in recent years. But we should not neglect to ask some historical questions or apply suitable methods of criticism from the Social Sciences. The origins of this series are in a practical research programme at the University of Kent, with an inclusive concern about ways of using the Bible. It is to be hoped that our series will offer fresh insights to all who, for any reason, study or use these books of the early Christians.

John M. Court
Series Editor

Preface

I began the research into Galatians which appears in this book in the early 1990s by considering Gal. 2.1–14 as an example of conflict in Mediterranean culture. Even then, however, a view I had reached earlier (Esler 1987: 87–89), that Peter had been advocating circumcision in Antioch (Gal. 2.14), was central to my position. In 1992 Dr John Court, the editor of the series of readings of New Testament texts in which this volume appears, kindly invited me to contribute a volume to it and then accepted my suggestion of Galatians.

Over the years I have published a series of essays exploring various parts of the letter (1994: 52–69; 1995c; 1996a; 1997); these were preceded by my delivering earlier versions in St Andrews and at seminars or conferences in Portland (Oregon), Sheffield, Sydney, Cambridge, Oslo and Chicago. On each occasion I profited from the responses of those present.

I have also greatly benefited from discussions with Richard Bauckham, Ron Piper, Michael Keeling, Jim Davila and Trevor Hart at St Mary's, and from very useful responses to written versions of some sections from John Barclay of Glasgow University and Mark Nanos, now at St Mary's. The views expressed here, however, are my responsibility and not theirs.

I have completely rewritten for the purposes of this book any material which has already been published, both to accommodate it to my developing views on theoretical aspects, such as interculturalism and social identity, and also to abbreviate or expand as appropriate. The material in Chapters 1, 6, 7 and most of Chapter 2 has not been published previously in any form.

Early in 1997, Dr Ralph Waller, the Principal of Harris Manchester College, Oxford, most helpfully arranged for me to spend a period of time at the college while I read and gathered some essential recent material on social identity theory in various Oxford libraries.

I am grateful, as ever, for the assistance and encouragement I have received from the staff at Routledge, especially Richard Stoneman, the senior editor responsible, Coco Stevenson, editorial assistant, and Sarah Brown, desk editor.

My wife Patricia has endured the problems of a partner preoccupied with a long-running project like this cheerfully and without complaint in spite of the busy demands of her own career.

Finally, I dedicate the book to our children, Dominic (12), Thomas (11) and Sinéad (9), who will see its completion as greatly improving the prospect of access to my computer for more enjoyable purposes.

St Andrews
St Patrick's Day 1998

Abbreviations

TEXT

ET	English Translation
JB	Jerusalem Bible
LSJ	Liddell, Scott and Jones, *Greek–English Lexicon*
MPG	Migne Patrologia Graeca
NEB	New English Bible
NRSV	New Revised Standard Version
NT	New Testament
OT	Old Testament
RSV	Revised Standard Version

REFERENCES

ABD	*The Anchor Bible Dictionary*
ASOR	American School of Oriental Research
BJRL	*Bulletin of the John Rylands Library*
BTB	*Biblical Theology Bulletin*
CurrTM	*Currents in Theology and Mission*
HTR	*Harvard Theological Review*
JBL	*Journal of Biblical Literature*
JJS	*Journal of Jewish Studies*
JRS	*Journal of Roman Studies*
JSJ	*Journal for the Study of Judaism*
JSNT	*Journal for the Study of the New Testament*
JSOT	*Journal for the Study of the Old Testament*
NovT	*Novum Testamentum*
NTS	*New Testament Studies*
OCD	*Oxford Classical Dictionary*
SBLDS	Society of Biblical Literature Dissertation Series

SBLSBS	Society of Biblical Literature Sources for Biblical Study
SJT	*Scottish Journal of Theology*
SNTS	Society for New Testament Studies
TDNT	*Theological Dictionary of the New Testament*
WUNT	Wissenschaftliche Untersuchungen zum Neuen Testament
ZNW	*Zeitschrift für die Neutestamentliche Wissenschaft*

Chapter 1

Reading Galatians

READING GALATIANS INTERCULTURALLY

Paul wrote his letter to the congregations of Galatia (located in Turkey) some time in the period from the late 40s to the mid-50s of the first century CE.[1] It is a short document, comprising six chapters and totalling only 149 verses, yet packed with historical, social and theological material of the highest significance. We are distanced from its creation, however, by nearly two thousand years and by a vast expanse of geographic and cultural space. How am I, a modern New Testament critic, to set about reading this letter at the dawn of a new century and a new millennium? Or how am I to set about explaining my reading to contemporaries who are equally distant from Paul and his Galatian audience? What does 'reading' even mean in this context?

Thirty years ago, perhaps, New Testament commentators could launch upon an interpretation of a text like Galatians reasonably untroubled by questions of method such as these, but that is no longer possible today. The pre-Socratic philosopher Heraclitus vividly expressed his belief in the dominance of change in human experience by saying that 'you could not step into the same river twice',[2] a position on the nature of reality summarised in the phrase *panta rhei* ('everything flows').[3] For someone involved in New Testament interpretation at present, *panta rhei* seems an apt summary in view of the rapid and continuous changes occurring in the field.[4]

Since at least the early 1970s the established mode of biblical criticism, the historical-critical method, which aims at retrieving the original meaning of biblical texts using historiographical techniques unrestrained by dogmatic beliefs, and which as far as the New Testament is concerned was largely developed by Ferdinand Christian Baur and David Friedrich Strauss in the 1830s and then refined by the source, form and redaction critics, has been under serious pressure. First, it has been challenged by the rise of literary criticism, which explores narrative and aesthetic dimensions of biblical texts commonly neglected by historical criticism and, very often, reacts against a perception of the Bible as an historical relic by seeking to find contemporary meanings in its pages. Second, social-scientific critics have argued that the historical method stands in need of fundamental overhaul, though not replacement, so as to bring within its scope the results of more than a century of research by anthropologists, sociologists and social psychologists.[5] Third, the whole enterprise of historical biblical criticism has come under postmodernist attack, for the reason that it allegedly represents one of the prime metanarratives of post-Enlightenment rationality, riddled, for example, with unsustainable claims to objectivity.

In spite of the flux which now characterises the field, most commentators hold a general position with respect to New Testament texts (such as Galatians), a still centre of a turning world, and it will be helpful if I briefly set forth mine here.[6] My guiding principle is to treat the New Testament texts primarily as communications from people (some of them known and some unknown) in first- and early second-century CE Mediterranean settings who had something of moment to say to other persons contemporaneous with them whom they thought would benefit from what was said.[7] They were the bearers of good news which they wished to pass on to others.

This may seem a rather commonsensical and unsurprising view to those unfamiliar with current debate in this area. Yet it sharply distinguishes my position from that of critics who favour focusing on the theological meanings to be gathered (or created) from the texts by readers in the present and who are attracted to the notion of the biblical texts as aesthetic artefacts (see Francis Watson 1994: 15). Critics such as these would be unhappy with the way my view privileges the elucidation of the meanings of biblical texts in the circumstances of their origin. In adopting this as my leading principle I have, in fact, situated myself on one side of a noticeable divide that has opened up in the field which, as we will soon see, largely mirrors a fundamental distinction in modern research as to how best to envisage the nature of communication and of 'reading' a text. Towards the end of this chapter I will set out a case that there are certain ethical implications to this dispute. On the other hand, I will make clear below my own position on how the meaning of biblical texts uncovered on the basis of this principle can function in our own setting.

Recognising and bridging the cultural divide

Inextricably linked to my position is the necessity of fully acknowledging the huge cultural gap between the New Testament authors and us. Unless we take steps positively to overcome this barrier, to comprehend the meanings of their utterances in their first-century contexts, we will never come near to understanding what they are saying, just as we discover today, if we travel or live among peoples of foreign cultures, that mere facility with the local language is no guarantee of understanding. Thus, we must also employ strategies for situating the words and gestures used in their very different cultural contexts; a wink might be an invitation to a pleasant liaison in one culture and a warning to keep away in another. If we do not face up to this cultural distance we remain at risk of ethnocentrically imposing our own taken-for-granted notions of reality onto a people who may simply not share them, of assuming that our understanding is their understanding. To reach some general comprehension of the distant culture of the first-century Mediterranean world we are able to profit from the work of anthropologists who have investigated contemporary societies which are remote in various ways from our own North Atlantic culture. Recent anthropological research into the Mediterranean area itself will be used extensively in this reading as one part of an array of social-scientific theory brought to bear on Galatians.

A good example of the issue at stake here arises with respect to a terminological point of some moment for this reading – the use of the words 'Christian', 'Jew' and 'Jewish' in connection with phenomena around the middle of the first century when Paul wrote Galatians. Some scholars have refused to use the word 'Christian' or 'Christianity' in relation to followers of Jesus in the first two generations after the Crucifixion because the Greek word *Christianos* only comes to be applied to them late in the first century.[8] But a more fundamental reason for avoiding these words is that because we are so familiar with 'Christian' and 'Christianity' we risk unconsciously imposing modern associations of these words on ancient data if we apply them to the early generations of the Jesus movement. Accordingly, these terms will not be employed in this reading with respect to phenomena in the first century CE, except where used in quotations. These words will, however, be used in other contexts in what follows, especially in relation to our contemporary situation.[9]

Yet scholars who avoid 'Christian' for the New Testament period continue to employ the expressions 'Jew', 'Jewish' and 'Judaism', to translate *Ioudaios* and *Ioudaismos*, notwithstanding the fact that they are affected by a similar anachronistic difficulty. Even though there has been great sensitivity in recent years to the need to recognise the diversity of outlooks and behaviour among Israelites in the first century CE (hence the frequent preference for 'Judaisms' over 'Judaism'), commentators have generally given little thought to the very appropriateness of 'Jew' and 'Judaism'. Yet our understanding of these words is inevitably shaped by events which occurred after the composition of the New Testament texts. Prominent among these events were the generation by the House of Israel of a new identity for themselves around orally transmitted legal traditions eventually codified in the Mishnah from 200 CE onwards, their fortunes in the medieval period and their fate in Nazi Europe. John H. Elliott, on the other hand, has argued recently that during the first century CE the effect of *Ioudaios* and *Ioudaismos* was to designate the ethnic group which originated in the geographical region known to the Greeks and Romans as Judea (from which the words are derived), with the word initially employed by outsiders but later becoming a self-appellation (Elliott 1997). Unfortunately, to translate *Ioudaios* as 'Judean', a solution recently adopted by the editors of the *Biblical Theology Bulletin*, is at present somewhat misleading in English, since we already use 'Judean' in a limited sense to designate the actual inhabitants of Judea. Accordingly, in this reading I will employ 'Israelite' (which was, in fact, a self-designation of the descendants of Abraham in the first century – see Rom. 11.1 and 2 Cor. 11.22), and, occasionally, the adjective 'Judaic', which does not seem to me to be affected by the same problems as 'Jewish', or I will simply transliterate the Greek words themselves.[10]

Once we have done our best to pierce the barrier of cultural difference between ourselves and the authors and original readers of the New Testament, the way is open for us to acquire a deep understanding of these utterances from another culture and to enjoy the richness of insight which comes from being an 'intercultural' person – able to stand with one's feet in two cultures and to analyse and assess one with respect to the other. There is a growing literature, to which I will refer below, which charts the nature and benefits of interculturalism. One aim of this reading of Galatians is to introduce this field as offering a promising new way of bringing biblical meanings into our contemporary experience. Biblical interculturalism represents a hermeneutics derived from social rather than philosophical sources.

We must, however, be open to the fundamental cultural diversity represented in the documents of the New Testament. At one level this reflects the geographic and ethnic variety encompassed in the Mediterranean region. In addition, although the New Testament texts originated there, in many vital respects they represent subversions of its culture. They are pervasively counter-cultural with respect to the world in which they were written. Accordingly, an important issue in a reading such as this is to acknowledge both the extent to which Paul reflects the Mediterranean culture in which he had been socialised while also recognising the degree to which he manifests a new, even subversive, culture based upon the unique impact of the Christian revelation. Indeed, to understand how far Paul diverges from cultural influences outside the Christian movement, we still need to appreciate them in their own terms; distinctiveness only manifests itself in contrast to the usual and the mundane.

Listening to our ancestors in faith

The particular communicators represented in the New Testament matter to me more than the other writers who survive from the ancient Mediterranean world. For the authors of the New Testament texts like Paul are my ancestors in faith; although remote in time and culture, they are the first extant witnesses of a new understanding of the relation of humanity and God which has continued to the present time so as to inform my own beliefs, values and identity. My attitude to these writers is rather like that of a family towards a distant cousin who arrives from across the sea bearing both a comforting sense of family identity and values but also harbouring certain outlooks and perspectives which are in discord with their own. They want to welcome their cousin into their midst, so as to renew their understanding of who they really are and what they stand for, while nevertheless wishing to make allowances for the extent to which his or her world and problems are not theirs.

These considerations lead to my reasons for adopting this approach. I cannot pretend to give a complete explanation in rational terms, as the reason lies as much in my own upbringing and identity as in any process of intellectual choice. Nevertheless, part of the answer rests on my view that although the Bible as a book plays a central role in Christian self-understanding, Christianity is not a religion of the book. Rather, Christianity is a religion of a series of revelatory acts to which certain texts bear witness in a manner which has subsequently been settled as authoritative (Grant with Tracy 1984: 177). The word 'biblicism' refers to gentler forms of the temptation to see Christianity as a religion of the book and 'fundamentalism' to the more extreme forms. Thus, for me at least, the biblical texts continually refer the reader to acts of divine revelation and to their significance for human beings beyond their pages. I am drawn to an interpretation which brings out this referential function, rather than one which is committed to understanding the texts *as texts*, which means as autonomous or quasi-autonomous imaginative worlds whose connection with their historical origins is not of much importance. Nevertheless, this view certainly does not entail that the form of the texts is not vital to the meanings they initially conveyed. Moreover, I believe that we should be ready to move to what the texts mean for us in the present, while maintaining that the earliest witness to the revelatory Christ-event found in the New Testament has primacy and later interpretations must be appropriate to it – at least in the sense of carefully engaging with the contextualised meanings conveyed when the texts were first published. I will explain my view on how canonisation of these texts affects the position later in this chapter.

The 'reading' attempted in this volume will focus primarily upon the meanings communicated by Galatians in its original context while also being alive to the manner in which such meanings can inform Christian experience in the present. For an intercultural interpretation must fix on two stages in the process of involvement with communications from another culture – first, the effort to comprehend them in their own terms and in their indigenous context and, second, the extent to which acquiring such insight leads to significant enrichment of our understanding in a whole range of areas, as the experience of a foreign culture is brought provocatively into dialogue with our own. For it is not enough to immerse ourselves in a foreign culture; sooner or later we usually come home and then we become the locus for a meeting between two cultures at odds with one another in various ways.

Having set out my broad approach to the reading, in the remaining sections of this Introduction I will develop four areas to pave the way for the detailed interpretation which is to follow in subsequent chapters: the broad approach to communication to be used; an elaboration of the model of intercultural communication which will be employed; the value of a historical reading in the face of recent attack; and, last, some hermeneutical and theological implications of the reading proposed.

TWO THEORIES OF COMMUNICATION: MESSAGE TRANSMISSION OR MEANING PRODUCTION?

I will first consider communication theory.[11] The modern study of communication is represented by two principal schools. The first, based on research conducted into the nature of communication using electromagnetic media (Shannon and Weaver 1949; Gerbner 1956), treats communication as the transmission of messages whereby one person affects or attempts to affect the behaviour or state of mind of another. It is concerned with how senders of messages formulate them for transmission (called 'encoding', although in a broad sense), how receivers make sense of them ('decoding', again in a broad sense), and with the channels and media of communication. It acknowledges the fact that receivers may construe a message in a sense different from that intended by the sender, so that whatever a sender intended, while important, forms only part of the phenomena of the communication. This may be referred to as the 'process' school of, or approach to, communication. The second school, stemming especially from the work of Swiss linguist Ferdinand de Saussure (1974), analyses communication as the production and exchange of meanings; it is concerned with how messages, especially texts, interact with people *to produce* meanings. Its main method of study is semiotics, the science of signs and meanings, and this is a convenient term by which to describe it (Fiske 1990: 2).

The process school draws upon the social sciences for resources to assist in its exploration of communicative *acts*, while the semiotics school utilises linguistics and the humanities (such as literary criticism) in its concern with *works* of communication. Thus, semiotics prefers the term 'reader' to 'receiver', since this suggests the greater degree of activity assumed under this approach, as the reader helps to create the meaning of the text by bringing to it his or her understanding and experience (Fiske 1990: 40). Nevertheless, even in the process model the use of the word 'reading' is quite appropriate for the interpretation of a written message, and the extent to which a person will conduct such a reading on the basis of his or her experience can be readily included in the theory. It is also quite consistent with this view to utilise a specific reading theory, such as those proposed by John Darr (1992: 16–36) or Bruce Malina (1996), since this merely constitutes the adaptation of the process theory of communication to the specific exigencies of a totally written communication emanating from a foreign culture.

From this admittedly brief outline of the two dominant theories of communication currently competing for attention, it will be apparent that my own approach to biblical interpretation lines up fairly closely with the process school, whereas the views from which I distinguished mine above broadly fall into the semiotics school. I do not wish to devalue the importance of semiotics and readily acknowledge that it will frequently offer useful insights in some areas; sometimes, indeed, both approaches may illuminate a particular problem (Fiske 1990: 4). A sensitivity to form and literary effect is often of critical significance in assessing meaning. The advantages of a semiotic approach are most obvious in the case of the gospels, given the narrative form they represent, while being far less clear with respect to the epistles. Nevertheless, even the gospels provide support for the process or purposeful message theory of communication. In the case of John's Gospel a statement at 20.30–31 unambiguously refers the reader to a reality beyond the text and to the extra-textual purpose of persuasion and witness embedded in it:

> Now Jesus did many signs in the presence of the disciples, which are not written in this book; but these are written that you may believe that Jesus is the Christ, the Son of God, and that believing you may have life in his name.
>
> (RSV)

A similar purpose of persuasion and confirmation appears in the dedication to Theophilus at the beginning of Luke's Gospel (1.1–4) and it is difficult, for me at least, not to imply such a perspective in the Gospels of Matthew and Mark, even though they contain no explicit statements of this kind.

In any event, to conduct the type of enquiry set out in this book – with respect to a letter actually directed to existing congregations in first-century Galatia – the process school plainly offers the most assistance. There are two particular issues with respect to which this is especially true. First, the historical dimension of the New Testament documents, that is, the extent to which their meaning is determined within their ancient Mediterranean contexts, is central to the process model but peripheral, at best, to the semiotic model. I have begun to set out the importance of history in this sense already and will expand upon this point later. Second, the process approach meshes closely with the practice of ancient rhetoric (aimed at persuading an audience to a particular view in a judicial proceeding, or on a political matter, or to a high or low estimation of a particular person) and the role of rhetoric will be a significant theme in this reading.

Within the terms of the perspective on communication I will adopt, therefore, the twenty-seven New Testament documents are the evidence for a process whereby, at a particular time and place, certain persons (the authors of the texts) reduced meanings into messages of a particular symbolic form, in this case the written word, for transmission to other persons (the express or implied recipients) and those written messages were in fact transmitted to them by delivery, as with actual letters like Galatians, or by publication, as with the gospels or other documents like the Acts of the Apostles and the Apocalypse, whereupon the recipients perceived and interpreted them, and possibly even acted on the basis of their interpretations. Furthermore, since all human communication takes place and is meaningful in particular contexts according to locally accepted standards of relevance, which is an insight lying at the heart of sociolinguistics (see Halliday 1978) but which also received philosophic support from Wittgenstein (1967), I consider that the context of these communications was of fundamental importance – both at the stage of the production of the messages ('encoding') and of their perception and interpretation ('decoding').

I will now set out the details of the model of intercultural communication to be deployed in this book, before defending the reading against current challenges to historical interpretation and justifying its importance for theology.

A MODEL OF INTERCULTURAL COMMUNICATION

The goal of interculturalism

It is possible to develop the process approach using insights generated in recent years by persons working on the nature and effectiveness of communication between persons of different cultures, a topic already introduced briefly above. This field has developed with the very practical purpose of helping persons (usually from North Atlantic cultures) with professional responsibilities in foreign cultures in areas such as voluntary work, drought and famine relief, medicine, nursing, teaching and business to understand and communicate with persons they encounter.[12] The relevance of this area of research lies in the fact that the cultural distance between us and the authors of the New Testament raises problems of comprehension analogous to those we experience when exposed to contemporary foreign cultures. It offers the prospect of providing techniques and strategies for understanding and assimilating the messages sent by our ancestors in faith – from another country and long ago.

It is worthwhile pausing for a moment to reflect upon the benefits of becoming competent in a foreign culture, of becoming an intercultural person. The movement from monoculture to interculture is a process of social and psychic growth whereby we come to integrate new elements of life with a clearer understanding of the nature of our own cultural conditioning (Gudykunst and Kim 1992: 255). We become more open to change and, having the perspective of each culture with which to assess the other, we become more capable of critical reflection on the values and institutions of both. The process is neither an easy nor a straightforward one. Nevertheless, the experience of immigrants and sojourners (which in the biblical tradition goes back as far as Abraham) proves that the goal of becoming an intercultural person is not an impossibly difficult one. To become intercultural with respect to the culture and counter-culture found in the New Testament offers the prospect of a similar enrichment of understanding, rendered critical in nature by the recognition that some of the problems facing our ancestors in faith who produced the documents were not ours and arose in relation to local values regarding issues such as slavery which are no longer part of our moral universe. Some of the more objectionable examples of first-century ideologies represented in the New Testament have recently been analysed by David Horrell (1995) and Raymond Hobbs (1995).

Modelling intercultural communication

To undertake the interpretation of Galatians offered in this book, it is necessary to set out in more detail the dynamics of the process of communication between members of different cultures. According to two leading writers in this field (Gudykunst and Kim 1992), the context of such communications can be divided into four distinct elements, which we may describe as 'influences': culture, groups and social roles, the individual and the environment.[13] To these I will add a fifth, which arises from the textual and structured nature of the communications under consideration: rhetoric and genre. I will now deal with each of these in turn, incorporating details specifically related to Paul's letter to the Galatians.

Culture

Every person carries within him or herself patterns of feeling, thinking, valuing and potential action which are learned during one's lifetime. These patterns constitute 'culture'. We may regard culture as a form of programming, while always bearing in mind the case argued strongly of late by British anthropologists Anthony Cohen (1994) and Nigel Rapport (1993), that individuals sometimes deviate from patterns of cultural conditioning and even manipulate them to their advantage. The process of enculturation begins within the family (where we are exposed to primary levels of socialisation, especially as far as learning who we are and how we should behave), and continues within the local community, at church and school (where we appropriate in various degrees rituals, symbols, cognitive traditions and further grounding in value systems), at work, in sporting and social clubs and so on.

We need to be open to the extent to which culture is shared within members of significant groups, where it refers to a broad system of knowledge common to the group and covering important values, symbols and ideas with reference to which the members interact with one another and with strangers in established settings and in new or ambiguous situations. At the same time, however, the variety of groups of all types into which human beings are enculturated, from the nation at one level to the family at the other, generates tremendous cultural diversity. The failure to recognise such diversity at the national level produces ethnocentrism – the assumption that the rest of the world is really like us (or if it is not, it should be) – which is not uncommonly exhibited by North Americans and Europeans with respect to persons of other national groups, as exemplified in 'the ugly American'.

In recent years a great deal of research has been conducted to isolate the variables which might be relevant to developing a taxonomy of national cultures. This research stems from the work of Dutch social scientist Geert Hofstede who in 1980 published *Culture's Consequences*, an analysis of over 100,000 questionnaires completed by the employees of a multi-national company (IBM) then operating in some fifty countries around the world. On the basis of his results Hofstede was able to isolate five variables which could be used to characterise the national cultures which were represented in his sample. These were:

1 the respective significance of the individual and the group, where 'individualism' refers to societies in which the ties between individuals are loose and 'collectivism' is the opposite and pertains to societies in which people from birth onwards are integrated into strong, cohesive ingroups, which provide protection in exchange for loyalty (Hofstede 1994: 51);
2 the differences in social roles between men and women;
3 the manner of dealing with inequality (with 'power distance' referring to the acceptance of inequality in a society, where 'high' power distance refers to a comparatively high tolerance of unequal power distribution, with its opposite being 'low' power distance [1994: 26]);
4 the degree of tolerance for the unknown; and
5 the trade-off between long-term and short-term gratification of needs (see Hofstede 1994: 23–138).

It is important to note that Hofstede found that individualist countries were far less common than collectivist and comprised mainly the USA, the nations of northern Europe and their ex-colonial offshoots, such as Australia and New Zealand. The countries around the Mediterranean formed part of the majority in being rather collectivist in orientation (1994: 53). Across the world, therefore, individualism was the exception not the rule. Interesting confirmation of this has come from another direction, in the work of the philosopher Charles Taylor, who has charted the ways in which the modern individualist self has developed in the last few centuries in northern Europe and countries which derive their culture from them in his book *The Sources of the Self* (1989).

Although Hofstede's study had its limitations (such as the fact that it was based on a fairly well-off and educated sample of persons from each country), it has stood up well in recent research. A Chinese study achieved results not too different from Hofstede, which suggests that the idea of classifying national cultures on the basis of certain variables is a reasonable one (Smith and Bond 1993: 38–46).

One does not need to accept the accuracy of the *particular* classification of nations on the strength of these variables offered by Hofstede to recognise the benefit they offer in assisting us to face up to cultural diversity and to expose ethnocentrism. This diversity suggests that we should hardly be surprised to find that New Testament texts presuppose – admittedly at a fairly high level of generality – a Mediterranean culture quite different from our own, late twentieth-century North Atlantic cultural patterns, as recently argued by several scholars, using models derived from anthropological research into modern Mediterranean countries.[14] This Mediterranean culture primarily relates to the earliest level of socialisation, acquired above all within families, and includes features such as a strong group orientation, patrilineal kinship patterns, the importance of honour as a primary value, the belief that all goods are limited and usually indivisible and the use of patron–client relations to overcome some of the consequences of that belief. Yet, as already noted, culture extends beyond this level to include elements acquired during worship and at school and work. In appropriate places, therefore, we will need to move beyond features such as these to take into account the role played by Graeco-Roman philosophical and literary influences, by Israelite law, (monotheistic) theology and tradition (for example, the figure of Abraham), and also popular views on religion, philosophy and ethics, while always recognising that Mediterranean cultural patterns pervasively underlie these phenomena as well.

Groups and social roles

The second influence on a communication is the set of groups to which we belong, the family above all, but also the town in which we live, our religious and ethnic affiliation and employment. This influence includes the social roles we fill, the extent to which these affect the way we see ourselves in relation to them and the way we interact with others. Groups are significant for our identity and day-to-day existence, but, as we have just seen, their level of significance varies greatly from culture to culture and we should not expect to find atypical North Atlantic individualism in New Testament texts. In Chapter 2 I will set out a social-scientific perspective known as social identity theory which has the potential to shed fresh light on Galatians by virtue of its interest in how groups interrelate and develop identity for their members in relation to one another. In Chapter 3 I will employ this theory, amplified in the area of the nature of boundaries which exist between groups where there is some element of ethnicity, to consider how tensions between the three groups which are affecting Paul's mission in Galatia – Israelites, gentiles, and Israelite and gentile Christ-followers – contributed to Paul's decision to write Galatians and the substance of the communication conveyed by it.

Individuality

The third influence is that of our own distinctive individuality. No two persons in the same culture are the same, even if members of one family, and such distinctiveness impacts on the communications they produce. The stress upon the cultural and social influences on communication in no way prejudices the importance of individuals in this process, even if the evidence for their involvement is often scarce in historical texts except for that of a few conspicuous figures.

To employ social-scientific research, moreover, does not entail neglect of the individual. Indeed Anthony Cohen has insisted on the importance of attending to the self in ethnography and stresses, for example, the extent to which individuals use group boundaries to achieve individual ends rather than being defined and delimited by them (1994). It is not easy, however, to emphasise the individual component in groups inaccessible to direct examination, such as those for whom ancient texts were written, and it is harder still for a text like Galatians where, in contrast with 1 Corinthians for example, not a single person in Galatia is named. Thus, although we will focus on the social dimensions of the data we should not forget the individuals comprising the groups discussed to whom we have no access.

Nevertheless, this recognition must not induce us to forget that some cultures, such as those of the Mediterranean region, tend to be much less given to individualism and much more group-oriented than ours and this must be borne in mind in considering any text originating in a foreign culture stamped with such a feature.

The environment

The fourth influence is that of the environment. Geographical location, climate, architecture and the physical aspects of lifestyle all condition the way in which we encode messages for transmission and decode them when received. The major environmental factors which will feature in my reading of the letter will be the unique nature of the Galatian setting and the importance of domestic architecture in the context of Paul's version of the gospel and his strategy for dealing with the problems at hand.

Genre and rhetoric

All of the four contextual influences just mentioned will be highly visible in any communication between persons of different cultures. The fifth influence however, of genre and rhetoric, is relevant inasmuch as the communications found in the New Testament texts are couched in the form of literary genres (such as Letter, Gospel, or Apocalypse) and frequently employ rhetorical techniques of persuasion. Although I am unwilling to read these texts primarily as literary creations, it is still necessary to come to terms with the literary form in which they are expressed, since this has a powerful effect on the meanings they communicate. For, as David Aune has correctly noted, literary genres and forms are not just 'neutral containers used as convenient ways to package various types of written communication. They are social conventions that provide contextual meaning for the smaller units of language and text they enclose' (1987: 13). The nature of epistolography in the ancient world, for example, is a lively field of research to which reference will be made below.[15]

The rhetorical aspect focuses on the extent to which New Testament texts are carefully structured communications delivered to particular audiences in ancient settings with the aim of persuading them to, or dissuading them from, a particular view or a particular course of action. The recent resurgence of interest in rhetoric, which closely links the form of a discourse to a particular situation and audience in which it is communicated, provides an important bridge between literary-critical and social-scientific approaches to biblical texts, as shown in Vernon

Robbins' significant efforts to bring the two fields together (1995, 1996).

I will propose below that an essential element in the reason for Paul's writing Galatians and for the content of the letter was to persuade his readers to adopt certain attitudes and to behave (or to refrain from behaving) in certain ways. In the ancient Graeco-Roman world a person who sought to persuade someone to a certain point of view or action usually employed rhetorical techniques. Rhetoric originated in the Greek city-state, the *polis*, of the fifth century BCE, where it played a vital role in the civic life in three broad contexts: the law courts (to persuade the jurors to adopt some view of an event in the past), the assemblies (to persuade the people to, or dissuade them from, some course of action in the future, such as the commencement of a foreign war), and in speeches of praise or blame (aimed at persuading an audience that someone was honourable or dishonourable). In due course, the types of rhetoric appropriate in these contexts came to be referred to as judicial, deliberative (or political) and epideictic (or encomiastic) respectively. So important was rhetoric that its theory was formulated at quite an early date by Greeks, such as Isocrates (died 338 BCE), Aristotle (384–322 BCE) in his *Rhetorica*, the author of the *Rhetorica ad Alexandrum* (written in 86–82 BCE),[16] and many others, who were followed by Romans like Cicero (106–43 BCE) and Quintilian (35 to the 90s CE).

Familiarity with rhetoric was universal among any educated person in the Graeco-Roman world. Although study of works like these formed a central part of the education of young men in the *gymnasia* (the universities of the time), great attention was also paid to preparatory rhetorical study at the pre-gymnasium or secondary-school level, which children undertook for a year or two once they had finished the primary level at about age 14 (Marrou 1956: 147, 238–242). Indeed, works of simplified rhetorical instruction called *progymnasmata* were developed for students at this level and examples survive by Aelius Theon, Aphthonius of Ephesus, Hermogenes of Tarsus and Menander Rhetor.[17] Moreover, public declamations by rhetoricians were a popular form of entertainment and virtually every speech made by an educated speaker in public or private was redolent with rhetorical figures and style. This meant that all those living in a city in the ancient Graeco-Roman world (which, as we will see in Chapter 2, included Galatia), even if they had not received a rhetorical education, were exposed at some time or other to the variety of rhetorical structures and styles (Aune 1987: 12–13). As a result, anyone who wished to persuade an audience to a particular view or action would inevitably have been impelled by this aspect of the culture to utilise rhetoric.

Until quite recently, however, many biblical commentators, like their colleagues in other fields, deprecated rhetoric as mere form, as verbal cleverness used to adorn the communication of ideas, and were unwilling to take it seriously in the interpretative task (Pogoloff 1992: 7–15). Although such a perception was fostered by a dispute between philosophy and rhetoric dating from Socrates' disagreement with the Sophists, the immediate antecedents for the trivialisation of rhetoric lay in the nineteenth century, notably in Germany, and were related to the development of the new scholarly disciplines which took place then (Kinneavy 1983; Rüegg 1993). We have now entered a period, however, in which a major reassessment of rhetoric is under way; in short, we are witnessing 'the recovery of rhetoric' (Roberts and Good 1993), both in terms of its impact in our own intellectual environment and a heightened appreciation of its status in the ancient Mediterranean world.

A significant impetus to this process was the 'New Rhetoric' of Chaim Perelman and Lucie Olbrechts-Tyteca (1969), who proposed that rhetoric had the capacity to reintegrate fields of human activity riven apart by Cartesian dualisms, especially that between mind and will. They argued that rhetoric aimed to induce particular actions, or assent to certain theses, by appealing to the whole range of human faculties, not just Cartesian rationality, in situations in which there might be no prior agreement on appropriate decision-making criteria (Vickers 1993: 39–43).

A central insight in the recovery of rhetoric has been the growing realisation that the scholarly disciplines, although ostensibly hostile to rhetoric, were actually constructed, legitimated and institutionalised using persuasive discourses directed at particular audiences. Moreover, the recognition that the disciplines are so dependent on rhetoric lessens the extent to which they can claim autonomy for their methodologies and paves the way for interdisciplinary conversation and co-operation. At the same time, although the return to rhetoric may seem to reflect the postmodernist attack on disciplinary metanarratives and their alleged foundations in rationality (Lyotard 1984), rhetoric rightly understood as a 'comprehensive and sophisticated mode of analysis' may actually be able to 'do much to counter the fragmenting and relativistic aspects of the postmodern condition'. It has the potential to contribute to the rehabilitation of 'grand' or 'totalising theories' which have a 'critical intent' (Roberts and Good 1993: 10, 12).

Coinciding with this interest in the general importance of rhetoric has been renewed attention to classical Greek and Latin literature on the subject and the extent to which rhetoric was employed in New Testament texts. One of the leading writers on Greek and Roman rhetoric,[18] George Kennedy (1963 and 1980), has also investigated the impact which rhetoric can have on New Testament interpretation (1984). In line with this trend, recent Pauline scholarship has increasingly recognised the influence of rhetoric in the letters the apostle wrote to his various congregations throughout the Mediterranean region (Betz 1979; M. Mitchell 1991; Pogoloff 1992; Witherington 1997) and the rhetorical dimensions of Galatians will be an important theme in this reading. While ancient rhetorical theory is often sufficient for reading the biblical texts, it is sometimes helpful to introduce insights from 'the new rhetoric'.[19]

A rhetorical approach to interpretation is particularly useful in a reading such as this for the reason that it is inseparably associated with the historical question of what a particular biblical text like Galatians meant for its first audience. This is seen in the foundational importance of what Lloyd F. Bitzer has called the 'rhetorical situation' of a communication, including a written one (1968). By this he means the situation which provokes the communication and profoundly shapes it and which comprises an 'exigence' (some imperfection in social affairs marked by urgency), an audience (persons capable of being influenced by discourse to change in some way or another) and certain constraints (such as persons, events, values, beliefs, interests) which have the power to restrain any decision or action needed to modify the exigence. As far as Paul's letter to the Galatians is concerned, the *exigence* consists of the fact that gentile members of the congregations he founded in Galatia are beginning to succumb to pressure to become Israelites through circumcision, together with problems internal to the congregations; the *audience* are those to whom he writes (who are largely gentile believers); while the *constraints* include the persons who are pushing them towards circumcision, Israelite traditions concerning righteousness, Abraham and gentile sinfulness, the propensity for dissension within the congregations and the perception of Paul current among them.

Since a rhetorical situation actually exists in the world of lived experience, and the purpose of the discourse is for the speaker or writer to persuade his or her audience to a particular decision, it is clear that they both share a real historical situation and this must be taken into account when interpreting the discourse. While none of this is to deny that presentation of the actual world in the text will have been 'reconstructed' by the author, it does place definite limitations on how far that reconstruction might diverge from reality as perceived by its intended audience. The claim by one critic (Vatz 1973) that no situation can have a nature independent of the rhetoric which the speaker chooses to characterise it plainly reveals the unacceptable side of the postmodernist turn to the subject and its weakness before a realist epistemology. Effective rhetorical discourse presupposes that the speaker and his or her audience share a basic understanding of the facts at issue and some measure of communality as far as beliefs and values are concerned.

We have now reached a point, therefore, where our interest in the historical dimension of Galatians, its meaning for its original audience, has been shown to require an investigation of the text as a discourse written in a particular rhetorical situation with the aim of dissuading its audience from various types of inappropriate behaviour or attitude. Such an approach is a step towards the production of an integrated understanding of Galatians in its actual and rhetorical setting, especially in the promise it offers of being able to shed light on the shape and strategies of Paul's argument.

In recent years there has been great interest in analysing Galatians from the standpoint of ancient rhetoric, beginning with an article by Hans Dieter Betz (1975), largely reproduced in his Galatians commentary (1979), which put the case that Galatians was structured along established rhetorical lines and exhibited the typical sequence of elements found in rhetorical handbooks and actual speeches.[20] Betz' views have inspired much discussion by, for example, Kennedy (1984: 144–152); Hester (1984 and 1991); Lyons (1985: 112–119); Gaventa (1986); Hall (1987 and 1991); Vouga (1988) and Smit (1989), to name only a few.

Betz assumed a very extensive appropriation of rhetoric in Galatians, so that he saw fit to erect arguments on the basis of formal comparison with rhetorical theory and practice to make points about the letter. A reaction to this approach has now begun to appear, however. At a general level, there is much force in the comment of Anderson that merely labelling some aspect of a Pauline letter with a Greek or Roman word from the language of rhetoric is of little assistance unless coupled with some pertinent observation as to its function in the text (Anderson 1996: 34).

More specifically, however, there is growing concern that rhetorical readings of Paul's letters exaggerate the extent of overlap between rhetoric and epistolography in the Graeco-Roman world. Thus, at a theoretical level, rhetorical handbooks do not deal with letter-writing as a sub-category of rhetoric until the fourth century CE, while the epistolary handbooks by authors such as the *Typoi Epistolikoi* and the *Epistolimaioi Charactēres*, attributed (incorrectly) to Demetrius of Phalerum and Libanius respectively, treat rhetoric as a different genre. Some letters extant from the period which are heavily rhetorical lack typical epistolary features, and vice versa (Reed 1994). Three important considerations undergird the difference between the two genres: first, the much larger number of contexts in which a letter might be relevant compared with the three standard occasions for a rhetorical speech; second, the fact that the addressees of a letter were as a rule much closer personally to the writer, since they were usually relatives or close friends, than in the case of a public oration; and, third, the need for greater simplicity of style in the case of a letter, where the receivers of the communication could not seek immediate clarification from the speaker. These factors counsel against any automatic application of rhetorical analysis to letters.

Nevertheless, very often the author of a letter, although addressing someone far away and not directly in front of him or her, possibly even a friend or relation, was working in a framework which was functionally similar to a rhetorical one. For example, (Pseudo-)Demetrius of Phalerum recognises the 'advisory' (*symbouleutikos*) as one of his twenty-one types of letters, used to 'impel (someone) to something or dissuade (someone) from something' (*Typoi Epistolikoi* 11). In response to an accusing letter, he notes that someone might reply with a 'defensive' (*apologetikos*) one (*Typoi Epistolikoi* 18) and this certainly resembles the judiciai setting in rhetorical theory. As already noted, the use of rhetoric was universal in the ancient Graeco-Roman world and it is hard to envisage how anyone wanting to mount a persuasive case in a letter, especially where the situation was close to being judicial, deliberative or epideictic, could possibly have been unaffected by it. Accordingly, a functional use of rhetorical style in letters is to be expected in such cases.

Paul himself reveals an explicit interest in the question of rhetoric in a significant passage, namely, 5.7–10. Having noted that they got off to a good start, he asks 'who got in your way so you were persuaded [*peithesthai*] not with respect to the truth?' (5.7). Persuasion lies at the heart of rhetoric and here Paul raises the disquieting fact that a persuasion is abroad in Galatia which is distracting them from the truth. In the next verse he denies that such persuasion (*peismonē*) is from God, 'the one who calls you'. Because this is the first appearance of the word *peismonē* in Greek its meaning is not easy to determine (Betz 1979: 265). Nevertheless, we may be confident that it covers argumentation, no doubt expressed with the benefit of rhetorical techniques which Paul may even be seeking to decry. After citing in v. 9 a proverb to the effect that a little yeast leavens the whole, which had a negative connotation, because fermentation was seen as corruption (Betz 1979: 266; Dunn 1993: 276), Paul continues the imagery of persuasion by saying, 'I am persuaded [*pepoitha*] in relation to you in the Lord that you will not think otherwise' (5.10a). Even though Paul blackens the rhetoric employed against his version of the gospel in Galatia, it is clear that he will have to meet it and, as we will see later in this reading, large parts of Galatians do make good sense as his response to argument put forward by the opposition.

The question of intention

One last point must be made on the nature of the process approach to communication, namely, that the actual intention of the 'encoder' of the message, although significant, is not necessarily of decisive weight. This is not because of some concern with the 'intentional fallacy', a notion which derives from the New Criticism of W. K. Wimsatt and Monroe Beardsley in the 1940s and holds that the question of authorial intention is one which should not be raised in relation to literary works of art. The origins of sensitivity to the intentional fallacy lie in the rejection of approaches to the meaning of literary works tied to the biography of the author and the turn to more text-centred and formalistic criticism earlier this century (Jefferson and Robey 1986: 81–82). In other words, the 'intentional fallacy' is at home in the semiotic view of communication and has little application to the process approach adopted here, or to analogous non-semiotic interpretations adopted by many New Testament critics for whom history matters.

On a process view of communication the reason that intention is not necessarily of great significance is quite different. Any intended meaning must be embodied in a message under the impact of the five influences mentioned above and this allows great scope for a distance between intention and finished effect. The message must then be 'decoded' by persons affected by the same five influences, which makes even more likely the chance of divergence between intended and interpreted meaning. Even at the stage of the first publication of the texts we must assume that meanings were culled from them which were not envisaged by the authors.

Yet the fact that the meaning one person encodes is not the same as the meaning another decodes should not cause us too much despondency. As one theorist has noted: 'To say that meaning in communication is never totally the same for all communicators is not to say that communication is impossible or even difficult – only that it is imperfect' (Fisher 1978: 257). Robert Young has recently mounted a strong case along similarly pragmatic lines for the effectiveness of intercultural communication in spite of various postmodernist challenges to it (1996).

Moreover, as we seek to determine how the communications of the New Testament were understood by their initial audiences it is inevitable that we will find some meanings which did not occur to the first readers or listeners. We can only aim for approximations of ancient meanings. Nor can we avoid the fact that all interpretation of an ancient document is a dialogue between the past and the present; the point is that using communication theory depends on accepting that there is a past with which we may enter into dialogue.

HISTORY, ETHICS AND POSTMODERNISM

The canonical challenge to historical criticism

The synthesis of the message, context and form of a New Testament text which is the object of investigation that is intercultural in nature falsifies the claim, made quite emphatically by Francis Watson (1994: 15–57), that historical criticism is only interested in the prehistory of the texts, the diachronic processes that produced the documents in the form in which we now have them. Watson makes this assertion:

> It has been agreed that the primary task of biblical scholarship is to reconstruct the diachronic historical processes underlying the text as it now stands. One searches the text for the clues it may (perhaps inadvertently) offer as to its own prehistory.
>
> (Watson 1994: 15)

Yet this is to cite a non-existent consensus and to interpret the entirety of historical criticism primarily in the light of source and form criticism, thereby missing the distinctiveness of recent scholarship which has sought to discern meaning in the interrelationship of text and context at the date of initial publication and which constitutes historical research of a very different type. This manner of interpretation, in exploring the meaning of the biblical books in the circumstances in which they were published, is sociolinguistic by instinct, not archaeological.

An important part of Watson's case against historical criticism depends upon his privileging the event of canonisation of the texts, and not their involvement in first-century historical reality, as rendering them theologically significant. He goes so far as to suggest that it is 'inherent in the genre of (biblical) canonical text to be transmitted in a form which has erased, to a greater or lesser extent, most of the particularities of its circumstances of origin' and to welcome this alleged fact, since it subordinates 'a merely historical curiosity' about what was happening to 'the ability of the text to function in quite different later circumstances' (1994: 40).[21]

His argument suffers from his neglecting the possibility that a recognition of the historical character of biblical documents contributed to their being canonised, a process not completed until the end of the fourth century (Schneemelcher 1991: 33) or even later (Kelly 1977: 60). Historical consciousness characterised the ancient period far less than has been the case since the Enlightenment, but an inchoate sense of history certainly existed then. After all, the Antiochene school of interpretation favoured a literal-historical approach (Grant with Tracy 1984: 63–72) and a style of interpretation which pursued the historical task of relating the meaning of texts to their initial settings was raised to a brilliant pitch in Ambrosiaster's commentary on the Pauline corpus (Esler 1995c: 311).

Another, more specific, way to make this point is to examine the main criterion which was employed in the early Church to which works were accepted into the canon, namely, apostolicity, the extent to which the early Church sought to ground its tradition in Jesus and the apostles (McDonald 1995: 229–232; Kelly 1977: 60). The apostolic criterion employed by the Church was 'based upon the presumption that, since the apostles were close to Jesus historically, they must have a better knowledge of him and his ministry than others might have had' (McDonald 1995: 232). Although we now doubt the attestation of many (though not all) of the texts to various apostles, the fact that they were so attested shows the powerful drive to link them to particular historical figures. A similar interest in the centrality to the canonisation process of distinguishing true from false traditions is evident in the rejection of the apocryphal Gospels and Acts (Schneemelcher 1991: 33).

In other words, rather than following Watson in drawing a sharp distinction between the historical and canonical status of the texts, it is more accurate to say that their historical dimension was assumed and confirmed in the very process of canonisation. In sum, Watson (influenced by Brevard Childs) misunderstands the nature of canonisation; he attributes a particular significance to the biblical writings by virtue of their canonical status, whereas the better view is that their canonical status reflects a decision taken by the Church as to their worth on a number of grounds, including their historical value. If the Church in the late fourth century, concluding a process which began much earlier with the collection of the four Gospels by Irenaeus (McDonald 1995: 168), canonised the documents because, *inter alia*, they were thought to be connected with the actual events concerning Jesus, why should we follow critics like Watson and Childs in replacing this criterion with the mere fact of ecclesial recognition?[22] The texts were canonised because they were, over some 300 years of use in the Church, judged to be significant; they are not significant merely because they have been canonised and assertions to the contrary represent an unfortunate type of biblicism. On the other hand, in preserving an interest in the historical character of these documents, especially the extent to which they speak of primal events beyond their pages, we are directly connected with some of the oldest instincts of Christian belief.

The postmodernist challenge to history

More fundamentally, however, in the last decade the historical-critical method, very much a creature of post-Enlightenment modernity and its trust in the virtues of rational analysis, has found itself exposed to the critical eyes of postmodernism, before whose gaze it represents a meta-narrative of Western rationality, an ordered and comprehensive account of significant phenomena, ripe for a radical shake-up, if not deconstruction.[23] Of particular concern to postmodernist critics is the extent to which historical criticism purports to be based upon the objectivity of Enlightenment rationality while actually reflecting power relations of the academy, the Churches or society at large. The movement from investigated object to investigating subject which is characteristic of post-modernism[24] inevitably privileges contemporary rather than historical meanings for biblical texts. Although in this it is similar to literary criticism, its distaste for theory and its propensity to replace criticism with performance and (occasionally narcissistic) self-display differentiates it from both social-scientific and literary approaches.

Nevertheless, the postmodernist challenge necessitates searching examination of one's epistemological orientation, especially in relation to the realist/idealist spectrum, and involvement in particular kinds of power relationships, together with a humble acknowledgement of the subjective factors operative in any interpretative enterprise. We may be heartened in all this by the fact that even Heraclitus, for all his interest in the flux of experience, still insisted that there was a measure to change, a stability which persisted throughout its course (Kirk and Raven 1971: 187). In the same vein, one recent group of postmodernist critics concede that taking postmodernism seriously, which for them necessitates acknowledging the various systems of power which have kept particular interpretative strategies (and not others) in place,[25] still 'entails heeding the continuing importance of traditional forms of biblical criticism' (the Bible and Culture Collective 1995: 11).

Ethics and historical interpretation

One other matter related to historical interpretation requires attention. As noted above, the overall view I take to the New Testament documents is that they are communications from our ancestors in faith to their contemporaries on matters they deemed of great moment. In this context it can be argued (and I do not put it higher than this) that we are under an ethical obligation to seek, at some stage in the process of interpretation, to hear and understand their own voices in the historical context in which they were uttered, rather than rejecting such meaning in favour of the meanings we might produce from a text alleged to exist autonomously in relation to the circumstances of its creation. E. D. Hirsch has described readings of the first type as 'allocratic', meaning the voice of the other (*allos*) is allowed to prevail (*krateō*), and the second as 'autocratic', since the reader disregards the other, so as to produce his or her meaning from the text (1982). Autocratic readings of historical texts imply an exclusion of particular persons (namely, the actual author and the actual intended readers) from the interpretative task and represent a flight away from realist and objectivist claims (even modest ones) towards subjectivist and idealist claims. Yet Hirsch has argued that whether one pursues an allocratic or an autocratic approach is not itself a question of epistemology, but ultimately depends on one's values and politics. Hirsch goes so far as to assert that unless there is 'a powerful overriding value in disregarding an author's intention, we who interpret as a vocation should not disregard it' (1976: 90).

Yet Robert Morgan has written:

> Texts, like dead men and women, have no rights, no aims, no interests
> . . . it is the interests or aims of the interpreters that are decisive, not
> the claims of the text as such. Any suggestion that a text has rights is a
> deception concealing someone else's interests.
>
> (Morgan with Barton 1988: 7)

This seems an uncharacteristic lapse on Morgan's part, for moral discourse is not exhausted by the language of rights. While our deceased parents certainly have no rights, who would deny that we have a duty to honour their memory? It is not stretching the notion of obligation too far to suggest that we should honour the memory of our ancestors in faith who composed the New Testament works and the memory of those who received them. Our duty here is even clearer than it is to the women in the Old Testament, many of them unnamed (like Jephthah's daughter in Judges 12 or the savagely abused woman in Judges 19), who are rightly attracting demands by feminist critics that their memories, at long last, be honoured. We will honour the memory of the gospel writers, Paul and the rest, and the actual human beings for whom they wrote, if we continue to work on the basis that we should initially seek to understand what they were trying to communicate to one another and then to let ourselves be interculturally transformed by those communications.

The choice seems to come down to this. Either, while fully recognising that our cultural conditioning obscures our understanding, we do our best to listen to others, simultaneously strangers and kin, who produced the texts so that we may encounter the provocatively different (and interculturally enriching) account of the world they might offer; or, alternatively, we silence their voices and read the texts to create new meaning for ourselves, either for aesthetic reasons, or because of interest in agendas derived from systematic theology, or simply because we have embraced a postmodernist emphasis on the enquiring subject. It is submitted that there are ethical dimensions to this choice.

Conclusion

In this reading, accordingly, the historical dimension of Galatians will continue to provide the stable point of reference amidst the flux, although attention to the issues just mentioned, which are contributing to the current condition of New Testament studies, will figure in the discussion. Although the reading is interested in the challenge posed by postmodernism, it is predicated upon a critical realist epistemology which believes that we can learn (with much humility and circumspection) about a world – either in the present or in the past – outside ourselves,[26] and upon the view that some construals of the biblical world (especially those deploying social-scientific and rhetorical insights) are more plausible than others, that ethical issues are involved in continuing to seek the original meanings of biblical texts, and that there are ways of introducing the fruits of historical-critical research into our contemporary experience, ecclesial and social, for example by following the path of interculturalism.

THE HERMENEUTICAL AND THEOLOGICAL ASPECTS OF AN INTERCULTURAL READING

We now begin our final task – to consider the ever-pressing challenge of what theological interpretation of the Bible should look like in a historically conscious age. For some critics, such as Brevard Childs and Francis

Watson, the historical method has simply failed to provide resources for theological reflection and should be largely abandoned in favour of an approach which fixes instead on the canonisation of the biblical texts as the source of their significance. In arriving at a theology which does not unacceptably jettison the historical dimension, heremeneutical questions insistently demand attention. How can we balance the pre-understandings and assumptions we bring to the texts from our contemporary situation against the provocative insight, based on their cultural distance from us, that we derive from historical research? What strategies are open to those who wish to credit the biblical texts with a higher degree of historical facticity than postmodernist critics would allow, while seeking to pursue the intercultural route charted above?

One useful strategy, although not the only one, is Hans-Georg Gadamer's 'game of conversation', where the interaction between text and interpreter, between past and present (Eagleton 1983: 71), assumes a life of its own, a logic of question and response, analogous to a conversation (Gadamer 1984). Furthermore, a specifically theological type of conversation, heavily interpretative in character, favoured by David Tracy, is to correlate the claim to attention of the biblical text and the theologian's understanding of his or her contemporary situation in one of three ways: as confrontation, similarity or identity (Grant with Tracy 1984: 170–174). The strangeness of the biblical world from that of the post-Enlightenment North Atlantic countries provides a powerful impetus to the confrontational mode of correlation. Moreover, as I have argued elsewhere (1995a: 14–19), the findings produced by social-scientific biblical interpretation mesh closely with George Lindbeck's understanding of religion (as a cultural system informing its adherents with a particular story of reality), while the symmetry between the two offers a way of enriching the process of intercultural correlation. Moreover, while Lindbeck's approach does not entail an insouciance to the importance of the foundational truth of Christianity for its adherents nor mean the end of an explicit concern to defend the universal significance of Christian truth claims, which are common misinterpretations of his view (Esler 1995a: 16–17), it does involve the recognition that most Christians have less interest in the issue of truth than in the way the Christian story shapes their ongoing experience. Lindbeck invites us to consider that the highly intellectualist interests of most European theologians, which are focused around ontological and epistemological issues, have caused them to neglect the theological implications of the dynamic integration of tradition and everyday experience (especially of a social kind) which is as

How does the text shape my experience?

Theology too implicated in modern Western intellectualism

vital to Christianity as it is to other religions. Oxford theologian Robert Morgan astutely sums up the position as follows:

> Christian faith makes truth-claims, and therefore faces questions about knowledge, including the relationship of our knowledge of God to the rest of our knowledge. But the relative lack of attention to these questions in the New Testament warns against giving them undue prominence in the conception of faith itself. Their importance for subsequent reflection should not obscure the less intellectual character of the primary religious response.
>
> (Morgan 1989: 5)

As far as Paul is concerned, the problems of a theology too implicated in modern Western intellectualism are apparent in the writings of N. T. Wright, who perpetuates the idealistic fallacy exposed by Bengt Holmberg nearly twenty years ago (Holmberg 1978) in advocating (and frequently attempting) the study of Pauline theology as a set of 'thought-forms and thought-patterns' abstracted from their rhetorical and social setting (Wright 1991: 16–17). With respect to Galatians, for example, Wright goes so far as to argue that the true gospel from which the Galatians have turned away consists of a particular 'sequence of thought' (1994: 232–233), rather than its constituting a much larger reality embracing theological ideas but also critically important social dimensions of the relationship between Israelite and gentile, as will be argued below.

Moreover, even interpretative processes of the type advocated by Tracy largely typify the activities of individual theologians, most obviously in a North Atlantic setting. Yet the base communities of Latin America and local groups elsewhere which they have inspired reveal a different pattern, one in which the correlation between scriptural interpretation and the scrutiny of the contemporary situation are conducted by the communities themselves, with some help from theologians functioning as consultants rather than creators of the theology. In these contexts the value of non-elite readings of biblical text becomes apparent. For, in the end, although New Testament interpreters may provide exegetical results which can be appropriated by local communities seeking to undertake correlations of the type just mentioned, it is only those congregations who can make the earliest Christian story, critically understood, their story (Esler 1995a: 14–19). The only realistic prospects of developing an intercultural understanding of New Testament experience are located in Christian communities.

Yet as David Tracy has pointed out in criticism of Gadamer, the

Golenhname!

process of conversation needs to encompass both retrieval from the biblical writings and also their critical analysis, a hermeneutics of suspicion, to uncover any systematic distortions besetting the tradition (Grant with Tracy 1984: 160–164), such as revealed by David Horrell's ideological critique of some of the Pauline and pseudo-Pauline correspondence (1995). The theological rationale for engaging in strategies of suspicion is that the biblical texts themselves do not constitute the salvation event but rather are witness to it and stand to be judged for their fidelity to it. This dimension excludes biblicism as a useful theological option.

In sum, my preference remains with a strong historical emphasis, while eschewing the sterilities of historicism and biblicism – by accepting the need for greater self-reflexivity and the production of results through intercultural dialogue more capable of enriching contemporary Christian (and non-Christian) life and theology than has traditionally been the case. I certainly do not pretend that my work is value free and write with the aim that the reading of Galatians offered here will be capable of feeding into contemporary liberative discourses, something I had in mind (though not so developed) in my earlier work on Luke's Gospel and Acts (Esler 1987: 220–223).

Chapter 2

Social identity and the epistle to the Galatians

WHERE, WHEN AND WHY GALATIANS?

My principal aim in this chapter is to explain the main area of social theory to be employed in the reading, which describes how identity is produced through intergroup dynamics, and to indicate how the theory relates to Galatians in general terms. Nevertheless, since social-scientific approaches to biblical interpretation should always be closely related to the ancient setting, it will be helpful if I briefly set the scene with a discussion of the destination and time of composition of the letter and a summary of why Paul came to write it in the first place. Detailed discussion of the context and Paul's response to it are reserved for later.

The broad context

As we will see, a reasonable amount of information can be deduced from Galatians as to the general circumstances prevailing amongst his addressees, especially the social and religious tensions, when Paul wrote the letter. We know enough to make a fair fist of setting the communication in the critical aspects of its context. To this extent, the precise destination and date of composition of the letter will not determine its interpretation. Nevertheless, a consideration of these issues, which must here be necessarily brief, will lay the foundations for an examination of the contents and context of the letter in certain specific respects using social-scientific perspectives.

We must begin with the fact that the letter is addressed to the congregations *of Galatia* (1.2) and that on one occasion Paul addresses his audience as (foolish) Galatians, *Galatai* (3.1). *Galatai* was the Greek word used for the Celts from beyond the Rhine who invaded regions of Macedonia, Greece, Thrace and Asia Minor in the period 280–275 BCE.[1] Ultimately, the Celts were successful in gaining control of a comparatively modest part of Asia Minor, much of it in Phrygian territory, consisting of a piece of land about 200 miles long and averaging about 100 miles wide, lying south of Bithynia and Paphlagonia, and stretching from Cappadocia and Pontus in the east to Phrygia in the west. The Celts who settled in this region consisted of three tribes, the Tolistobogii, the Tectosages and the Trocmi, respectively inhabiting the western, central and eastern parts of this region, thereafter called Galatia. The main centres of each of these tribes, forts more than towns, were Pessinus, Ancyra and Tavium.[2]

Rome initially intervened in Asia Minor during its war with the Seleucid king, Antiochus III. In 189 BCE, after the Romans had defeated Antiochus in Asia Minor in the battle of Magnesia, the consul Manlius Vulso took the opportunity to invade Galatia and reduce its warlike inhabitants to complete submission (Scullard 1961: 255–263). Rome became far more involved in 133 BCE when the Attalid kingdom based on Pergamon was bequeathed to it. By 44 BCE, when Julius Caesar was assassinated, the Galatian leader, Deiotarus, had succeeded in seizing control of the whole of the region occupied by its three tribes, the first time this had been achieved (Strabo, *Geography*, 12.5.1). He died in 41 BCE. Following intervention by Antony and then Augustus, one Amyntas, the former right-hand man of Deiotarus, ended up as king of the whole of the tribal region of Galatia, together with parts of Lycaonia (including Isaurica), Cilicia Tracheia, much of Pisidia proper and Phrygian Pisidia. On the death of Amyntas in 25 BCE, the Romans annexed all of this land as the province of Galatia (Levick 1967: 25–31). But the province was enlarged even further as other dynasts died, by the addition of Paphlagonia in 6–5 BCE, Pontus Galaticus in 3–2 BCE, Comana Pontica in 34–35 CE and Pontus Polemoniacus in 64–65 CE (Levick 1967: 63).

The region presented a very complex mix of ethnic and cultural influences. The forces of hellenisation had hardly begun in this region prior to the arrival of the Celts among the largely Phrygian population and for the next 250 years proceeded fairly slowly (S. Mitchell 1993: 85–86), except with respect to a knowledge of Greek, which must have become fairly common (S. Mitchell 1993: 174). Celtic, once introduced however, persisted as an oral language for centuries, at least until the time of Jerome (S. Mitchell 1993: 50). In about 210 BCE the Seleucid king, Antiochus III, moved two thousand families of *Ioudaioi* from Mesopotamia to the fortresses and most important places of Phrygia and Lydia to help quell revolts in those regions. He also directed that they should be able to use their own laws and to remain free from molestation by anyone

(Josephus, *Jewish Antiquities*, 12.147–153). Although they were settled outside Galatia, they were obviously in a position to move into Galatia when times were ripe. That they had done so early in the Roman period is shown by the fact that Augustus ordered a decree protecting the rights of *Ioudaioi* in Asia to be erected in his temple in Ancyra, in the centre of Galatia (Josephus, *Jewish Antiquities*, 16.165).

Yet the influence of Rome was by far the most significant. Strabo's description of Galatia in Book 12 of his *Geography*, completed about 18–19 CE yet reflecting sources from the previous century on which it was largely based (S. Mitchell 1993: 81), mentions various walled garrisons (*phrouria*), some of which functioned as emporia, but no cities. Augustus acted to fill this breach by establishing cities soon after 25 BCE in Pessinus, Ancyra (which became the Roman headquarters of the province) and Tavium (S. Mitchell 1993: 86). Roman magistracies were instituted in the cities along the lines of the *Lex Pompeia* (S. Mitchell 1993: 86–89). Nor was it long before the imperial cult was established in the province and festivities such as gladiatorial combats and fighting with wild animals were instituted to celebrate it. Colonies were also set up in various parts of the province, most of them in the south, with new establishments at Antioch, Cremna, Parlais, Olbasa, Comama, Lystra, Iconium and Ninica, and colonies within existing settlements in other places (Levick 1967). Roman tax collectors moved in, and with them Roman and Italian businessmen who frequently purchased land to allow local landowners to pay the tax. In time, more and more of the province fell into Italian hands by this means (S. Mitchell 1993: 154). These factors, along with road building, monetarisation of the economy and new modes of exploiting the land had a significant impact on the life and culture of the province.

We would expect that from the infusion of Greek and Roman influences into the province the inhabitants would have become familiar with the typical features of Mediterranean culture already identified, namely, group orientation, honour (the index of group regard) and shame, limited good, patron and client and so on. We would expect, however, that some of these features, such as group orientation, may have characterised Celtic society anyway, given that they are common in most pre-industrial and non-North Atlantic cultures. In fact, we have ancient evidence about the Celts which confirms this. Thus, Athenaeus reports that the Celts had bards who recited their praises in company and privately (*Deipnosophistae*, 6.246), and that at dinner they sometimes engaged in fights, occasionally to the death, over who was the best among them and therefore entitled to the finest portion of the meal (*Deipnosophistae*, 4.154). Diodorus Siculus also reports that during meals they seized upon any matter for disputation and then challenged one another to single combat (5.28). All this suggests that they had a developed sense of honour and eagerly engaged in contests in relation to it.

The destination and date of Galatians

If one asks what Paul had in mind by the 'Galatia' and *Galatai* mentioned in the letter (1.2; 3.1), two answers are possible. Either he was referring to the old area of Celtic tribal occupation in the north of the province and to its inhabitants just as Strabo does by use of these words a number of times in Book 12 of his *Geography*, or he had in mind the province as a whole, the vast area which covered Celtic Galatia *stricto sensu*, the parts in the south which had formed part of the kingdom of Amyntas, and the areas lying further north along the Black Sea, Paphlagonia and the areas of Pontus added by 35 CE. Ramsay (1922: 179) and, more recently, Hemer (1989: 299–305) demonstrated that both Galatia and *Galatai* were used at this period without any derogatory implication to refer to the province and the provincial population.

The first option has come to be called 'the North Galatian hypothesis', although it is not a very accurate expression and it would be better called 'the tribal Galatia hypothesis'.[3] Those who adhere to it regard Paul as having written the letter to otherwise unknown communities presumably located in places like Pessinus, Ancyra and Tavium, and therefore necessarily not to towns elsewhere in the province, in its southern or northern parts.

To opt for the second meaning of Galatia logically means that Paul could have been writing to congregations anywhere in the province, from the Black Sea in the north to the Mediterranean in the south. We could reasonably call this approach 'the provincial Galatia hypothesis'. In fact, however, those who favour it radically reduce the huge range of possible destinations it encompasses to propose 'the South Galatian hypothesis', by arguing that in the letter 'Galatia' covers only the places situated in the province expressly mentioned in Acts as visited by Paul, namely, Antioch, which is geographically located in Pisidia (Acts 13.14–50; 14.19, 21), Iconium (Acts 13.51–14.6, 19, 21; 16.21) in Phrygia, and Lystra and Derbe in Lycaonia (Acts 14.6–21; 16.1–5). There are no positive arguments in support of this restrictive position; the nomination of these cities as the destination of Galatians merely arises as a possibility once one grants that Galatia and *Galatai* had a meaning broader than the tribal one and then looks to Acts for Galatian sites outside the tribal area. Yet the problems which Paul encountered in these cities as described in

Acts do not correlate with the issue he had to deal with in Galatia, namely, pressure by Israelite Christ-followers for gentiles to be circumcised if they wished to continue belonging to the congregations. Moreover, whereas all of the congregations Paul has in mind seem to share the same experience and he can even envisage one person in particular as a trouble-maker (5.10), Derbe is 286 km. (172 miles) from Antioch in Pisidia, which makes it rather unlikely that they had anything so specific in common or that Paul would want to deal with them collectively.[4]

Why then has the 'South Galatian hypothesis' been formulated? In essence, it is a product of scholars who have a high opinion of the value of Acts as an historical source and who wish to correlate what Paul says about his activities with what Luke says. Oddly enough, however, even in Acts Paul is described as passing through 'the Galatian territory' (in context plainly referring to the tribal area) on two occasions which could have given him an opportunity to found congregations there (Acts 16.6; 18.23), but for some reason this information has not been given much weight by the South Galatia advocates.

A further consequence of the 'South Galatian hypothesis' is that Pisidian Antioch, Iconium, Lystra and Derbe all feature in the 'first missionary journey' recounted in Acts 13–14 and this provides support, so it is said, for postulating an early date for Acts, say in the mid- to late 40s, rather than a late date, in the early to mid-50s of the first century CE.

The position a critic takes on this topic largely depends on what attitude he or she takes to the worth of Acts as a source in relation to Paul's own account of his activities – for which Gal. 1.15–2.14 provides the fullest, although hardly ample, evidence. Some of the difficulties emerge when one considers that Paul describes three journeys to Jerusalem (two as undertaken and one proposed)[5] whereas Acts speaks of five[6] and it is extremely difficult, as John Knox has argued (1989: 43–52), to reconcile Luke's account with that of Paul in spite of skilful efforts by some scholars to do so.[7] Although there can be no doubt that Luke preserves many important individual pieces of information about Paul and his mission and usually gets details of the political and legal context right, his overall framework does convey to many, myself included (Esler 1987), the impression that it has been shaped to serve his own ends. Thus, as one example, Acts 15 has too many features in common with the Jerusalem council as described by Paul in Gal. 2.1–10 to be based on another meeting in the holy city,[8] yet Luke seems to have retrojected it back into an earlier period in Paul's career and to have conflated with it information of a later compromise on the problems of table-fellowship between gentiles and Israelites, which produces an impression of harmony on this issue much earlier than it could ever have been established. It is beyond the scope of this reading, however, to add anything further on this vexed issue in New Testament scholarship.

Nevertheless, it is a matter of great significance that Paul and Acts offer roughly convergent testimony on a matter bearing directly on the destination of the letter. Paul says in Gal. 4.13 that he preached the gospel to them *on an earlier occasion* (and the Greek word *proteron* used here could mean this was the first time) 'because of a weakness of the flesh'. This presumably indicates that he was on his way somewhere else but was forced to go to Galatia through illness and took the opportunity to preach to them when he was there. The most likely scenario for such a diversion (and no such illness is mentioned in Acts in connection with the South Galatian cities) is that he was travelling on the Cilician road which ran east–west south of Galatia and rather than proceeding along it, went north into the Celtic tribal region. In Acts 16.6–7, set at a time when Paul had just moved from Derbe to Lystra and other towns further on (that is, along the Cilician road), Luke tells us that 'they travelled through Phrygia and the Galatian territory having been prevented by the Holy Spirit from preaching the word in Asia'. In other words, they were intending to continue on westward to Asia and a sudden intervention pushed them north. This is so similar to what Paul says as to raise a strong argument that the two accounts relate to the same events.

Murphy-O'Connor, who runs this argument most persuasively, notes that the first major town they would have come to in tribal Galatia was Pessinus (1996: 159–162, 191–193). Even if Paul also visited other parts of Galatia, Pessinus has the strongest claim of any town in the whole area to be a destination for Paul's letter and its inhabitants to be among the *Galatai* he rebukes in 3.1. We know from Strabo that Pessinus was an important emporium in the area (especially in connection with sheep-raising) and that it contained a famous temple of Cybele, mother of the gods. After the foundation of the province of Galatia in 25 BCE it was one of the centres for the imperial cult and we actually have epigraphic evidence of banquets, sacrifices and gladiatorial combats conducted there in the period 31–37 by Galatian priests of the divine Augustus and the goddess, Roma.[9] Parts of Pessinus (modern Balahissar), including an imperial temple-theatre complex from the reign of Tiberius, have been excavated, although the temple of Cybele lies under a mosque (S. Mitchell 1993: 105).

Adopting the tribal Galatian hypothesis based on the agreement of Gal. 4.13 and Acts 16.6–7 tends to push back the date for the letter, possibly into the 50s. Although nothing really turns on the exact date as

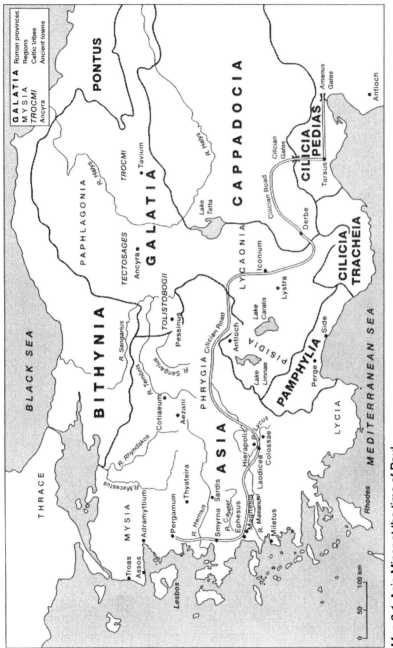

Map 2.1 Asia Minor at the time of Paul
Source: Murphy-O'Connor, J. (1996) *Paul: A Critical Life.* Oxford: The Clarendon Press.

far as the reading offered in this book is concerned, I favour the view that 1 Thessalonians was written before Galatians, principally for the reason that there are no signs whatever of the righteousness issue in 1 Thessalonians. This omission may be explicable on the basis that Paul was writing to a purely gentile audience in Thessalonika untroubled by proponents of circumcision and, as I will argue in Chapter 6, that righteousness was a later and contingent development in his thought. Yet once he had become engaged with righteousness it assumed such importance for him (as we see in Romans) that it is difficult to imagine him thereafter writing a letter with a reasonable amount of social and theological content (such as 1 Thessalonians) without mentioning it.

Paul's problem

As Paul begins to dictate the letter to his scribe,[10] he faces a major problem. Some time previously he had carried the gospel to Galatia. Accompanied by dramatic manifestations of the Holy Spirit, Paul preached the salvation available in Christ, and founded urban communities whose membership included Israelites and gentiles, free persons and slaves, men and women. Essential to his message, his gospel, was that the gentile members were not obliged to be circumcised or to take on the other duties of the Mosaic law, that they were not, in short, required to become Israelites. Nothing was to prevent the association of all within the confines of his congregations.

But now his achievement in establishing the communities in Galatia is under threat from pressures originating from both outside and inside. First, he has learned, we know not how or when, that the gentile members are under pressure to be circumcised, possibly at the behest of persons representing or sympathetic to the leaders of the Christ-movement in Jerusalem. They are in danger of abandoning the gospel he preached in favour of a different 'gospel', which Paul insists is not really a gospel at all (1.6–7). One aspect of the case his opponents are mounting in Galatia is that only through taking on the Mosaic law can the gentile members acquire 'righteousness' (*dikaiosynē*). Some of the gentiles, it seems, have even started to succumb to these demands by adopting lesser requirements of the law relating to the observance of feast days (4.10). Second, he has discovered that the members of his Galatian congregations are behaving towards one another, or have the potential to behave, in a manner quite contrary to his hopes and expectations.

Yet not only are people in Galatia claiming that Paul's version of the gospel is defective in not demanding gentile circumcision, but they are attacking his own status as an apostle, in contrast with the leaders in Jerusalem.

To make matters worse, this was not the first time this type of problem had arisen. On a previous occasion, in Antioch, before his mission in Galatia, he had run into heavy opposition to his form of mixed Israelite–gentile community and to his version of the gospel. There too the opposition had a connection with the leaders of the movement in Jerusalem, in that case James and Peter (the latter of whom had actually broken off table-fellowship with the Antiochean gentiles), even though they had previously agreed at a meeting in Jerusalem that circumcision was not necessary for gentile converts. Although he had publicly rebuked Peter, he had not persuaded the church in Antioch that he was in the right. Now, once again it seems, he faces a similar or even identical threat as far as his Galatian congregations are concerned. He gives vent to very strong animosity to the rival teaching and to its proponents, for example, by expressing a wish that anyone preaching a gospel different from his be accursed (1.8–9) and that those advocating circumcision might castrate themselves (5.12).

GROUPS AND IDENTITY IN GALATIANS: SOME DATA

Paul addresses his letter to 'the congregations (*ekklēsiai*) of Galatia' (1.2). His concern from the start is with groups and throughout the epistle he uses expressions to describe his addressees which are always plural and largely collective in nature. The most important of them is 'brothers', appearing in nine places (1.11; 3.15; 4.12, 28, 31; 5.11, 13; 6.1, 18), but there are others, such as 'foolish Galatians' (3.1), and 'my children' (4.19). Matching such language are other collective designations which he seeks to bring into relationship with his audience, including those rescued by Jesus Christ from the present evil age (1.4), believers in Christ Jesus (2.16), 'those seeking to be justified in Christ' (2.17), 'sons of God' (3.26), 'seed of Abraham' and promised heirs (3.29), 'sons' (4.6), 'children according to the promise of Isaac' (4.28), children of Sarah (4.21–31), people led by the Spirit (5.18), people of Christ (5.24), 'house members of the faith' (6.10), 'a new creation' (6.15) and 'the Israel of God' (6.16).

Whatever else they do, all of these designations, both the established ones like 'Galatians' and 'brothers' and the second type which Paul argues are also applicable to his audience, supply answers to the question, 'Who are we?', which could be shared by his addressees. As such, they serve to highlight aspects of the *identity* of the members of the congregations, since identity essentially refers to that which makes us distinctive human beings, in other words, our sense of who we are. The rich array of language and argument relating to identity, here presented in collective forms, is one of the most striking features of this letter, although this is a topic rarely taken up by commentators.

Paul never addresses an individual in Galatians or refers to one in his audience, although there may be a veiled reference to someone causing them trouble at 5.10. The only named living individuals he mentions are himself, starting with his opening at 1.2, although even there he adds 'and all the brothers who are with me', and Cephas/Peter, James, Barnabas, Titus and John in the autobiographical section (1.11–2.14).

We should not forget, however, that the groups to which he wrote were composed of individuals, each with a distinctive identity which encompassed more than the fact of belonging to the congregations. We gain a fleeting glimpse of this at 6.1 when he does address them as individuals, 'Look to yourself'. They each differed depending on whether the person was *Ioudaios* or *Hellene*, slave or free, man or woman (these last three factors being mentioned by Paul at 3.28), poor or not so poor, young or old, educated or uneducated, and so on, with each having a personal story to tell. Yet, just as in 1 Thessalonians, we do not come to know about or even learn the name of a single one of them, which is quite unlike the position in 1 Corinthians. The point is that Paul seeks to communicate with his audience in their capacity as obviously or demonstrably belonging to collectivities linked by some significant characteristic, above all their status in relation to God, Jesus Christ or the Spirit, but also their current geographic location, their kinship (here fictive in nature) *vis-à-vis* each other or illustrious ancestors like Abraham and Sarah and, for some of them, their ultimate place of origin in Judea (indicated by the use of *Iudaismos*, *Ioudaia* and *Ioudaios*). In short, Paul considers that the characteristics differentiating the persons to whom he writes should somehow be submerged in their oneness in Christ (3.28).

In addition to the congregations, Paul refers to other groups, especially Israelites, sinful gentiles and those advocating circumcision of the gentile Christ-followers (6.12–13),who in various ways constitute a threat to the collectivities he has founded in Galatia. The chief danger seems to be that the gentile members will succumb to pressure to be circumcised and adopt the Mosaic law, a step which will allegedly result in 'righteousness' (*dikaiosynē*) for those taking it. Much of what Paul says in Galatians is aimed at combating this position, as will emerge more fully below.

Yet the danger to the groups of Christ-followers comes not only from those we might for the moment call outsiders, but also from within. An important section in the letter indicates that the internal nature and functioning of the congregations is at risk from certain dispositions and types of behaviour (5.13–6.10). The extent to which such problems relate to the group organisation of the Galatian believers will be taken up later.

THEOLOGY AND SOCIAL CONTEXT IN GALATIANS

The phenomena just introduced are very prominent aspects of the letter to the Galatians. A central argument in this reading, to which I will repeatedly return, is that the important things which Paul has to say that are 'theological' in nature, which I will here define broadly as referring to his understanding of God's plan for humanity and how his audience should align themselves with it, are deeply entwined in these group-oriented characteristics. Paul's theology in Galatians was developed in a particular *social* context and to investigate what it might have meant to those first exposed to it we must seek to understand the nature of this contextualisation.

Although most modern commentators readily concede that the letter is not a theological treatise and that Paul's theology must be gathered from what is, after all, an occasional piece of writing, they seldom address the full implications of its connection with the social dimensions of the Galatian context.[11] This failing is most clearly seen in the widespread yet unstated assumption that a critic interpreting Galatians requires no specialist assistance from the disciplines which address the social aspects of human existence, the social sciences, although a more egregious form of error is represented in the view of N. T. Wright that Paul's thought-forms and thought-patterns can be usefully discussed separately from social (and rhetorical) setting (1991: 16–17). Once we recognise that Paul's theology comes embedded in a particular social context, we should also acknowledge that it makes little sense to employ sophisticated techniques in some areas and yet not call for expert assistance – and here that means from the social sciences – to understand the social context.

Two specific issues arise here. While an appropriate treatment of context will necessitate spending some time exploring contemporary social-scientific research, it is noteworthy that so many critics who, for example, devote years to the archaeology of the first-century Mediterranean, have no time at all for this task, apparently on the basis that the material side of culture deserves their disciplined scrutiny but the social side does not.

Perhaps we are faced here with a mixture of intellectual inertia and the usual disinclination of academics to cross the purity boundaries which they draw around their particular disciplines, as Vernon Robbins has accurately pointed out (1995: 275). Second, an investigation of Galatians employing social-scientific research will not be reductionist, so long as it does not seek fully to explain the theological in terms of the social but rather aims holistically to do justice to both aspects of the work's complex meaning. Offering a more sophisticated account of context may well encourage modes of enquiry which do not at their outset privilege theological questions and which, indeed, re-situate familiar textual data in possibly surprising new frameworks. Such will be the case in this reading. Nevertheless, where the overall aim of the investigation is to satisfy a theological aim of the intercultural type set out in Chapter 1, it is difficult to see why such characteristics should lead this reading to fall condemned as reductionist.

AN OUTLINE OF SOCIAL IDENTITY THEORY

The theory and its general application to Galatians

There are many areas of social-scientific theory which one could employ to shed light on Galatians. Different critics could choose different approaches depending on which they perceive to be most useful for interpreting the data and the extent to which the results likely to be obtained will assist with wider hermeneutical aims. The need to take seriously the cultural difference between ourselves and the ancient Mediterranean world by use of anthropological insights which have profiled the cultural distinctiveness of the region remains of bedrock importance (Malina 1993). Nevertheless, since the cultural features typifying the Mediterranean operate for its inhabitants at the primary level of socialisation, it is to be expected that some more precise area of social-scientific theory might assist in understanding the specific shape of the communication in Galatians.

In this reading I will principally rely on the theory of social identity developed by social psychologist Henri Tajfel in the 1960s and 1970s, during much of which he was at the University of Bristol, England.[12] Tajfel died in 1982, but his work has been influential with co-workers and students of his such as John Turner, Dominic Abrams and Michael Hogg, and its continuing importance can be seen in the contributions in a recent Festschrift in his honour (Robinson 1996). This theory will guide the overall shape of the reading and the other social-scientific perspectives will be introduced in relation to it. In selecting social identity theory for this central role, I have firmly in mind the data relating to groups, group identity and intergroup conflict which were set out earlier in this chapter, for all of these factors are addressed in the theory. In addition, however, the theory deals with issues of identity which are closely compatible with the intercultural approach to New Testament interpretation set out in Chapter 1 and, moreover, with George Lindbeck's understanding of religion as a cultural system informing its followers with a particular account of reality which figures prominently in that approach (Esler 1995a: 1–20). I have now been working with Tajfel's insights for some years, having employed them initially in a paper on the Matthean beatitudes in 1994, which to the best of my knowledge marks the debut of this theory in New Testament interpretation,[13] and more recently in an essay dealing with Galatians 5–6 (Esler 1996a). In the rest of this chapter I will set out the theory and suggest its relevance to the letter in general terms, while leaving more detailed treatment of some of the issues for later.

Social identity theory adopts a position in relation to the continuing problem of the relationship between the individual and the group. In 1924, American social psychologist, Floyd Allport, classically expressed the reductionist view that a group must be treated as dissolved into the individuals that composed it. This meant that the group had no distinct conceptual status apart from those individuals and that social psychology as a discipline did not study the group as such but the interactions between the individuals concerned. Social psychology was really part of the psychology of the individual. This approach, whose origins in the highly individualist USA – where it still enjoys some popularity – will occasion little surprise, was strongly attacked by European social psychologists from the 1960s onwards, with Henri Tajfel and Serge Moscovici leading the charge. Scholars such as these founded *The European Journal of Social Psychology* to forge a non-reductionist form of the discipline and strove to address more adequately social dimensions of human behaviour neglected or ignored by the Allport school. The Europeans insisted that the critical question was how, that is, through what psychological processes, society at large or a group in particular managed to install itself in the mind of individuals and to affect their behaviour (Hogg and Abrams 1988: 12–16). At this point it is worth noting that Paul's interest in Galatians in advocating certain group-oriented expressions to his individual readers/listeners represents precisely the type of phenomenon which the European social psychologists sought to explain.

Social identity theory first appeared in published form in an essay by

Henri Tajfel in 1972.[14] Here he argued that groups needed to establish a positively valued distinctiveness from other groups to provide their members with a positive social identity. The bedrock empirical foundation for this view was the 'minimum group experiments', which were inspired by studies conducted by Sherif in boys' summer camps in the USA in the 1950s. This research, some of it laboratory-based, indicated that merely categorising people as belonging to one group or another produced social comparison with other groups which, in turn, led to notable forms of group behaviour, with members favouring one another and discriminating against the members of outgroups. Hot on the heels of these phenomena came the processes of social conflict and social change. In realising who we are in terms of group membership, we come up against those groups in our environment whom we are not. Tajfel observed that our sense of belonging to a group actually had three dimensions:

1 'the cognitive dimension', which is the simple recognition of belonging to a group;
2 'the evaluative dimension', which covers the positive or negative connotations of belonging;
3 'the emotional dimension', which refers to attitudes members hold toward insiders and outsiders.

(Tajfel 1978: 28)

Although not made much of by Tajfel, one feature of a group which may contribute greatly to the cognitive dimension of belonging and also help to foster the evaluative and emotional dimensions in a positive way is a distinctive orientation towards the future. Thus, among the Hausa people of the Sudan there is a group of Muslims who live their whole life as if they are on a pilgrimage, a *haj*, to Mecca even though most of them never get there. Travelling light, their entire existence is oriented to a future arrival which they may never experience. The future becomes a legitimating charter for life in the present (Yamba 1992). Other groups perceive a glorious destiny in store at a more determinate point in the future. Good examples of this are millenarian movements such as the cargo cults of Melanesia and the flying saucer cults of the USA in which the belief that the members are soon to experience a creation radically renewed or to be transported to a better world actually provides the whole rationale for belonging.[15]

The general relevance of this theory to Galatians is clear. Paul is concerned with maintaining the distinctive identity of his congregations in relation to the Israelite and gentile outgroups. Moreover, he wishes to defend their distinctiveness not so much by reminding them of the fact of their membership (the cognitive dimension) as by developing the evaluative dimension through drawing out the positive aspects of belonging to the ingroup which accepts his version of the gospel as compared with the negatively evaluated outgroups. Here we see the applicability of the insight of social identity theory that all evaluative statements are comparative, since how good we are depends on how we rate against others (Hogg and Abrams 1988: 16). As we will see below, Paul's strategy in Galatians pervasively involves processes of comparison and evaluation. The emotional dimension also emerges – in the frustration mixed with warmth (see 4.19–20) he expresses towards his converts, on the one hand, and the antipathy he harbours towards those who are disturbing them, on the other.

A detailed model of the nature of the processes of intergroup comparison is central to social identity theory and will be described below, after the certain aspects and implications of the theory have been explored.

The place of the individual in social identity theory

Tajfel defined social identity as 'the individual's knowledge that he belongs to certain social groups together with some emotional and value significance to him of group membership' (1972: 31). The concept deals with group belonging, but since it involves not merely a person's knowledge of a group's attributes but has self-evaluative consequences, it is also psychological (Hogg and Abrams 1988: 7). It is plain from the desirable nature of the collective designations that Paul is intent on pressing on his Galatians that he wants them to evaluate more positively the fact of their membership. Yet the collective elements of identity which Paul is recommending can only be appropriated by individuals. The apostle will be successful only when the forms of identity with which he is concerned have become phenomenologically real psychological states in the hearts and minds of the individual Galatians, with the result that they have begun to evaluate themselves differently.

To see more clearly how the balance between the social and the psychological operates in this theory, I will set out briefly the model of the self in social identity theory. For social identity theorists the self-concept has two separate components, social identity and personal identity (Hogg and Abrams 1988: 24–25). Each aspect of identity comprises a number of identifications. The social identifications are derived from belonging to groups, such as nationality, sex, ethnicity, occupation, sports teams; thus a person might identify him or herself as Scottish, as a member of a particular family, as a Christian, as a teacher and so on. Personal identifications, on the other hand, usually denote specific individual attributes and are generally grounded in relationships with specific individuals or objects: she is a daughter of Flora, a friend of Duncan, a lover of Mozart. Each such identification contains numerous self-descriptions: thus, as Scottish s/he may say s/he is a hill-walker, community-oriented, enthusiastically celebrates Hogmanay, is fond of single malt whisky, and so on. As the daughter of Flora, she may describe herself as irritated by her mother's dress sense, but influenced by her generosity, as devoted to her siblings, etc. (See Figure 2.1.)

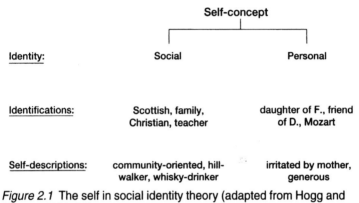

Figure 2.1 The self in social identity theory (adapted from Hogg and Abrams 1988: 24)

It is clear that this model fixes upon aspects of the self which are socially derived, either from groups or close and enduring interpersonal relationships, so that little attention is paid to aspects such as individual moral dispositions, emotional make-up, abilities and interests which may characterise a particular person.[16] It would not be difficult to include these in a more comprehensive picture of the self, if that was required by the nature of the data, which it is not for Galatians. Nevertheless, the whole thrust of social identity theory is that under certain conditions 'social identity is more salient than personal identity in self-conception, and that when this is the case behaviour is qualitatively different: it is group behaviour' (Hogg and Abrams 1988: 25). A key proposition of this reading is that in Galatians Paul is seeking to insist on the value of certain collective forms of identity in the self-conception of the individual Christ-followers to whom he writes and their distinct personal identities have little bearing on his task, except to the extent that certain aspects of identity with at least a modest personal component might serve to promote (5.22–23; 6.1–6) rather than frustrate (5.19–21) this aim.

Group norms

Within the perspective of social identity theory norms are values which define acceptable and unacceptable attitudes and behaviours for group members. By bringing order and predictability to the environment they help members to construe the world and to determine appropriate behaviour in new and ambiguous situations. Accordingly, norms maintain and enhance group identity (Brown 1988: 42–48).

When critics speak of the 'ethics' in various New Testament texts,[17] they generally have in mind phenomena which are treated as norms in social identity theory. However, there are significant differences in how these phenomena are handled. First, New Testament critics often refer to ethics as if they were readily capable of being extracted from the texts in which they appear for separate analysis, so that they become distinct objects of investigation. Social identity theory, on the other hand, treats norms as *aspects* of identity. Second, whereas existing approaches to New Testament ethics are very concerned with the actions of individuals, following Tajfel's lead means that we favour a strongly group-oriented understanding of norms, with the focus on their role in how the identity of the ingroup is created, maintained and even strengthened.

I will illustrate these distinctions with an example from my own experience. Prior to the changes introduced by the Second Vatican Council, the Roman Catholic Church forbade its members from eating meat on Fridays. This ban did not merely constitute a rule the breach of which by any individual Catholic was sinful, it also served to stamp the membership with a distinctive identity. It formed one of a panoply of measures, only some of which related to norms, which told Catholics who they were in contrast to outsiders.

Social identity theory and the ancient Mediterranean world

Social identity theory has recently been developed and fine-tuned in ways which we must now consider. Social psychologists Hinkle and Brown (1990) have pointed out that a few studies conducted in the 1980s have indicated that the intergroup comparisons – which earlier research in the field suggested would be a readily occurring and spontaneous phenomenon – did not always happen. While not challenging the value of the theory, Hinkle and Brown have sought to determine more precisely the circumstances under which comparisons are implicated in social identity. Their enhancements of the theory actually make it even more suitable for application to the ancient Mediterranean world.

They begin with the fact, perhaps not sufficiently taken into account in the rather homogeneous samples used in the laboratory research, that groups differ greatly from one another in many ways: size, function, emotional significance, and so on. Such factors may have an important bearing on whether a group does compare itself with others or not. They have isolated two variables in identifying when intergroup comparisons are likely to be significant in people's behaviour and when they are not. The first is the question of individualism *vis-à-vis* collectivism in the culture in question and the second is the extent to which the group exhibits a comparative or non-comparative ideology.

The individualism/collectivism spectrum

Their first variable refers to 'the extent to which cultures emphasize interpersonal competition, individual achievement and separation from the in-group versus co-operation within the group, collective achievements and close ties with in-group members' (Hinkle and Brown 1990: 65–66). In Chapter 1 we discussed recent efforts, stemming from the work of Geert Hofstede in 1980, to develop taxonomies of national cultures on the basis of a small number of variables. Of Hofstede's five variables, the individualist/collectivist one has been found most useful by other researchers (Smith and Bond 1993: 38–46). As we have already seen, North Atlantic countries tend to be individualist and are rather unusual in this respect, whereas Mediterranean countries form part of the large majority in being collectivist. In addition, Harry Triandis, of the University of Illinois, has persuasively argued that the individualist/collectivist spectrum manifests itself in distinct orientations among groups within a national culture and even at an individual level as idiocentric (self-directed) or allocentric (other-directed) personalities (1988, 1989). In this view, we are helped in assessing how the self is likely to be construed in any given culture by knowing whether individualism or collectivism dominates there.

Hinkle and Brown reasonably propose that collectivists are more likely than individualists to be concerned with how the groups to which they belong are faring in relation to other groups; in other words, collectivists are more likely to engage in the process of intergroup comparison. The reason for this is that an individualist has far less staked on the contribution group-belonging makes to his or her identity than someone imbued with a collectivist outlook and is less likely to be committed to benefits which accrue from intergroup comparison.

The implications of this view for Galatians are clear. Given that individualism is only common in the post-industrial modern countries having a North Atlantic culture, we would naturally assume that the Mediterranean societies of the first century CE, which form the larger context of Galatians, were at least as collectivist as modern ones, but probably more so, given the effects of the recent exposure of contemporary Mediterranean peoples to individualist influences from Northern Europe, especially in an age of mass media, such as television. Indeed, anthropological research conducted in the region since the late 1950s, brilliantly modelled by Bruce Malina in *The New Testament World* (1993), focuses on its group orientation as one of the most prominent of the ensemble of features which comprise Mediterranean culture. In this respect the work of Malina and other critics who find this research helpful for interpreting the Bible falls securely into place as a small part of the much larger enterprise in the adumbration of regional and national cultures inspired by Hofstede. This makes all the more obviously ethnocentric and anachronistic the work of commentators who persist in disregarding the collectivist orientation of Old and New Testament texts.

Group ideologies

Hinkle and Brown recognise, however, that one could envisage a group in a collectivist culture which is not particularly given to intergroup comparison, such as a therapy group or a writer's guild, just as in some individualist cultures groups such as football teams and political parties may be intensely concerned to compare themselves with and achieve supremacy over other groups in the environment. This means that a second dimension requiring attention is whether a comparative or non-comparative ideology pervades a group or the context in which it finds itself. Some contexts naturally encourage a comparative ideology, such as a sporting competition between a number of teams, or an election being hotly fought by a number of parties, and in these cases, research has demonstrated, the processes of intergroup comparison flourish (Hinkle and Brown 1990: 67).

The significance of this for present purposes rests in the strongly competitive nature of Mediterranean society, ancient and modern, a feature which anthropologists describe as 'agonistic', from the Greek *agōn*, meaning a contest. This competitiveness is brought about by the symbiosis of two aspects of the culture. First, there is the position of honour as the central social value for both individuals and groups and the fact that one way in which honour is acquired is by actively striving to get the better of

agonistic competitiveness emerges @ the crossroads of honour & limited good.

one's equals (as long as they are not kin) in all aspects of life. The second is the prevalence of the notion that all goods exist only in finite and usually indivisible portions, which means that one person or group can only enjoy an accretion of some good at the expense of some other person or group. This phenomenon is called 'limited good' and is similar to the modern concept of the zero sum game (Malina 1993: 103–112). Thus, there is only one birthright for Isaac to hand on and Jacob makes sure he is the son who receives it, as Esau learns to his cost (Gen. 25.29–34); in fact, Isaac even has only one blessing (Gen. 27.30–40).

Another very clear example can be seen in Judges 7.1–8 when Yahweh ensures that the Israelite army is reduced from 32,000 to a derisory 300 so that there may be no doubt that he is due the honour for defeating Midian. Closer to Paul is the statement of Philo of Alexandria that the honour and regard given to deified mortals reduces the honour paid to the true God (*de Ebriarte*, 110). So too John says of Jesus, 'He must increase, I must decrease' (John 3.30). In the Graeco-Roman world, the popular belief in limited good is well expressed in the remark of Iamblichus, 'People do not find it pleasant to give honour to someone else, for they suppose that they themselves are being deprived of something' (Diels 1935: 400). Similarly, Plutarch describes a person hearing an outstanding speaker and expressing envy at his success, 'As though commendation were money, he feels that he is robbing himself of every bit that he bestows on another' (*On Listening to Lectures*, 44B).[18]

The coexistence of the pivotal nature of honour and the limited good provides a strong stimulus to the development of ideologies and occasions of intergroup comparison. Thus, a group which gets the better of a rival in some contest earns honour for itself while leaving its competitor in a state of shame.

In this perspective, righteousness, Abrahamic descent, the presence of the Spirit and freedom which are so important in Galatians constitute resources which Paul wants his audience to be confident reside among them rather than with those outside his congregations.

Paul maintains that these goods are both finite and indivisible; there is no room in his argument for the idea that they might be shared with the Israelites. Thus he reasons that the members of the congregations are justified by faith not by works of the law (2.16); that those who believe are the sons of Abraham (3.7); that the Spirit came to those who heard the faith proclaimed, not to those who fulfilled the works of the law (3.2, 5); and that the believers in Christ enjoy freedom as the children of Sarah, in contrast to Hagar's children who are in slavery (4.21–5.1). Accordingly, the letter illustrates a typical Mediterranean contest over scarce resources of the sort which satisfies the second condition which Hinkle and Brown posit as necessary for comparison between groups to occur.

THE PROCESSES OF INTERGROUP COMPARISON AND CONFLICT

Now that we have proposed that the letter to the Galatians in its Mediterranean context satisfies the two conditions which Hinkle and Brown suggest as necessary for a group to venture upon intergroup comparison, even if that eventually leads to conflict, we may explore the detailed dynamics of this process according to the theory. A diagram summarising the position will be provided at the end of this discussion (see Figure 2.2 on p. 55).

The stimulus to the development of the theory in this area came from the early realisation by Tajfel and others that groups usually differed in very significant ways in areas such as size, power, access to resources and prestige – all of which were capable of being perceived as, in varying degrees, legitimate or illegitimate, and mutable or immutable – and that the theory needed to account for such variations. The relationship between Paul's Galatian congregations and other groups in their environment, Israelites especially but also gentiles, certainly entailed diversity of this kind in ways to be discussed later.

To understand the process of intergroup comparison, with conflict as its most extreme form, it is helpful to mention that there is a continuum which stretches from purely interindividual behaviour at one end to purely intergroup behaviour at the other. Purely interindividual behaviour is determined solely by reference to the personal characteristics of those involved and not in relation to any social categories; such behaviour is rather difficult to imagine. Purely intergroup behaviour consists of a total suppression of any features personal to the individuals concerned and focuses solely on membership of social groups; a good example is the anonymous slaughter of a civilian population by an enemy bomber pilot releasing a ton of high-incendiary bombs on their city. The behaviour characteristic of Galatians reveals a strong intergroup aspect with barely any sign whatever of interindividual conduct. Not one person in the Galatian congregations is mentioned by name. At one point Paul may even suggest that he does not know the identity of a person causing the disturbance (5.10), unless this is a way of emphasising that his status will not protect him from judgement.

The area of the theory dealing with intergroup comparisons begins with the position of a group which has a status lower than that of another group or groups. The lower the status of a group in relation to other groups with which it might be compared, the less contribution it can make to positive social identity (Tajfel and Turner 1979: 43). In Galatia, for example, it seems that a significant number of the members of Paul's congregations consider or are being urged to consider that their status as such is inferior to that of the Israelite outgroup. The fact that the advocates of this view are maintaining (even if Paul disagrees) that their position still comprises 'gospel' and does not involve abandoning Christ brings home to us the importance of the social dimension of the comparison in contrast to the theological. In other words, as gentile Christ-followers they have a threatened or even negative social identity in relation to that of the house of Israel. Social identity theorists next proceed to develop a range of responses possible for a group with a low status in elaboration of the principles already considered. Depending on circumstances, two broad possibilities are open to those who are unhappy with their negative social identity as members of one group in comparison with another group and who seek to improve their position – 'social mobility' and 'social change'.

Social mobility

The first, which is regarded by those pursuing it as a movement from lower to higher status, is simply to leave their group and join the other, an option referred to by Tajfel as *social mobility*. This option depends on a measure of permeability existing across intergroup boundaries (Hogg and Abrams 1988: 54), a topic of considerable complexity which will be developed in detail in Chapter 3, with help from another area of social-scientific theory – the understanding of the nature of ethnicity proposed by anthropologist Fredrik Barth. Yet social mobility has its difficulties. First of all, external constraints, such as extremely negative evaluations of one's colour, religion, gender or socioeconomic level espoused by the group to which one aspires, will sometimes make crossing the intergroup boundary very difficult. The occasional sectarian murder in Northern Ireland of the Catholic or Protestant partner in a mixed relationship illustrates the problem. In a pre-industrial, collectivist and honour-oriented culture such as that of the ancient Mediterranean, where there was an expectation that people would remain within existing social categories, social mobility was a much more unusual phenomenon than in modern North Atlantic societies, although it was certainly not unknown. A soldier who worked his way up through the ranks of a Roman legion to become a centurion received a payment of 25,000 denarii on retirement which was enough to make him eligible to join the local aristocracy sitting on provincial town councils. Occasionally, however, a dominant group will engage in tokenism by enlisting a few members from subordinate groups as a way of weakening their cohesiveness and ability to act together (Hogg and Abrams 1988: 56). In addition, a dominant group will at times engineer the demise of subordinate groups by allowing their members mass admission.

Second, there is often the internal constraint which consists of the disapproval that flows from one's original group towards those who wish to disidentify themselves from it. Groups often exert pressure on members to prevent them from leaving. In this case, individual social mobility is not so much unavailable as undesirable (Tajfel and Turner 1979: 45).

How may we relate Galatians to the phenomenon of mobility? Paul faces the problem in Galatia that a powerful group of Israelites, probably associated with local synagogues and using Israelite Christ-followers as their agents, are willing to admit all of the gentile members of the communities he founded there, so long as they are circumcised. The Israelites are offering mass admission as just outlined, probably supported by the argument to the effect that the gentiles have a lower status as members of the Pauline congregations than they would if they adopted a strategy of individual mobility by acquiring a much more positive identity through circumcision and adherence to the Mosaic law. Such a step would mean the gentiles disidentifying themselves from the Pauline *ekklēsiai*, which could lose their cohesiveness or even disintegrate as a result. Moreover, these members also have before them the option of reassimilation into the gentile world from which they came. Mobility in two directions is plainly available to them. Yet Paul considers either course would mean a derogation from the gospel he has taught. For this reason he engages in the second obstacle to intergroup mobility, that of exerting pressure on them not to join the outgroups which beckon. Galatians represents a case where mobility is possible but is subject to an internal constraint in the form of strong opposition from an ingroup leader.

Social change

The second broad possibility open to the members of an ingroup who seek to acquire a more positive social identity consists of effecting a positive re-evaluation of the ingroup in relation to hitherto dominant outgroups, which Tajfel referred to as *social change* (Hogg and Abrams

1988: 27). This response assumes the impermeability of intergroup boundaries and the relative impossibility of moving from a low- to a high-status group. Such a strategy appears in Galatians because although Paul urges the gentile members not to be circumcised and join the Judaic outgroup, nor to revert to modes of existence typifying the gentile world, a large part of his case that these are possible but undesirable options depends upon his making membership of the congregations more attractive in terms of the positive social identity which individual members obtain through belonging to them.

Social change offers two specific modes of promoting a more positive group identity: *social creativity* and *social competition*. The basis for the distinction is the possibility of change in the actual nature of the comparative relationship between ingroup and outgroup. According to Tajfel, the crucial factor here is whether it is possible to conceive of 'cognitive alternatives' to the current arrangements (Tajfel and Turner 1979: 45). Thus, two football teams at the top of a competition from the previous year can certainly envisage an alteration of their comparative position in the coming season, whereas Black Americans in certain parts of the USA before the civil rights movement of the 1960s would have found it much harder to do so. If there is any doubt as to whether such change is possible (which is often the case in intergroup relations) we may find members of one group pursuing tactics which exemplify both social creativity and social competition. Paul adopts this policy in Galatians.

Social creativity

Social creativity designates the case where the subordinate group does not aim for any change in its actual social position or its access to objective resources in relation to the dominant outgroup, but practises other strategies for improving its social identity which involve redefining or altering elements in the comparative situation (Tajfel and Turner 1979: 43). Tajfel referred to this as a 'secure comparison', meaning one predicated upon a stable relationship between ingroup and outgroup with no alternative arrangements in view. The theory offers three ways in which social creativity may take place:

1 The ingroup might compare itself to the outgroup on some new dimension. In Galatians, for example, Paul reminds his audience that the Spirit and associated miraculous phenomena arrived among them from proclamation of the faith, not through works of the (Mosaic) law (3.2, 5). Within the perspective of social identity theory, accordingly, we

are able to suggest that the ingroup's experience of the Spirit, which is an important theme in Galatians, repays consideration as contributing to a more positive social identity. Tajfel and Turner (1979: 43) suggest that the success of an inferior ingroup in managing to legitimise some aspect of its identity in this way may threaten the dominant outgroup's superior distinctiveness and possibly encourage an increase in intergroup tension. This latter point is an interesting one as far as Galatians is concerned, especially in relation to the possibly hostile reaction to Paul's success at the Jerusalem conference (Gal. 2.1–10), which is discussed in Chapter 5.

2 The ingroup may redefine the value of some existing comparison so that what was previously regarded as a weakness is now seen as a strength. One modern example is the 'Black is beautiful' assertion which flourished in the USA in the 1960s. Freedom seems to function in this way in Galatians. Paul seems obliged to counter some suggestion abroad that freedom in Christ leads to sin: 'You were called for freedom, brothers, only not freedom as an opportunity for the flesh' (5.13; 2.17). This disturbing possibility may well underlie some of the arguments of those advocating circumcision, so that he must insist at some length (in Gal. 5.13–6.10) that freedom, properly understood (as slavery to one another in love, 5.13), should foster a positive sense of identity, not a negative one: 'For freedom Christ has set us free; therefore keep firm and do not again take on the yoke of slavery' (5.1). I will cover this issue in Chapter 8.

One form of redefinition of particular interest for Galatians, as we will see in Chapter 8, is the assertion that true positive values, desirable group norms, are the very antithesis of those espoused by the dominant groups in the environment (Brown 1988: 250–251). A modern example of this was evident in the hippy counter-culture of the 1960s.

3 The ingroup may fix upon some other outgroup with which to compare itself rather than the dominant outgroup, on the basis that 'compared to these people, on the other hand, we look rather good'. Paul engages in something like this strategy in Galatians when he says: 'We are Jews by birth and not gentile sinners' (2.15).

Social competition

Social competition refers to the efforts by the subordinate ingroup to improve its actual social location *vis-à-vis* the dominant outgroup, especially in relation to their respective access to status and resources. Here there is pressure to alter the *status quo*, since those who disagree with the terms of the comparison, which will usually mean that they evaluate their social identity more negatively than if they considered the comparison legitimate, will want to do something actually to change the situation. Members try 'to reverse the relative positions of the ingroup and outgroup on salient dimensions' (Tajfel and Turner 1979: 44). Direct competition of this kind presupposes that alternative arrangements are possible, so that the comparative relationship is unstable or 'insecure'. Not just the subordinate group, but also the dominant and high-status group will experience an unstable identity in such a case. With respect to the latter, Tajfel and Turner note: 'Any threat to the distinctively superior position of a group implies a potential loss of positive comparisons and possible negative comparisons, which must be guarded against' (1979: 45). Such threats are often caused by the activity of the subordinate group. This strategy will usually produce antagonism and conflict between the groups. In a strongly group-oriented setting such as that of the ancient Mediterranean, where all goods were thought to exist in finite and indivisible amounts, competition in respect to them is likely to have been more intense than in modern North Atlantic cultures which are individualistic and which, at least since the days of Adam Smith, have been at home with the notion of expanding productivity.

In Galatia, as a result of Paul's evangelism, an unstable comparative relationship has come into existence between the communities of Christ-followers and the local *Ioudaioi*. I will leave an examination of the precise reason for this until Chapter 4, but suffice it to say that something about the mixed gentile–Israelite nature of the Pauline congregations has induced among the Israelites a belief that their social identity is at risk and that they need to insist quite strongly on its positive nature. Paul, although communicating with gentile and Israelite Christ-followers and not Israelites themselves, directly counters such claims – by arguing that a number of desirable attributes, such as righteousness and descent from Abraham, rightly belong to his congregations and not to the Israelites to whom they might otherwise seem to be related. He is seeking to reverse the respective positions of the two groups in relation to these dimensions. Moreover, Paul also attributes to the Judaic outgroup negative characteristics, such as its involvement in the realm of 'the flesh' in stark contrast to his communities' experience of the Spirit, and he develops this contrast with some vigour. Accordingly, Galatia offers very explicit examples of social competition.

Paul's treatment of righteousness, Abrahamic descent and flesh versus

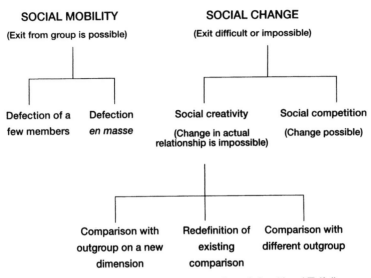

Figure 2.2 Processes of intergroup comparison (after Henri Tajfel)

spirit also leads us into the last area of social identity theory requiring attention in this chapter – stereotyping.

Stereotyping

We are continually faced with an abundance of complex information flowing in from our environment concerning other human beings. To allow us to adapt our thinking or behaviour to this situation we need to simplify or systematise such information. One common way we achieve this is to develop schematic mental images of certain categories of person. These images are stereotypes and the process just described illustrates their cognitive aspect, in helping us to perceive and interpret reality. But since we usually share stereotypes with others socially proximate to ourselves, they also have social functions, in various ways affecting how groups to which we belong respond to other groups (Tajfel 1981: 144–147). Prior to the development of social identity theory, much research had been conducted into stereotypes which can be summarised into five areas:

1 People are ready to characterise large human groups on the basis of a few rather crude attributes;
2 these stereotypes are very hard to change;

3 they are learnt at a very young age;
4 they become more pronounced and hostile with a rise in tension between groups; and
5 they are harmful when enunciated in the context of social conflict.

(Hogg and Abrams 1988: 67)

Hogg and Abrams describe stereotypes within the framework of social identity theory as:

> generalizations about people based on category membership. They are beliefs that all members of a particular group have the same qualities, which circumscribe the group and differentiate it from other groups. A specific group member is assumed to be, or is treated as, essentially identical to other members of the group.

(Hogg and Abrams 1988: 65)

Stereotypes are very often associated with evaluation and there is a strong tendency to attach positive evaluations to one's ingroup and negative evaluations to outgroups. 'Stereotyping is a fundamental and probably universal bias in perception' with important consequences for behaviour (Hogg and Abrams 1988: 66).

For Tajfel and those following him, stereotyping is produced by classifying stimuli into two categories in a particular way – by accentuation. To allow us to simplify and manage the numerous stimuli coming in our direction from the social environment we tend to accentuate their characteristics, that is to say, we exaggerate both the similarity of phenomena within each of two categories and the differences between categories. This creates a situation where things are more black and white, and less grey and ambiguous.

We apply these processes to ourselves as well as to others, which means that we engage in self-categorisation and self-stereotyping, the latter in areas such as personality traits, behaviour and behavioural norms, attitudes and beliefs. Moreover, ingroup stereotypes tend to be positive ones, since they strengthen the sense of belonging of the various individual selves making up the group, while stereotypes of outgroups are often negative (Hogg and Abrams 1988: 68–74).

Examples of stereotypes from Galatians include 'gentile sinners' (2.15), 'sons of Abraham' (3.7), 'sons of God' (3.26), 'those wishing to be under law' (4.21), children of the present-day Jerusalem (4.25), 'children according to the promise of Isaac' (4.28), 'children of the free woman' and 'children of the slave girl' (4.31), those led by the Spirit (5.16), those performing works of the flesh (5.21), 'those of Christ' (5.24), those wish-

ing to make a good showing in the flesh (6.12), those who are circumcised
(6.13) and 'the Israel of God' (6.16). Many of these expressions have
already been referred to in the list of collective expressions provided
earlier in this chapter. This is no coincidence, for Paul's way of thinking
about groups was deeply stereotypical, as indeed was that of first-century
Israelites, as we will soon see.

It is especially important for what follows in this reading to note that
the extent to which stereotyping will be used to sharpen ingroup/
outgroup differentiation will depend on the local context of the interaction. In particular, Hogg and Abrams reasonably suggest that a group
with a restricted repertoire of positive social identities will vigorously
strive to maintain them:

> They will cherish what identities they have, fiercely preserving their
> positive aspects vis-à-vis outgroups, and engaging in pronounced
> ingroup/outgroup differentiation. They will engage in prejudice,
> extreme and rigid stereotyping probably accompanied by overt
> behavioural discrimination.
>
> (1988: 74)

That is, ethnocentrism, or 'own-group-enhancing stereotypic differences', will flourish 'under conditions in which intergroup distinctiveness
is perceived to be becoming eroded and insecure, or when social conditions are such that low status is perceived to be illegitimate and change-
able' (Hogg and Abrams 1988: 77). The various forms such reactions
may take were discussed above. Paul both faced this phenomenon in
Galatia in the hostility towards his mixed gentile–Israelite congregations and also contributed to it himself in relation to Israelite (and
gentile) outsiders.

Chapter 3

Context and rhetoric in Galatians

In the previous chapter we considered the more general aspects of the geographic and chronological setting and the problems Paul faced in Galatia, as a foundation for describing social identity theory and its broad application to a communication so taken up with its author telling his audience who they really were. We must now relate these perspectives more closely to the specific context of the letter, since a fundamental tenet of this reading is the extent to which a communication has meaning within a particular social setting. The primary aim of this chapter, therefore, is to focus on what I will argue is the critical issue for the relationship between Paul's ingroups and the Israelite outgroup and the respective social identities experienced by them – the nature, operation and status of certain group boundaries in Galatia.

At the same time, however, we must continue to develop our picture of the rhetorical form of Paul's response to the Galatian situation. Context and rhetoric are closely linked, since the speaker (or writer) must carefully align his or her communication with the nature and setting of the problem at hand to have any hope of persuading the audience to a particular point of view. In Chapter 1 I presented a case for reading a *letter* like Galatians as a first-century communication employing the rhetoric of the period. The present need, however, is to explore the relationship between Galatians as a communication written to make an impact in a particular social context and rhetoric as the means for achieving such an end, a relationship encapsulated in the notion of the 'rhetorical situation' of the letter as explained in Chapter 1. In the first part of this chapter I will develop two aspects of the use of rhetoric in the letter, the broad nature of the rhetoric employed and a defence of drawing historical conclusions from a rhetorical document like this in relation both to the circumstances in Galatians contemporaneous with Paul's writing

Galatians and the autobiographical account in 1.11–2.14. In the remaining two parts I will discuss two aspects of the context, namely, the exigence and audience of the rhetorical situation, as described in Chapter 1.

RHETORIC IN GALATIANS

Deliberative or judicial rhetoric?

Our earlier discussion suggests that when Paul began to dictate the letter to respond to the problems in Galatia his resort to rhetorical techniques of persuasion would have been virtually unavoidable, just as it was for another first-century Jewish author, Josephus, who fell into the style of epideictic oratory when composing his autobiography.[1] For this reason, although the lack of a formal relationship between rhetoric and epistolography renders it an exercise of dubious value to enquire whether Galatians is judicial *per se* (see Betz 1975, 1979) or deliberative *per se* (see Smit 1989), it is certainly worthwhile to investigate whether, as a functional matter, the letter is primarily apologetic, being concerned with Paul's status, especially as an apostle, or primarily deliberative, as interested in persuading his audience to, or dissuading them from, some course of action or viewpoint. In addressing this issue, which has actually been live in Pauline scholarship since the fourth century CE (Gaventa 1986: 310), we might expect to be helped more by a work such as Aristotle's *Rhetorica*, since it discusses the issues in a very open way and with ample reference to large social contexts, than many of the rhetorical works written after Aristotle, which, although illuminating, became increasingly technical and formulaic.

A number of prominent features of Galatians have stimulated discussion as to whether it should be seen as predominantly deliberative or judicial. The chief of these are (what might loosely be called) the autobiographical aspects of the letter.[2] Galatians begins, after all, with an emphatic assertion by Paul of his apostolic status:

1.1 Paul an apostle, not from human beings nor through a human being, but through Jesus Christ and God the Father, who raised him from the dead,
1.2 and all the brethren who are with me, to the congregations of Galatia:
1.3 Grace to you and peace from God our Father and Lord Jesus Christ,

1.4 who gave himself for our sins to deliver us from the present evil age, according to the will of our God and Father;
1.5 to whom be the glory for ever and ever. Amen.

Then, after a brief section in which he castigates the Galatians for turning towards another gospel (1.6–10), he further asserts that the gospel he proclaims has a divine and not human origin (1.11–12) before continuing with a long narrative describing his own conversion and relating certain points in his subsequent career, especially his involvement with Cephas, James and the Jerusalem Church, culminating in a dramatic confrontation with Cephas in Antioch (1.13–2.14).

Hans Dieter Betz classified Galatians, in a strict rhetorical sense, as judicial, as constituting an 'apologetic letter' in which Paul sought to defend himself against charges brought by his Galatian opponents as prosecutors in an imaginary courtroom where the jury was the letter's addressees (1979: 24). Central to this case was the passage from 1.12–2.14, which Betz construed as the *narratio*,[3] the statement of facts at issue which formed, of necessity, a central part of virtually every judicial speech, since it was upon the relevant facts that the jury reached its verdict.

Although this view secured some support,[4] most scholars, quite rightly, rejected it. George Kennedy, one of the great authorities on ancient rhetoric (1963 and 1980), offered a succinct yet compelling critique (1984: 144–152). A *narratio* could appear in deliberative and epideictic speeches; hence the presence of 1.12–2.14 in Galatians did not sound in favour of its judicial nature. Furthermore, *narrationes* in judicial speeches concerned the facts directly at issue in the case and this was not the case with Paul's autobiographical passage. Second, and even more significantly, Gal. 5.1–6.10 (to which we will return later) was exhortatory in nature and such material played no part whatever in judicial oratory, although exhortation was common in deliberative and epideictic speeches; Betz' attempts to circumvent this difficulty were highly artificial and unconvincing. Last, and perhaps most important, the subject of Galatians simply could not support Betz' case, for Paul's principal aim (as appears in his conclusion at 6.12–16) was not to persuade the Galatians that they should alter their judgement of him, but that they should not get circumcised. In keeping with the point of deliberative rhetoric, Paul is really interested in altering the Galatians' views and behaviour with respect to the future, not in achieving the judicial aim of having them form a view of something which has occurred in the past. A similar line has been adopted by Lyons (1985: 112–119); Gaventa (1986); Hall (1987); and Vouga (1988), who points out that the Demosthenes' *de Corona* is a good classical example of a deliberative speech containing a *narratio*; and Smit (1989).

Virtually all of the scholars who have participated in this debate have, however, assumed an ease of incorporation of rhetorical features into epistolary style which underestimates the differences between the two genres, as discussed in Chapter 1. They have sought to make quite specific points about the letter using stylistic features culled from rhetorical treatises and the *progymnasmata*. As already noted, the better approach is to accord due credit to the differences between speech-making and letter-writing, while always acknowledging that given the pervasive influence of rhetoric in the Graeco-Roman world someone writing a letter in a context similar to one of the three standard rhetorical occasions would tend to adopt, at least in a broad sense, features appropriate to the occasion. Accordingly, it is reasonable to ask whether the function of Galatians is deliberative or judicial or even epideictic,[5] since this raises the important issue of Paul's main purpose in writing the epistle. Broadly speaking, although the arguments advanced by Kennedy for its being deliberative in nature, here meant in a functional not a technical sense, are persuasive, it will be useful to tease out the implications of this result a little, especially with respect to Gal. 1.12–2.14, since this passage must have some relationship to the broad intentions in this communication.

Rhetoric and history

Such an investigation takes us back to the significance of the historical dimension of the text, that is, the relationship it bears to the context in which, and for which, the message it contains was communicated, which is a crucial aspect of this reading. The extent to which a work like Galatians that utilises rhetoric can yield historical information has recently come under attack, however, and the project needs to be defended against at least two types of criticism. Most radically, Robert Hall has argued that since certain ancient rhetoricians urged writers of *narrationes* to re-interpret history in the interest of persuasion not truth and since Paul is employing rhetorical techniques, Galatians must be discounted as an historical source (1991). In other words, since Paul uses rhetoric you have to be careful about believing anything he says. Not quite so extreme is the case made by George Lyons (1985), that it is wrong to adopt the 'mirror-reading' espoused by Tyson (1968) and others, which consists of holding that where Paul utters strong antitheses (1.1, 10–12) or denials (2.5, 17, 21) he is responding to specific charges. According to Lyons, the specific charges proposed are often quite arbitrary when set against the possibilities thrown up by the data and, more significantly, much of the material thought relevant can be explained as rhetorical amplification not necessarily related to any precise charges. I will respond to Hall and Lyons in turn, although it is worth noting at once that the arguments of both exhibit a heavier investment in the specific features of rhetoric than may be justified in the case of an epistolary communication.

Robert Hall's scepticism as to the factual accuracy of Galatians

Hall's scepticism as to the truth of what Paul says is quite unjustified. First of all, he assembles a number of statements about the *narratio* without distinguishing between *narrationes* in judicial as opposed to deliberative speeches and relies on Quintilian, the *Rhetorica ad Herennium*, Cicero and the pseudo-Aristotelian *Rhetorica ad Alexandrum*, without mentioning Aristotle's superior work *Rhetorica*. Yet it is risky to assume that what is said regarding a judicial speech applies to a deliberative one, for as Aristotle explained:

> Political [sc. deliberative] rhetoric is given to less unscrupulous practices than forensic, because it treats of wider issues. In a political debate the man who is forming a judgment is making a decision about his own vital interests. There is no need, therefore, to prove anything except that the facts are what the supporter of the measure maintains they are. In forensic [judicial] oratory this is not enough; to conciliate the listener is what pays here. It is other people's affairs that are to be decided, so that the judges, intent on their own satisfaction and listening with partiality, surrender themselves to the disputants instead of judging between them.
>
> (*Rhetorica* 1354; ET by Roberts 1924)

This is just common sense; applied to a *narratio* it means that an audience is more likely to smile at specious falsehood when their own interests are not affected (judicial context) than when they are (deliberative context). Given this view, we would not expect Paul's Galatians to be too tolerant of his pulling the wool over their eyes, nor expect him to think he could.

Second, there are actually references in the rhetorical literature, precisely to the opposite effect claimed by Hall, which insist on the need for factual accuracy in *narrationes* like that found in Galatians 1 and 2. In a section devoted to political speeches, the *Rhetorica ad Alexandrum* states that we must 'either narrate events which have happened in the past or recall them to the minds of our hearer' and continues a little later as follows in relation to a scenario closely related to the journey to Jerusalem Paul describes in Gal. 2.1–10:

> When therefore we are reporting the details of an embassy, we must make a lucid statement of everything that was said, in order that our speech may carry weight . . . next, if we have been unsuccessful, our object will be to make our hearers think that the failure of the negotiations was due to some other cause and not to our negligence . . . This [sc. our success] they are ready to believe, if, not having been present at the negotiations, they observe the zeal displayed in our speech in omitting nothing but accurately reporting every detail. So when we are describing the results of an embassy, we must for the reasons which I have stated report everything just as it happened.
>
> (*Rhetorica ad Alexandrum* 1438a; ET by Forster 1924)

The author further explains that the speaker needs to be clear, concise and convincing, yet the latter factor is not meant as a licence to falsify the facts, but rather to ensure that the audience 'may not reject our statements before we have supported them with proofs and justifications'. Where the facts are improbable, and the limitation is significant, the author states that we must bring forward reasons which will make them plausible and, moreover, we 'must omit anything the occurrence of which seems too improbable' (ibid.: 1438b). Thus, although embarrassingly unlikely facts may be left unsaid (something also permissible under evidentiary rules of English common law, which permit any factual statement against one's interest to be left unsaid), there is no justification offered here for falsification of facts.

Third, even Hall concedes the view of Quintilian that facts too widely known must be admitted (1991: 312). Yet much of what Paul says in Gal. 1.13–2.14 was well and truly in the public domain; this applies in particular to the crucial facts of his three dealings with members of the Jerusalem Church – on his two visits to Jerusalem and at Antioch. All of this could have been checked against his version of events. As for the matters personal to himself, he is in fact remarkably reticent, thereby failing to follow the advice later to be given by Quintilian – that one should invent what could not be disproved (Quint. 4.2.93).

Fourth, there is the distinctive nature of Paul's audience. They were not some amorphous body of citizens unrelated to him whom he needed to persuade to a particular course. In group-oriented ancient Mediterranean culture there was no necessary shame in misleading such people for your own benefit. No, he was writing to the congregations he himself had founded, people whom he repeatedly addresses as *adelphoi*, 'brethren', fellow 'house members of the faith' (6.10), his own family in Christ. By Mediterranean standards it would have been disgraceful to dissemble to persons such as these and nothing which Hall cites from the rhetoricians suggests otherwise. There is no justification whatever for thinking Paul acted so wickedly within the ethical conventions of his day as to have done so.

George Lyons' attack on 'mirror-readings' of Galatians

As to Lyons' argument, it is certainly reasonable to be cautious about drawing too specific an inference as to what historical phenomenon, if any, might underlie Paul's emphatic antitheses, denials and questions. Clearly, some mirror-reading interpretations have pushed the evidence beyond breaking-point, especially as to the identity of Paul's opponents. We must always be ready to consider whether there is a rhetorical reason for some particular statement. This is not to say, however, that we should abandon seeking to contextualise Pauline assertions in mid-first-century CE Galatia. The alleged weaknesses and inconsistencies which, Lyons argues, affect existing attempts to relate Paul's message to his Galatian context do not mean that a reasonable case cannot be made, only that we need to approach the problem differently, through injecting some social-scientific realism into the discussion. In particular, we need to employ a new framework of socially realistic and reflective questions (such as those deriving from Mediterranean anthropology) with which to investigate the text, rather than the hunches of modern European individualists, as has hitherto been the case.

Lyons himself recognises that 'trouble-makers' were at work in Galatia, that Paul faced opposition there and that the Galatians were in peril of falling away from the true gospel (1985: 170–176). Lyons' view is characterised by an unwillingness to get much more specific than this. Yet his own fairly sceptical position has its problems. His emphatic denial that we can know anything much about the opposition neglects important questions thrown up by data such as the reference to present-day Jerusalem being in slavery (4.25), the possible reference to a known person at 5.10, the circumcisers' connection with the cross (6.12) and, finally, the question about Paul's advocacy of circumcision at 5.11. The fact that no one has yet come up with entirely satisfactory answers to the dilemmas posed by data such as these does not justify our throwing up our hands with the despairing cry that it is all too hard. This is especially the case where methodological advances offer the promise of side-stepping old obstacles to understanding.

The real weakness with Lyons' position, however, lies in his use of ancient rhetorical theory. His argument, *in nuce*, is that Paul's antithetical constructions represent, not his defence against charges raised against him, but rhetorical constructions used for purposes of emphasis and clarity; they serve the positive function of affirming his position, rather than the negative one of responding to charges against him (1985: 105–112). The foundation for his position is an article by Abraham Malherbe which seeks to relate Paul's autobiographical remarks in 1 Thess. 2.1–12 to similar statements by the Cynic philosopher Dio Chrysostom (*c.* CE 40–120) in his *Oration* 32 in which, according to Malherbe, Dio is not defending himself against specific charges that he was a charlatan but just using antithetic formulations to characterise himself as the ideal Cynic (Malherbe 1970).

Lyons supports this view of the rhetoric of the situation with the argument that a further reason for rejecting the defensive nature of Paul's statements of this kind is that the letter is deliberative not forensic in nature, as claimed by Betz (Lyons 1985: 112–119). The latter point rests on an assumption that deliberative speeches did not contain passages in defence of the speaker and may be disposed of quickly, since it is abundantly clear that the makers of deliberative (political) speeches frequently had to present their own character favourably as a way of persuading their audience of the merits of their case:

> the orator must not only try to make the argument of his speech demonstrative and worthy of belief; he must also make his own character look right and put his hearers, who are to decide, into the right frame of mind. Particularly in political oratory, but also in lawsuits, it adds much to an orator's influence that his own character should look right and that he should be thought to entertain the right feelings towards his hearers.
>
> (*Rhetorica*, 1377b; ET by Roberts 1924)

As a general observation, it is clear that Lyons has left out of consideration the extent to which the primary level of socialisation in Mediterranean society involved the inculcation of a fierce sense of competitiveness with all who were not family or close friends. Although some critics have been remarkably slow to listen, Bruce Malina has been urging readers of the New Testament since 1981 to take seriously the extent to which first-century Mediterranean society was a fiercely competitive one, riven with envy directed at one's successful competitors.[6] Solid confirmation of this phenomenon can be found throughout Graeco-Roman literature, but there is actually an extensive theoretical treatment of the subject in Aristotle's *Rhetorica* (1370b–1371a; 1384a; 1387a–b), who says blankly at one point: 'We compete with our equals' (1384a), and at another:

> Envy [*phthonos*] is pain at the sight of such good fortune as consists of the good things already mentioned; we feel it towards our equals; not with the idea of getting something for ourselves, but because the other people have it. We shall feel it if we have, or think we have, equals; and by 'equals' I mean equals in birth, relationship, age, disposition, distinction, or wealth . . . So too we compete with those who follow the same ends as ourselves: we compete [*philotimountai*] with our rivals in sport or in love, and generally with those who are after the same things; and it is therefore these whom we are bound to envy above all others.
>
> (*Rhetorica* 1387b–1388a; ET by Roberts 1924)

This meant that Paul would necessarily face opposition to his success wherever he went and would need to be quick to defend himself against it. His own engagement with this type of outlook is evident when he states that he was advanced in *Ioudaismos* beyond many contemporaries of his age (1.14). In this context, Lyons' proposal that Paul's rhetoric could operate merely to emphasise his meaning, that he could send a message to his congregations without really needing to counter the envious attacks he could expect from others in Galatia, represents a socially unrealistic imposition of modern individualist notions on ancient texts where they are quite inapposite.

For this reason, Lyons is also unwise to rely on Malherbe's essay on 1 Thess. 2.1–12 in making his case, since Malherbe himself may have misconstrued Dio in much the same way – by failing to appreciate the savagely competitive nature of ancient Graeco-Roman society which meant that Dio could anticipate criticisms which could be made of him as a Cynic. Has Malherbe interpreted Dio in the intellectualist fashion typical of many modern European scholars, by divorcing him from the conflict-ridden Mediterranean culture where the possibility of attack by others envious of one's success was, as Aristotle pointed out, an ever-present reality? After all, Malherbe essentially depends upon verbal similarity between a section of Dio Chrysostom's *Oration* 32 and 1 Thess. 2 without closely examining the meaning of the language in these two distinct contexts.

But even more fundamentally, the dichotomy Lyons draws between a mode of interpretation which attempts to relate particular statements by Paul to conflict in Galatia, on the one hand, and the characteristics of rhetoric on the other, is a false one. For it ignores a significant strand of ancient Graeco-Roman rhetoric which advised that speakers should incorporate into their speeches references to the case they thought was being made against them, with such material constituting a firm basis for something very like the mirror-readings which Lyons decries.

In ancient rhetoric 'anticipation' (*prokatalēpsis* or *prolēpsis*; *praesumptio*) was 'the method by which we shall counteract the ill-feeling which is against us by anticipating the adverse criticisms of our audience and the arguments of those who are going to speak against us' (*Rhetorica ad Alexandrum*, 1432b). The rhetorical work just cited explains anticipation like this, in a section which is said to apply to all kinds of oratory:

> If you are the object of misrepresentation, the misrepresentation must be connected with yourself or the subject on which you are speaking or your actual words. Misrepresentations of this kind can date either from the present or from the past. If then one is under suspicion of wrongdoing in the past, one must employ anticipation in addressing one's audience and say: 'I am well aware that a prejudice exists against me, but I will prove that it is groundless.' You must then make a brief defence in your proem, if you have anything to say on your own behalf, or raise objections to the judgments which have been passed upon you.
>
> (*Rhetorica ad Alexandrum*, 1436b–1437a; ET by Forster 1924)

Anticipation is a prominent theme in the *Rhetorica ad Alexandrum*[7] and is mentioned by other rhetoricians.[8] Quintilian says that it is of extraordinary value in judicial speeches (9.2.16), although he acknowledges that sometimes the second speaker may capitalise on the practice by ridiculing the case which would allegedly be made by the defence (5.13.43–50).

The clearest example in Galatians is found at 5.11: 'If I am still preaching circumcision, why am I being persecuted?', where the inexplicable suddenness and lack of context for this remark really allow of only one explanation: Paul is anticipating a claim which has already been made against him that he himself preaches circumcision (and therefore is acting hypocritically in opposing the gentile Christ-followers being circumcised). Similarly, Paul's assertion in Gal. 1.1 that he is an apostle through divine and not human agency, which has no parallel at such a place in any other letter by him, and the claims that he seeks to please God not human beings (1.10), that his gospel had a divine, not human, origin (1.11–12), and that after his conversion experience he went off to the Arabia Felix without speaking to anyone (1.16–17), also read very well as anticipations. Paul is moving to anticipate the claim that his authority and his gospel are merely human (and therefore should not stand in the way of the different gospel being preached now that he has left Galatia). I will seek to demonstrate in Chapter 5 of this reading how the autobiographical section in 1.13–2.14 can be construed very easily as anticipation by Paul either of attacks on his authority or character or as anticipation of charges which may be made against him.

Yet, as is plain in the quotation from *Rhetorica ad Alexandrum* above, anticipation extends beyond the character of the speaker to an attack on the arguments which could be brought against his case, and much of what Paul says about the relationship between law and righteousness in the letter can be seen as an anticipation of the views of those advocating circumcision in Galatia. Moreover, this kind of approach meshes nicely with the other data in the text which even Lyons cannot dismiss as the rhetoric of emphasis, such as the explicit statements about circumcision or the circumcisers at 5.2–3, 12, 6.12–13.

Conclusion

Accordingly, it is reasonable to conclude that Paul's rhetoric is closely matched to the factual context of his mission in Galatia, both in terms of the fundamentally agonistic nature of the culture, the general dimensions of the problem there and the precise demands of the rhetorical practice of anticipation. This is not to say that understanding the contextual clues in the text is an easy business, nor to deny that much of the work in the field to date is flawed, but rather that we are certainly entitled to think that far more can be deduced about the situation in Galatia from the way Paul presents his argument than Hall or Lyons would have us believe. The challenge is to employ social-scientific insights to try to avoid some of the pitfalls into which previous scholars have fallen, and to bring the theory and practice of rhetoric more adequately to bear upon the letter. The immediate task, which will occupy the rest of this chapter, is to conduct a more detailed investigation of those features of the Galatian context of the epistle which we have characterised as the exigence and audience of the letter. In the remaining chapters a large proportion of the text will be examined section by section, roughly following the order of Paul's delivery. The ongoing theme of this examination will be the analysis of the letter as a communication from another culture, an understanding of which holds out the prospect of intercultural enrichment of the type discussed above.

THE EXIGENCE OF THE LETTER

Rhetorical situation

To reiterate the discussion in Chapter 1 of this reading, the rhetorical situation of a communication encompasses three elements: first, some serious imperfection in social relationships (an 'exigence') which provokes and shapes the communication; second, an audience of persons capable of being influenced by discourse to change in some way or another so as to have an effect on the exigence; and, third, various constraints (including persons, events, traditions, values, beliefs, interests) having the power adversely to affect any decision or action needed to modify the exigence. As we will see, however, there is considerable overlap between the three and their isolation as distinct elements in the rhetorical situation is conceptually convenient rather than corresponding to any hard and fast division in actual human experience. I will discuss the first two elements in the remaining parts of this chapter and take up the main constraints which constituted the third element in Galatia, such as the authority accorded to Israel's scripture, at various places later in this reading, especially in Chapters 6 and 7.

Since all three elements are deeply implicated in the general social realities of the ancient Mediterranean region and the more specific dynamics of the Galatian area discussed in Chapter 2, considering them will require assistance from the social sciences so as to maximise the extent to which questions put to the text and the overall framework of the investigation will be socially appropriate and not just intuitive guesses derived from modern European individualism. In particular, social identity theory offers a way of comprehending all of the phenomena which are covered by the three elements of rhetorical situation. A large part of the chapter, indeed, will offer an amplification of the role that ethnic boundaries play in the development and maintenance of social identity through intergroup conflict.

The nature of the task means that in this chapter we will have to focus on passages from various sections of text (especially 1.1–2.14; 4.12–19; 5.1–12; 6.11–13 and 15–16), with the aim of reading the letter more in its own order left until later chapters.

Paul's Gospel and its rival

The exigence of the letter to the Galatians consists of some pathological condition affecting social relationships among Paul's addressees which has provoked him to write and which has influenced the content and form of his communication. More precisely, since Paul is geographically distant from Galatia, the exigence consists of what he has heard of some problem or problems from unnamed intermediaries. Although his know-ledge of the situation as he writes is limited, we may assume that he had a general awareness of what was going on from his previous visit there and a more particular grasp of recent developments from his informants, since if there was no reasonable correspondence between his message and whatever was transpiring in Galatia, his writing and despatch of the letter would have been a waste of time.

Paul begins Galatians in a manner found nowhere else in his cor-respondence – with an assertion that his apostleship was the result of divine *and not human* initiative:

> Paul an apostle, not from human beings nor through a human being, but through Jesus Christ and God the Father, who raised him from the dead.
>
> (Gal. 1.1)

The best explanation for such a beginning is that there were some in Galatia who were insisting that human beings – and not God – were responsible for Paul's status as an apostle and that Paul is compelled to confront such an allegation at the very outset if he hopes to persuade his readers to his point of view. Recent attempts to undermine such a view as exemplifying an allegedly illicit 'mirror-reading' of the text come up against the fact of anticipation as recommended by ancient rhetoricians who, as we have seen, were well aware of the close connection between the messenger and the message and the need for both to come across to the audience in the most favourable light for the communication to be persuasive. Paul's strong feelings concerning events in Galatia are also shown by his omission of the customary thanksgiving and prayer at the start of the letter.[9]

Gal. 1.1 does not speak of the circumstances which might have led to Paul's apostolic status being questioned. Yet only four verses later, after a greeting which includes a statement of the salvific significance of Jesus' death and a doxology (1.2–5), he expressly raises the exigence in this way:

> 1.6 I am astonished that you are so quickly turning from [*metatithesthe*] him who called you in grace [of Christ] to a different gospel.
> 1.7 Not that there is another gospel, but there are some who trouble [*tarassontes*] you and want to pervert the gospel of Christ.

1.8 But even if we, or an angel from heaven, should preach to you a gospel contrary to that which we preached to you, let him be accursed.

1.9 As we have said before, so now I say again, if any one is preaching to you a gospel contrary to that which you received, let him be accursed.

Paul is most aggrieved that they are in the process of betraying (as shown by the present tense of *metatithesthe* in 1.6) the one who called them, either God (Matera 1992: 45) or Christ or perhaps Paul himself (Betz 1979: 46), by turning to a different gospel. He gives us a few details later of how he had commenced preaching among them because he had been suffering some weakness, perhaps an eye complaint (Elliott 1990b), which they cheerfully endured, not rejecting him, but receiving him like an angel of God, like Christ Jesus (4.12–15). But now it is as if he is their enemy (4.16). The sense of betrayal is great.

Whoever was urging adoption of a different gospel would have needed to assert that God was behind this version and not Paul's, and one means to this end was to deny any divine warrant for his authority, a notion he contests in the very first verse of the letter. Accordingly, whatever gospel means in 1.6, it exists in an 'agonistic' context, that is, one prone to conflict, where the message and the person who conveyed it to them are closely linked. In a strongly group-oriented society, Paul naturally complains of their disloyalty and vigorously attacks those who are encouraging it.

Moreover, the highly competitive nature of this culture means that it is most unlikely that people would have been causing trouble in Galatia by arguing against Paul's message, without expressing hostility to the man himself. Paul faced opponents, not just rival opinions. That the opposition was engaged in *ad hominem* attacks on Paul is suggested in 1.1 and indicated explicitly by the fact that he must deny the charge that he himself was still preaching circumcision (5.11). Views to the contrary, such as those of J. Louis Martyn (1986) and George Lyons (1985), rest on gentler modern habits of dispute (particularly in the Academy) and are socially unrealistic when applied to the agonistic Graeco-Roman world of the first century CE so evident in Galatians. The cultural difference between us and Paul in this regard is emphatically shown by the fact that twice in 1.8–9 he actually wishes a curse on those urging acceptance of another gospel, while at 5.12 he comes up with the more extreme suggestion of self-castration.

In verse 7 Paul corrects what he has just said by denying that the other version on offer in Galatia really is the gospel and by asserting that those causing the disturbance are seeking to pervert the gospel of Christ. From this it seems clear that the trouble-makers are claiming the word gospel for their position and that they are Christ-followers of some sort, although we will see that there may have been persons of a different kind standing behind them.

The demand for circumcision

Yet how do these rival gospels differ? What do they entail? We may immediately dispense with any notion that we are dealing with thought-forms or thought-patterns separable from social context. For there seems little doubt that the primary distinction between the two gospels, at least for congregations with a mixed population of Israelites and gentiles, is that Paul's does not require believers in Christ to be circumcised and join the house of Israel, whereas the advocates of the other gospel demand precisely this. At 5.10 we find the only other use of the verb 'trouble' (*tarassein*) in Galatians apart from the instance at 1.7 and there it is used of some unnamed person who is mentioned in close relationship to the activities of the circumcisers (5.11–12). There is a close connection between circumcision and taking on all the Mosaic law at 5.2–5. Similarly, at 2.5 Paul uses the expression 'the truth of the gospel' in respect of the position he previously maintained (allegedly for the sake of the Galatians) in Jerusalem in the face of people wishing to impose circumcision. It is possible that the alternatives mentioned at 2.7–8, namely, 'the gospel of the uncircumcised' and 'the gospel of the circumcised' would have been taken by his Galatian audience as aptly distinguishing his version from that of his rivals, although the chasm between them was not necessarily as obvious at the time of the Jerusalem meeting as it later became. We gain a particularly valuable insight into the identity of the circumcisers in Gal. 6.12–13, which I will consider in a moment.

Circumcision and social identity

The heart of Tajfel's theory explored in Chapter 2 of this reading is the investigation of how groups establish a positively valued distinctiveness *vis-à-vis* other groups so as to provide their members with an attractive social identity. Paul's opponents are inviting the gentiles among his addressees to take on the social identity of Israelites, an identity with many desirable attributes, by initially accepting one of the key elements which made that group distinctive, circumcision. At the same time, since those advocating such an action are describing their position as gospel, they must be maintaining that it does not entail the gentiles abandoning Christ. Paul must contest this appeal. His initial reaction is to castigate the alternative on offer as a perversion of the gospel proposed by persons who deserve to be cursed (1.7–9). His fuller response consists mainly of a demonstration that a more positive identity is to be found among the type of congregation which he originally founded in Galatia, but he also insists that to become an Israelite while purporting to follow Christ actually means rejecting the significance of his death for salvation (2.21).

Who were those favouring circumcision?

The statement in the letter which reveals most about the activities of the circumcisers, at least as Paul sees them, occurs near its end:[10]

> 6.12 Those who want to make a good showing in the flesh are the ones who are compelling you to be circumcised, and only in order that they may not be persecuted for the cross of Christ.
> 6.13 For even those who are circumcised do not themselves keep the law, but they want you to be circumcised so that they may base their claims to honour on your flesh.

Gal. 6.12 brings into prominence something which is widely unappreciated, that Paul's opponents regard circumcision as the solution to a problem, not the problem itself – which is left unspecified here. Yet another revealing feature of this verse is Paul's suggestion that those seeking to have his addressees circumcised are doing so in order to avoid being persecuted (*mē diōkōntai*) *for the cross of Christ*. This can only mean that they have some association with the cross of Christ, that they are in some sense followers of Christ, which accords with the fact (already noted) that they present their position as gospel, but that other persons will persecute them unless they see to it that the gentile Christ-followers are circumcised. Clearly the cross itself is not the problem; their connection with it will be permitted if the gentiles are circumcised. Leaving aside for the moment the nature of the problem which is producing the pressure for circumcision, it seems most likely that its advocates are Israelite members of the Galatian communities, but that they are themselves being threatened – either by Israelite Christ-followers from elsewhere (similar to the people from James in Jerusalem who arrived in Antioch and produced enough fear on Peter's part for him to withdraw from table-fellowship with gentiles [Gal. 2.12]), or by local Galatian Israelites, or by a coalition of both of these groups.

The involvement of representatives from the Jerusalem Church, although resisted by some,[11] is strongly suggested both by the close parallel, to which I will return later, between the situation in Antioch and in Galatia and by the fact that at 4.25 Paul states that 'the present day Jerusalem is in slavery (*douleuei*) together with its children'. Since Jerusalem figures in the letter on three occasions previous to this condemnation as the locus of the form of faith in Christ represented by Peter, James and John (1.17, 18 and 2.1), it is difficult not to consider that the church in the holy city is tainted by this description. After all, it was precisely in Jerusalem that Paul had to fight off an attempt to enslave him and his converts (*katadoulōsousin* – 2.4), no doubt by imposing circumcision on the gentiles in their ranks.

To be most effective, the threat of persecution (*diōkein*) mentioned by Paul in 6.12 would need to involve recourse to the disciplinary procedures available in the synagogue or to other means whereby Israelite authority was enforced. This is in keeping with what Paul says elsewhere in the letter. After all, before he turned to Christ, he himself 'persecuted the church of God' (*ediōkon tēn ekklēsian tou theou*) and tried to destroy it (Gal. 1.13). He was probably exercising some sort of authority vested in the house of Israel, perhaps akin to the letters from the high priest to the synagogues in Damascus he is described as requesting in Acts 9.2. His denial at 5.11 that he 'still preaches circumcision' – in a context which must mean in relation to gentile Christ-followers and not to gentiles at large – raises an inference that he did so at some stage in the past. The only plausible period for such activity by Paul is before he became a Christ-follower. Whatever it was that motivated Paul to persecute the church (a question too infrequently asked by New Testament critics), possibly involving insistence on circumcision for the gentile members, the fact of such persecution testifies to the interest among Israelites at large, that is, among those who were not part of the Jesus messianic movement, and within a few years of the Crucifixion, of a grave concern with some aspect of its activities and a desire to terminate or modify them. Accordingly, Robert Jewett's proposal (1970–1971), that lying behind the push to circumcise was the arrival of Israelite zealots from Palestine stirred into action by the activities of the Roman rulers there in the late 40s and early 50s of the first century, not only lacks specific evidence in support, but is unnecessary in the light of Paul's behaviour in the 30s. I consider that the precise cause of offence was Israelite opposition to the practice of Israelite and gentile Christ-followers sharing the same food, wine and vessels in eucharistic meals, for reasons I will discuss in Chapter 4.

One final point must be mentioned here. The Israelites or envoys from Jerusalem insisting that the local Israelite Christ-followers have the gentiles circumcised must have had grounds to believe that this result was possible. This could only have been the case if those to whom they were applying pressure had some connection with the gentiles of a kind which would allow them to exercise their powers of persuasion and be held responsible if they failed. In the circumstances, the only plausible context for such social proximity was the congregations Paul had founded. The circumcisers were Israelite members and their targets gentile members.

Yet none of this goes very far towards profiling the various groups in Galatia and the relationships between them, nor explores the reason for the attempts to have the gentiles circumcised. After briefly mentioning one other aspect of the exigence of the letter, I will deal with the groups represented in Galatia in what remains of this chapter and the latter issue, concerning a Judaic prohibition on intimate forms of table-fellowship, in the next.

The problems 'internal' to the Galatian congregations

The remaining area of the exigence requiring attention is the distortion in social relationships among the congregations which Paul seeks to address in Gal. 5.13–6.10. Many commentators have found it difficult to reconcile Paul's interest in apparently 'internal' questions in Galatians 5 and 6 with the main concern of his letter, regarded as the 'external' or boundary-sensitive demands for circumcision. In Chapter 8 I will argue that from a social-scientific perspective the so-called internal and external issues are, in fact, closely interconnected, especially because notions of social and personal identity are central to both, even with respect to material in this section of the text traditionally labelled as 'ethical'. For the moment, however, since this discussion can be separated, at least conceptually, from that of the audience of Paul's communication, it may be left till later while we proceed to this second aspect of the rhetorical situation of Galatians.

THE AUDIENCE

As noted in Chapter 1 of this reading, we are operating with a model of communication which envisions it as a process whereby the person sending the message intends it to have an effect on the recipients, and this corresponds to the basic aim of ancient rhetoric – to persuade others to a particular viewpoint or course of action. To be effective in this regard, a communication must relate to the nature of the persons who will receive it and to the varied realities of the situation in which they find themselves. We are also seeking, as explained in the previous chapter, to interpret such a communication as related to the maintenance of a desirable and distinctive social identity in a setting of intergroup conflict. Accordingly, it is necessary to explore the identity, characteristics and circumstances of the groups who comprised Paul's audience and the other groups in their environment with whom they needed to relate.

The Israelite diaspora in the first century CE

Paul arrived in Galatia bearing the message of a new religious movement which had originated among the Israelites in Palestine some twenty years or so earlier and he apparently won converts from among local Israelites and gentiles. Since the relationship of his gospel to contemporary patterns of Israelite belief and practice lies close to the heart of the message he conveys in this letter, a suitable starting point for a consideration of his audience is with the striking phenomenon of the Israelite dispersion, or 'diaspora', across the Mediterranean world of the first century CE.

Several million Israelites lived outside of Palestine at this time (Barclay 1996a: 4), when the total population of the Roman empire was probably only about sixty million.[12] The diaspora had begun as early as the forced deportation of sectors of the Palestinian population to Assyria and Babylon in the eighth and sixth centuries BCE, but the conquest of the East by Alexander, which resulted in large numbers of Judeans moving to Egypt around and after the time of his death in 323 BCE, marked the beginning of the diaspora on a grand scale. 1 Maccabees 15.16–23 is a circular letter written by the Roman senate in 139–138 BCE in support of privileges of the *Ioudaioi* which indicates their presence in Egypt, Syria, Pergamon Caria, Lycia, Pamphylia and a number of Greek cities and islands. By the first century CE, Philo, an Israelite from Alexandria, could report that there were communities of *Ioudaioi* as far away as Bithynia and the remote corners of Pontus (*In Flaccum* 281–282). The Mediterranean diaspora and the literature which it produced has recently been the subject of a major treatment by John Barclay (1996a).

There is some evidence for the siting of Israelites in Asia Minor generally in the New Testament period which has been well treated by Trebilco (1991), although very little is known specifically about the positions in the cities (on either the tribal or provincial Galatian hypotheses) which may have contained the communities for which Paul wrote

Galatians. As Barclay notes, most of the evidence we do possess for Asia Minor comes from those parts which at some time or other lay within the Roman province of Asia and this excludes large areas such as Bithynia, Pontus, Galatia, Cappadocia, Cilicia and Pamphylia (1996a: 260). Nevertheless, it is possible to follow Trebilco in making some generalisations about the presence of Israelites in Asia Minor which probably extend to the cities relevant for Galatians. As noted in the previous chapter of this reading, there is evidence for the presence of *Ioudaioi* in Asia Minor as early as the third century BCE (when 2,000 families from Babylon and Mesopotamia were settled by the Seleucid king, Antiochus III, in Lydia and Phrygia)[13] and their existence in flourishing and organised communities can be documented for centuries after the turn of the era. The evidence presented by Trebilco does not support the picture of tightly knit and introverted Israelite groups (except perhaps in the period of significant hostility between them and the cities of Asia Minor in the period 49 BCE to 2 CE), but rather indicates regular interaction with gentiles, which included a fair degree of involvement in city life (even if this did not usually extend to citizenship), together with signs of considerable respect by gentiles for Israelites, as manifested in their becoming patrons of Israelite institutions or even attending synagogues as God-fearers (Trebilco 1991: 183–190). And yet the Israelites managed to maintain a distinct identity in what was first a pagan and later a Christian environment and this suggests that they must have maintained effective boundaries of some sort between themselves and the outside world. The discussion to be undertaken below will take into account both the level of interaction between Israelites and gentiles and the fact that they did not lose their distinctive identity. This brings us to the point where examination of the data can be promoted by the use of social-scientific ideas and perspectives – in this case those relating to the role of boundaries in ethnic interaction within a broader framework of social identity theory. In John Barclay's formulation, they may have become acculturated but they were not assimilated (1996a: 92–98).

Ethnicity and boundaries: an anthropological perspective

In Chapter 2 I outlined a theory relating to social identity which can be applied to virtually any type of group that exists in relationship to another group or other groups. Sometimes, however, the theory needs to be fleshed out to take account of some specific dimension of the groups under discussion. One such factor is the ethnic character of at least one of the groups, since this will bear upon the nature of the intergroup

relationships and the stereotyping of ingroup and outgroup. Since Israelite ethnicity was important in the Galatian context of Paul's communicative efforts, we will now incorporate a discussion of this issue into the
wider theory dealing with social identity.

Boundary maintenance in an ethnic setting[14]

From a social-scientific perspective, the existence of groups of people
who called themselves *Israelitai* after a putative ancestor, Israel, and who
were referred to by their contemporaries as *Ioudaioi* ('Judeans') from the
geographic area of the eastern Mediterranean – Judea – from which
they were thought ultimately to hail, living among gentiles in places as
far from Palestine as Galatia, demands attention be paid to the whole
question of ethnicity. This factor contributed significantly to their distinctiveness as a group and must be taken into account in considering
how they related to other groups.

Two dominant trends as to the meaning of ethnicity are visible in
recent research (see Brett 1996b: 12–15; Esler 1996a). The first – associated with commentators like Edward Shils (1957) and Clifford Geertz
(1973) and representing an anthropological approach to social phenomena which stresses the extent to which individuals are shaped by the
groups and institutions to which they belonged – focuses on what are
perceived to be cultural or 'primordial' features of ethnicity, such as
kinship and a common territory, language and religious tradition, which
together allegedly produce a powerful and abiding affiliation. The fact
that a person born in Northern Ireland happens to be Catholic or Protestant will have a powerful effect on how he or she sees the world and
progresses in it. The second, newer, trend, which illustrates the recent
tendency among anthropologists (such as Anthony Cohen and Nigel
Rapport) to emphasise the role of individuals in manipulating social
arrangements for their own ends, was articulated by Fredrik Barth in his
celebrated introduction to *Ethnic Groups and Boundaries* (1969) and reverses
the relationship between a sense of belonging and associated cultural
features. Given this view, ethnicity is not primordial (Eller and Coughlan
1993).

Although Barth is still interested in cultural features of the sort just
mentioned, he treats them as the result rather than as the essence of
ethnicity, as the diverse modes of expressing an underlying sense of
collective identity. In this perspective, we may treat the cultural indicators of ethnicity as discourses chosen by a group to maintain a fundamental apartness which its members cherish – usually in the context of a

dynamic relationship with other groups which has sharp political connotations, even though Barth himself may have neglected the political
dimension (Jenkins 1996: 102). Since Barth sees the individual members
of an ethnic group continually at work formulating the means whereby
they express their distinctiveness, it is fair to say that he locates ethnicity
'firmly in the realms of the interactional, the transactional and the symbolic' (Cohen 1993: 1). Accordingly, although ideologies of collective
descent frequently underpin ethnicity, in reality it is negotiable.

Barth begins by criticising the notion that ethnic differentiation and
the cultural diversity it sustains are derived from geographic or social
isolation. He offers two reasons. First, boundaries persist despite the flow
of personnel across them in various forms of social intercourse and,
second, stable and persisting social relations can be preserved across such
boundaries and are often maintained precisely on the basis of dichotom-
ised ethnic statuses (1969: 9–10). His theory would therefore lead him
to oppose the idea that the maintenance of a distinct Israelite ethnic
identity in diaspora communities like those in Galatia rested on social
isolation, and Trebilco's research confirms such a view for the *Ioudaioi* of
Asia Minor.

Barth's own approach has several interconnected parts. First of all, he
proposes that ethnic groups are categories of ascription and identification employed by the persons involved with a view to organising interaction
between themselves and others. In this perspective, a second central issue
is to examine the different processes involved in generating and maintaining ethnic groups. This, thirdly, pushes one towards a close examination
of ethnic boundaries and boundary maintenance (1969: 10).

Barth's view entails the consequence that boundary maintenance,
meaning how the actors themselves envision and maintain the boundaries, assumes a central importance. Boundaries are not the product of
cultural difference, as Geertz and Shils suggest, but rather elements such
as a distinctive culture (which can include an alleged descent from some
notable ancestor and religious tradition) should be seen as the product or
result of social differentiation. Cultural features do not matter for 'objective' reasons, but because they are the features which the actors themselves regard as significant in establishing boundaries (Barth 1969: 9–14),
in fostering their sense of distinctiveness. This means that a sense of
one's separateness as a distinctive group is antecedent to the (changing)
ways in which that separateness is expressed.

As Richard Jenkins has pointed out, Barth's analysis is applicable to
social entities other than ethnic ones (1996: 91). For the foundation of
Barth's view is that group identity is a product of collective internal

definition whereby in relating to significant others we, as a group, mobilise identifications of similarity and difference and in so doing generate group identities (Jenkins 1996: 83). Understood in this sense, group identity becomes 'ethnic' when the cultural features selected to maintain distinctiveness rely upon factors such as common ancestry, geographic provenance or language.

Interesting confirmation for this aspect of Barth's theory lies in the fact that cultural and organisational features which at one stage signal boundaries can change without loss of the ongoing distinction between insiders and outsiders or a sense of ethnic affiliation (Barth 1969: 14).[15] There may even be a substantial change of personnel, with some people leaving the ethnic ingroup and others joining it, without loss of its distinctive status (1969: 21; Jenkins 1996: 65), a phenomenon relevant to Paul's strategy in Galatians, as we will see. All this reveals how akin boundaries are to processes.

Needless to say, the distinction between that which constitutes ethnicity and its contingent expressions is easier to make at a conceptual plane than amid the complexities of lived experience and it will at times be appropriate to talk of a dialectical relationship between the two (Jenkins 1996: 97). Nevertheless, the real force of the distinction becomes apparent at a time when particular cultural expressions of ethnic identity are changing or where there is pressure for them to be changed, so that the negotiable nature of the indicia of ethnicity becomes quite visible.

Since collective identities are developed actively through processes of interaction with other groups, we must be careful in using the very word 'boundary' since it can convey inappropriate notions of impermeability. One commentator has noted that the processes which create 'boundaries' are best seen as temporary check-points rather than concrete walls, even though in particular settings they may become routinised and institutionalised (Jenkins 1996: 99).

According to Barth, certain cultural features operate as emblems of ethnic distinctiveness, whereas others are downgraded or ignored. The cultural features which do serve to highlight ethnic differentiation fall into two broad types. First, there are *overt signals or signs*, features which people deliberately adopt to show identity (for example, dress, language, architecture and lifestyle). Second, there are *basic value orientations*, the norms of morality and excellence used to assess performance. The second aspect is important for its connection to the issue of identity: 'Since belonging to an ethnic category implies being a certain kind of person, having that basic identity, it also implies a claim to be judged, and to judge oneself, by those standards that are relevant to that identity' (Barth 1969: 14).

This area can be further developed with the aid of a useful distinction drawn by Anthony Cohen between two senses in which insiders perceive a relevant social boundary. He distinguishes between (a) the public face and 'typical' mode of the boundary, which means the sense insiders have of a boundary as it would be perceived by people on the other side, and (b) the private face and idiosyncratic mode, the insiders' own sense of community – as refracted through all the complexities of their life and experience. The former comes close to Barth's 'overt signals' and the latter to his 'value orientations'. Of utmost importance for the discussion in this chapter, and also that concerning the Mosaic law later in this reading (Chapter 7) is Cohen's view that the private and idiosyncratic mode is more important than the public mode, for here we have people thinking about and symbolising their community in relation to the richness of its inner life (Cohen 1989: 74–75). An example from my own experience will illustrate this point. Prior to the Second Vatican Council, at a time when Roman Catholics in Australia were openly differentiated from the rest of the population by overt acts such as their refusal to eat meat on Fridays, there was a devotion popular among boys and girls of school-age which consisted in their going to Mass on the first Friday of nine consecutive months. This devotion often meant early morning cycle rides to church in mid-winter and it was not something which one spoke about to Protestant friends. Catholics knew that this devotion was quite important in building their sense of identity *vis-à-vis* the rest of society, of constructing the private mode of community understanding in Cohen's analysis, while they were equally aware that it played no role in the public one.

Prescription and proscription in ethnic boundaries

Yet it is important to realise that even though Barth regards boundaries as permeable, in that they allow 'osmosis' through them, the ethnic group can only sustain its existence if there are at all times some respects in which interaction is prohibited:

> Stable inter-ethnic relations presuppose . . . a set of prescriptions governing situations of contact, and allowing for articulation in some sectors or domains of activity, and a set of proscriptions on social situations preventing inter-ethnic interaction in other sectors, and thus insulating parts of the cultures from confrontation and modification.
>
> (Barth 1969: 16)

Without some proscriptions, the *ethnos* would simply merge with other groups in its environment. Accordingly, nothing in this discussion dispenses us from determining which cultural features reflect the boundary between Israelite and non-Israelite at any given time. A common strategy for ethnic groups is to frown on connubium and commensality with outsiders, while allowing other forms of interaction, a strategy which can be seen, for example, in the Indian caste system as far as intermarriage is concerned and in certain types of table-fellowship. In the next chapter I will set out my case for arguing that in the first century CE one proscribed activity for Israelites was intimate table-fellowship with gentiles, while certain trading and social links were permitted.

Israelite ethnic identity in the *Letter of Aristeas*

All of this is highly significant for understanding the status of diaspora *Ioudaioi*, including those in the complex ethnic mixture characterising Galatia. It suggests that the differentiation of the world into ingroups and outgroups is the vital thing, with the panoply of Judaic cultural features being the product or result of this. Emic statements which come very close to this are found in the *Letter of Aristeas*, an Israelite text which was probably written in Egypt in the second century BCE, although it may be a century or two older (Barclay 1996a: 445). The *Letter of Aristeas* broadly deals with how the Septuagint (the Greek translation of a version of the Hebrew Bible) came into existence, but it touches upon many other areas of interest, including an explanation and defence of the Mosaic law, especially as it related to food, putatively made by the Jerusalem high priest Eleazar to the gentile Egyptians whom Ptolemy had sent to the holy city in search of competent translators (*Letter of Aristeas*, 128–171). Although the text may only ever have had an Israelite audience, Eleazar's statement is important as offering the sort of legitimation for the law which Israelites of the time thought would have been suitable for well-disposed gentiles. There is no other explanation of the law as detailed as this extant in the literature of the diaspora. It is not too much of a jump to imagine that similar things might have been said to the Galatian gentiles by those urging them to become members of the House of Israel.

Eleazar begins by observing that people are influenced by those with whom they associate, so that they become miserable and perverted by consorting with the wicked (*kakoi*), but pass from ignorance and amend their lives if they mix with the wise (*sophoi*) and prudent (*phronimoi*) (130). This means that the world is stereotypically divided into two broad groups which fundamentally shape the behaviour of their members and that it is vital to locate oneself in the right one. This notion had a long history in Israel, as we will see later in connection with a discussion of Proverbs 10–15 in Chapter 6. Eleazar's legitimation of the law, therefore, takes group differentiation as its starting-point, with associated accentuation of important behavioural phenomena into two sharply defined categories in the manner proposed in social identity theory.

In the previous chapter we noted that where a group has a limited repertoire of positive social identities it may rely strongly on processes of group differentiation through stereotyping. The position of Israelites in the diaspora was frequently ambiguous. Although there were forms of interaction between them and their gentile neighbours – in trade for example – they were not able to take part in the flourishing local cults of their host cities and may have been in some places, such as Alexandria (Barclay 1996a: 48–51), precluded from citizenship. These disadvantages would have lessened the number of positive roles available to them in a manner likely to foster the stereotypical reinforcement of features, such as behavioural norms, which differentiated them from outgroups.

In this perspective, we are not surprised when Eleazar continues by mentioning that Moses enjoined piety (*eusebeia*) and righteousness (*dikaiosynē*) specified in terms of negative and positive commandments (*Letter of Aristeas*, 131). These qualities summarise the main types of discourse which will be used in what follows to characterise Israelite distinctiveness, with *eusebeia* relating more to relationships to God and *dikaiosynē* to those with other human beings (as evident towards the end of this passage, where mention is made of exercising 'righteousness towards all human beings, while remembering that God is sovereign', 168). Thus, Eleazar starts by picking out cultural features which Barth refers to as 'basic value orientations', rather than 'overt signals and signs' to designate Israelite ethnic distinctiveness and identity.

It is worth noting at this point that the fact that *eusebeia* and *dikaiosynē* can be interpreted as contributing to Israelite identity does not count against their ontological or ethical reality. That Israel builds its identity in worshipping Yahweh and acting in certain normative ways is quite consistent with the existence of such a God and the worth of its ethics. In other words, the introduction of social-scientific perspectives does not entail the reductionist explanation of data in terms of one theoretical framework, but the fuller exposition of the complex of meaning which exists in the text, by highlighting aspects often ignored.

First of all, Eleazar says, Moses taught that God is one and that his power is manifested in everything, so that no one can escape detection

(132–133). Moses went on to show that all other human beings 'except us' consider there are many gods, although they are more powerful than the effigies of stone and wood they create and revere as gods (134–135), which reveals their folly (136–138).

While the discourse of monotheism was a central feature of the Israelite religious tradition distinguishing them from their neighbours, it is interesting to consider whether it did function as the core of the Israelite *ethnos* in the manner advocated by anthropologists before Barth or whether it can be construed as one of the most important cultural expressions of an antecedent Israelite identity. In other words, was monotheism primordial or was it a boundary phenomenon subject to negotiation throughout the history of Israel in the manner proposed by Barth? This brings us to a hotly contested area in Old Testament and intertestamental scholarship, with some commentators, such as Jeffrey Tigay (1986) and Larry Hurtado (1988), arguing for Israelite monotheism in both First and Second Temple periods, while others, such as Peter Hayman (1991) and Margaret Barker (1987, 1992), advocate the continuing importance in the religious tradition of other divine figures. This is not the occasion to reach any firm view on such a large dispute. Nevertheless, a case can certainly be made that even if Yahweh alone was worshipped in cultic contexts, as Hurtado argues, the fact that throughout Israelite history we come across quasi-divine rivals (like Leviathan and Behemoth) whom Yahweh defeated, a heavenly court and even angelic figures with mediatorial roles indicates continuing discussion within Israel over Yahweh's position. This suggests that monotheism was a subject open to some degree of negotiation in the ongoing formulation of Israelite identity in a manner which provides support for Barth's position.

In any event, no final view need be reached on this point since while monotheism is not a live issue in Galatians, the law most certainly is. In this regard we come next to a remarkable passage in which Eleazar clearly confirms that what mattered was the maintenance of Israelite apartness and that the Mosaic law functioned to provide the cultural apparatus which would secure this end, although without specifying the precise cultural features in mind:

the law-giver [sc. Moses] . . . fenced us about [*periephraxen hēmas*] with impregnable palisades and walls of iron, so that we might in no way mix with [*epimisgōmetha*] the other nations [*ethnōn*], pure [*hagnoi*] in body [*kata sōma*] and soul [*kata psychēn*], released from vain ideas, reverencing the one almighty God over the whole creation.

(*Letter of Aristeas*, 139, my translation)

The text then develops the idea that whereas other human beings are concerned with food, drink and clothing, Israelites are totally taken up with the sovereignty of God (140–141). Whether we wish to interpret the monotheism in this section of the text as primordial or follow Barth in construing it as one of the cultural features expressing ethnic distinctiveness, it is clear that acknowledgment of one God does not do service at a purely theological level but contributes to the sense of belonging to the Judaic *ethnos*, in contrast to the other ethic groups who were polytheist and impure. That the Israelites call themselves 'people of God' (*anthrōpoi theou*, 140) has pronounced social as well as theological implications. Again, however, to insist that Judaic monotheism does not exist in a theological vacuum is not to challenge the ontological reality that we may wish to attribute to Israel's God, but rather to outline the social context in which that reality is experienced.

Eleazar continues as follows:

> Therefore, lest we should become perverted [*diastrophas lambanōmen*], by sharing the pollution of others [*mētheni synalisgoumenoi*] or by associating with evil people [*homilountes phaulois*], he hedged us around on all sides with types of purification [*pantothen hēmas periephraxen hagneiais*] in matters of food and drink and touch and hearing and seeing [*dia brōtōn kai potōn kai haphrōn kai akoēs kai horaseōs*] as legal requirements [*nomikōs*].
>
> (*Letter of Aristeas*, 142, my translation)

This passage reinforces the essential need for Israelites to be in the good as opposed to the evil group distinguished earlier (130). Now, at last, the nature of the Mosaic 'palisade' is mentioned. It is a mode of purification, especially as far as food and drink are concerned, a means of ensuring the reality of group identity in contra-distinction to an undesirable outgroup. This is very close to Barth's view.

It is noteworthy that although practices concerning food and drink, and touch, seeing and hearing, constitute fairly visible aspects of lifestyle, in short, cultural features of the type Barth labels as overt signals or signs, the flow of the discussion suggests their relevance to the piety and righteousness introduced earlier (131). This connection is made explicit soon after, when we are told that certain ordinances to do with unclean animals have been made 'for the sake of righteousness' (*dikaiosynēs heneken*), to promote holy meditation and the perfection of our habits (144). As an example, Eleazar cites the requirement to eat tame rather than wild birds (145–146), which is a sign that Israelites should not oppress anyone and should practise righteousness (147–149). The text links overt cultural signs of identity, like food laws, with value orientations under the broad banner of righteousness in a context which continually stresses Judaic distinctiveness from the sinful outgroup. Hence it is difficult to avoid the conclusion that righteousness functions to label and celebrate an ensemble of elements of Judaic identity.

Even more illuminating is the admittedly far-fetched way in which Eleazar suggests that the cleft nature of the hoof of clean animals symbolises a separation, apartness or division (*diastolē*) in all the actions of his people with a view to what is right (150). The next passage reveals how righteousness is bonded to the experience of sharing the identity of a privileged group sharply differentiated from a wicked outgroup:

> Therefore he compels us to do everything in a manner apart [*meta diastolēs*] with a view to righteousness [*pros dikaiosynēn*] . . . He further [sc. indicates] that we have been kept apart [*diestalmetha*] from all human beings. For most other human beings defile themselves with intercourse and practise notable injustice [*adikian*], with countries and whole cities priding themselves on these things. For not only do they have intercourse with males, but they even defile mothers and daughters. But we have been kept apart [*diestalmetha*] from this behaviour.
>
> (*Letter of Aristeas*, 151–152, my translation)

One final point concerning the *Letter of Aristeas*. In legitimating, that is explaining and justifying, the Mosaic law for the benefit of Ptolemy's envoys, Eleazar (and the unknown author of the text behind him) offers an account of the boundary between Israelites and gentiles which must be predicated on the assumption that the latter group were ignorant of many of the details provided. This illustrates Anthony Cohen's distinction between the full sense of a boundary, encompassing more of the inner life and values of the group, which insiders have, compared with that of outsiders, which tends to focus on the obviously visible phenomena to do with lifestyle, dress, festivals and so on.

Israelites and gentiles in Galatia

These social-scientific perspectives, developed in relation to the *Letter of Aristeas*, are very helpful in assessing the three groups in Galatia critical to the discussion – gentiles, Israelites and Christ-followers (some of them gentiles and some Israelites) – and the boundaries between them. To consider the nature of the interrelationships between these groups we will begin with the origins of the situation – the arrival of Israelites in Galatia. Prior to this event, which we assume but about which we have no actual evidence, Galatia contained gentiles of many types, especially the native Phrygian population and the more recent Celtic invaders, together with some Greeks, but all no doubt had in common an acceptance of the polytheistic religious practices of Asia Minor. The arrival of the Israelites must have produced a decisive change in the local social dynamics. For in Galatia, as elsewhere, they were determined to preserve their group identity, so closely tied to monotheism, cultural features of lifestyle, tradition and values, largely encapsulated in the demands of the law, which expressed and supported it, even though survival in this culture meant some measure of interaction with the local gentiles. Figure 3.1, showing a processual and permeable boundary with some modes of interaction permitted and some proscribed as just discussed, represents the initial stage, after the arrival of Israelites in Galatia.[16]

We have already addressed the nature of the boundaries which must exist between an ethnic group and the other groups in its social environment if the former is to preserve a distinctive identity. Permeable boundaries are required which permit some measure of interaction while prohibiting others. This means that we must always determine what social interactions first-century Galatian Israelites permitted between themselves and the surrounding gentiles, and which they forbade. What then are we to make of the view expressed in an influential article on this subject by the prominent Pauline scholar James Dunn (1983)? He argues that because there was a variety of social relations between first-century Israelites in the diaspora and their gentile neighbours, especially God-fearers (those who regularly went along to synagogue to revere God), this

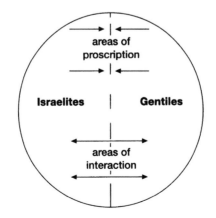

Figure 3.1 The Israelite/gentile boundary in the diaspora

meant that some Israelites would have been happy to modify resistance
to practices such as actually dining with gentiles:

> there would be a broad range of social intercourse between faithful
> Jew and God-fearing gentile, with strict Jews avoiding table-fellowship
> as far as possible, and those less scrupulous in matters of tithing and
> purity willingly extending and accepting invitations to meals where
> such gentiles would be present.
>
> (Dunn 1983: 147)

Like many New Testament critics, Dunn is operating here on the basis of
an implicit model of social relations, in this case one which suggests that
if an ethnic group mixes socially with outsiders in some areas it will
proceed to do so in others. Yet this view falters before Fredrik Barth's
position (1969), based on disciplined social-scientific research, which
holds that the maintenance of ethnic identity depends on the existence
of some areas where intercourse is prescribed and others where it is
proscribed. Prescriptions and proscriptions coexist simultaneously; the
former do not lead to a relaxation of the latter. Accordingly, the unstated
model underlying Dunn's view is contradicted by informed opinion in
the field and any case resting upon it must be regarded as suspect. This
does not mean that cultural features which figured in ethnic boundaries
are not at times subject to negotiation and modification; that this is so
forms an important part of our case. The point is that one cannot argue
from social interaction in one area to a breakdown of proscription in
another. It is necessary to determine in any particular setting what was
proscribed and what permitted on the evidence available.

Moreover, an important dimension of the reading offered in this book
is that there was one particular proscription on Israelite–gentile relationships in Galatia (and the diaspora generally) in the first century CE
which must be appreciated if we are to comprehend the case which Paul
seeks to make in this letter – the prohibition on Israelites dining with
gentiles in the full (and, for current purposes, only relevant) sense of
sitting around one table and sharing, that is physically handing around,
bread and wine. This question will be addressed in the next chapter.

The establishment of Pauline congregations in Galatia

The fact that Paul had converted both Israelites and gentiles in Galatia
to faith in Christ and integrated them into the communities where there
was, ideally at least, neither *Ioudaios* nor *Hellene*, neither slave nor free,
neither male nor female, but they were all one in Christ Jesus (3.28),

meant that there was now to be a new social and religious entity on the scene. Paul unambiguously asserts that the Christ-followers constituted a third group, set over against both the Judaic and the gentile worlds:

> 6.15 For neither circumcision counts for anything, nor uncircumcision, but a new creation.
> 6.16 Peace and mercy be upon all who walk by this rule, upon the Israel of God.

As we have seen in Chapter 2, he employs a rich array of expressions in the letter to distinguish the identity of this third group, his new creation and Israel of God. It is to its members that Paul writes.

Yet the richness of the language Paul deploys to assert their distinctiveness prompts the question as to just how firmly established was this new identity. How successfully had the Christ-followers, both Israelites and gentiles, managed to distinguish themselves from the robust and probably well-regarded Israelite communities in the cities of Galatia, especially when they had accepted an Israelite Messiah through the power of one of his Israelite apostles? To what extent had they abandoned the practices which characterised the bleakly competitive and envy-ridden Mediterranean world of first-century Asia Minor, including the Celtic part of it in tribal Galatia? Had their original status as either Israelites or gentiles become irrelevant to their present existence or were the boundaries between themselves and those in those groups who had remained unaffected by the preaching about Christ becoming dangerously unstable, with the ultimate risk that the gentile members might become Israelites or that either type of Christ-follower might lapse into the reprehensible behaviour typical of the honour-ridden Mediterranean? In short, had they become a third and separate group with a stable and desirable social identity at all?

It will be helpful to set out the position with the help of Figure 3.2, which covers the three groups relevant to the discussion and the boundaries between them (understood in the manner set out above).[17] This diagram represents the culmination of three stages of group development: first, solely gentile; second, gentiles and Israelites; and, third, gentiles, Israelites and Christ-followers. A comparison of this with Figure 3.1 above is instructive. Whereas before the arrival of Paul, there were two groups with one boundary between them, now there are three groups and three boundaries.

The segment CBAC represents the congregations, drawing members from both Israelites and gentiles (designated by the other two segments), which have only come into existence as a result of Paul's missionary

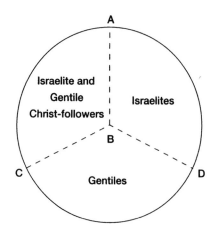

Figure 3.2 Israelites, gentiles and Christ-followers

activities. From the perspective of social identity theory these Christ-followers constitute an ingroup *vis-à-vis* two outgroups, Israelites and gentiles. Paul distinguishes his addressees from these outgroups in many ways, but on two occasions he does this explicitly by pointing out that what matters is neither circumcision nor uncircumcision but faith working through love (5.6), and the new creation and Israel of God which result (6.15). There are no more distinctions between *Ioudaios* and *Hellene* (3.28). I have suggested elsewhere that a useful social-scientific way to characterise the nature of the Pauline communities is as sectarian bodies in relation to Israel (Esler 1987: 89), an approach which, *inter alia*, fixes upon the fact that there is usually exclusivity of membership as between the sect and the dominant religious group from which it has sprung.[18] As we will see in Chapter 8, however, there is considerable tension among the Christ-followers; they do not comprise an harmonious group.

Second, the Israelites are an ingroup in relation to two outgroups, Christ-followers and gentiles; prior to Paul's arrival the Israelites had encountered only the latter as an outgroup.

Third, the gentiles are an ingroup with respect to the Israelites and Christ-followers, although we obtain no sense of their perspective on the situation in Galatia as we do for the other two groups.

As for the boundaries – understood as processes and not barriers as previously explained – between these three groups, first we have the Israelite–gentile boundary (BD), which actually predated Paul's preaching by centuries. First-century CE Israelites strongly differentiated themselves from gentiles whom they treated as embedded in sinfulness, mainly because of their involvement in various forms of idolatry, as we have already observed in the *Letter of Aristeas*. Paul's (inevitable) acceptance of this outlook as an Israelite himself emerges clearly at Gal. 2.15: 'We ourselves, who are *Ioudaioi* by birth and not gentile sinners'. From our previous discussion, we may be confident that Israelites like Paul had a full appreciation of the richness of this boundary, especially the extent to which it covered ethical as well as more public and ceremonial features, that is, Barth's 'value orientations' as well as 'overt signs and signals', while appreciating that gentiles would have had a much more externalised understanding of its nature.

The other two boundaries, however, are more important for understanding the context of the letter. Some of the Christ-followers were Israelites when they converted and the rest were gentiles, so that we need to take into account the possible influence of residual affiliations with these source groups, or even, in the case of the former, an ongoing relationship with the synagogue. In other words, the boundaries were at risk of exhibiting permeability of an illicit type (as far as Paul was concerned) if the proscriptions necessary for the congregations of Christ-followers to continue as distinctive groups broke down.

The principal focus of Paul's concern in this letter is the boundary represented by the line AB, which separates his Christ-followers from Israel. The Israelite members of his congregations, whom other Israelites regard with suspicion for the reason to be considered in the next chapter, are under pressure from the wider Israelite community (6.12–13) either to eliminate boundary AB altogether by securing the circumcision of the gentile members or, in effect, to cross back again by breaking off relationships with them (4.17). The latter approach had previously been adopted by Peter, Barnabas and the other Israelite Christ-followers in Antioch (2.11–14), probably as a means of achieving the long-term goal of forcing the gentiles to accept circumcision (Esler 1995c), as will be argued in Chapter 5. In any event, the gentile members are under intense pressure to be circumcised. Their succumbing to such pressure could be regarded in two ways in the light of the notion of social mobility discussed in Chapter 2 of this reading. If all gentile Christ-followers were circumcised, this would constitute defection *en masse* from the Pauline congregations, since the boundary would be dissolved altogether. If only a few defected, they would be regarded as having crossed the line and entered the Israelite outgroup. Although there is no evidence that any gentiles in Galatia have yet been circumcised, there are signs that this boundary is subject to an existing type of permeability – which Paul also disavows – in that the gentiles have started to engage in Israelite festivals and holy days (4.10).

We can be confident that Paul's (internal) sense of the boundary AB was a rich one, given the variegated identity of groups he had formed, whereas he must have been aware that Israelites had a much more superficial understanding of it, given their preoccupation with the issue of circumcision.

The line CB is the boundary between the Christ-followers and the gentiles. The gentiles among the Pauline congregations had once been on the other side of the boundary, engaged in various kinds of idolatrous practice, to which Paul refers in the letter (4.3, 8). Paul sees some of the gentile Christ-followers as being at risk of crossing back over into the realm of gentile idolatry (4.9; 5.20). Just as significantly, Paul is concerned in Galatians 5–6 with the fact that the members of his congregations are falling into the viciously competitive practices characteristic of the Mediterranean region. Their failings in this area indicate that there are dangerous signs of permeability in this boundary in illicit respects, which is something to be discussed in Chapter 8.

Chapter 4

The problem with mixed table-fellowship

In the previous chapter I developed social identity theory in the area of ethnic boundaries as a means to examine essential features of the exigence prompting Paul to write to the Galatians and the nature of the groups among his audience. During this exposition I foreshadowed that the particular issue which generated Israelite hostility to the Pauline type of mixed community was the practice of eucharistic table-fellowship, characterised by the participants sharing, that is, passing round from hand to hand, the one loaf and the one cup. In this chapter I will set out a case for why that would have caused sufficient offence in the first century CE to explain the opposition Paul encountered to his evangelism and the pressure on his gentile converts to be circumcised, not only in Galatia contemporaneously with his writing the letter, but previously in Jerusalem and Antioch.

I initially developed a particular approach to this subject at some length in my work on Luke's Gospel and the Acts of the Apostles (1987: 71–109), by proposing that, in general, Israelites in the first century CE did not dine with gentiles in the full sense just mentioned. I argued that this prohibition is reflected very clearly in Acts and Galatians and that its presence is implied in Mark 7 and Matthew 15. While my views have provoked a variety of responses, in particular a spirited (though, as we will see, ineffective) attack by E. P. Sanders (1990a), I still adhere to the position I outlined in 1987. My developing theoretical understanding of the issues at stake in such a form of ethnic interaction and further consideration of the ancient sources has, indeed, encouraged me to argue the point with more confidence. I consider the ban on full table-fellowship to be a matter of fundamental importance for the history of the early Christian-movement and in understanding some of its products, including the letter to the Galatians – in relation both to the incident at Antioch some time in the past (recounted in 2.11–14) and to the problem in Galatia Paul is seeking to address.

In the first section in this chapter I will briefly rehearse the data on which my argument was based and suggest the need to distinguish evidence for the fact of a prohibition from the various frameworks (both emic and etic) within which one might seek to explain it. The second section will contain a critical assessment of the response of E. P. Sanders (and of C. Hill) to my case and a further development of the overall argument. The third section will investigate the importance of the biblical laws against idolatry as underlying the ban as far as first-century Israelites were concerned. The fourth section, finally, will reassess some of the ancient evidence for the ban in the light of the previous discussion in this chapter and the theory on social identity and ethnic boundaries explored in previous chapters.

THE FIRST-CENTURY BAN ON MIXED TABLE-FELLOWSHIP: THE NATURE OF THE ARGUMENT

An outline of the data and argument

I began my 1987 investigation by using anthropological insights developed by Mary Douglas, Louis Dumont and Edmund Leach to raise the possibility that the highly developed purity concerns manifested by ancient Israel may have represented a symbolic replication of Israel's precarious position as an *ethnos* in the midst of a threatening world, in particular by rendering problematic table-fellowship between Israelites and gentiles (Esler 1987: 73–6). I made clear that such a possibility arose not merely because of the existence of the food laws, but also for the reason that commensality, given that it was 'an action expressing the warmest intimacy and respect', involved 'a most serious dereliction from the fundamental objective of preserving the separate identity of the Jewish people' (ibid.: 76). In this introductory context I mentioned that in the Indian caste system the taboos relating to food specified what foods might be eaten and with whom.

Having thus employed the social sciences merely to raise the question and not to answer it, I turned to Greek, Roman and Judaic sources bearing upon the first century CE 'to establish as a matter of historical fact that such an attitude (sc. of 'opposition of Jews to table-fellowship with gentiles') did characterise the Judaism of this period' (ibid.: 76). After critically considering the views of two critics who countenanced the notion that some Israelites did eat with gentiles (ibid.: 76–77), I moved on to argue that the ancient evidence indicated 'that as a general rule Jews did refrain from eating with gentiles' (ibid.: 77).

Hecataeus of Abdera (322–285 BCE) had claimed Israelites engaged in an unsocial and intolerant way of life (*apanthrōpon tina kai misoxenon bion*).[1] Apollonius of Molon (who was writing in the first half of the first century BCE) saw *Ioudaioi* as atheists and misanthropes unwilling to associate with (*koinōnein*) other people.[2] Diodorus of Siculus (writing 60–30 BCE) is the earliest Graeco-Roman author to mention specifically that Israelites did not engage in table-fellowship (*trapezēs koinōnein*) with any other *ethnos* (*Bibliotheca Historica*, 34.1.2). Pompeius Trogus (straddling the turn of the millennium) noted that Israelites did not live with (and the word he used could mean 'dine with') strangers.[3] At the beginning of the second century CE, the Roman historian Tacitus asserted that *Iudaei* ate apart (*separati epulis*), slept apart and avoided intercourse with foreign women (*Histories*, 5.5.2). Finally, Philostratus (writing in the late second and early third century) repeated the charge that Israelites did not share meals with other people: they have discovered a life apart and do not share a table with other people [*mēte koinē pros anthrōpous trapeza*], nor join in libations, prayers or sacrifices' (*Vita Apollonii*, 5.33).

I located evidence in Israelite sources for a similar refusal to eat with gentiles in the full sense under discussion in Dan. 1.3–17, Judith 10–12, Esther 14.17 (in part of the apocryphal additions), Tobit 1, and a number of non-scriptural Israelite works, the *Letter of Aristeas*, the *Book of Jubilees* and *Joseph and Asenath*, and in the Mishnah and Talmud, which I will consider again below.

There is also direct evidence in two passages in Acts for just such a prohibition. The first consists of what Peter says to Cornelius and his kinsmen and close friends:

> You yourselves know how illicit [*athemiton*] it is for an Israelite to associate with [*kollasthai*] or to visit [*proserchesthai*] any one of another nation; but God has shown me that I should not call any man common or unclean.
>
> (Acts 10.28)

The word *athemiton* is a strong word which can even refer to idolatrous practices.[4] The implications of Peter's baptism of Cornelius are brought out in the second relevant passage in Acts, namely, the charge levelled against Peter when he reports on his conversion of Cornelius to the Church in Jerusalem:

> So when Peter went up to Jerusalem, the circumcision party [*hoi ek*

peritomēs] criticized him, saying, 'Why did you go in to uncircumcised men and eat with [*synesthiein*] them?'

(Acts 11.2–3)

Although Cornelius was an exemplary God-fearing gentile dedicated to acts of charity to the Israelite people (Acts 10.1–2), this made no difference to his status as an uncircumcised pagan with whom one should not eat; Peter does not even mention this fact in his reply to the criticism (11.4–17). The particular problem in Acts 10–11 is connected with an Israelite eating in a gentile's house, but we will see later that the issue encompasses other situations as well. A problem with table-fellowship of some kind at least also underlines the fact that Peter and Barnabas and the other Christ-following Israelites of Antioch discontinued the practice out of fear of the circumcision party (*hoi ek peritomēs*, Gal. 2.11–12). This New Testament data is widely neglected in the discussion.

The conclusion I drew after considering this evidence (Esler 1987: 78–84, some details of which will be discussed below) was that 'as a general rule Jews did refrain from eating with gentiles' (ibid.: 77) during this period, or to put the matter more precisely:

> The antipathy of Jews towards table-fellowship with gentiles, in the full sense of sitting around a table with them and sharing the same food, wine and vessels, was an intrinsic feature of Jewish life for centuries before and after our period.
>
> (ibid.: 84)

The essential qualification of table-fellowship in this full sense was necessary in view of my interest in the eucharistic meal (ibid.: 87–88, 91, 92, 96, 102–103, 104, 108), where those present shared one loaf and one cup as the indispensable form of such fellowship (*koinōnia*), as revealed in 1 Corinthians:

> The cup of blessing which we bless, is it not a participation [*koinōnia*] in the blood of Christ? The bread which we break, is it not a participation [*koinōnia*] in the body of Christ? Because there is one bread, we who are many are one body, for we all partake of the one bread.
>
> (10.16–17)

I made clear in my 1987 treatment that I was not suggesting that there were not some Israelites who breached the rules regulating their relationships with the outside world – after all, Acts 16.1 was evidence for an uncircumcised son of an Israelite woman and a Greek man. My point in this area was that 'Jews who permanently gave up the prohibitions which distinguished them from gentiles ceased to be Jews' and that Israelites who did fudge the boundaries 'came under heavy pressure to conform or to abandon Judaism altogether' (1987: 86), pressure of the kind to which Paul himself is described as succumbing in Acts 16.1–3. In this context, circumcision of gentiles engaging in table-fellowship was, from an Israelite perspective, the solution to the problem, not the problem itself.

The distinction between phenomenon and explanation

During my 1987 discussion of the ancient evidence I kept broadly separate evidence for the phenomenon of the prohibition from a consideration of its etiology. Initially, I sought to demonstrate the 'opposition of Jews to table-fellowship with gentiles' as a historical fact (1987: 76), that 'as a general rule Jews did refrain from eating with gentiles' (ibid.: 77), and after I had discussed the evidence at length (ibid.: 78–84), and concluded that a ban on table-fellowship in the full sense did exist (ibid.: 84), I proceeded briefly to address what might have been the reason for it when nothing in the Mosaic code specifically forbade such table-fellowship (ibid.: 84–86). Although in commenting on two of the ten items of Israelite evidence for the ban (but none of the six Graeco-Roman authors) I did raise in passing the question of possible cause,[5] I reiterate that in dealing with this data from outside of the New Testament I separated evidence for the prohibition from a consideration of its cause. It will be helpful for the subsequent discussion in this chapter if I expand somewhat on this distinction.

To treat evidence for a phenomenon separately from its possible foundations accords with the methodology employed in Berger and Luckmann's *The Social Construction of Reality* (the text which provided my overall theoretical framework in 1987, although I did not then employ it for this particular purpose). In this text Berger and Luckmann, inspired by the work of Alfred Schütz, focused on the taken-for-granted world of common-sense knowledge, the paramount reality of everyday life. Yet once features of the everyday world have been described phenomenologically they are susceptible to being situated within a number of possible provinces or frameworks of meaning. Although some of these intepretative frameworks might come from indigenous, insider or 'emic' accounts, while others are outsider, social-scientific or 'etic' explanations, the distinction between them (and the mundane realities which they seek to explain) is an important one. Accordingly, having isolated the *phenomenon* of a ban on full Israelite–gentile table-fellowship in the first-century Mediterranean world, one may then seek to account for it – and in either emic or etic ways. It is noteworthy that the two Acts passages cited above, Acts 10.28a and 11.3, contain statements of the prohibition, while Acts 10.28b takes the extra explanatory step from an emic perspective, with reference to gentiles being common or unclean.

In this context I originally offered two, essentially emic, explanations: first, an Israelite sensitivity to eating foods provided by gentiles for fear that the vessels used to prepare them had been polluted through contact with foods proscribed by Leviticus and, second, ritual impurity of gentiles themselves (1987: 85–6). In the latter regard I followed G. Alon in locating the origin of gentile impurity in the extension of the impurity of the idols they worshipped to the gentiles themselves. Acts 10.28b could be thought to support this view.

Etic explanations for the prohibition could be offered along the lines of the need postulated by Mary Douglas to defend the Israelite *ethnos* ever threatened by the surrounding impurity of the gentile world, or using Barth's understanding of boundaries as important not for 'object-ive' reasons, but because the Israelite insiders regarded them as signifi-cant in establishing a differentiation *vis-à-vis* outsiders which prescribed some modes of intercourse while proscribing others (Barth 1969: 9–14).

In recent years another emic explanation has occurred to me as an important cause for the ban, that it was seen by first-century Israelites as a *direct application* of the biblical laws forbidding idolatry, such as those in Exod. 23.13, 24, 32–33 and 34.12–16; Deut. 7.1–6, 25–26 and 12.2–3, and so on, and I will return to this issue later. A similar conclusion has also been reached independently of me by Peter Tomson, a rabbinics scholar, whose position I will also discuss below.

DEVELOPING THE ARGUMENT: A RESPONSE TO E. P. SANDERS

My case for a prohibition on table-fellowship of the relevant sort ran into strong opposition from E. P. Sanders (1990a) and Craig Hill (1992: 118–125).[6] By critically considering his response to my position I will be able to develop the general case for a prohibition and also expose the weak-nesses in Sanders' argument which has been quite influential in the recent discussion in this area.[7]

Sanders' 1990a essay 'Jewish Association with gentiles and Galatians 2:11–14' combines his renowned grasp of the ancient data with a failure to appreciate some of the implications of the evidence and a notable misinterpretation of my position. The title is revealing; like James Dunn, Sanders believes that evidence of social intercourse between Israelites and gentiles in the first century CE relates directly to the question of whether table-fellowship took place between them. Yet such a view potentially runs into the problems discussed in Chapter 3 of this reading. To recapitulate briefly, Fredrik Barth has argued that ethnic groups only survive in the presence of other groups if there are some areas where intercourse is permitted and some where it is forbidden, so that prescription and proscription coexist, with the existence of the former certainly not leading to the relaxation of the latter. While Sanders' model of the social dynamics involved is an implied one, in this case his familiarity with the data, especially the significance of gentile idolatry, has saved him from Dunn's error, noted in Chapter 3, of assuming that if an ethnic group has interactions with outsiders in some areas it will proceed to do so in others. For Sanders diverges from Dunn in recognising that there were some zones of prohibited intercourse between Israelites and gentiles. Thus, he argues, many 'Jews':

> rubbed shoulders with gentiles because of their work. More significantly, many Jews admired gentile institutions, education, and culture, and they sought to participate. Jews also prized their own culture, and they wanted others to appreciate it. To attract gentiles, to make them sympathetic to the Jewish way of life, Jews had to be open to them. Most knew that the only real problems with associating with gentiles were idolatry and the biblical food laws . . . Different people balanced mingling and separatism in different ways, and doubtless in most communities and families there were customs that removed the burden of anxious decision-making from the shoulders of individuals.
>
> (Sanders 1990a: 185)

Inasmuch as Sanders allows some areas of contact and others of proscription, it is possible to relate this statement to Fredrik Barth's framework of ethnic interaction outlined in Chapter 3.

Sanders has in common with my position a belief that what was at issue in Antioch was the practice of mixed table-fellowship itself (although one would hardly gather from the tone of his discussion that we had anything in common), rather than some difficulty with the manner in which it was conducted, for example in the original suggestion of Dunn that the attempted imposition of pharisaical purity laws was at stake (1990a: 129–182).[8] Sanders rejected Dunn's proposal outright, since purity rules of this type did not apply outside Israel (1990a: 172),[9] a point also made by Tomson (1990: 228–229). Sanders and I differ to the extent that whereas I argue for an Israelite prohibition on the practice, he favours the view that there was no law on it, but that strict Israelites might worry about the effects of fraternisation with gentiles (because the association might lead to contact with idolatry or transgression of one of the food laws), just as James worried that too much fraternisation with gentiles would have bad results and that Peter's mission would be discredited if he were seen to engage in it himself (Sanders 1990a: 186).

Sanders has, however, misrepresented my position – and this in ways which stand in the road of understanding Paul's communication to the Galatians. First of all, he suggests that I had argued that Israelites avoided social intercourse with gentiles altogether, table-fellowship included.[10] At the end of my 1987 discussion I made it quite clear that I was not for one moment suggesting that Israelites did not have social intercourse with gentiles, but that table-fellowship in the full sense of sharing food and wine (which was the only one under consideration) was a special case. My own view was clearly expressed in what Sanders had before him:

> Such aloofness is not, of course, incompatible with Judaism's having exuded a great attraction for many thoughtful gentiles. But although Jews were happy to mix with gentiles in synagogues or possibly even in market-places or streets, eating with them was a very different matter. Eating was an occasion fraught with the possibility of breaching the purity code, one of the most crucial aspects of the Mosaic law for the maintenance of the separate identity of the Jewish *ethnos*. The antipathy of Jews towards table-fellowship with gentiles, in the full sense of sitting around a table with them and sharing the same food, wine and vessels, was an intrinsic feature of Jewish life for centuries before and after our period.
>
> (Esler 1987: 84)

This observation closely reflects Fredrik Barth's view, discussed above, that the maintenance of any ethnic boundary depends upon some intercourse being allowed and other types being proscribed. In another section of my book (1987: 145–157) I had even proposed that, as far as the history of the earliest communities was concerned, it had been association between Greek-speaking Israelites and their gentile acquaintances, even friends (ibid.: 156), whom they encountered in synagogues in Jerusalem, which led to the first admission of gentiles (ibid.: 145–163, especially 157–158). Sanders' discussion of the social intercourse between Israelites and gentiles in the first and second centuries (1990a: 179–180) is quite consistent with my argument, despite his suggestion to the contrary (1990a: 180).

A second weakness with Sanders' response is that he fails to recognise the division in my argument between the phenomenon of a prohibition on table-fellowship of the type with which I was concerned and various possible modes of explanation for it. He forces my discussion of the matter at issue into an *explanatory* framework which distinguishes between a problem concerning food and a problem concerning people (ibid.: 176). This distinction (an emic one which derives from ancient sources) relates to the causal and not the phenomenological level when one is asking whether or not first-century Israelites would have sat at a table with gentiles sharing food and vessels with them. Prior to addressing my position he had considered at some length the question of whether first-century Israelites thought gentiles as such were impure (ibid.: 172–176). Yet while I did consider the purity status of gentiles in relation to the ancient sources outside the New Testament, I did so in passing, in relation to two out of sixteen items of data when I was gathering evidence for the fact of the ban, and then briefly as one possible explanation for the prohibition (1987: 85–86)[11] after I had set out the factual evidence for it (ibid.: 76–84). But in discussing this evidence and in offering a view on causation I did not suggest a problem with the food itself, nor was I concerned to express my own argument in relation to this distinction between problematic persons and problematic food. In spite of this, a prominent theme in Sanders' criticism of my argument is to the effect that I initially see the problem as one concerning gentiles (Sanders 1990a: 176) but later confuse 'the issue of the people with that of the food' (ibid.: 178). Nevertheless, Sanders' criticism, misplaced as it is, has encouraged me to make the distinction between phenomenon and cause more prominent in this context.

A third (and major) problem with Sanders' case is that he has apparently overlooked the issue mentioned in the last sentence of the quotation cited above from my 1987 treatment – that my concern was with meals where the participants sat at one table and shared the same food, wine and vessels. My interest was (and is) only in table-fellowship of this particular type, since this was the type which characterised the eucharistic meal (1987: 87–88). (Paul makes clear the importance of sharing food and wine in the context of the Lord's Supper in 1 Cor. 10.16–17, since that was the only meal indispensable to Paul's model of Christian community, as becomes clear at 1 Cor. 11.17–34, especially v. 22, although I did not cite these passages in 1987.) Sanders (and most of the commentators influenced by him) notably fails to relate his argument to the only form of table-fellowship of any consequence for the discussion – the Eucharistic variety where the participants shared food, wine and vessels. A meal in common like this, characterised by a marked intimacy in the way it was conducted, which is the only type I had (or now have) under consideration, is obviously to be distinguished from other situations in which persons in the same context are eating and drinking, but doing so in parallel, inasmuch as they share among themselves neither food, nor wine, nor vessels. The latter situation hardly deserves to be called 'eating with' or to have the expression 'table-fellowship' attached to it and as far as I can see, moreover, has no bearing on any significant issue in the New Testament. Thus, Sanders curiously ends his review of Esther and the other biblical passages I had raised with the statement: 'The point of all these exemplary stories of how to eat with gentiles is that Jews should sit and eat their own food or only vegetables' (1990a: 177), as if that view weighed against my position. But it merely serves to confirm it, since Sanders thereby acknowledges that genuine table-fellowship was illicit, while focusing on the case of Israelites and gentiles eating parallel rather than common meals which was not the subject of my discussion and which has no significance for the interpretation of Paul, or Luke, or any other New Testament writer.

Greek and Roman table-fellowship

At this point it will be helpful to examine briefly the main Greek and Roman forms of commensality to assess what non-Israelite inhabitants of the first-century Mediterranean world would have made of meals attended by Israelites consuming their own food and wine and served by their own servants, which Sanders equates with table-fellowship.

Greek meals were conducted in a special room, called the *andrōn*, or men's room, which was square in shape and contained between seven and fifteen couches, on which the diners – two per couch – reclined with equal status. The sense of architectural harmony and proportion was central to the social values expressed in the meal (Bergquist 1990). A large jar, a *kratēr*, in which wine was mixed with water, occupied a central place in the room and was the focus of the event (Lissarrague 1990). The meal had two stages, the *deipnon*, when the food was consumed, and the *symposion*, the time for serious drinking, talking and entertainment. The *symposion* began with libations to the gods, *spondai*.[12] The libations covered both a libation from the unmixed wine in the *kratēr* (Lissarrague 1990: 204–205) and individual libations by the diners, a custom which went back to the Homeric period (*Odyssey* 13.53–56; Xenophon, *Symposium*, 2.1). The diners were supplied with wine mixed with water in proportions determined by the host which was served from the *kratēr* to the guests in equal proportions. An attendant obtained wine from the *kratēr* in a jug (*oinochoē*) and poured it into the broad, flat cups (*phialai*) which those present used for drinking and making libations. At the end of the session there was a procession (*kōmos*) through the streets which demonstrated the power and cohesion of the group of guests (Murray 1996b). These meals were strongly androcentric; respectable women did not attend them, although hetaerae and entertainers did.[13]

The Roman banquet, or *convivium*, was modelled on the Etruscan version of the Greek *symposion* (Murray 1996a). It differed from the Greek prototype in a number of respects. The dining room (*triclinium*) contained three couches each capable of holding three reclining guests. The couches were arranged around a square table, one side of which was left free for the service and, unlike the equality of the Greek *symposion*, they were arranged in a strict hierarchy of honour, with the couch of honour being that opposite the empty side of the table, and on it the most honourable position was on the right hand (Carcopino 1941: 265–266). Respectable women, and sometimes a man's clients, were present. Although the emphasis was on eating rather than drinking, the Romans also used a central mixing jar (*cratera*) for achieving the correct proportions of water and wine for distribution to all the guests (Carcopino 1941: 269). Lastly, the Roman *convivium* was embedded in social and family structures.[14]

Now imagine a typical Greek or Roman meal where there are a group of *Ioudaioi* present, dining off their own table, with food they have brought along themselves and served by their own servants, and drinking wine not from the communal mixing-jar but from their own supplies, a situation which in Sanders' view constitutes 'table-fellowship'. Clearly such a group would not only have been socially anomalous but would have gone a long way to destroying the conviviality of the occasion. It is not too much to suggest that the fellowship of the meal would have been destroyed. Their failure to partake of the common wine would have been particularly destructive of the symbolic unity created around the *kratēr*. But an Israelite failure to refuse the meal or part of it could also easily have given offence. There is a fragment of Epictetus which states: 'Now when we have been invited to a banquet, we take what has been set before us; and if a person should bid his host to set before him fish or cakes, he would be regarded as eccentric [*atopos*].'[15] The word *atopos* means not only 'unusual', but also 'unnatural', 'disgusting' (Gooch 1993: 43), and it is very likely that this is how a Greek or Roman would have reacted to an Israelite who either asked for some special meal or produced his own food and wine at the feast. There is one other piece of evidence which may confirm this. In his blistering attack on *Iudaei* in his *Histories*, 5.5.2, Tacitus says of them:

> adversus omnes alios hostile odium. Separati epulis, discreti cubilibus, proiectissima ad libidinem gens, alienarum concubitu abstinent; inter se nihil inlicitum [Towards all others [they feel] hatred and enmity. They sit apart at meals and they sleep apart, and although they are a race most given to lust, they abstain from intercourse with foreign women; among themselves nothing is unlawful].

Now while *separati epulis* could imply that they have their meals in a separate place, it is also possible that it means that although dining in the same place as gentiles, they sit at separate tables. If so, Tacitus still regards this as a sign of their alleged hatred of all other people. He certainly does not see it as a sign of fellowship.

This investigation makes it likely that Greeks and Romans who took part in a dinner with Israelites who were sitting at a separate table and eating their food and drinking their own wine, served by their own servants in what was, in fact, a parallel meal, would not have considered this table-fellowship. There is no justification for Sanders to regard it as such.

THE LAW AGAINST IDOLATRY AS ONE CAUSE FOR THE BAN

Recently I have proposed another emic way of accounting for the prohibition (1994: 67–68), as a means of avoiding idolatry (cf. Exod. 23.13, 24, 32–33 and 34.12–16; Deut. 7.1–6, 25–26 and 12.2–3). I will now explore this possibility a little more, never forgetting that it is an explanation which can be conceptually distinguished from the phenomenon of the prohibition. My initial interest in causally linking the prohibition to a concern over the risk of idolatry was encouraged by my coming across an important piece of evidence in the Tosefta *'Abodah Zarah*, 4.6 in the saying of Rabbi Shimon ben Elazar (of the late second century CE) to the effect that Israelites who dined in a gentile's house committed idolatry, even though they ate their own food and wine and their own servants served it to them.[16] I have since discovered a helpful consideration of this passage by Peter Tomson (1990), to which I will return in a moment.

Gentile wine, especially, caused peculiar difficulties. The Mishnah (especially the tractate *'Abodah Zarah*) and the Gemara, although they very often indicate the necessity of differentiating between gentiles as social or business associates on the one hand and as idolaters on the other (Porton 1988: 241–258), demonstrate an extraordinary sensitivity to the problems posed by gentile wine, which was generally regarded as routinely dedicated to pagan gods by the offering of a small libation (Burkert 1985: 70–73). Not surprisingly, libation wine was forbidden to Israelites (see *m. Demai*, 6.10).

Furthermore, there was always the risk that gentiles might secretly turn Israelite wine to which they had direct access into libation wine. Thus, the Mishnah notes that if an idolater were helping an Israelite to take jars of wine from one place to another and the wine had been watched by Israelites, its Israelite use was permitted, but if the wine had not been consistently watched so that the gentile had an opportunity to open the jar and make the wine a libation offering to his god, it could not be consumed (*'Abodah Zarah*, 5.3). The Mishnah gives many similar examples of the dangers of allowing gentiles access to open containers of wine, lest they turn it into a libation (*'Abodah Zarah*, 5.4–7). There is even a case in the Mishnah warning of the danger for an Israelite sitting at a table with a gentile – but each with their own jar of wine – lest the Israelite leave the table and in his absence the gentile offer a libation to a god from his wine (*'Abodah Zarah*, 5.5).

Explicit Israelite concern with deceptive practices occurring in the context of a meal can also be seen in the Mishnaic injunction not to utter 'Amen' to a blessing over food made by a Samaritan unless it had been audible throughout (*Berachoth*, 8.8), no doubt to avoid the risk that the Samaritan had muttered something which included a forbidden phrase such as 'Blessed be God who dwells on Mount Gerizim'.[17]

If an Israelite were in a gentile house there would always be the gravest risk that any wine served would be libation wine and perhaps this is one causal factor explaining why Peter tells Cornelius that it is *athemitos* (contrary to divine will) for an Israelite to visit gentiles (Acts 10.28) and why other members of the Jerusalem community take umbrage at his having done so and also having eaten with them (Acts 11.3). The reason Peter himself offers for the prohibition at Acts 10.28b does not explicitly mention idolatry, but, as we have noted above, *athemitos* is a strong word which can carry precisely this flavour.

In addition, however, it cannot be said that an Israelite could safely entertain a gentile in his house merely because the wine had previously been under Israelite control. The Mishnaic examples just given indicate how much vigilance would be necessary to ensure that the gentile did not tamper with the wine to be drunk by an Israelite. The sharing of one jar would be very risky and the passing around of one cup quite perilous.

On the other hand, as noted above, the Tosefta *'Abodah Zarah*, 4.6 is even stricter in suggesting that Israelites who dined in a gentile's house committed idolatry, even if they ate their own food and wine and their own servants served it to them. Peter Tomson has published a significant treatment of how meals with gentiles were treated in the Halakha (the legal traditions) from the Tannaic period, the first and second centuries CE (1990: 230–236), which pays particular attention to the Tosefta passage.

After reviewing some of the literature on the question of whether table-fellowship was possible between Israelites and gentiles in each other's homes, Tomson considers the sources which suggest that it was possible for an Israelite and a gentile to sit at a table together, and even drink wine, as long as there was no chance that the Israelite was drinking wine which had been turned into a libation offering to a god. An example is *m. 'Abodah Zarah*, 5.5, which I cited above. He refers to stories about Rabbi Meir (mid-second century) indicating that Israelites and gentiles could have good relations by taking precautions to avoid hala-khic difficulties over wine. Tomson believes that from this type of trad-ition 'it appears to have been quite possible to enjoy table-fellowship with gentiles, either in Jewish or gentile homes' (1990: 233). Yet what he calls 'table-fellowship' I would call a 'meal in parallel', since there can have been no passing around of one cup or one loaf, such as characterised the Eucharist. Nor, as we have seen, would ancient Greeks or Romans have thought of such a practice as table-fellowship. That is, this evidence actually confirms my case for there having been a prohibition on table-fellowship of the relevant type!

Moreover, Tomson goes on to note that the Tannaim, the first- and second-century rabbis, were not unanimous on this matter, and quotes the negative view on table-fellowship in *t. 'Abodah Zarah*, 4.6 attributed to Rabbi Shimon ben Elazar (actually a student of Rabbi Meir) which I have referred to above:

> R. Shimon ben Elazar says: Israelites outside the land worship idols in purity. How? If a non-Jew prepared a wedding feast for his son and sent out to invite all Jews in his town – even if they have food and drink of their own and have their own servant waiting at them, they worship idols. Thus it is said: '[. . . Lest you make a covenant . . . when they sacrifice to their gods and] when one invites you, you eat of his sacrifice'.
>
> (Exod. 34.15)

Since we are dealing with a diaspora situation the problem cannot be with the purity rules as such, so that the word 'purity' is used meta-phorically (Tomson 1990: 234). Another saying attributed to Rabbi

Shimon ben Elazar is that a person caused exile to befall his children if he ate with gentiles at table (*b. Sanhedrin*, 104a). Hence we have the curious situation where Rabbi Shimon ben Elazar and his teacher Rabbi Meir represent divergent views on table-fellowship, with the former regarding them as idolatrous even though they were really meals in parallel rather than in common. Tomson offers a historical understanding for this, by tracing the strict view back to the House of Shammai before the destruction of the Temple in 70 CE and the liberal view back to the House of Hillel (1990: 235). There may be some connection between the view expressed by Peter in Acts 10.28 and the line taken by Rabbi Shimon ben Elazar; even though Peter does not explicitly raise the problem of idolatry, it is implied in the word *athemitos* as already noted.

On the strength of this analysis, Tomson suggests that the dispute at Antioch reported in Gal. 2.11–14 was ultimately related to a conflict between these two views, with Peter and Barnabas and the men from James behind them representing the strict view which was motivated by a fear of idolatry, while Paul took the other view (1990: 236). This proposal is compatible with my own position to the extent that it insists on the centrality of fears concerning idolatry as the cause of the tension. But it is necessary to make some qualifications. First of all, the practice of the Eucharistic meal meant genuine table-fellowship, with sharing of food, wine and vessels, and not a parallel meal of the type later advocated by Israelites of a more liberal persuasion. Accordingly, it went far beyond what even Rabbi Meir would later permit. Second, Paul supported mixed table-fellowship not because he favoured a different scribal opinion, which (as just noted) did not extend as far as meals of this sort in any event, but because for Israelites and gentiles to share in the one loaf and the one cup was a central feature of the gospel he preached, the legitimacy of which was sealed in the experience of the Spirit (see Gal. 3.1–5). I have recently argued in relation to Acts 10.44–48 that the final seal on the admission of gentiles into the early communities of Christ-followers, which legitimated their entry into table-fellowship with Israelite members, was the manifestation by the gentiles of charismatic gifts in mixed congregations (Esler 1994: 37–51). I consider that Gal. 3.1–5 suggests that Paul also interpreted the reception of the Spirit in the same way.

These considerations allow us realistically to postulate that there was, or was perceived by Israelite outsiders to be, a grave danger that a gentile from whom an Israelite took a cup of wine at a Eucharistic meal could have converted the wine into an offering for his god by making a surreptitious libation from it, thereby putting the Israelite in peril of idolatry

(Esler 1994: 67). Segal, who is aware of the problem with wine, suggests that 'if a Jewish Christian were observing rules about wine, he or she might have insisted that the Eucharist be dispensed by a Jew to avoid the problems associated with a gentile serving wine' (1990: 232). But this idea does not solve the problem, since even if an Israelite handed the cup to each of the participants in turn, one of them had only to turn the wine into a libation offering for all who followed to be caught up in the idolatry. Segal's proposal is also anachronistic in its image of one person distributing the bread and wine as in most modern Eucharistic services. Paul's practice envisages the passing round of one cup and one loaf (1 Cor. 10.16–17).

It is interesting to note in this context that Sanders makes a vital concession, apparently without realising its significance for mixed table-fellowship of precisely the kind in question, that 'There was no barrier to social intercourse with gentiles, as long as one did not eat their meat or *drink their wine*' (1990a: 178) (my emphasis). On a number of occasions he mentions Israelite concern to avoid idolatry, for example that connected with libation wine. Here he has conceded the case that I am now seeking to press. An Israelite follower of Christ at a Eucharistic celebration who took the cup of wine from a gentile ran the very risk that what he or she was receiving was gentile wine, if a secretive dribble of a drop or two had previously rendered it an idolatrous libation to a pagan god. No doubt the trust shared by the members of the congregation usually meant that this risk was very small, but as far as Israelite outsiders were concerned, there was no consideration of this kind to diminish the potential for committing inadvertent idolatry in the manner I have suggested above.

Finally, in spite of his mentioning the problem with the wine, Sanders has missed the vital passage in *t. 'Abodah Zarah*, 4.6.[18]

ISRAELITE EVIDENCE FOR THE PROHIBITION

In the light of the foregoing discussion it will be useful to look again at some of the Israelite evidence for the prohibition, the *Letter of Aristeas* in particular. I need not rehearse the Graeco-Roman evidence mentioned at the beginning of this chapter. Even Sanders concedes that these passages reflect some sort of social reality associated with Israelite exclusivism, with some of them singling out eating as an example of it: 'Jews were in general less willing to mix than were the other peoples of the empire' (1990a: 180).[19]

I will now reassess the case I have argued above in relation to some of the primary evidence for the prohibition, beginning with some of the Old Testament and apocryphal data upon which I rely. Dan. 1.3–17 contains evidence for the phenomenon of a prohibition on genuine table-fellowship *and* offers as a reason problems with the Babylonian king's food and the wine. The same can be said of Judith 12, where the heroine sits at table with Holofernes, but consuming her own food and drink served by her maid, not the food and wine he has laid on (12.19). Again, this is a meal in parallel, not table-fellowship. A passage from the apocryphal additions to the book of Esther (14.17) is to similar effect: 'Your servant has not eaten at Haman's table, and I have not honored the king's feast or drunk the wine of libations' (NRSV). Here we have further evidence of a prohibition on genuine table-fellowship, and the problem with libation wine seems prominent as a reason. This is similar to my 1987 view, in criticism of which Hill comments as follows:

> Plainly, the dominant concern is loyalty to Jewish dietary laws. It is only by extension that it may be thought to apply to dining in the presence of Haman as well as eating the food provided at his table. The exemplary character of the other heroes consists of their obedience to food laws alone.
>
> (Hill 1992: 120)

Apart from noting that Hill, too, is locked into the problematic persons versus problematic foods dichotomy which he has presumably derived from Sanders, my initial objection to this view is its irrelevance. Like Sanders, Hill confuses evidence of a phenomenon with evidence as to its rationale. It is enough for my argument that the text presents loyal Israelites refusing to engage in table-fellowship with gentiles in the full sense under discussion. The precise reason for such refusal, be it 'dietary laws' or anything else, is a separate issue. But even on the question of the basis for this outlook, Hill falls into error. Nothing in the passage he cites suggests Esther is avoiding foods banned by the dietary code in Leviticus. The wine of libations, expressly mentioned, is not something within the food laws at all. Its connection, a vital one in this context, is with the prohibition on idolatry. It may be that Haman's food was acceptable within the Levitical provisions but still impermissible because tainted with idolatry. Exactly the same could be said of Tobit, who refused to eat the food of the gentiles even though his brothers and fellow Israelites did (Tobit 1.11).

The position is similar in the extra-scriptural Israelite works. *Joseph and Asenath* relates how when Joseph was entertained at the house of

Asenath's parents, who were gentiles, 'they set a table before him separately, because he did not eat with [*sunēsthie*] the Egyptians, as this was an abomination to him'. We observe here a strongly expressed refusal to engage in genuine table-fellowship with gentiles. While the actual reason for this being an abomination to Joseph is not specified, the attitude itself is similar to that expressed in the other texts already discussed. Sanders reasonably proposes that the author of this work wanted to 'convince the readers not to eat with gentiles and (the main goal of the work) not to marry them without insisting on full conversion'. So far, so good. He then adds, however, 'This is not sociological evidence that Jews did not eat with gentiles or marry them; on the contrary, the author was trying to check a practice he considered threatening' (Sanders 1990a: 177). This argument has a prima facie appeal which evaporates on closer inspection. There were always Israelites who disobeyed the Torah and others who called them back to its observance. No one suggests this means the Torah did not exist. The same can be said of the prohibition against the intimate sharing of a meal with gentiles. Whatever the basis for the rule, one cannot reasonably doubt its existence merely because it is propounded by a particular author. Are we to believe that whoever wrote *Joseph and Asenath* was the only Israelite of the time who found table-fellowship in the full sense with gentiles wrong? The mere fact that there may have been Israelites who did not eat with gentiles and who (like the author of *Joseph and Asenath*) encouraged others not to do so cannot constitute evidence against the existence of a prohibition on this practice. Lastly, Sanders' treatment of this text is at least superior to that of Hill who has little to propose in relation to it, except for the unhelpfully generalised suggestion that it is best explained as an 'apologetic gloss' on Genesis 43.32, which states that the Egyptians had a horror of dining with the Hebrews (Hill 1992: 120).

The next extra-scriptural passage comes from chapter 22 of the *Book of Jubilees:*

> Separate thyself from the nations,
> And eat not with them: . . .
> For their works are unclean,
> And all their ways are a pollution and an abomination and
>   uncleanness.

Sanders is adamant in rejecting the witness of this book, by reason of its association with the sectarian literature from Qumran and its extremism:

> There is no more reason to think that Jews in general accepted its

admonitions about gentiles than to suppose that they accepted its solar calendar.

(1990a: 177)

In 1987 I noted the connection of this text with the narrower type of Israelite observance represented at Qumran, while suggesting that on the question of the appropriate attitude to gentiles it expressed a view shared by many, if not most, Israelites of the second century BCE (1987: 83). The actions taken by Antiochus IV Epiphanes in 167–164 BCE to prohibit religious practices central to Israelite religion, after all, would have stimulated anti-gentile sentiments in this period. The two issues to which Sanders refers are, moreover, quite different in character, since table-fellowship with gentiles related to the boundaries between Israelite and non-Israelite, whereas calendrical disputes differentiated Israelite from Israelite. In addition, the passages already discussed are consonant with this injunction in *Jubilees* not to eat with gentiles, at least in the subject sense. Hill suggests that the fact that 'an extreme document like *Jubilees*' finds it necessary to inveigh against table-fellowship with gentiles raises a doubt as to whether such a prohibition was part of normal behaviour (1992: 120). Even if this were correct – and it is mere surmise, given the tendency of religious communities to reiterate primary affirmations even in quiet times in order to maintain group identity – it is an objection without real force. As already argued, the existence of a rule and its occasional, or even frequent, breach are not inconsistent. No one suggests that in the case of the Torah; why should it be regarded as persuasive in this context? As long as such a rule was regarded as in existence, various Israelites at different times could mount a campaign of one type or another to see that it was enforced.

The *Letter of Aristeas*

As far as the non-scriptural texts are concerned, the most revealing is the *Letter of Aristeas* which in one section describes how the Israelite translators of the Hebrew scriptures into Greek dined with the (gentile) King of Egypt for seven days. In 1987 I was of the opinion that this was further evidence of an Israelite ban on table-fellowship in the full sense under discussion and I adhere to that view. Indeed, my closer inspection of the relevant passage, in its wider context in the work and in the light of Fredrik Barth's approach to ethnicity which I discussed in the previous chapter, encourages me to be somewhat more emphatic on this point. I will now set out why.

The relevant passage of the *Letter of Aristeas* describes a banquet called by the King of Egypt in honour of the arrival of Israelite scholars from Palestine who were to translate Hebrew scriptures into Greek. Although this is certainly a case where we find at least one gentile (the king) eating a meal in the same room as Israelites, in 1987 I argued that this did not count as evidence against a prohibition on genuine table-fellowship. In spite of criticism by Sanders and Hill, I adhere to that view, although I will now pose a somewhat developed version of the argument.

The context of the passage needs mentioning. The section of the work dealing with the banquet begins with the reception of the translators in Alexandria (*Letter of Aristeas*, 172–181), continues with a description of the preparations (182–186), and then moves on to the meal itself, which actually stretches over seven days and is largely taken up with the wise answers the translators give to questions posed to them by Ptolemy (187–294). Yet immediately before this section there is an explanation and defence of the Mosaic law, spoken by Eleazar, the high priest in Jerusalem, in response to an enquiry made of him by Ptolemy's envoys (128–171). Although I discussed this illuminating defence of the Israelite law in Chapter 3 of this reading, it is helpful to reiterate here that the initial rationale for the law as explained by Eleazar is to keep Israel separate from evil people (130). Monotheism, ethical norms and the law all operate as an impregnable fence and an iron wall to keep the Israelites from having dealings with other nations (139). Here we see an emic explanation of ethnic distinctiveness very similar to the etic account of Fredrik Barth. Specific attention is paid to one particular aspect of this wall:

> Therefore, lest we should become perverted [*diastrophas lambanōmen*], by sharing the pollution of others [*mētheni synalisgoumenoi*] or by associating with evil people [*homilountes phaulois*], he hedged us around on all sides with types of purification [*pantothen hēmas periephraxen hagneiais*] in matters of food and drink and touch and hearing and seeing [*dia brōtōn kai potōn kai haphrōn kai akoēs kai horaseōs*] as legal requirements [*nomikōs*].
>
> (*Letter of Aristeas*, 142)

Although a number of *causative factors* are referred to in this passage, such as gentile pollution, the Levitical food laws, prohibitions on drink stemming not from Leviticus but presumably from the laws against idolatry, and so on, the actual *phenomenon* (to use the distinction I introduced earlier) whereby there are restrictions on certain types of social intercourse comes through loud and clear. Accordingly, when one proceeds to the description of the banquet just after this, it would be surprising to interpret it, as do Sanders and Hill, as in any way supportive of Israelite laxity in the area of table-fellowship with gentiles. As John Barclay has recently pointed out, although the *Letter of Aristeas* is in many ways an eirenic document meant to portray mutual respect between Israelites and gentiles (Barclay 1996a: 144), the author is still determined to insist on the validity of Israelite separateness. This suggests 'that if Jews and gentiles are to mix in friendly social intercourse, it has to be *on the Jews' terms*' (1996a: 147). In this context, the reader is led to expect that the banquet will confirm, rather than prejudice, the legitimation of Israelite apartness set out immediately before, and this expectation is, in fact, entirely satisfied.

The king begins by saying that he wishes 'to dine today with you' (*deipnēsai sēmeron meth' hymōn* [*Letter of Aristeas*, 180]). It should be noted that he does not use *synesthiein*, the usual word for 'to eat together' to cover the type of table-fellowship I am arguing was banned in the first century (cf. Acts 11.3; Gal. 2.12), but rather employs an expression wherein the use of the verb without a prefix and the insertion of an adverb between it and the phrase 'with you', creates an impression of a rather less intimate form of table-fellowship. Pelletier's translation captures this nuance nicely: 'Aussi ai-je décidé de dîner ce soir en votre compagnie' (1962: 187). Nevertheless, the king immediately adds that all things would be duly prepared for them in accordance with their usages, and for him with them (*kamoi meth' hymōn* [*Letter of Aristeas*, 181]), the latter expression repeating the one used in his initial invitation and again distinguishing between him and them. There can be little doubt that he adds this rider to allay any fears they may have had that the banquet would not accord with Israelite customs.

The head steward then summoned Dorotheus who had charge of such guests and ordered him to make the necessary preparations. We now learn that the king had arranged that there were persons appointed to ensure that visitors from every state (*polis*) would have their own particular customs with respect to food, wine and seating requirements (*ta pota kai brōta kai strumnai*) honoured in his banquets. Accordingly, when visitors arrived, such officials would ensure that preparations were made in accordance with their customs (*kata tous ethismous*) so that they were not put into a difficult situation (*kata mēthen dyscheiraintes*) and could enjoy themselves. Dorotheus had the responsibility (*prostasia*) for Israelite guests. Although the text does not say so, it may imply that Dorotheus himself was an Israelite. We learn earlier in the text that Israelites were employed by Ptolemy as soldiers and as courtiers worthy of trust (*tēs peri tēn aulēn pisteōs axious* [*Letter of Aristeas*, 38]). More specifically, however, as

Hadas notes: 'Dorotheus is of the theophoric type (sc. of name) favoured by Jews' (1951: 171). The name appears in an inscription from Rome in relation to someone who is probably an Egyptian Israelite and in two Israelite inscriptions from Cyrenaica (Horbury and Noy 1992: 234–235, 324). Having an Israelite in this position would certainly eliminate or lessen many complications.

There were stores of food kept separate (*diamemerismena*) for banquets for Israelite guests and Dorotheus laid some of these out for the feast. Couches were arranged in accordance with the king's order, in such a way as to honour his guests, in two rows, with half reclining on couches on his right and 'the rest behind his own couch' (*tous de loipous meta tēn heautou klisian*). Thus, the king is expressly said to recline on his own couch; there is no contiguity between him and the Israelites.

Before the meal started, the king bade Dorotheus to perform the customary rites of all visitors from Judaea. This meant dispensing with the usual services of the sacred heralds, the ministers of sacrifices and those who offered prayers (*kateuchai*) and simply asking the oldest of the Israelite priests present to say a blessing. Given the ubiquitous practice of making libations at Greek meals, we can safely assume that this was something which was dropped in honour of the Israelite guests.

Finally, all the service at table was done by Dorotheus' staff, among whom (*en hois*) were royal pages (*basilikoi paides*) and persons who had been honoured by the king. The text does not tell us what sort of people were on Dorotheus' staff, but they could well have been Israelites. These servants may have been among those appointed courtiers too (*Letter of Aristeas*, 38). Such was also the case with Daniel and his companions in Babylon, after all. In Mediterranean culture, moreover, it would be usual for Dorotheus to bring his own relatives into service (one aspect of keeping everything in the family) and if he was an Israelite we can reasonably assume his servants were too, either for this reason, as far as some of them at least were concerned, or simply to avoid questions being asked about the food and drink.

Thus, the situation is very similar to the way Judith managed to dine safely with Holofernes, although she was sitting at his own table. The Israelites are spatially separated from their gentile host (so there is no sign of any food or drink being passed from him to them or vice versa), they are eating specifically Israelite food and drink (no doubt wine), which has expressly not been subject to any rites akin to libation to pagan gods, and those ministering to them are possibly Israelites. This situation is not table-fellowship in the relevant sense, characterised by the intimate sharing of food and wine, and, in fact, is designed precisely to avoid it.

Moving on from this phenomenological level to the issue of causation, moreover, whatever the possible reasons for the prohibition might have been, either idolatry from drinking gentile libation wine (either overt or surreptitious), or eating prohibited foods, or coming into contact with impure gentiles, all of which are mentioned a little earlier (at 142) as noted above, the dining arrangements in the *Letter of Aristeas* avoid an infringement of any of them.

Accordingly, this was a meal conducted in parallel, not in common; it did not constitute table-fellowship. This critical point is lost on Sanders, although he was responding to a less developed version of my argument than that offered here. After waving his finger at me once more for confusing 'the issue of the people with that of the food' (a charge for which, as noted above, I have a rather good alibi), he states:

> Even more curiously he asks 'whether food or wine were passed between the king and the Jews', and concludes that 'he ate his and they ate theirs' (82). The passage quite clearly says that he ate theirs.
>
> (Sanders 1990a: 178)

His use of 'curiously' indicates the extent of his failure to contrast an essential feature of the account – that there is no table-fellowship of the relevant type – with Paul's determination that Israelites and gentiles in his congregations *would be permitted* to sit at one table and to pass around one loaf and one cup.

Hill's reply to my 1987 view on the attitude evident in the *Letter of Aristeas* is briefer than his teacher's:

> Esler's reference to the separatism of the Jews at the Egyptian court is simply wrong; the king and the Jewish translators together ate Jewish food.
>
> (Hill 1992: 120)

Brief, typically confident, yet erroneous, Hill's idea of what one needs for a successful dinner-party must differ from mine and, moreover, from that of first-century Greeks or Romans (whose banquets were characterised by the consumption of wine from a common mixing-jar which was subject to libations) since there was no 'eating together' in these meals at all. The respective parties may have been eating Israelite food in the same room, but the lengths taken to avoid the possibility that the Israelites, sitting at their separate tables, would come into contact with food or wine touched by the king (or by other gentiles previously) strongly evidences a prohibition on table-fellowship of the relevant type. The situation described in the *Letter of Aristeas* is an even more extreme case (by virtue of the spatial separation of those eating) of the type of dinner in India between members of different castes; the only way this can safely be conducted, which means without prejudice to maintaining the rigid boundaries between the various groups, is to have a Brahman, a member of the highest caste, do the cooking.

CONCLUSION

Accordingly, I stand by my 1987 case for the existence of a prohibition against Israelites engaging in table-fellowship with gentiles of a kind which involved the passing around between those present of bread and wine. One plausible reason for this was that it risked the commission of idolatry in breach of biblical commandments. That is to say, we are not just dealing with a concern for the effects of too much fraternisation, but with what was perceived to be a direct breach of the Torah. I will rely upon this conclusion at numerous points in the rest of this reading.

Chapter 5

Paul, Jerusalem and Antioch

In Chapters 3 and 4 I considered the events and circumstances contemporaneous with Paul's writing Galatians which constituted the 'exigence' of the letter in the language of rhetorical analysis. Yet one of the
striking features of the letter is that in a continuous section – of 28 verses
out of a total of 149 – Paul speaks of events in the past (1.11–2.14).
Beginning with a statement that his gospel had no human origin but
came to him through a revelation concerning Jesus Christ (1.11–12),[1] he
launches into an autobiographical account with a mention of his earlier
career as an eminent Israelite persecutor of the church of God (1.13–
14), a description of how God chose to reveal his son 'in me' so he might
preach the gospel among the gentiles (1.15–16) and a statement of his
journey immediately thereafter to Arabia and return to Damascus (1.17).
He then recounts his first trip after these events to Jerusalem, where he
saw no one except Cephas and James the Lord's brother (1.18–20), his
departure to Syria and Cilicia and the response to his evangelism (1.21–
24), his second visit to Jerusalem with Barnabas and Titus and the events
that occurred then (2.1–10) and, last, the incident in Antioch when Peter
and the other Israelites broke off table-fellowship with the gentiles, leading to his rebuke of Peter when he saw that he was not walking according
to the truth of the gospel (2.11–14).

A reader of the letter must inevitably ask why Paul should include this
statement of past events in a letter written to the Galatian congregations
some time later. How were the two situations related? What was it about
the earlier events, if anything, which bore on the Galatian exigence of
the letter?

As we have seen in Chapter 3, the ancient rhetoricians used the word
'*narratio*' to describe a statement of past facts in a speech and such a
feature could occur in a deliberative communication (as here) even if
more common in a judicial one. Thus, although Aristotle notes at one

point in the *Rhetorica* that one cannot have a *narratio* in a technical sense in a political speech, only in a judicial one, where it covers facts directly relevant to the facts at issue in the case, typically the guilt or innocence of the defendant (1414a), he later acknowledges that occasionally there can be a *narratio* in a deliberative speech, but 'it will be of past events, the recollection of which is to help the hearers to make better plans for the future. Or it may be employed to attack someone's character, or to eulogise him' (1417b; ET by Roberts 1924). Paul utilises both of these possibilities for a *narratio* in a deliberative speech. Although the *narratio* must have some relevance to the events in Galatia, if Galatians was predominantly judicial in function, which I have argued it is not, it would deal with the facts at issue in Galatia, not with events in Jerusalem and Antioch some years earlier (Esler 1994: 59–60). This still leaves for later consideration, however, the important question of the precise relationship between Paul's account of these earlier events and the situation he is facing in Galatia as he dictates the letter.

We have also argued that we need not be unduly sceptical about the historical accuracy of what Paul says (*pace* Robert Hall) nor be disinclined to regard Paul as responding to actual or anticipated criticism (*pace* George Lyons) in line with the rhetorical device of anticipation.

THE PAULINE GOSPEL

Before looking at particular sections of 1.11–2.14, it is worthwhile noting the importance of one issue, that of the genuine gospel, which constitutes a unifying theme running through this narrative. Paul has already expressed grave displeasure that his audience are so quickly turning away from the gospel he taught to another which is not the gospel of Christ but a perversion of it (1.6–7). Anyone who preaches such a 'gospel', even if it be an angel from Heaven, is to be accursed (1.8–9). Building upon the theme of his divinely authorised apostleship with which he began at Gal. 1.1, Paul insists that he is intent on pleasing God not human beings, even if he did so in the past, otherwise he would not be Christ's slave (1.10). At this point he asserts:

> For I would have you know, brothers, the gospel which I preach is not human in nature, for I did not receive it from a human being, nor was I taught it, but [I received it] through a revelation of Jesus Christ.
> (Gal. 1.11–12)

He refers to this gospel a number of times in what follows, sometimes using the noun *euaggelion*, 'good news', 'gospel' (2.2, 5, 7, 14), sometimes the verb *euaggelizesthai*, 'to preach the good news', 'to proclaim the gospel' (1.16, 23)[2] and, on one occasion, both (1.11). God chose to reveal his son in him so that he might preach Christ among the gentiles (1.16);[3] the members of the Judean churches glorified God when they heard he was preaching the gospel of the faith which he once tried to destroy (1.23–24); he laid before the congregation in Jerusalem the gospel he proclaimed among the gentiles (2.2); he resisted the efforts of false brothers intent on imposing the yoke of slavery (no doubt meaning circumcision) so he might preserve 'the truth of the gospel' for the Galatians (2.5); some at least of those in Jerusalem acknowledged that he had been entrusted with the gospel of the uncircumcision just as Peter had been entrusted with that of the circumcision and that God was at work in both apostolates (2.7–8); and, last, that in Antioch he rebuked Peter when he saw that he was not walking according to 'the truth of the gospel' (2.14).

What is the point of these many repeated references to his gospel? We must first recall that Paul's gospel, as we argued in Chapters 3 and 4, goes beyond a collection of ideas about Christ and his redemptive work to embrace essential ways in which that message was contextualised, in particular, in a mixed congregation of Israelites and gentiles who engaged in table-fellowship of one loaf of bread and one cup of wine in spite of strong Israelite opposition to this practice, probably from fear of the risk of idolatry it entailed. Israelite antipathy to mixed table-fellowship was the reason for the pressure on his Galatian gentiles to be circumcised. The position of those who are offering a perverted version of the gospel does not primarily entail a difference over theology but a demand that Paul's gentile converts be circumcised and join the Israelite *ethnos*. Now while Paul is well aware that such a step has profound theological implications, especially in that if the law is necessary for righteousness Christ died in vain (2.21), he must confront the pervasive social context in which this issue is set. For Paul, in fact, the 'truth of the gospel' (2.5, 14, and nowhere else in his writings) means the freedom with which his Israelite and gentile converts can be members of the same congregation without having their 'freedom' replaced with the demands of the Mosaic law. Paul's strategy in the face of this challenge is twofold, first, he establishes for himself and his gospel a divine authority *ab initio* (which is a powerful means to defend the legitimacy of his mixed communities), and, second, he mentions occasions in the past when representatives of the Jerusalem Church either had the chance to object to his gospel and did not, actively considered it and agreed with its worth, or acted inconsistently with it. The existence of the rhetorical feature known as *anticipation* renders it highly likely that this strategy was designed to confront in advance claims that his gospel lacked requisite authority or that he had in the past subordinated himself to the Jerusalem Church – and should do so now. For the reasons I set out in Chapter 3, the case put forward by Lyons against such a conclusion constituting an illicit 'mirror-reading' of the letter is unpersuasive. Yet the real issue for Paul is not his own status; that is only relevant to the extent that his gospel may suffer by association with him. He assumes his opponents will attack the messenger in order to disable the message. His ultimate aim is to dissuade the Galatian gentiles from becoming Israelites. His insistence on his own divine authority is directed to underpinning the gospel he proclaims. Furthermore, from the perspective of social identity theory we may suggest that the way in which he insists upon a divine warrant for himself and his gospel and categorises the rival on offer in Galatia as no gospel at all, but just a perversion of it, reflects the process of stereotyping. By this means he is able to generate a powerful positive social identity for his type of congregations and impute a very negative one to the competition.

PAUL'S CONVERSION AND EARLIER CAREER (GAL. 1.13–17)

In Gal. 1.13–17 Paul recounts events which are traditionally referred to as his conversion and their aftermath:

> But when it pleased him who had set me apart from my mother's womb and called me through his grace, to reveal his son in me so that I might proclaim him among the gentiles, immediately – without consulting anyone and without going up to Jerusalem to those who were apostles before me – I went away into Arabia and again returned to Damascus.

The stress in these verses falls more on what he did after God had chosen to reveal Christ in him, than on the revelation itself – which appears in a temporal clause preceding the main clause of the sentence. This fact and the details given make Paul's account very different from that which Luke provides in Acts 9.1–31. Nevertheless, the location of the 'conversion' is the proximity of Damascus in either case.

What was the nature of this 'conversion'? Critics such as Alan Segal still see a continuing role for the word in relation to Paul's experience (1990). Did it mean that Paul had transferred to a new 'religion'? Recently Krister Stendahl has denied that it did, preferring indeed to

refer to Paul's 'call' or commissioning rather than conversion, especially
on the basis that the language Paul uses contains a number of allusions
to the way in which Old Testament prophets described their call and
Paul is thereby seeking to emphasise his continuity with the God and
religion of Israel, not to sever his connections (1977: 1–23). Thus, Isaiah
says:

> Yahweh called me before I was born,
> from my mother's womb he pronounced my name.
>   (49.1; JB)

And again:

> It is not enough for you to be my servant,
> to restore the tribes of Jacob and bring back the survivors of Israel;
> I will make you the light of the nations
> so that my salvation shall reach to the ends of the earth.
>   (49.6; JB)

Jeremiah says of his commissioning:

> The word of Yahweh was addressed to me, saying:
> 'Before I formed you in the womb I knew you;
> before you came to birth I consecrated you;
> I have appointed you as prophet to the nations'.
>   (1.5; JB)

Other scholars, such as W. D. Davies (1977–1978), agree that Paul did
not think of himself as moving into a new religion but as having found
the final expression of Israelite tradition.

This is an issue where it is clearly necessary to sort out some theoretical issues, especially those clinging to the notion of belonging to a
religion, before seeking to characterise the nature of Paul's actions and
orientation. The first point is to reiterate the need to distinguish between
emic and etic levels of analysis, between the ways – no doubt various and
contested – that first-century persons such as Paul might have understood the phenomenon and the views modern observers trained in the
social sciences might form of it. As Segal correctly points out, conversion
itself is an etic word (1990: 285). Second, when we are operating at the
etic level we need to deploy theoretical resources which will be helpful for
the task.

Even from an emic perspective it is plain that the way in which Paul
seeks to characterise his new orientation, by describing himself as called
like Isaiah and Jeremiah, cannot be the end of the issue, since his

Israelite contemporaries who opposed his activity were easily able to deny such claims: 'He would say that, wouldn't he?' From a first-century perspective, other Israelites could refute Paul's self-description by asserting that he taught diaspora Israelites apostasy from Moses, especially by encouraging them not to circumcise their children, a charge Luke reports in Acts 21.21. Or they could say that his eating with sinful gentiles made him one of them, an accusation which may underlie his protestation to the contrary at Gal. 2.15. John Barclay has recently undertaken an excellent study of such charges against Paul (and similar ones made in this period) in terms of the deviance theory of Howard Becker which brings out the significance of the debate about Paul among first-century insiders. Becker proposes that deviance is constructed in the process of social interaction. In this perspective, deviance is not a quality inherent in the acts a person commits, but the consequence of the successful application of the label 'deviant' (Barclay 1995). Thus, ' "apostasy", like other deviant labels, is essentially a matter of perspective' (Barclay 1995: 118). Israelites of different views could react differently to the enigmatic figure of Paul in their midst. If he was viewed by his contemporary Israelites as an apostate, he was (historically speaking) an apostate (1995: 123).

Deviance and labelling theory is a sociological means of discussing differing first-century reactions to Paul's post-Damascus orientation. But there are other theoretical resources available which are somewhat more remote from emic understandings. One of them is the sociology of sectarianism, which has been applied to 1 Peter by J. H. Elliott (1990a), to Luke–Acts by myself (1987), to John's Gospel by D. Rensberger (1988) and to Matthew's Gospel by J. A. Overman (1990), to name some of the critics who have employed this theory. I will not rehearse the theory in detail here,[4] since I intend to rely on it only in a fairly general way. It is possible to devise models which trace the development of a new movement, which I refer to as a 'reform movement', within an existing religion through various stages until, at last, it has reached a stage of such significant differentiation and dissociation from that religion that it is appropriate to refer to it as a sect (Esler 1987: 46–53; 1994: 13–17).[5] In my view, that point comes when joint membership of the original religion and the reform movement is no longer possible, paradigmatically expressed in the secession or expulsion of the new group. On this model the critical question is whether this point has been reached or not. I have previously suggested (1987: 88–89) that the religion being advocated by Paul in Galatia had become sectarian in relation to Israelite religion, inasmuch as the mixed table-fellowship practised in his congregations involved a demolition of the boundaries between Israelite and non-Israelite which were necessary for the preservation of the Israelite *ethnos* and stirred up hostility sufficient to have Israelite members break off relationships with the gentiles. The exclusion of gentiles is explicitly recognised in Galatians at 4.17. On this etic approach, Paul's opponents, on the other hand, were seeking to keep the new religious orientation begun by Jesus Christ as a reform movement within Israel.

Yet how would we assess Paul's position immediately after God revealed Jesus Christ in him (1.16)? In particular, could this have been sectarian in the sense just discussed? The answer to this question depends in part on the nature of the Church of God (*ekklēsia tou theou*) which existed before Paul and which he had been persecuting and trying to destroy (Gal. 1.13; also 1 Cor. 15.9; cf. Phil. 3.6). A question closely related to this is Paul's motivation for his persecuting the church, a question too infrequently considered in any detail, which I will only be able to mention here briefly.[6] That Paul did persecute the church has a far-reaching significance for our understanding not only of his own career and how it bears on Galatians, but also of the origins of early Christianity generally. The persecution indicates that at a very early time the new movement had acquired a distinctive identity in relation to mainstream Israel and also that something about this distinctiveness caused grave offence to zealous Israelites like Paul.

But what was the reason for the offence? Hultgren suggests it was '"the faith", the positive proclamation of the church, the message of Jesus as messiah crucified and risen' (1976: 102), but this view is very unlikely because this proclamation was not a problem in Galatia, since the circumcisers themselves in some way adhered to the 'cross of Christ' for which they would escape persecution if they brought the gentiles into the House of Israel (Gal. 6.12), and there is no reason to think the cross itself had caused difficulties earlier. We need something else, and something more related to practice, rather than messianic beliefs which, in any event, would not necessarily have caused offence during this period given its diversity of messianic speculation (Smith 1967: 262).

→   In my view, the critical issue is whether gentiles had already started to join the Christ-movement. Some scholars have been attracted to the idea that it was Paul who first began to admit them. This seems unlikely, however. Paul does not say he inaugurated the mission to the gentiles, nor is the claim made in the Acts of the Apostles. Even if Acts is not historical in crediting Peter with the admission of the first gentile Christ-follower, in the form of the centurion Cornelius in Acts 10, its portrayal of the receipt of the Holy Spirit as the stimulus for the acceptance of gentiles (Acts 10.44–48) has a good claim to historical plausibility (Esler 1994: 37–51). Such a phenomenon could have occurred at any time in the earliest stages of the movement, even in Jerusalem, where God-fearing gentiles, marginalised from full participation in the Temple cult, may have mixed with diaspora Israelites in the first congregations and been exposed to the liberating impact of the gospel and the onrush of the Spirit on Israelite and gentile alike (Esler 1987: 145–161).

But in addition to these considerations there is evidence in Galatians directly in point. At one very revealing point (5.11) Paul asks, 'If I am still proclaiming circumcision, brothers, why am I still being persecuted? Surely, the scandal of the cross would be removed?' Although opinions differ,[7] the most natural explanation for this question about circumcision is that Paul is admitting that he had at one stage preached circumcision but does so no longer. He may have in mind the period when he once pleased human beings, whereas he now pleases God (Gal. 1.10). But in what context, we must ask, did Paul once preach circumcision? In spite of Matt. 23.15 ('Alas for you scribes and Pharisee hypocrites, because you cross the sea and the dry land to make a single proselyte, and when he becomes one you make him a child of Hell twice as much as your-selves'), the better view is that first-century Israelites did not actively seek to make proselytes (McKnight 1991). Moreover, the very fact that Paul asks the question at 5.11 suggests that the charge that he is still circumcis-ing is being raised in support of the present activities of the Galatian circumcisers. The second statement in 5.11, about removing the scandal of the cross, refers to Paul's view mentioned earlier, that for someone who preaches circumcision and claims righteousness comes from the law, Christ died in vain (2.21).

When one puts these considerations together, the most plausible con-text for Paul's preaching of circumcision was his persecution of the church before he turned to Christ. And what would stimulate him to preach circumcision? Only the fact that the church already comprised mixed congregations of Israelites and gentiles who were engaged in some deeply offensive practice for which the solution was circumcision of the latter. Even at this early stage the most likely candidate as the problem which elicited this solution was the eucharist of shared loaf and shared wine. If so, mixed Israelite–gentile table-fellowship served sharply to differentiate one segment of those who followed Jesus as the Christ from very early in the post-Easter development of the movement.

That Arabia was Paul's first destination (Gal. 1.17), something not even mentioned in Acts, may have been motivated by Old Testament prophecies which isolated this as the area in which the future influx of gentiles into God's holy people would begin, as Richard Bauckham has recently argued (1996). Yet Arabia could hardly contain no Israelites and if Paul began preaching the gospel there it is likely that the problem of mixed groups of Israelites and gentiles would have been with him from the very beginning of his ministry.

An objection might be raised to this argument from the way the history of the Christ-movement is presented in Acts. How could Paul's conversion be related to his decision to enter a form of the Christ-movement characterised by Israelites and gentiles engaging in mixed table-fellowship when Acts describes his conversion in Chapter 9 but that of the first gentile, at Peter's hands, in Chapter 10? And did not the Council of Jerusalem, long after Paul's conversion, specifically endorse this initial admission of gentiles in which Peter was involved (Acts 15.1–29)? My answer to this is twofold. First, I accept, as intimated above, that it is historically probable that the receipt of the Spirit by unbaptised gentiles was the stimulus to their being accepted into the communities and into eucharistic table-fellowship with Israelite members (Esler 1994: 37–51). I also fully accept that the problem which the Jerusalem church associated with gentile conversion was that of mixed Israelite–gentile table-fellowship (Acts 10.28; 11.1–3). These realities underlie the Cornelius story. Nevertheless, I have very little confidence in Luke's presentation of Cornelius having been the first gentile to convert, with Peter being the agent of this event. My reasons for this view are set out elsewhere (Esler 1987: 95–96, 107). Thus, I do not consider that the way Luke recounts the Cornelius story stands in the road of there having been gentile converts prior to Paul's conversion whose inclusion into eucharistic table-fellowship with Israelite Christ-followers deeply offended Israelite sentiment. Second, equally grave doubts surround the Lucan account of the Council of Jerusalem in Acts 15 (Esler 1987: 97–98). This passage reads best to me (although I cannot develop my reasons here) as a version of the events reported far more accurately in Gal. 2.1–10. Luke has both retrojected his account of what transpired in Jerusalem back into an earlier stage of Paul's ministry than is historically possible, and also significantly reworked the facts (especially by the insertion of the four requirements in Acts 15.20 and 29), so that he may present Paul as having conducted most of his mission after the embarrassing question of the status of gentiles in the movement had been settled once and for all. Given the quite extraordinary and insufficiently appreciated fact that as late as the eve of his departure for his final visit to Jerusalem Paul was in doubt whether his collection would be acceptable to the Jerusalem church (Rom. 15.31), I consider there is good reason to doubt that, at least at this stage, he had been reconciled to its leaders in the manner described in Acts 15.

On the basis of this discussion we are able to conclude that the church which Paul persecuted had a distinct identity and had already become sectarian in relation to Israel in the sense described above; that is, Israelite activists like Paul took the view that its mixed Israelite–gentile nature was so offensive that it could not be allowed to exist in its present form but must be destroyed. The means chosen was to have the gentile members become Israelites. This would have left a group of Israelites who acknowledged Jesus as the Messiah and who constituted a reform movement within Israel. Accordingly, in the light of this analysis, the action of God in choosing to reveal Christ in Paul so that he could preach the gospel among the gentiles and Paul's acceptance of this mission meant that he was moving from Israel to a sect outside Israel, no matter that he dressed up this transition in language drawn from the commissions of Isaiah and Jeremiah. Paul himself recognised how far he had moved from Israel when he wrote – at a point in his career not too distant in time from the composition of Galatians – that he was 'not under the [Mosaic] law' (1 Cor. 9.20). Accordingly, the charge that he taught apostasy against Moses reported at Acts 21.21 came close to being correct, even if he never went so far as to advise Israelites not to circumcise their children. Hence it is reasonable to speak of Paul's 'conversion'.

Finally, all this means that the problem over mixed table-fellowship and the proposed solution of circumcision was a feature of one strand of the Jesus movement before Paul joined it and at the time of his writing to the Galatians. It now remains to consider the intermediate events in Jerusalem and Antioch described in Gal. 2.1–10. I have elsewhere set out my views on this matter in some detail (Esler 1995c) and will now offer an abbreviated version of my argument.

THE JERUSALEM AGREEMENT AND ITS BREACH IN ANTIOCH (GAL. 1.18–2.14)

Setting the scene (1.18–24)

Paul offers a very schematic outline of his career after his return to Damascus (1.17). Three years later he went up to Jerusalem, remained there for a fortnight and, as he solemnly asserts, got to know (*historēsai*)[8] Peter, but of the other apostles saw only James, the brother of the Lord (1.18–20). In spite of attacks by Lyons on 'mirror-readings' of Galatians, the natural assumption is that Paul speaks in these terms as a way of countering suggestions that he had been more closely linked with or subordinate to the leaders in Jerusalem than had actually been the case. Paul's language here is another instance of anticipation.

After this he went off to the regions of Syria and Cilicia. We need not assume that he restricted himself to this area, merely that this was where he took up his work after his visit to Peter. Throughout the period after his departure he was not personally present among the churches of Judea (1.22),[9] but they heard of his work and glorified God for the fact that the person who had formerly tried to destroy the faith was now preaching it (1.23–24).

The Jerusalem agreement (2.1–10)

A model of Mediterranean social relations

To see the point of Paul's account of the events in Jerusalem during his second visit there after his conversion it is necessary to shed modern, individualistic attitudes derived from a North Atlantic culture and seek to interpret them in the light of the group-oriented and conflict-ridden culture of the Mediterranean. Research conducted in the region in the last four decades or so by anthropologists like Peristiany (1965), Pitt-Rivers (1965), Bourdieu (1965), Campbell (1964) and Peristiany and Pitt-Rivers (1992), especially as summarised and applied to the New Testament by Bruce Malina (1993), offers invaluable assistance in adopting cultural models more attuned to the social realities of the region. In addition, Malina and Neyrey have recently developed this approach by exploring the very different ways in which personality was expressed in the ancient Mediterranean world, especially in rhetorical techniques and literary genres, and they have applied their insights to the manner in which Paul presents himself in Gal. 1.12–2.14 (1996: 19–63).

As already noted, honour is the central good in this culture; thus Xenophon observed that human beings differ from animals in desiring the honour of their fellows (*Hiero*, 7.3). Honour can be ascribed to one, for example, by being born into a noble family, or can be actively acquired from others by successfully bettering them in the social pattern referred to as challenge-and-response, which was originally formulated by Pierre Bourdieu (1965) and helpfully reworked by Malina (1993: 33–37). Usually it is a game played by men who are not related or close friends, since it takes place in the public space where men interact and it is most dishonourable for family members to compete with one another.

Cases like the interaction between Peninnah and Hannah in 1 Samuel 1 – which does accord with the pattern – are the exceptions which prove the rule on both counts. In addition, moreover, challenge-and-response is usually played by social equals. So deeply was challenge-and-response embedded in ancient Graeco-Roman culture that Plutarch even recognised a social ill called *dysōpia*, meaning too easy a willingness to enter into challenge-and-response, especially over trivial matters.[10] This phenomenon has no real parallel in North Atlantic culture; it is only possible in cultures which combine a belief in honour as the primary social value and the notion that all goods, honour included, are limited.

Challenge-and-response has a number of stages. First, there is the challenge, which is a claim to enter the social space of another; it may either be positive, to gain a share of that space through a compliment or a request for help, or negative, to dislodge the other from his space, with an insult or a physical assault. Second, there is the manner in which the person challenged assesses its terms; is his honour put on the line or not? Third comes his response, which will take one of three forms: (a) a deliberate and scornful refusal to do anything in response; (b) acceptance of the challenge through a counter-challenge, for example, by an insult or a physical assault on the challenger; and (c) a passive refusal to act, although this may be construed by the audience as a cause of dishonour. The fourth stage is the public verdict, which attributes honour to the challenger or the person challenged. The loser suffers shame by this process.

Sometimes a person is unable to reply, or reply successfully, to a challenge at the time it is made, with the result that his honour is left 'in a state of desecration' (Pitt-Rivers 1965: 27). Until satisfaction can be obtained, and this could take virtually any length of time, the aggrieved person will be filled with the desire for revenge. The need to wreak vengeance on one's enemies to end the dishonour caused by their actions is, and was, one of the most powerful factors motivating Mediterranean social relations. There is a very good example of this in the account of the Ammonite war in 2 Samuel 10–12. Upon the death of the Ammonite king, David sends ambassadors to pay his respects to the new king (2 Sam. 10.1–2). But the Ammonites grievously insult them and send them back to David (2 Sam. 10.3–5). This inevitably causes offence and leads to Israel commencing war against Ammon (2 Sam. 10.6–7), which is only successfully concluded when David finally captures their capital (2 Sam. 12.29–31). It is interesting that David's failure to take personal responsibility for removing the slight to Israel and Israel's god, in that he entrusts most of the work to Joab, leads to all the problems caused by his being in Jerusalem 'at the turn of the year, when kings go out to war' (2 Sam. 11.1) and seeing Bathsheba from his roof. In the end, Joab only manages to get David out of Jerusalem to lead his army in the final assault on Ammon by telling him that he has captured the water-town and will take the rest of the city and call it after his own name unless David takes over the command (2 Sam. 12.26–28). Not only is this section of 2 Samuel structured around an insult offered to Israel which is ultimately avenged, but David is presented as a king who gets into serious trouble because of his failure to seek vengeance on Ammon and restore the honour of Israel himself.

As far as oral exchanges are concerned, it is useful to note the results of research by J. Pitt-Rivers. A person commits his honour to what he says, for example by way of a statement of past events or a promise as to the future, only if his words represent his sincere intentions, 'If his true will was not behind the promise or the assertion, then he is not dishonoured if he fails to fulfil the promise or turns out to have lied' (Pitt-Rivers 1965: 32–33). This means that a man can lie and deceive without forfeiting his honour and this is very often seen in the way members of one group treat another. In John's Gospel, for example, Jesus apparently lies to his brothers (7.1–10). When they suggest he should go up to Jerusalem for the feast of Tents (7.3–4) he says he is not going to (7.6–8) and then goes up secretly (7.10). No dishonour can be attributed to Jesus, however, because although they were his natural kin they did not have faith in him (7.5). Accordingly, they were not members of his group and he had no duty to tell them the truth.

None of this means that you cannot call a man a liar in public, but you can only do so if you can demonstrate that he previously committed his honour to the accuracy of the statement or promise; otherwise, you run the risk of making a fool of yourself by having been deceived. One way to try to get round this problem and to tie a person to the truth of his statements is to obtain an oath from him:

> By invoking that which is sacred to him – his god, the bones of saints, his loyalty to his sovereign, the health of his mother or simply his honour – he activates a curse against himself in the eventuality of his failure to implement his oath or, at least, he ensures that public opinion is entitled to judge him as dishonoured.
>
> (Pitt-Rivers 1965: 34)

Gal. 2.1–10 in the light of this model: making the agreement in Jerusalem

Fourteen years later Paul again returned to Jerusalem, with Barnabas and taking Titus along too (2.1). He went there in accordance with a vision (2.2), which excludes any possibility that he was summoned by the Jerusalem authorities. If we adopted social scenarios derived from modern North Atlantic culture, we might not find anything too startling in Paul's opening remarks. But within the framework of Mediterranean culture the picture is very different. Titus was an uncircumcised gentile (2.3). Excluding the fanciful possibility that every time they had an ordinary meal, let alone a Eucharistic one, Paul and Barnabas sent him off to eat somewhere else, his presence with them, sharing table-fellowship of the sort which would raise Israelite hackles, probably because of the risk of idolatry, raised in microcosm the whole essence of Paul's gentile mission and the problem which other Israelites considered to attach to it. The many critics who consider that the issue of table-fellowship did not come up during the Jerusalem visit but only later in Antioch have given insufficient attention to the fact that the problem was raised loud and clear as soon as Titus arrived with Paul and Barnabas.

By bringing Titus to Jerusalem, Paul was challenging the Jerusalem community; he was, in a literal sense, entering their social space. He may have construed this positively, as a claim to share that space, but some, at least, of the Israelite followers of Christ in the Holy City, would have construed it negatively, as an attempt to elbow them from that space. Titus' uncircumcised presence was a grievous insult to all those who thought only members of the House of Israel could belong to the new movement. The sense of conflict which surrounded this visit can be seen in the military imagery which Paul employs in relation to it and its aftermath in Antioch, which will be mentioned below.

Paul tells us that he had a *private* meeting with those who seemed to be something (2.2). Although he may wish to suggest by this that he was concerned for their reputation and wished to minimise the offence occasioned by bringing Titus with him and Barnabas, it is difficult to take the remark too seriously since we can safely assume that the busy gossip mills of a pre-industrial city like Jerusalem would soon have let everyone interested know that Paul and Barnabas were in town with a gentile. Similarly, in the Acts of the Apostles, the Israelites see Paul with Trophimus, a gentile from Ephesus, in the city, and wrongly assume he has brought gentiles into the Temple (Acts 21.27–29).

Paul asserts he 'laid before' the leaders 'the gospel which I preach among the gentiles . . . lest I am running or ran in vain' (2.2). We should be wary of any notion that Paul was seeking the approval of the Jerusalem authorities or suggesting that his status was less than theirs. The verb he employs for 'lay before' (*anatithēmi*) carries no such connotation, and it is unlikely that a gospel which he gained directly from a divine revelation (Gal. 1.15–17) could be in any way deficient. Moreover, an essential part of Paul's case must have involved the claims that God had been at work in this apostolate (2.8) and had bestowed grace upon it (2.9). The expression 'lest I am running or ran in vain' probably conveys apprehension, but that of the Jerusalem leadership, not Paul. The best way to interpret 2.2 in line with the agonistic nature of the meeting is that Paul is saying 'Look at the results of my work and tell me where I have gone wrong!' This is his way to stifle criticism of his evangelism, not to solicit approval or accreditation for it.

Paul now proceeds to record the results of the meeting. First of all, Titus was not compelled to be circumcised (2.3). This is sometimes taken to mean that he underwent circumcision voluntarily, but this possibility is extremely difficult to reconcile with what Paul says elsewhere in the letter.[11] The fact that Titus was not circumcised is obviously a point relevant to Paul's argument that the Galatians should not allow themselves to be circumcised. But there is more to it than this. Paul is also indicating that having bearded the lion in his den by bringing Titus to Jerusalem, he got away with it. Here we see Mediterranean man revelling in typical fashion in relation to his success over his adversaries.

In vv. 4–5 he gives us a revealing glimpse of the nature of the dispute and the bitterness of the antagonism. He mentions false brothers (*pseudadelphoi*) secretly smuggled in (to his meeting with the leaders) who slipped in to spy on 'our freedom which we have in Christ Jesus so as to enslave us' (2.4). These were probably hardline Israelite Christ-followers who wanted all members of the congregations to be Israelites. Although it is sometimes suggested that they were Israelites who were not part of the movement, their probable close connection, even identification, with those described as 'the circumcision group' in 2.12 (who also appear in Acts 11.3) and the fact that Paul refers to them in language so similar to that used of the people at 6.12 who are Israelite Christ-followers make this interpretation unlikely.[12] Not for one moment did he yield to the false brothers, Paul insists, before adding his reason in a way which tears the veil of time by suggesting that what he did on this occasion in the past was for the benefit of the Galatians – 'in order that the truth of the gospel might remain *for you*' (2.5). The 'truth of the gospel' here refers to the practice of his congregations containing Isaelites and gentiles sharing table-fellowship with one another without the latter having to take on circumcision and the yoke of the Mosaic law. This was the freedom referred to in the previous verse.

The model of Mediterranean social relations set out above suggests that the defeat of the circumcision group in Jerusalem would have left them steaming with the desire for revenge. Their honour had been besmirched by Paul's very obviously getting the better of them and in this culture we expect that they would seek to turn the tables on Paul, just as Israel did on Ammon in 2 Samuel 10–12. The strong language Paul uses to denigrate them in 2.4 may well reflect the intense nature of the antipathy between him and them. That 'those who seemed to be something' in the Jerusalem congregation imposed no requirement on Paul (2.6), other than that he remember the poor (2.10), could only have deepened their sense of shame. When Paul left Jerusalem, he would have been well advised to watch his back.

The Jerusalem leaders even went so far as to enter into a compact with Paul and Barnabas. Since God had been active with Peter among the circumcised and with Paul among the uncircumcised (2.7–8),

> James and Cephas and John, those who seem to be pillars, gave me and Barnabas right hands of fellowship, so that we among the gentiles, they among the circumcised.
>
> (Gal. 2.9)

The precise implications of this agreement have been much discussed. In the Greek, the word order is: 'they gave right hands [*dexias edōkan*] to me and Barnabas of fellowship [*koinōnias*]'. Commentators usually speak in general terms of the exchange of right hands being a way of symbolising a contract in the ancient world (Betz 1979: 100; Dunn 1993: 110). This is unhelpful. None of the contracts recognised in Roman law, for example, required a handshake, as can be seen in the account of contracts given by the second-century CE Roman jurist Gaius (*Institutes*, 89–162).[13] They were formed either by delivery of an object, by (a strict form of) words, by writing, or by consent (Gaius, *Institutes*, 89). Because the last category, consensual agreements, required no formalities of words or writing they could be entered into even when the parties were at a distance from one another,[14] so that handshakes *inter partes* were excluded. The suggestion of Sampley, that the *koinōnia* in Gal. 2.9 is equivalent to one of the four types of Roman consensual agreements, the *societas*, or partnership,[15] is inconsistent with this characteristic of a *societas* that it was constituted by 'bare agreement' (*nudo consensu* [Gaius, *Institutes*, 154]). Greek law, moreover, was less inclined to favour informal consensual agreements and often insisted on writing (Nicholas 1962: 194–195).

The actual source for the arrangement in Gal. 2.9 lies elsewhere, in the Septuagint, where, in 1 and 2 Maccabees, the precise expression 'give right hands' occurs eleven times.[16] In almost all of these cases a person who is in a superior position, usually in a military context, gives the right hand to people who are virtually suppliants, who 'take it', as a way of bringing peace to a conflict. It is not a gesture made between equals, as claimed by Betz (1979: 100). This context brings out some surprising dimensions to Gal. 2.9. We should not read this verse as an expression of balance and amity between the parties. Rather, James, Cephas and John condescend to Paul and Barnabas by acting as if they are in a superior position to them in a conflict and are graciously offering a cessation of hostilities. This is the force of 'giving right hands'. Paul and Barnabas clearly took the hands that were proffered to them, but Paul expressly dissents from the superiority implied in the gesture by describing the three Jerusalem leaders, in the same verse, as (only) seeming to be pillars.

The explanation for the word *koinōnia* somewhat awkwardly at the end of the verse is that it is an appositive genitive – Paul and Barnabas were offered a peace 'which consisted of fellowship'. Moreover, the use of this word to categorise the peace which had now been established suggests that it was meant to refer to future relationships between the parties (see also Dunn 1993: 110), not to what the parties may have already had in common.

Yet what did the parties have in mind by *koinōnia*? Although many commentators opt for some general notion of fellowship (Betz 1979: 100; Dunn 1993: 110–111; Matera 1992: 77), something more specific than this is needed here to give some point to the agreement. Paul uses *koinōnia* thirteen times in his correspondence[17] and while it always has a core meaning to do with sharing or common participation, its precise implications vary considerably. In Gal. 2.9 it must mean something which the three pillars themselves are capable of providing or at least guaranteeing; this means we may eliminate the use of the *koinōnia* in relation to the Holy Spirit or Jesus Christ or faith in him (1 Cor. 1.9; 2 Cor. 13.13; Phil. 2.1; 3.10; Phlm 6). Second, it cannot have the sense of the sharing of physical goods in relation to the collection found at Rom. 15.26; 2 Cor. 8.4 and 9.13 since this only concerned Paul, not James, Cephas and John. Third, the general senses of 'association' which occurs at 2 Cor. 6.14 or 'co-operation' at Phil. 1.5 seem too vague to satisfy the requirement that Paul and Barnabas were actually benefiting from the agreement. This leaves the use of *koinōnia* at 1 Cor. 10.16 in connection with Eucharistic table-fellowship. Moreover, *koinōnia* was commonly used in the ancient world to denote table-fellowship, even in cases where human beings shared sacrificial meals with the gods (Hauck 1966b: 798–800). Choosing this interpretation is attractive for two other reasons. First, it means that the Jerusalem leaders entered into a peace with Paul and Barnabas in a form which precisely answered the problem Paul had provocatively raised by his visiting the city with Titus, namely, the mixed table-fellowship of his diaspora congregations. Second, immediately after this agreement we find Peter in Antioch first engaging in table-fellowship with the gentile believers there and then discontinuing this practice. Interpreting *koinōnia* in the way proposed here means that Peter's visit to Antioch constituted the specific implementation of the agreement. After all, since the parties had agreed that Paul and Barnabas would pursue their mission among the gentiles and Peter among the circumcised (Gal. 2.9), some explanation is needed for Peter's visit to Antioch (where Paul was active) after the Jerusalem meeting, and the possibility that this was intended as a way of putting the agreement very visibly into effect is an appealing one.

A noteworthy feature of the agreement of Gal. 2.9 is that Paul and Barnabas did not obtain any oaths from the pillars to bind them to its performance. As noted above, taking an oath is a device in the Mediterranean region for ensuring that a person will stick to his promise. Ancient Greek and Israelite oaths served essentially the same purpose, with breach of an oath bringing a curse down on one's head (Schneider 1967). The Old Testament provided that oaths could be made on Yahweh's name (Deut. 6.13; 10.20) and that false swearing was an abuse of his name (Exod. 20.7; Lev. 19.12). Oaths could either be made to assert the truth of a statement of facts or to seal the truth of a promise made as to future conduct (Schneider 1967: 458), with the latter type, for which there are examples in the Old Testament (Josh. 1.12–22; Judg. 21.1–5; Neh. 10.29), being the one theoretically relevant to strengthen the Jerusalem agreement. It is worth noting that on two of the eleven occasions in the Septuagint where 'right hands' were given, oaths were taken as well (1 Macc. 6.61 and 2 Macc. 4.34), although in both cases the oaths were promptly broken.[18] That Paul himself was not adverse to giving oaths can be seen from the example of one at Gal. 1.20 and others elsewhere in his letters.[19] Nevertheless, there were some misgivings expressed about oath-giving (Jer. 5.2; Zech. 5.3–4; Sir. 23.9–14).

In any event, James, Cephas and John gave no oaths. Nor are we told if Paul had sought them. The reason they do not figure in the account of the agreement may have been the prohibition on oaths which is associated with traditions concerning James (James 5.12), and which appears in Matt. 5.33–37, in what may be a stratum of that text derived from a similar Israelite strand of the movement, perhaps even originating with Jesus himself. The consequences of Paul not binding the pillars by an oath will be addressed below.

We must assume from Gal. 2.11 that after the meeting, Paul, Barnabas and Titus travelled to Antioch (presumably the place from where they had gone to Jerusalem) and that Peter went there some time afterwards. Paul begins the passage with a note of Peter's arrival followed by a summary of his response to him: 'I opposed him to his face, because he was condemned' (2.11). The language here is very revealing. The expression 'to oppose someone to their face' (*anthistēnai kata prosōpon*) is a biblical one used where people resist a determined military assault, usually without success.[20] Accordingly, Paul is suggesting that Peter made a frontal attack, in other words, that the hostilities previously settled in Jerusalem had now been resumed, and that he had resisted. Yet he may also be intimating by the biblical context of this idiom that he was ultimately unsuccessful against Peter.

Paul then proceeds to explain how this confrontation came about. Initially Peter ate with (*synēsthien*) the gentiles, but following the arrival of certain people from James he withdrew and separated himself from fear of the circumcision group (2.12). The rest of the *Ioudaioi*, even Barnabas, joined him in his hypocrisy (2.13). But when Paul saw that he was not walking 'according to the truth of the gospel', he said to him in front of everyone: 'If you being a *Ioudaios* live like a gentile and not like a *Ioudaios*, how can you compel the gentiles "to Judaize" [*Ioudaizein*]?' The meaning of *Ioudaizein* is disputed and I will return to it in a moment.

How are we to understand this extraordinary chain of events? How do they relate to the agreement previously reached in Jerusalem? What did the people from James say to Peter to make him break off table-fellowship? What did they have against the practice? In what lay Peter's offence as far as Paul was concerned? What was Peter actually seeking the gentiles to do? Given the massive amount of attention these four verses have received, it is impossible to offer a summary of scholarship here. My aim is to seek to explain the meaning of the incident at Antioch in the light of the model from Mediterranean culture set out above with occasional reference to other views.

Our starting-point is the situation Paul left behind in Jerusalem. He had extracted an agreement from the Jerusalem leaders without giving away anything himself. True, he had consented to remember their poor, a responsibility that we know from his references to the collection[21] he took very seriously, but this was not much of a concession. On the preferable view of the Greek in 2.10, he *was eager* (*espoudasa*) to do this anyway, rather than that he *hastened* to do it.[22] His point is that he would have done it even without any action by the pillars, so that they really got nothing in return from Paul for the promise of fellowship. If so, the honour of the leaders had been left in an ambiguous position, since they were open to the charge that they had let Paul get the better of them. The false brothers who vigorously advocated circumcision found themselves in an even worse position, since they had been soundly defeated. When Paul left Jerusalem, they would have been driven to wreak vengeance upon him. As already noted, persons in this culture who are shamed to this extent do not forgive or forget. Their best hope for revenge was certainly to have the leaders reverse the agreement they had reached with Paul and to insist on circumcision as necessary for gentile converts. With Paul and Barnabas, and later Peter, out of the city they would have been left with James and John upon whom they could exert pressure to revoke the agreement. Presumably, their line would be to persuade the two leaders that their own honour had been desecrated by the agreement and that things must be put right. It is probable that they also backed up their arguments with some sort of threat, possibly to bring to bear on anyone actually engaging in table-fellowship with the gentiles the sort of force, whatever its precise nature, which Paul himself had once deployed against 'the church of God' (Gal. 1.13).

In this scenario, the advocates of circumcision were successful, because some time after Peter had reached Antioch they prevailed upon James to send him a message to break off table-fellowship. That Peter did so 'from fear of the circumcision group' (Gal. 2.12) is a reflection of the power which they (like Paul before them) had been able to bring to bear on the congregations. This is a socially plausible explanation for Peter's sudden change of behaviour. It also means that the agreement reached in Jerusalem had been directly revoked. I have already argued that it is extremely unrealistic to assume that the question of table-fellowship could somehow not have come up during the Jerusalem meeting.

There is strong confirmation of a complete breach of the agreement by Peter (and James behind him) in Gal. 2.14 when Paul says 'But when I saw that they were not walking straight with respect to the truth of the gospel, I said to Cephas . . .'. The only other time in his correspondence that Paul uses the phrase 'the truth of the gospel' is at Gal. 2.5 where it refers to what Paul protected for the Galatians against the foray of the false brothers. In other words, he is now equating Peter, Barnabas and the other Jewish Christ-followers in Antioch with the false brothers who had tried in Jerusalem to enslave the gentiles under the Mosaic law in that he presents both sets of opponents as equally a threat to 'the truth of the gospel'. Peter and the others had now adopted the view previously expressed by the circumcisers in the Holy City. Although suppressed in Jerusalem, it had now re-emerged in Antioch.

Moreover, if Peter had come to accept the position of the false brothers, he must have reached the view that circumcision was necessary for the gentiles as the price of readmission to the congregation in the full sense, meaning Eucharistic fellowship.[23] In other words, when Paul asked him how he could compel the gentiles to 'Judaize', he meant how could Peter force them to become *Ioudaioi*, members of the House of Israel, through circumcision. This view is quite rare in the field, with most scholars being unwilling to accept its consequence, that Peter and James had unequivocally broken the Jerusalem agreement. The most common interpretation is that Peter was seeking the imposition of something less drastic than circumcision, such as certain Jewish customs.[24] Perhaps modern notions of fair play have affected the ability of many critics to interpret the incident in a manner which is at home in Mediterranean culture. Certainly at least one ancient commentator, and a very well-informed one at that (Esler 1995c: 311), Ambrosiaster, who was active in the late fourth century CE, favoured the view that Peter was advocating circumcision of the gentiles, since in commenting on Gal. 6.13 Ambrosiaster relates the trouble occurring in Galatia when Paul was writing to what Peter had previously attempted in Antioch (Esler 1995c: 311; Vogels 1969: 66). A number of other considerations support this view.

First, circumcision was the goal of the circumcision group, from fear of whom Peter withdrew from table-fellowship (2.12); it would be odd if having acted in response to the threat he perceived they represented he aimed for a result other than the one they wanted.

Second, there are three connections which Paul draws between the closely related series of events in Jerusalem and Antioch and the one he faces in Galatia which suggest that the problem and the solution to it proposed by Israelite Christ-followers were the same in each case. These considerations are: (a) as noted earlier in this chapter, ancient rhetoric required a *narratio* in a deliberative speech to have some relationship to the matter at issue, and the fact that in each situation Paul had come up against a demand that his converts be circumcised is an excellent candidate for such a connection; (b) Paul portrayed his action in Jerusalem as having been motivated to protect the truth of the gospel for the

Galatians (2.5), so that the truth previously threatened by circumcisers in Jerusalem and then in Antioch (2.14) is once again at risk from the same peril; (c) in 4.25 Paul tells the Galatians that Jerusalem is in slavery with her children and this is closely equivalent to the views he expresses against the false brothers in 2.4 and extends to Peter and the rest in 2.13.[25]

Third, it is difficult to account for Paul's immediate transition in Gal. 2.15–16 to a discussion of justification by faith and not works of the law, which certainly include circumcision, if this topic is not the same as that raised by Peter's demand of the gentiles.

There is one apparent obstacle to the argument developed here that Peter resiled from the agreement in Antioch. It is the circumstance that Paul does not tax him with precisely this offence, *of breaking his promise,* rather he accuses him of inconsistent behaviour in first eating with the gentiles and then ending such fellowship upon the arrival of the people from James. There are two answers to this. The first fixes on the suggestion that the precise meaning of the fellowship agreed to in Jerusalem (2.9) was table-fellowship of the sort Peter abandons in Antioch; given this view the breach of the agreement was self-evident and Paul did not need to labour the point to his audience.

The second answer rests in Mediterranean attitudes to honesty and dishonesty as discussed earlier. In this culture people commit their honour to a promise only through their sincere intentions. If their true will was not really behind the undertaking, they are not dishonoured by going back on what they have promised. Moreover, a charge of promise-breaking can be answered by asserting that one had not really intended to carry out the promise, even if this is a convenient rationalisation after the event akin to the child's ploy, 'I had my fingers crossed'. Thus, actions speak louder than words in this culture because they are more likely to reflect a person's real intentions. The only way to have confidence that someone really stands behind their word at the time it is given is by taking an oath to the truth of the undertaking.

But Paul, for whatever reason, had not obtained an oath from James, Cephas and John. Not only did he have no way of knowing if they had committed their honour to the agreement, but he risked making a fool of himself if he agitated this issue, inasmuch as he had been misled by their unsupported promise. The best he can do is to accuse Peter of misbehaviour in first dining with gentiles and then breaking off this contact. Here he relies on the good Mediterranean principle that actions speak louder than words. When Peter came to Antioch he dined with gentiles, so that his actions and intentions were aligned. This meant that Peter was living 'like a gentile', but such was the result of the Jerusalem agreement. Peter was in Paul's zone of operations putting into effect the arrangement that gentiles and Israelites could share intimate forms of association in the congregation without the former needing to become Israelites. By ceasing this practice he stands condemned for acting inconsistently with what he knew to be the agreed and correct position. The language Paul uses supports this view. Having mentioned Peter's withdrawal (2.13), he says that the other *Ioudaioi* 'joined him in this deceptive inconsistency' (*synypekrithēsan*) and that Barnabas 'was similarly led away by their deceptive inconsistency' (*synapēchthē tē hypocrisei*). The verb *hypokrinomai* and the related nouns *hypokrisis* and *hypocritēs* were used in classical Greek originally in the sense of 'answer' or 'interpret', and later came to be applied to acting in theatre. To a limited extent for the classical authors, but then almost without exception in the Septuagint, for first-century authors like Philo and Josephus and elsewhere in the New Testament, these words acquired a negative sense (Wilckens 1972). They do not, however, convey the meaning of 'hypocrisy', the parade of virtue as a disguise for wrongdoing (Wilckens 1972: 565), but rather suggest reprehensible play-acting, the disjunction of intention and action in serious matters. As used by Paul in Gal. 2.13 they convey the sense that Peter, Barnabas and the other Israelites are now acting a part which does not accord with their true intentions as revealed earlier when they did engage in table-fellowship with the gentiles. These earlier intentions and actions, moreover, were in accord with 'the truth of the gospel', in that they exemplified the freedom of the gentiles from the demands of the Mosaic law which characterised Paul's apostolate, so that when the Israelite members broke off table-fellowship they diverged from this truth (2.13) and this elicited Paul's criticism of Peter (2.14).

The fact that when condemning Peter in front of everyone Paul uses the present tense: 'If you being a *Ioudaios* live like a gentile and not like a *Ioudaios*, how can you compel the gentiles to become a *Ioudaios*?' does not prejudice this argument.[26] If Paul used a past tense – 'if you lived like a gentile' – he would be conceding to Peter that he had irrevocably altered his ideas and actions. The present tense, on the other hand, sharpens the point of Paul's attack by animating an insinuation that Peter's present manifestation of *Ioudaismos* in withdrawing from the gentiles is merely a pretence, since his adoption of gentile ways really represents his true position.

There is discussion as to whether the words of Paul's address to Peter end at 2.14, which is my view (and that of Betz 1979: 113–114 and Dunn 1990b: 172), or extend to 2.21, as many others hold (Verseput

1993: 51). Although I will not rehearse the argument I have developed elsewhere on this point (Esler 1995c: 309–310), it is worth noting here how far off the mark is the claim that the brevity of Paul's statement, if it does end at 2.14, makes little sense. Given the distinctive nature of the Mediterranean outlook on honesty, Paul's statement at 2.14 was by far his best point. The passage at 2.15–21 begins his generalised and theological reflection on the issues which had been at stake in Antioch, written for the benefit of his Galatian audience. I will discuss them in the next chapter.

Lastly, we must ask whether Paul did succeed in persuading the Israelites among the Christ-followers that he was in the right. The better view is that he did not, since if he had it is difficult to see why he would not have played such a trump card in seeking to dissuade the Galatians from being circumcised.[27] As already noted, the biblical expression used by Paul at 2.11 for his response to Peter's actions, 'I opposed him to his face', usually occurs in a context of unsuccessful resistance. Paul's problem as he writes the letter is that a war which flared up in Antioch, where he lost the initial engagement, has now broken out again in Galatia, possibly indeed through the actions of combatants who have been encouraged by his previous defeat.

Chapter 6

Righteousness as privileged identity

RIGHTEOUSNESS IN GALATIANS

The data

Having recounted how he rebuked Peter at Antioch (2.11–14), Paul launches upon a new topic in a manner translated in the Revised Standard Version as follows:

> We ourselves, who are Jews by birth and not gentile sinners, yet who know that a man is not justified by works of the law but through faith in Jesus Christ, even we have believed in Christ Jesus, in order to be justified by faith in Christ, and not by works of the law, because by works of the law shall no one be justified.
>
> (2.15–16)

The words translated here as 'justified' (a different translation will be offered later) are passive forms of *dikaioō*, which appears three times in v. 16. The theme which Paul so begins at 2.15–16 is further developed in 2.17–2.21, initially with a firm denial that the aim of being justified (*dikaioō*) in Christ when coupled with our personal sinfulness makes Christ a minister of sin (2.17). Then come strong assertions of Paul's death to the (Mosaic) law to achieve life in God, of his crucifixion with Christ and Christ's life in him, and of his current life in faith in the Christ who handed himself over on his behalf (2.18–20). Finally, Paul disavows rejecting God's grace, inasmuch as if *dikaiosynē* (a noun cognate with *dikaioō* meaning 'justification' or 'righteousness') came through the law, then surely Christ died in vain (2.21).

It is worthwhile noting at once that the passive form of the verb *dikaioō* and the noun *dikaiosynē* are brought into close proximity in 2.15–21 and, furthermore, that they are virtually equivalent to the extent that they both designate that which derives from faith in Christ, who died to save but not from the law. The instance of *dikaiosynē* at Gal. 2.21 looks, indeed, like a climax of what has been said previously in relation to *dikaioō*. The verb *dikaioō* is used in the present tense in Gal. 2.16, in the aorist tense (which is employed to denote single events, usually in the past) in 2.16 and 2.17 and in the future tense at 2.16, which is probably an allusion to Psalm 143.2 where it relates to judgement before God, although that idea is not made explicit in v. 16 and there is certainly no justification for assuming Paul had the *final* judgement in mind here.[1]

After a section reminding the Galatians that they received the Spirit through faith and not works of the law (3.1–5), which carries the clear implication that the Spirit is like righteousness in being a benefit derived from faith, Paul returns to righteousness language in connection with a discussion of Abraham and the curse of the law (3.6–14). Here he insists that Abraham's faith was accounted to him as righteousness (*dikaiosynē*, 3.6), that scripture foresaw that God would 'justify' (*dikaioō*) the gentiles by faith (3.8) and that those relying on the law are cursed and that it is evident that no one is justified (*dikaioō*) before God by the law, because 'the righteous person [*dikaios*] will live by faith', a citation of Hab. 2.4 (3.11). Both instances of *dikaioō* are in the present tense.

The verb crops up again at 3.24 (aorist tense) and 5.5 (present tense), in both cases to speak of what comes from faith and not from the law. The noun *dikaiosynē* recurs at 3.21, where Paul disconnects it from law, and at 5.5, in a similar context, but with Paul now speaking of how we await 'the hope of righteousness' through the Spirit by faith.

In addition to the areas of overlap already noticed in Gal. 2.15–21, we observe that the noun and the verb are brought into close proximity in 3.6–11 and 3.21–24 and into very close proximity in 5.4–5, while the verb and the adjective (*dikaios*) actually occur together in 3.11. Such connections constitute strong prima facie grounds for proposing a single explanation for these terms, although many commentators, as we will see, prefer a variety of meanings. Unfortunately, there is no modern verb to correspond with 'righteous' and if we find it necessary to preserve the unity of the semantic field we may adopt for our verb either the old form 'rightwise' (now admittedly enjoying something of a revival in this context) or E. P. Sanders' useful neologism 'to righteous' (1983: 6). An alternative proposed below is to translate the passive of the verb as to be or become righteous.

Righteousness in the wider context of Galatians

Having now considered the basic data on righteousness in Galatians, it will be helpful to set the subject within the broad context of the letter which we have already considered. This will provide a framework both for the critical discussion of existing approaches in the next section of this chapter and to pave the way for my own reading of righteousness as legitimate identity, which will follow.

The gentile members of the Galatian communities contemplating circumcision considered that they would acquire righteousness as a result. This view rests largely on the fact that on no fewer than six occasions in the letter (2.16 [thrice]; 2.21; 3.11; 3.21) Paul asserts or implies that righteousness does not come from law.[2] Fairly unequivocal evidence for this also comes from 5.2–4:

> Now I, Paul, say to you that if you are circumcised, Christ will be of no advantage to you. I again bear witness to everyone who is circumcised that he is obliged to keep the whole law. You are severed from Christ, you who are righteoused [*dikaiousthe*] by the law; you have fallen away from grace.

Here Paul's statement presupposes that his addressees believed that they would be 'righteoused' through circumcision and acceptance of the law.

Since the advocates of righteousness were maintaining that it was to be gained from circumcision, it follows that they must also have thought that it was not to be found among gentiles. It is clear from 2.15 that Paul was well aware that Israelites considered gentiles sinful and he shared their view, at least as far as idolatrous *goyim* were concerned (see also 4.8). From this it followed that a person could only be or become righteous by crossing the boundary separating Israelites from gentiles to join the House of Israel.

That the gentile members believed, or were at risk of believing, that righteousness was obtained in this way must have resulted from persuasion by Israelite Christ-followers, since these were the Israelites with whom they had the closest dealings. Yet these Israelite members were themselves under pressure from other Israelites to end their anomalous boundary violation with gentiles (Gal. 6.12–13). This means that righteousness must have been at home in the wider Judaic community. The discussion of the law in the *Letter of Aristeas* which we examined in Chapter 3 brings out this position quite unambiguously; there righteousness was depicted as essential in designating the condition of Israelites *vis-à-vis* the gentiles. In this perspective righteousness was inextricably connected with being an Israelite, with an identity to match, which included the possession of a collection of superior ethical norms which were very distinctive in the Graeco-Roman world. In Galatia it was an aspect of general Israelite experience and belief being urged by the Israelite members of the congregations on the gentile believers due to the pressure being exerted on the former group by the wider Judaic community. Therefore, it is most unlikely to have been some feature peculiar to the theology or experience of Israelite Christ-followers as suggested, for example, by Betz (1979: 115–116).

Moreover, the advocates of the Mosaic law must have been presenting righteousness as something desirable. The circumcisers are holding out righteousness as the desirable end produced by the law; righteousness is the prize they have put on offer. To an extent, Paul shares this view. That he is intent on presenting righteousness as a benefit of belonging to his congregations is apparent in the way he moves to a discussion of the gift of the Spirit in 3.1–5, immediately after he has opened up the topic of righteousness. Moreover, he does not suggest for one moment that righteousness is not worth having, only that it must be obtained by faith in Jesus Christ and not through the law. Our understanding of righteousness, therefore, must be consonant with its evident appeal and attractiveness.

This does not mean, however, that the righteousness which he argues comes from faith in Christ is exactly the same as that being proposed by his opponents. Righteousness was something about which rival groups could compete, a situation also evident in Matt. 5.20, even though the Matthean understanding of righteousness was different to the Pauline (Przybylski 1980). There was nothing to prevent there being two versions of righteousness on offer in Galatia which had some common element while differing in other respects in accordance with their different social locations. The result of this is that while Paul is certainly at issue with his Galatian opponents as to the proper method of acquisition or achievement of righteousness, there may also be some variance in the meaning of the expression on his lips and theirs. In other words, although righteousness, as it has initially been urged on the gentiles from Israelite quarters, cannot have a specific significance for believers in Christ (as already noted), the version of its meaning advocated by Paul to his Galatian audience as he responds to pressure may acquire such a flavour. It was a reality capable of redefinition in the struggle between the groups.

Finally, since Paul is talking to people who already belong to his congregations, we are dealing with an issue which relates to how the members will enhance or even perfect their existing membership. As far as Paul is concerned, the issue does not relate to how people 'get in', but deals with the character of their ongoing membership, with 'staying in'. At the same time, even though the advocates of circumcision may well have been asserting that circumcision was essential to membership, to 'getting in' rather than to 'staying in', they are likely to have been portraying righteousness as a fruit of entry, part of the glorious condition which came from being a member of a people with ancestors as illustrious as Abraham, not as a condition of entry. Nothing in Galatians suggests that the advocates of circumcision were insisting on righteousness as essential to entry or as a requirement for continuing membership. It was the prize one gained through circumcision.

LANDMARKS IN THE DISCUSSION OF RIGHTEOUSNESS IN GALATIANS

From the time of the Reformation to the present there has been intense interest in Paul's understanding of righteousness or justification, as principally expressed in his letters to the Galatians and Romans, by both the Church and the Academy. As recently as 1978, Hans Hübner could still assert that ' "justification by faith" is what Paul is ineluctably concerned to talk about' (1984: 7). Considerations of space, however, prevent my offering a detailed history of discussion on this topic, a task undertaken by others in any event (Anderson *et al.* 1985: 17–48; Westerholm 1988: 15–86; Thielman 1989: 1–27). Nevertheless, it is necessary to offer a critical survey of some of the highlights of this research so as to set the scene for the very different interpretation of righteousness to be offered in the current chapter of this reading, one which will fix on its role in maintaining the distinctive identity of the Galatian congregations.

Martin Luther

Martin Luther's agonised preoccupation in his early years with the impossibility of being able to stand before God with a clear conscience in spite of the rich and increasingly corrupt array of penitential practices offered by late medieval catholicism was a powerful stimulus for him to reject these practices, as he did most graphically by nailing his *Ninety-Five Theses* to the door of Erfurt Cathedral in 1517, and to develop a theology which related salvation directly to the grace of God apprehended in faith rather than by human good works. He encapsulated his insights in the expression 'justification by faith', although that notion went back as far as Augustine (Anderson *et al.* 1985: 17–19). Luther argued that when we accept Christ into our hearts by faith God accounts us as righteous, so that we obtain remission of our sins and achieve righteousness. Sin is still present in us, but God disregards it, or prevents it being imputed to us, for Christ's sake. This means that the Christian is at one and the same time justified and a sinner (*simul iustus et peccator*).

For Luther then, 'justification by faith' meant the remission of sins – obtained by faith and not human works – which allowed one the joyful and quiet conscience he had previously craved (Dillenberger 1961: 111–112). Luther developed this view from his reading of Galatians and Romans and although he knew Paul was talking about the Mosaic law, he considered that the same must apply all the more to works which mere human beings might devise. Ultimately, the papist, the Israelite, the Turk and the heretic were all alike as they believed that God would be favourably disposed towards them if they performed particular actions and angry with them if they did not (Dillenberger 1961: 106–107).

Krister Stendahl

Krister Stendahl began what has proved to be a seminal article (first published in 1963) for disentangling Paul from Lutheran interpretations of his work with the assertion that in the history of Western Christianity and culture Paul had been hailed as 'a hero of the introspective conscience' (1977: 78). He noted that in Protestant Christianity, especially, the struggle of the ruthlessly honest man with his conscience, with Martin Luther as the prototype, had become identified with the awareness of sin in the Pauline letters. Yet, he suggests, it is exactly at this point that we can discern the greatest difference between the first and the sixteenth centuries, when individualism and the introspective conscience had begun to take root, as a result of factors like the Augustinian inheritance, especially through the influence of the *Confessions* of Augustine, and medieval penitential devotions, to which we may also add the cultural revolution of the twelfth century (Gurevich 1995).

For Paul, in fact, had a rather robust conscience. In Philippians 3 he speaks of his life before he turned to Christ and even claims in v. 6 that, as far as the righteousness (*dikaiosynē*) required by the law was concerned, he had been 'blameless' (*amemptos*), a word which suggests the ethical dimension of the concept among first-century Israelites. It is virtually impossible to find any sign of concern in Paul for the events of his past, except that he persecuted the Church. He can refer to his past without any reference to a plagued conscience such as Luther possessed. Against this might be put what he says in Romans 7, but here Stendahl (like most other commentators) accepted the position espoused in 1929 by W. G. Kümmel to the effect that the 'I' voice in this passage was not Paul himself, but humanity in general under the law (see Westerholm 1988: 52–64). The formula *simul iustus et peccator* does not apply to Paul.

The broad and largely persuasive view of Stendahl, then, is that whereas Paul was concerned about the possibility of gentiles being included in the messianic community, his statements came to be read as answers to the quest for assurance about human salvation out of a common human predicament (1977: 86). In 1977 Stendahl reiterated his view that Paul did not regard the Israelite–gentile problem as illustrative of some universal human plight and its resolution:

> The doctrine of justification by faith was hammered out by Paul for the very specific and limited purpose of defending the rights of gentile converts to be full and genuine heirs to the promise of God to Israel.
>
> (1977: 2)

Alleged Jewish legalism

One of the most unfortunate notions ultimately to develop from Luther's position and subsequent Protestant/Catholic controversy was that first-century Israelites were characterised by a religion of works–righteousness, wherein God was believed to weigh fulfilment of the law against transgressions to determine who would be saved. This was alleged to lead either to despairing uncertainty of redemption on the one hand or a boasting certainty of it on the other. This line on Israelite religion, as originally noted by G. F. Moore (1921, 1927), seems to have been imported into New Testament scholarship by F. Weber in 1880 and thereafter found its way into the influential writings of Bousset and Schürer. Moore argued that the Judaism of Paul's day was actually characterised by grace and sincere devotion to God, not by striving for merit and boasting in achievement.

E. P. Sanders

In a major contribution to the discussion based on an extensive survey of Judaic literature from the ancient period and published in 1977, E. P. Sanders largely confirmed Moore's view, while insisting that underpinning the religion of first-century Israel was a belief in God's election of his people and his establishment of a covenant with them. Performing the works of the law functioned to keep Israelites within the covenant, not to earn salvation (1977: 1–428). Sanders designated his position 'covenantal nomism' and he has won widespread scholarly support for it (Thielman 1989: 17).

As far as Paul went, Sanders proposed that he did not begin with a critique of Israel, by claiming that it pursued righteousness in the wrong way (by works), but rather that his starting-point was the experience of salvation which came from faith and participation in Christ, from which vantage-point he was able to argue for the inadequacy of the law and to deny that it led to righteousness (1977: 431–523). Unlike Luther, who moved from plight to solution, Paul moved from solution to plight. This does not mean that Paul did not have a strong sense of the sinfulness of our condition before and without Christ's sacrificial death (see Gal. 1.4). One problem for some scholars, such as Hooker (1990b), with Sanders' distinction between Israelite covenantal theology and Paul's doctrine of participation in Christ was that it drove a deep wedge between Paul and Israel, so that his interest in the eventual conversion of Israelites to Christ which appears in Romans 9–11, for example, became very difficult to comprehend. Yet to argue for alleged intellectual similarities between Paul and Israel in areas such as salvation and covenant – as Hooker does (1990b) – runs the risk of underestimating the profound social chasm which had opened up between Paul's congregations and mainstream Israel, as discussed in previous chapters of this reading.

Sanders' most detailed statement of his understanding of Paul's outlook on righteousness is found in his 1983 work *Paul, the Law and the Jewish People*. He reiterates that Paul's position is dominated by his Christology and soteriology, but develops his earlier case by arguing that the apostle employs righteousness language to describe the movement of gentiles into the body of those who will be saved, rather than their behaviour or condition once they have achieved this. Righteousness language is about 'getting in', not 'staying in' (1983: 6). The passive form of *dikaioō* 'is used to denote the act of transfer' (1983: 10). In Sanders' view, the 'subject of Galatians is not whether or not humans, abstractly conceived, can by good deeds earn enough merit to be declared righteous at the judgement; it is the condition on which gentiles enter the people of God' (1983: 18). On the other hand, Sanders qualifies all this by attributing a rather circumscribed meaning to 'entry'. He asserts that he does not mean that the requirement of faith alone for entry is just a fleeting one that has no significance for continuing life in the people of God; he is speaking of 'entry' in 'the sense of what is essential in order to be considered a member *at all* (1983: 20). This qualification makes his position rather confusing. On the one hand he is talking about transfer into the people of God, and on the other a 'membership requirement' (1983: 52). Not surprisingly, some commentators have missed this nuance and suggest he is talking about 'getting in' when the problem in Galatians concerns 'staying in' (see Witherington 1997). It is not necessary, however, to spend more time here analysing Sanders' argument, since (as noted above and to be developed below) righteousness cannot be construed as a condition of entry or a requirement of continued membership on the lips either of Paul or his opponents, since to both of them it denotes a prize of belonging.

J. A. Ziesler: making or declaring righteous?

In an influential 1972 monograph J. A. Ziesler presented a distinctive interpretation of righteousness in Paul to the effect that he employs the verb *dikaioō* in a 'declaratory', 'forensic' or 'relational' sense meaning 'to declare righteous' or 'to acquit' (especially in the context of the Last Judgement), even if there is no actual change of behaviour, no actual righteousness (the Lutheran meaning), while the noun *dikaiosynē* and adjective *dikaios* have 'behavioural' or 'ethical' meanings, 'the state of being made righteous' or 'made righteous', so that there is a real change in behaviour (1972: 1–2). This interpretation runs up against the initial problem that, as noted above, the actual usage in Galatians suggests, at least prima facie, that the verb, noun and adjective are used together in similar contexts and express much the same meaning.

There is another issue, however, which goes to the very basis of the distinction between declaring and making righteous which Ziesler finds in both Paul and extra-Pauline Jewish literature. This distinction is a common one in Pauline studies and derives ultimately from Reformation controversy, with the first alternative being frequently linked with the Protestant position and the second with the Catholic. Ziesler regards his position as mediating between Protestant and Catholic viewpoints: Christians are both justified by faith (acquitted, restored to fellowship) – the forensic or relational sense – and righteous by faith (leading a new life in Christ) – the ethical sense.

Three fundamental objections can be made to this distinction. First, it simply assumes that 'ethical' is an appropriate designation for first-century phenomena. Yet we bring to our modern use of this word a number of presuppositions based on our familiarity with it as a well-established and independent area of human discourse which may be quite inappropriate when applied to an ancient Mediterranean context, where kinship, religion, politics and economics were far more closely interconnected than they are with us. Indeed, as already seen in Chapter 2, within the framework of social identity theory 'ethical' norms function to establish and maintain group identity, not as independent entities. Second, and connected with the point just made, Ziesler's distinction rests on the unexamined assumption that 'ethical' behaviour exists independently of its recognition or acknowledgment by others. The basis for this view is our experience of moral values, derived, for example, from religious tradition or philosophic ethics with universal application (such as those of Kant or the Utilitarians), which transcend the values of any particular group. In this context there is no necessary connection between acting 'ethically' and being regarded by others as doing so. Yet in a group-oriented society such as that of the ancient Mediterranean the position was quite different. Anthropologists have revealed that in a cultural area like the Mediterranean, where the role of the group in the creation and maintenance of individuality is so much more prominent than among modern individualistic North Atlantic peoples, qualities and virtues such as honour (and arguably righteousness) essentially exist to the extent that they are credited to people by others. Given this view, to declare righteous and to make righteous are one and the same.

The third objection involves the careful use of legal terminology, which is regrettably uncommon in this field. Most legal systems distinguish between criminal and civil law. In a criminal case the defendant stands to be punished (for example, by death or imprisonment) if found guilty of the charge, so that his or her personal status is at issue. In such a case, where the charge is not proven it is English usage to say that the person has been 'acquitted' or 'found innocent', while if the case is proven the defendant will be 'found guilty' or 'condemned'. In a civil case, on the other hand, one party is usually seeking to obtain property or damages from the other. An appropriate English expression for successful plaintiffs in civil cases is that they have 'received verdict in their favour' and it is quite inapposite to say they have been 'acquitted' or 'found innocent'. The difficulty with ancient Jewish law in this regard was that, although it did distinguish between criminal and civil cases in many respects, it used the same language to describe successful and unsuccessful parties in both types of case.[3] For this reason it is necessary to translate the verb in a general way so as to cover both types of result.[4] It is quite wrong, although almost a universal practice, to translate *dikaioō* as 'acquit' or 'declare innocent', since this only covers criminal cases.

In a civil case, moreover, the finding would have meant that the losing party handed over property to the winner, who was therefore actually 'put in the right', and this result went far beyond a mere declaration of status. The Mediterranean tendency mentioned above for desirable personal goods to be socially created suggests that it is reasonable to regard a party's condition as *dikaios* as something which flows from the verdict, not as a pre-existing status merely recognised by the judges. This is especially clear in a civil case where an intrinsic aspect of winning a case in most instances is to receive property not previously in one's possession.

All of these objections to the dubious ethical/relational distinction in discussions of righteousness will be relied upon below, both in reassessing Old Testament material on righteousness and in considering how it applies to Galatians.

At times Ziesler recognises that 'a sharp distinction between ethical and forensic is not possible' (1972: 52–53), that they are inseparable (ibid.: 56), but he is prepared to tolerate this rather than pausing to question the very status of the relationship/ethics dichotomy into which he attempts to hammer the biblical data. Even Przybylski, who takes Ziesler to task for inadequate treatment of the Qumran and Tannaitic evidence in his treatment of righteousness (1980: 6–7), follows him in employing this suspect distinction between 'norm' and 'relationship' (1980: 9–12).

The righteousness of God

A lively focus in recent discussion, stimulated in particular by an essay by Ernst Käsemann (1969b), has been 'the righteousness of God' (*dikaiosynē tou theou*). Although this expression is not found in Galatians, the statement that 'through faith God "righteouses" [*dikaioi*] the gentiles' at Gal. 3.8 raises some of the issues involved and necessitates a brief introduction of the topic here and further mention in later discussion.

The expression appears several times in Romans (1.17; 3.5, 21, 22, 25, 26; 10.3 [twice]). Käsemann regarded it as a central theme in Pauline theology (1969b: 168), although reason will soon be given to doubt this view. The earliest instance of *dikaiosynē tou theou* in the Pauline correspondence, however, is at 2 Cor. 5.21, where Paul makes the remarkable statement: 'For our sake he [God] made him to be sin who knew no sin, so that in him we might become the righteousness of God'. Käsemann notes that here the phrase describes 'the reality of the redeemed community' (1969b: 169), with which I agree, subject to raising a question for later discussion as to whether 'identity' might be more appropriate than 'reality'.

In 1 Cor. 1.30 we seem to have a related idea when Paul says: 'Because of him [God] you are in Christ Jesus, who became wisdom from God [*apo theou*] for us, righteousness [*dikaiosynē*], sanctification [*hagiasmos*] and redemption [*apolytrōsis*]', assuming that the last three realities are also 'from God'. It is possible that this instance is from a pre-Pauline hymn (see Käsemann 1969b: 169; Reumann 1982: 31), although it lacks the clear reference to an earlier tradition so evident at 1 Cor. 15.3–5. At Phil. 3.9 mention is made of 'righteousness from God' (*dikaiosynē ek theou*).

Controversy rages as to whether the phrase is (a) an objective genitive, meaning the righteousness which is valid or acceptable before God and which he offers as a gift; (b) a subjective genitive, meaning the righteousness which proceeds from God and is thus a divine activity or attribute; (c) a genitive of authorship (which really combines objective and subjective elements), meaning the righteousness which goes out from God and is the basis of his relationship with humanity; or (d) a genitive of origin, meaning the righteous status of a person which is the product of God's action in 'righteousing' (Reumann 1982: 66). Käsemann's position represents a rejection of the objective genitive explanation in favour of the genitive of subject. Bultmann's perspective seems closer to the genitive of author (1964).

There is no instance in the Old Testament of the precise phrase *dikaiosynē tou theou*. According to Käsemann, the closest analogy is in Deut. 33.21 (LXX): 'The Lord has wrought righteousness' (*dikaiosynēn kyrios epoiēsen*), yet it is extremely curious that he missed the nine instances of the expression 'your [sc. God's] righteousness' in Psalm 119 (Psalm 118 LXX). Käsemann argued that the Deut. 33.21 example underlay the subsequent development of the phrase into a fixed and semi-technical one before Paul, especially in apocalyptic settings, as shown, for example, in the fact that the exact Hebrew parallel *sedeq el* is found in Qumran in the *War Scroll* (1 QM 4.6) and the phrase is also found in the intertestamental text, the *Testament of Dan* (6.10). In addition, it appears independently in Matt. 6.33 and James 1.20. Whereas Bultmann (1964) had seen God's righteousness as a gift, Käsemann also urged that it conveyed the power of God and referred to God's loyalty to the community, which required a reciprocal response of obedient service. Although many would agree with this position (Fitzmyer 1982: 207), the question remains as to how the concept is to be construed if we adopt a different framework than that common among New Testament commentators, by introducing notions of social identity in the context of the ancient Mediterranean world.

PAULINE RIGHTEOUSNESS – A REACTIVE TEACHING?

William Wrede and Albert Schweitzer

As long ago as 1907 William Wrede propounded the following view on the importance of righteousness for Paul:

> The Reformation has accustomed us to look upon this as the central point of Pauline doctrine; but it is not so . . . it only appears where Paul is dealing with the strife against Judaism. And this fact indicates the real significance of the doctrine. It is the polemical doctrine of Paul, is only made intelligible by the struggle of his life, his controversy with Judaism and Jewish Christianity, and is only intended for this.
>
> (Wrede 1907: 123)

It seems to me that Wrede was essentially correct in this view. I seek to argue that righteousness language was only adopted by Paul in defence of claims being made by Israelites or Israelite Christ-followers in certain of his communities, such as in Galatia. In other words, it was forced on his communities by his opponents. Paul certainly needs to respond to Israelite claims being made in Galatia as to the importance of the law and the Abrahamic tradition. The issue of righteousness arguably arose in precisely the same way. Albert Schweitzer also came to a similar view (1931: 205–226). He regarded the doctrine of righteousness by faith as 'a subsidiary crater' formed within the rim of the main crater: 'the mystical doctrine of redemption through the being-in-Christ' (1931: 225).

Many commentators reject the notion that righteousness was a reactive teaching by Paul which did not express the core of this theology. A typical response, offered by Dahl (1977: 101–106) and Reumann (1992: 753–754), is to suggest that the version of righteousness favoured by the trouble-makers had a significance for believers in Christ which pre-dated Paul. This seems misguided, since whether or not righteousness had some pre-Pauline use in such circles, which is a not unreasonable if not necessarily demonstrable notion, the better view is that what Paul faced in Galatia was a purely Israelite understanding of this notion.

The contrast with 1 Thessalonians

To argue that righteousness was something which Paul added to his proclamation in the face of insistence on its importance by Israelites or Israelite Christ-followers necessitates that we pay considerable attention to 1 Thessalonians. Many (myself included) regard this as Paul's earliest letter, but even if it is not it contains an invaluable indication of the shape of his thought when his gentile converts were not faced with pressures to be circumcised. One of the striking features of 1 Thessalonians is the extent to which its 'theology' (which I will use as a term of convenience although conscious of the dangers of imagining one can isolate Pauline 'theology' from what we would refer to as his position on social relations) differs from that which appears in his other letters, all of which were probably written later or in contexts where circumcising activity had occurred. Of particular importance is the absence of righteousness language, of words having a *dik-* root, especially *dikaioō, dikaiōs* and *dikaiosynē*. Also missing are *dikaiōma* and *dikaiōsis*, while the adverb *dikaiōs* appears only once, at 1 Thess. 2.10, to describe Paul's initial conduct among the Thessalonians and is not relevant to this discussion. How is such a phenomenon to be explained?

Since in 1 Thessalonians Paul is addressing purely gentile believers ('you turned from idols', 1 Thess. 1.9), this letter seems to corroborate the view of Wrede and Schweitzer, that righteousness was not vitally important to Paul, but was a theme adopted by him in a situation only when he was in dispute with Israelites or Israelite Christ-followers or in controversy over the law.

One answer to this argument, which on the face of it seems quite a reasonable one, is to propose that non-appearance of righteousness is explicable on the basis that the subject was not relevant to the situation in Thessalonika which had impelled Paul to write the letter. Marshall takes this view (1982: 175), as does Havener, who considers that we should not assume that between 1 Thessalonians and Galatians 'Paul developed a whole new way of thinking theologically', but merely that the prominence of the *parousia* for so many of the Thessalonians constituted an issue which did not require discussion of righteousness (1981: 110). Uprichard even suggests that we can assume that the Thessalonians had 'been taught about justification and there was, therefore, no point in raising the issue' (1979: 19).

To test such answers to the absence of righteousness language in the letter, we must look fairly closely at the text of 1 Thessalonians. If Paul simply does not raise issues which in Galatians are related to righteousness, those answers might be persuasive. Yet if he does, while employing different ideas and language in connection with them, we would have strong evidence for righteousness not having been an essential element of Pauline teaching as so often argued.

To allow a more precise focus of our discussion, it will be helpful to bear in mind the main aspects of existence and destiny for believers in Christ to which Paul will eventually link righteousness when writing to the Galatians, namely, faith (Gal. 2.16), the significance of the death of Jesus (2.21), the believer's status in Christ (2.17; 5.4), life (3.11), the experience of the Holy Spirit (3.1–14) and, although the theme is very underdeveloped in Galatians, the last days.[5]

Galatians-type issues in 1 Thessalonians independent of righteousness

We will begin with three preliminary points, dealing with the fact that Paul fails to make the connections between righteousness with other subjects evident in Galatians, before moving on to the main area of evidence, where Paul seems deliberately to choose language other than that of righteousness.

First, it is worth noting that although there are thirteen references to faith in 1 Thessalonians, eight times using the noun *pistis* (1.3, 8; 3.2, 5, 6, 7, 10; 5.8) and five times the verb *pisteuō* (1.7; 2.4, 10, 13; 4.14), it is significant that Paul never links it with righteousness. Whereas if he had simply failed to mention faith we might have surmised from Galatians that it was something he brought up in conjunction with righteousness, his actual usage in 1 Thessalonians precludes any necessary connection. Faith stands independent of the question of righteousness.

Second, Paul makes it as clear in 1 Thessalonians as he does in Galatians that the power of the Spirit was evident when he preached the gospel (1.5; cf. Gal. 3.2) and characterised the life of those who believed it thereafter (1.6; cf. Gal. 3.5), yet never seeks to relate the Spirit to righteousness, as he does in Gal. 3.1–14.

Third, there is the significance of the death of Jesus, to which Paul refers on three occasions (1.10; 4.14; 5.10). The last of these incorporates an explicit reference to the soteriological significance of the death of Jesus.[6] It is possible that these passages reflect pre-Pauline tradition (Best 1972: 218). Yet even if they have been adopted rather than formulated by Paul they must reflect his own beliefs. In this context it is highly significant that none of them refers to righteousness in a way parallel, for example, to Gal. 2.21. Even the instance at 5.10 is unaccompanied by any righteousness talk.

Faith and love as the explicit substitute for righteousness in 1 Thessalonians

But not only does Paul raise Galatians-type issues in 1 Thessalonians without mentioning righteousness, in one place he deliberately omits the concept from his source. This alteration constitutes the strongest evidence in support of the views of Wrede and Schweitzer. Near the start of the letter Paul mentions being mindful of the Thessalonians' 'work of faith [*pistis*], labour of love [*agapē*] and endurance of hope [*elpis*]' (1.3). This triad of faith, love and hope, which is also found elsewhere in the New Testament,[7] seems to have been first formulated in circles of Christ-followers, possibly by Paul himself (Best 1972: 67), possibly by others before him (Bruce 1982a: 12), to encapsulate fundamental elements of the movement. Thus, in the third verse of 1 Thessalonians, we come across a description of elements of the experience of following Christ which would have mapped out for ex-idolaters in Thessalonika the horizontal and vertical dimensions of their experience in a new and imposing way. We are so used to the emphasis on faith, hope and love in the subsequent traditions of Christian piety that we have lost the sense of their original freshness when thus brought into conjunction. While Paul no doubt primarily has in mind the circumstances when he first preached the gospel to the Thessalonians, we may assume that his readers would understand that these three realities – faith, hope and love – should continue to characterise their condition in the world.

In the present discussion the critical issue arising from his introduction of faith, love and hope is whether it serves as a description of the condition of being a Christ-follower for which he later (or elsewhere) substitutes the notion of being righteous (*dikaios*), since this would suggest that righteousness language was introduced in particular contexts and was not necessarily central to his message. In fact, however, the second mention of the triad of faith, hope and love in the letter, at 5.8, allows us to reach a far stronger conclusion than this. When Paul says 'let us who belong to daylight keep sober, putting on [*endusamenoi*] the breastplate of faith and love [*thōraka pisteōs kai agapēs*] and the hope of salvation for a helmet [*perikephalaian elpida sōtērias*]', he has in mind either Isa. 59.17 or Wis. 5.18 (which is presumably dependent on Isaiah), or both. The Isaian passage reads: 'He put on [*enedusato*] righteousness as a breastplate [*dikaiosunēn thōraka*] and placed the helmet of salvation [*perikephalaian sōtēriou*] on his head', while the one from Wisdom has: 'He will put on righteousness as a breastplate [*endusetai thōraka dikaiosynēn*], and he will don true judgment instead of a helmet'. Paul has changed the phrase 'breastplate of righteousness' to 'breastplate of faith and love', while adding the word 'hope' to the expression 'helmet of salvation', which he otherwise retains. Paul's treatment of the Greek source(s) means, first, that faith and love, the two aspects of the triad most involved in present reality (they are also used together at 3.6 in relation to the recent disposition of the Thessalonians), represent a way of describing the condition of being a Christ-follower analogous to that expressed by 'righteousness'. Second, however, the alteration indicates that in writing to gentiles he has deliberately chosen to substitute the former for the latter, presumably because he found righteousness inappropriate for such an audience. This redactional alteration, even in isolation from other data, goes a long way to undermine the explanations offered by Marshall, Havener and Uprichard for the absence of righteousness language in 1 Thessalonians. There is other evidence, however, needing to be cited, that takes the form of an alternative semantic field which Paul deploys to speak of the present and future existence of the Christ-follower in 1 Thessalonians.

Sanctification language in 1 Thessalonians

A noteworthy feature of 1 Thessalonians is how little information Paul provides as to the state of his addressees before they came to believe, which supports the proposal of E. P. Sanders, previously discussed, that Paul moved from solution to plight, rather than from plight to solution, as argued by Bultmann (1952: 270–285, 301) and others. Certainly he describes the Thessalonians as idol-worshippers (1.9) and his use of the word *akatharsia*, at 4.7, meaning the uncleanliness and immorality of gentile life, may indicate how he envisaged their prior life (Hauck 1966a: 428–429), yet he never says they were sinners (*hamartōloi*) or involved in sin (*hamartia*). He is much more concerned with their current situation as believers and the glorious future in store for them.

Apart from the language of faith and love, the most important semantic field which Paul employs to designate the condition of the Thessalonians, in the present and the future, is that of 'being made holy' (*hagios*), or 'sanctification'. This notion is represented by the verb *hagiazō* (5.23), used elsewhere by Paul at Rom. 15.16 and 1 Cor. 1.2; 6.11 and 7.14, and the rare nouns *hagiasmos* (4.3, 4, 7), which only appears in three other places in the Pauline letters (Rom. 6.19, 22; 1 Cor. 7.14 [twice]), and *hagiōsynē* (3.13), which is found elsewhere in Paul at Rom. 1.4 and 2 Cor. 7.1.[8] That *hagiasmos* refers to a present reality is clear from 4.3 and 4.4, where it is connected with avoidance of fornication, and 4.7, where it is contrasted with *akatharsia*. These instances demand that we give due recognition to the role which this word has to draw boundaries between the idolatrous and immoral gentiles outside the congregation (the *ekklēsia*, 1 Thess. 1.1), the realm of *akatharsia*, and the holy existence to be expected inside.

On the other hand, the noun *hagiōsynē* and the verb *hagiazō* are used with respect to the believers' future destiny, in the first case of the need for them to keep their hearts blameless in holiness (*hagiōsynē*) at the coming of Jesus with his holy ones (3.13) and, in the second, in a prayer that God will make them holy (*hagiasai*) and that their body and soul will be kept blameless at his coming (5.23). These references should not just be categorised as 'eschatological' as if that were the end of the story, since (as noted in Chapter 2 of this reading) the destiny which a group believes to be in store for its members also constitutes an essential dimension of its identity.

This aspect could be analysed using Mary Douglas' exposition of purity as concerned with boundary creation and enforcement,[9] but in this reading we must point to the extent to which sanctification language serves to establish and maintain a particular type of social identity for the gentile believers of Thessalonika along the lines of Tajfel's theory. It functions to encapsulate the identity of the ingroup of Thessalonian believers in Christ in contrast to the idolatrous outgroup: 'For God has not called you for impurity but in sanctification' (4.7). Moreover, it does so in the manner already discussed in Chapter 2, inasmuch as the norms and destiny which are part of this identity exist in blunt opposition to that which prevails in the gentile world outside. A sure sign of the importance this language has to denote the identity of Christ-followers in this letter is that Paul refers to those of them who will appear at the coming of Jesus as 'holy ones' (*hagioi*, 1 Thess. 3.13), a usage without parallel in Galatians where the word *hagios* ('holy') does not even occur.

Support for the view that Paul regarded this sanctification language as peculiarly appropriate to gentiles exists in the fact that in Rom. 15.16 and 1 Cor. 7.14 forms of the verb *hagiazō* are applied, respectively, to a gentile gift and to gentiles themselves.

Accordingly, this language seems to constitute a semantic framework appropriate to gentiles which parallels that of righteousness used by Paul in Galatians, where he had a mixed Israelite–gentile audience in mind. This constitutes another factor in support of the view of Wrede and Schweitzer that righteousness cannot have been of fundamental importance to him.

A Matthean comparison

There is an interesting parallel to this situation in the case of Matthew. Przybylski argues that Matthew uses *dikaiosynē* as a provisional concept, only in contexts where Jesus is involved in polemical situations or dealing with an audience with some non-disciple component, never in non-polemical contexts (1980: 116). Matthew sees the righteousness language as a point of contact with first-century Judaism, but as inadequate to express the salvation which comes with Jesus. So he replaces 'righteous-ness' with 'will of God' and 'righteous one' with 'disciple' (1980: 122). If Matthew, with the strong Jewish background to his traditions, found *righteousness* an inadequate concept for his audience, how much more likely is Paul to have done so when dealing with a gentile congregation?

Conclusion

Since we have discovered from this investigation that in 1 Thessalonians, where he had a gentile audience, Paul not only failed to mention right-eousness but, in a context where he could have raised it, consciously and deliberately chose to use other language – that of faith and love, and sanctification – we conclude that righteousness was not at the heart of Paul's thought. It was not something he was 'ineluctably concerned to talk about' (Hübner 1984: 7), nor should it be seen as the key to under-standing Pauline theology (Käsemann 1969b: 168). Instead, it was a subsidiary teaching deployed only in certain situations, where there was an issue as to the manner in which Israelites and gentiles could coexist in the same community. Thus, the view of Wrede and Schweitzer has been vindicated. But we are yet to explain just why it was that Paul adopted the language of righteousness in contexts where the relationship of Israelite and gentile was a problem.

RIGHTEOUSNESS IN THE OLD TESTAMENT: A NEW APPROACH

In Chapter 3 I interpreted the *Letter of Aristeas* as a text written for diaspora Israelites (but in a way they imagined would have made sense to gentiles) which revealed that the role of the law was to separate the Israelite ingroup from the sinful gentile outgroup and to establish a dis-tinctive identity for God's people (*anthrōpoi theou* [140]), with righteous-ness functioning to denote important aspects of that separateness and identity. This approach to righteousness as a glittering prize of being

Israelite is closely consistent with the views that the advocates of circumcision were apparently airing in Galatia, as explained earlier in this chapter. It now becomes necessary to determine if there is a biblical context for this perspective, since we need to be sure that the *Letter of Aristeas* is not atypical in its outlook but that it expresses a central concern of Israelite tradition for which our best evidence is the Old Testament which, in its Greek version, clearly formed part of the battleground in Galatia.

In the Septuagint, the semantic field covering words which contain a reference to righteousness, as indicated by their possessing the root *dik-*, is a large one. The most common of the group is *dikaios*, which occurs some 375 times according to the Septuagint Concordance of Hatch and Redpath, not counting alternate versions. Next comes *dikaiosynē*, with some 350 instances. Third is *dikaiōma*, with 130 examples, which can be passed over in the present discussion,[10] and, last, *dikaioun*, with only some 45 examples.

Dikaioō

We will begin with the verb. The meaning of *dikaioō* has been critical in the discussion. As noted earlier, it is the most common of the *dik-* root words in Galatians, appearing eight times. The following expresses a common view as to its meaning:

> In the LXX *dikaioun* is primarily a forensic term, and it is the legal and forensic sense which Paul adopts: God acquits the sinner, God declares a person to be just.
>
> (Matera 1992: 93)

This is a very common view, even though some scholars in the past argued on the basis of traditional word study techniques that the evidence for a forensic sense of the verb in the Septuagint was much slighter than is generally supposed (Lagrange 1931: 123–133; Snaith 1944: 166; Watson 1960). Moreover, we have already seen that there are good reasons for questioning the distinction into 'forensic' and 'ethical' senses of righteousness language and for rejecting the translation of *dikaioō* as 'acquit'. A survey of the instances of this verb in the Greek Old Testament, to which I will now proceed, shows that sometimes it is used in a judicial setting literally, but sometimes metaphorically (for example, with respect to Yahweh's judgements) and, furthermore, that there are significant instances of *dikaioō* which lack any judicial connection, literal or metaphorical, and where the correct meaning, especially where the verb is in the middle voice,[11] is simply 'be righteous'. I will argue below that the latter meaning is the dominant one in Galatians.

There are only eight examples of *dikaioō* having a literal legal sense with respect to the action of the judge (Exod. 23.7; Deut. 25.1; 2 Sam. 15.4; Ps. 82.3 [81.3 LXX]; Isa. 1.17; 5.23; Ezek. 44.24; Sir. 42.2). This is hardly a large number when one considers how many scholars assert that the primary meaning of the word is 'forensic'. Of the first six examples, for which there is an extant Hebrew text to compare, the verb translates the hiphil of *tsādaq* in all cases except Isa. 1.17 (where the Hebrew is *rīb*). Watson notes that *dikaioō* is unfailingly chosen to translate the hiphil of *tsādaq* (1960: 257). In half of these six instances, moreover, it is primarily civil suits which are in view, typically because they concern the need to do justice to the poor and needy, which will mean awarding them property (see Ps. 81.3; Isa. 1:17 and 5.23). In these examples 'to acquit' and 'to declare innocent' are entirely inappropriate English translations, since we need something like 'to put in the right', or 'to award verdict in favour of'.

The next group is that in which *dikaioō* is used of God's action in judgement, where the word is being used metaphorically: Ps. 18.9 (19.9 LXX); Ps. 142.2 (143.2 LXX); Mic. 7.9; Isa. 43.9, 43.26, 50.8 and 53.11. Once again, this is not a large number of cases and it is necessary to bear in mind that since the literal reality underlying them goes beyond what in English we call acquittal or declarations of innocence we should be slow to translate these examples in such terms. It is interesting to observe that in only two of these (Isa. 50.8 and 53.11) does the Greek verb translate the hiphil of *tsādaq*, which we have seen is closely linked to human judicial activity. In all the others, except Mic. 7.9 (where the Hebrew is *rīb*), the underlying Hebrew is the qal of *tsādaq*, possibly signalling a distance between divine and human activity in the eyes of the authors of the original Hebrew passages.

There are many other instances where the meaning of 'being put in the right', or 'being regarded as in the right' or 'righteous' occur in contexts divorced from legal proceedings although it might be thought that there is a judicial flavouring to them. Examples include Gen. 44.16; Job 33.32 and Ps. 72.13.

Lastly, we come to the examples which, in various degrees, have drifted free of such judicial imagery, sometimes in connection with human beings and sometimes with God. A good example from the canonical Old Testament is the use of the word *dikaioō* by Judah towards Tamar at Gen. 38.26, where the expression *dedikaiōtai ē egō* means 'she has acted more righteously than I' or, simply, 'she is more righteous than I'.[12]

Other non-forensic cases occur at Jer. 3.11 and Ezek. 16.51–52 (thrice), since there the meaning is to prove or show someone to be righteous in a general sense.

But the most interesting examples of this type are found in the apocryphal Wisdom text Siracides, a work which Paul knew well,[13] specifically at Sir. 1.21, 7.5, 10.29, 13.22, 18.22, 23.11, 26.29 and 34.5, many of which are future passives which probably translate qals of *tsādaq* in the lost Hebrew original (Watson 1960: 262). Ziesler, quite remarkably, categorises all of these as 'forensic' (1972: 74), a designation appropriate to none of them. The concern of all of these texts is whether a person will be, or be regarded as, *dikaios* in a general sense and in one's present existence, not whether he or she will be successful in judicial proceedings, terrestrial or eschatological. As we will see later, there is a strong interest in the Wisdom literature to promote the desirability of being *dikaios*.

Thus, at Sir. 1.21 it is said that 'a furiously angry man will not be able to be regarded as *dikaios* [*dikaiōthēnai*], for the sway of his anger will be his fall'. No judgement is in view, simply the fact that a man like this could not be regarded as *dikaios*, since he is doomed for disaster. At Sir. 7.4b–5 the speaker exhorts his listener not to seek the seat of honour from the king, 'nor to present yourself as righteous [*dikaiou*] before the Lord, nor to boast of your wisdom before the king'. We see here, typically of a Mediterranean culture where virtues exist to the extent that significant others accredit them to their claimants, that the author is alive to the problem that a person might seek royal warrant for a claim to possess a significant social good of being righteous. There are no judicial connotations. The extent to which one's condition as righteous depends upon the view of significant others and its similarity to honour in this regard emerges even more unequivocally in the saying at Sir. 10.29: 'Who will maintain [or regard] as righteous [*dikaiōsei*] the person who sins against his own soul and who will honour him who dishonours his own life?' There is a similar case at Sir. 13.22: 'When a rich man takes a fall, many help him; he says things which should not be spoken and people treat him as righteous [*edikaiōsan*]'.

The most striking occurrences in Siracides are those where it is not easy to determine whether the meaning of the passive of the verb is 'be regarded as righteous' or just 'be righteous'. As we have already seen, this is what we would expect in this culture where you possess personal values largely to the extent that others agree you possess them. Thus, does the passive form of the verb in the statement at Sir. 18.22: 'Do not defer until death [*dikaiōthēnai*]' mean 'to be regarded as righteous' or 'to be or to become righteous'? Watson comments that the verb here is the equivalent of 'become righteous' (1960: 262).

Equally interesting is Sir. 23.11: 'A man who makes many oaths will be full of iniquity and the scourge will never depart from his house . . . and if he swears in vain, he will not be counted as righteous [*dikaiōthēsetai*], for his house will be full of calamities', for here *dikaiōthēsetai* comes very close to meaning simply 'will (not) be righteous'. The same can be said of Sir. 34.5: 'He who loves gold will not be treated as righteous/be righteous [*dikaiōthēsetai*]'.

We will round off this discussion of the biblical evidence with cases where *dikaioō* is used with respect to how God will be regarded by human beings: Ps. 50.4; Isa. 42.21; Sir. 18.2. There is clearly no forensic aspect to these cases, for God is not judged. The point is to assert that God will be regarded as righteous or, in this culture much the same thing, will be righteous and the source of righteousness (cf. Isa. 45.23–25).

From the first century CE comes further evidence for the passive of *dikaioō* meaning 'to be righteous' in the fact that there are five passages from 2 Baruch (21.9, 11, 12; 24.1, 2) and one from 4 Ezra (12.7), texts which were probably written in Hebrew or Aramaic and then translated into Greek and subsequently into Latin (and other versions), where the passive of *justificare* means 'be righteous' (Watson 1960: 264–265).

To conclude, the 'forensic' interpretation for *dikaioō* favoured by so many commentators has been shown to rest on a flimsy foundation in the Septuagint, while the particular translation of 'acquit' or 'to declare innocent' has nothing to say for itself at all. The word has a wide range of meanings and very often it has no judicial connotation and simply means 'to be regarded as righteous' or, as Lagrange maintained, 'to be or to become righteous' (1931: 123–133). It is noteworthy that Watson, who seeks to counter the scepticism of Lagrange, acknowledges that it is 'beyond dispute' that the 'LXX translators used the passive of *dikaioō* to translate the qal of *tsādaq* in a number of passages where the Hebrew verb means "appear righteous", "be shown to be in the right", even "be righteous"', but then seeks to discount the significance of this finding by asserting that such diversity (away from the usual forensic interpretation) was caused by difficulties in translating the Hebrew original (1960: 264). Yet this view, even if correct, would be quite irrelevant to the phenomenon of first-century Israelites, like Paul and his Israelite contemporaries, usually working with a Greek version and drawing upon the rich semantic resources it contained.

These results have very important implications for how we interpret what Paul has to say on righteousness in Galatians. They necessitate, however, determining what 'righteous' itself might have meant.

Dikaios and Dikaiosynē

The examination of the *Letter of Aristeas* in Chapter 3 revealed an approach to righteousness as a salient and desirable feature of Israelite identity (including, but going beyond, normative behaviour and destiny) which served to distinguish Israelites from the evil, polluted, unjust and polytheistic peoples among whom they lived. That this characteristic Israelite division of the world into a pure ingroup and a sinful outgroup was part of Paul's own outlook is evident from Gal. 2.15: 'We are *Ioudaioi* by birth and not gentile sinners'. It is a matter of great consequence for the argument of this chapter that the sections of the biblical tradition which seem to express most powerfully this social contrast do so in relation to the words *dikaios* and, to a lesser extent, *dikaiosynē*, as we will now see.

A consideration of the pattern of usage of *dikaios* and *dikaiosynē* in the Septuagint soon reveals an interesting phenomenon – that there is a heavy concentration of these words in the Psalms and Proverbs.[14] More specifically, however, the psalm with the greatest number of instances of *dikaios* is Psalm 36 (Psalm 37 LXX), which has nine, while Proverbs 10–15 account for fifty-one. There is a close connection between these works. Both Psalm 36, which 'is not so much a psalm as a collection of proverbs' (Weiser 1962: 15), and Proverbs 10–15 feature a noticeable reliance on the form of antithetical parallelism, where the condition of the righteous is continually contrasted with that of the sinner. Examples include: 'For the arms of sinners shall be broken; but the Lord supports the righteous' (Psalm 36:17) or 'The memory of the righteous is praised; but the name of the ungodly person is extinguished' (Prov. 10:7). The noun *dikaiosynē* also occurs in these works (at Ps. 36.6 and about a dozen times in Proverbs 10–15) and is closely linked to the condition of being *dikaios*; it is something of a portmanteau word whose contents are unpacked with reference to particular aspects of the existence of the *dikaios*.

It is reasonable to propose that if a first-century Jew had wanted to point to biblical warrant for the division of society into holy insiders and sinful outsiders, the type of Wisdom evident in Psalm 36 and Proverbs 10–15 would have provided the richest source and one which, moreover, was worked out in large part in the language of righteousness.[15] Although many of the proverbs in this collection represented by

Proverbs 10–15 are pre-exilic, it is possible that its current form dates from exilic or post-exilic times when Israel had developed a sharper sense of its differentiation from the gentiles with whom it competed for a place in the world. It is interesting to consider what significance *dikaios* might have carried at that time. Nevertheless, our focus here is on how Israelites of the first century CE would have understood what it meant to be a *dikaios* in their own context.

What we must investigate, therefore, is what such a first-century enquirer would learn from these texts as to what it meant to be a *dikaios*, a 'righteous person'.

I will begin with two common views as to the meaning of this word. Schrenk considers that in the Septuagint it refers to satisfying duties to God and the theocratic society, therefore having a righteous cause before him.[16] This is close to the forensic meaning already mentioned in connection with the verb *dikaioō*, especially to the extent that it seems to have a future judgement in view, while also having a covenantal aspect. Ziesler argues that the adjective (and the noun) have a connection with proper action within the covenant established between God and his people.[17] To keep this chapter within manageable limits, I will deal only with Proverbs 10, while submitting that the same applies to Proverbs 11–15, to which I will make occasional reference.

Proverbs 10

Prov. 10.2 contains the assertion that *dikaiosunē* delivers from death. This is the only instance of this word in Proverbs 10, but there then follow sixteen examples of *dikaios*, with that which is asserted of the *dikaios* being placed in antithesis to a statement concerning the *asebēs*, or ungodly person, on eleven occasions, and in contrast to some other quality on three occasions (such as foolishness at 10.18 and 21 and injustice at 10.31). We will deal with the positive statements first. The details predicated of the righteous person can be roughly divided into two broad categories: his current condition and his destiny. In the first and by far the larger category we learn that the blessing of the Lord is upon his head (10.6, 22), there is a fountain of life in the hand of the *dikaios* (10.11), his works produce life (10.16), his lips cover enmity (10.18), know sublime truths (10.21) and drop graces (10.32), his mouth drops wisdom (10.31), his tongue is tried silver (10.20) and his desire is acceptable (10.24). The following statements can be included in the second category: the soul of the *dikaios* will not be famished by the Lord (10.3), his life is preserved by instruction (10.17), he escapes the storm when it

passes by (10.25), joy rests a long time with him (10.28), he will never fail
(10.30) and his memory will be praised (10.7).

This positive picture is drawn in remorseless contrast to the condition
and destiny of the person who is not *dikaios* and who is referred to as
'ungodly' (*asebēs*) thirteen times in this chapter (in antithesis to *dikaios* in
every case except 10.15 and 10.27),[18] 'senseless' (twice at 10.18 and 21)
and 'unjust' (10.31). The dichotomy between the righteous and the
ungodly is similar to that set out in the *Letter of Aristeas* and would have
reflected the existence of any Israelite living in the diaspora.

Yet although the antitheses create a powerful contrast between the
righteous person and the godless one, they do not do so by primarily
specifying particular types of ethical conduct or different results of
impending divine judgement which differentiate the two groups, even
though a contrast between ethical and unethical behaviour forms part of
what is being conveyed, just as was the case with *dikaiosynē* in the *Letter of
Aristeas*.

The first thing to notice is that none of the sixteen instances of *dikaios*
in Proverbs 10 refers to the covenant or to the judgement of God and
very few prescribe or proscribe particular types of behaviour. One
proverb with some ethical significance is 10.31:

> The lips of the righteous know what is acceptable,
> but the mouth of the wicked what is perverse.

There are a few more like this in Proverbs 11–15 (cf. 11.5; 12.17; 13.5, 9
and 11).

Furthermore, it is perhaps possible to read some of these proverbs as
containing exhortations to be good. Take as an example:

> The wage of the righteous leads to life,
> the gain of the wicked is sin.
>
> (Proverbs 10.16)

This may perhaps be interpreted as 'if you are righteous (the meaning of
which is unspecified), you will be rewarded; if sinful, you will suffer
various forms of disadvantage'.[19] Such a view distinguishes between an
assumed core meaning of *dikaios* and the consequences of being this type
of person. Yet it is clear that a paraenetic interpretation of this kind
cannot exhaust the meaning of the proverb. There is, after all, no reason
why it should not also be taken as a simple statement of fact, that the
righteous person lives. Much the same can be said of 10.2:

> Treasures gained by wickedness do not profit,
> but righteousness delivers from death.

Many of these proverbs, however, cannot be construed paraenetically.
Take as a typical example:

The tongue of the righteous is choice silver,
the mind of the wicked is of little worth.

(Proverbs 10.20)

It would be rather artificial to say that the expression 'the tongue of the
righteous is choice silver' could be reduced to an exhortation of the form
'be righteous so you may speak well'. First of all, such a process represents a disregard for the natural sense of the proverb, especially for the
indicative mood in which it is expressed; it is questionable to read a
statement 'A is B' not as a way of telling you something about A, but as a
disguised form of 'Be A so you can have B'. Rather, that which is predicated of the *dikaios* serves to amplify and extend our understanding of
what it means to be *dikaios*, yet without in any way defining such a person
or specifying the nature of his or her behaviour. The statement in 10.20,
as in so many of the proverbs, is a metaphoric one and here we see the
customary function of metaphor to allow us to reinterpret a familiar
phenomenon (here, the tongue or speaking capacity of the *dikaios*), the
primary subject of the metaphor, by association with its secondary subject (here, choice silver). Moreover, the use of metaphor of this type
indicates that the function of the assertion is as much to provide appro-
bation for the *dikaios* as to describe him or her in any functional way.

Accordingly, although the descriptions of *dikaios* in these proverbs recognise that the notion has both an ethical content and consequences for
the future (although in a general rather than an eschatological sense) as
well as the present, they cannot be characterised in the manner of
Schrenk and Ziesler. The meaning of *dikaios* in Proverbs 10–15 tran-
scends forensic/covenantal or ethical interpretations. The characteristics
attributed to the righteous do not define them, nor specify in any functional sense what they actually do, but rather commend them as having a
desirable set of qualities and gifts and a desirable destiny.

Almost all of what is predicated of the righteous person could, in fact,
be summarised by the assertions that 'righteousness will deliver from
death' (10.2) and that 'the blessing [*eulogia*] of the Lord is upon the head
of the righteous' (10. 6, 22). The exact notion of life, or escape from
death, is mentioned explicitly a number of times (10.2, 3, 11, 16; 11.6,
19, 30; 12.28). Moreover, many of the proverbs describe ways in which
the *dikaios* will be blessed, even if the word *eulogia* itself does not appear.

We conclude, therefore, that the effect of these descriptions is not to
indicate what is right in God's eyes or what constitutes faithfulness to

him, certainly not to specify any type of desirable behaviour, even if some of the statements do have ethical dimensions, but rather to identify and commend a particular type of person as singularly graced with life and blessings in sharp contrast to another sort of person who is not. In effect, the *dikaios* is the exemplary Israelite, exhibiting numerous admirable qualities and likely to receive a rich crop of blessings from God. Tajfel's notion of social identity, which expressly incorporates ethical norms and can also be developed to cover future orientation but extends beyond both of these features to specify a more complete reality, seems to offer a fruitful interpretative framework. In this perspective, the word *dikaiosynē* used in 10.2 has the meaning 'the condition of the *dikaios*', 'the blessed condition of being a good Israelite', with all the connotations just mentioned. There is an equivalence between the adjective and the noun.

If the *dikaios* is the exemplary Israelite, the *asebēs* is primarily the worthless, God-forsaking gentile. This phenomenon is explicable in terms of that part of Tajfel's model dealing with the way group identity is developed in a context of intergroup conflict. The members of the ingroup define themselves with respect to groups to which they do not belong, and generate a stereotyped picture of the outgroups as a way of strengthening their social identity. This consideration applies both to Israelites of the first century CE who could have turned to this text for guidance and group self-understanding, but also to earlier audiences of Proverbs 10–15, for whom the plethora of antitheses were probably rooted in the social realities of diaspora experience in Babylon or around the Mediterranean.

The most remarkable evidence that the *dikaios* statements do not so much indicate what is right in God's eyes or specify particular types of desirable behaviour as identify a type of positive group identity occurs at 14.34: 'Righteousness exalts a nation [*ethnos*], but sins [*hamartiai*] diminish tribes [*phulas*]'. Here we have an emic expression of the division of social reality into a nation which is righteous on the one hand, with the other tribes which are enmeshed in sin on the other, which our etic analysis has already led us to suggest underlies the righteous/ungodly schema. Group identity is constructed and maintained by stereotyping outgroups. At the same time, 14.34 gives unequivocal expression to the circumstance that honour and well-being are attached to this identity but not shared by outsiders. Thus, we are dealing with privileged social identity.

Lacking a coherent social theory such as Tajfel's which is capable of providing a plausible social location for the antitheses, William McKane, in his significant work on Proverbs, goes astray in assuming that the

'extreme tidiness' of the doctrine underlying the *dikaios/asebēs* antithesis
(that for the righteous person this is the best of all possible worlds) 'is an
indication of its sterility and its disengagement from mundane realities',
a sign that it has disconnected itself from life and has left all problems
behind (1970: 16). Once Tajfel's model has been applied to the data, we
discover good grounds for believing that, in an ancient Mediterranean
world dominated by fierce intergroup competitiveness, exactly the opposite was the case.

The understanding of righteousness which appears in the Wisdom
literature as set out above largely satisfies the specifications for the notion
in Galatia which we have set out, that is, as a notably privileged aspect of
being a Israelite which would exert its allure on the gentile members of
the congregations. While it cannot be said that this discussion proves
positively that such usage underlies the controversy in Galatia, it is clear
that this context for righteousness is an available one, can be connected
easily with many of the main issues and avoids the problems which
thickly cluster around alternative explanations, especially those which
are 'forensic' in nature.

THE MEANING AND FUNCTION OF
RIGHTEOUSNESS IN GALATIANS

The contest for righteousness

To establish a theoretical base for describing the meaning and function
of righteousness in Galatians, the penultimate task in this chapter, we
will utilise an aspect of Tajfel's model of social identity, set out in Chapter 2. 'Social competition' occurs when a subordinate group seeks to
improve its position in relation to a dominant group with respect to
scarce resources such as status. It occurs when members of the subordinate group are dissatisfied with the usual terms of comparison and wish to
change them, which will necessitate reversing the respective positions of
the groups on salient dimensions. This is precisely Paul's position as far
as righteousness is concerned. His opponents are arguing that the dominant Israelite group will provide for any who will join them – through
circumcision and acceptance of the Mosaic law – that prestigious asset
called righteousness. Paul counters this claim head-on by arguing that
righteousness belongs with the congregations of Christ-followers, not
with the Israelites.

That he should have chosen this path at all is noteworthy. He could have
simply agreed that righteousness was a purely Israelite phenomenon and

instead opted for defining the identity of the gentile believers in terms of the language of sanctification which he employs in 1 Thessalonians. The fact that he did not pursue this option was probably a result of the evident appeal of the prize of righteousness; its advocates were finding so ready an ear for their arguments (cf. 4.10) that Paul was simply unable to abandon this trophy to the opposition. No, he must wrest it from them for his congregations, never mind how challenging the objective might be.

Although righteousness functioned as an Israelite identity-descriptor which transcended the ethical requirements imposed by the law, it was an aspect of it, as can be seen in Proverbs 10–15 and the *Letter of Aristeas*. The norms associated with righteousness were regarded as an important means whereby Israel separated itself from unclean and polytheistic gentiles. To wrench righteousness from its Israelite home, so that *dikaios* now meant 'the blessed Christ-follower' and not 'the blessed Israelite', Paul had to highlight certain of its elements which related to the fact and blessings of belonging to God's people (which are very visible in Proverbs 10–15) while steering clear of its *torah*-based ethics, even though that left undecided the critical question of how one kept gentile sinfulness at bay. We will now see how he does this, although the full picture will require a consideration of Gal. 5.13–6.10 in relation to this last issue in Chapter 8, where we will note the remarkable fact that in offering his congregations ethical guidance, albeit as an aspect of the social identity he is urging upon them, Paul entirely eschews the language of righteousness.

Righteousness in Gal. 2.15–21

When Paul takes up the subject of righteousness in Galatians at 2.15, his initial assertion – 'We who are *Ioudaioi* by birth and gentile sinners [*hamartōloi*]' – immediately evokes the radical distinction between *Ioudaios* and gentile so essential to the maintenance of Israelite identity in the diaspora which we have seen was the likely context for the righteous/ungodly antitheses of Proverbs 10–15. This statement summons before his audience the fundamental theological and social divide between Israelite and non-Israelite and demonstrates that nothing he will say is intended to challenge the reality of gentile sinfulness, stemming from polytheism, which his gentiles had abandoned on conversion although they have now begun to display recidivist tendencies (4.8–11). More than this, however, Paul insists upon his own status, from birth (and not, presumably, for only a part of his life following conversion), as a member of the Israelite ingroup in contrast to its sinful alternative.[20] He is anxious to ensure that there is no doubt that he is speaking with the authority of one who is not and never has been a part of the sinful gentile world. Implicit in such belonging is the reality (or at least the possibility) of righteousness, which was a way of describing and celebrating the legitimacy of Israelite identity. We know that the universe in which he is moving is one in which good Israelites manage to remain *dikaios,* in the present and the future, in spite of the sinfulness characterising their environment.

Yet his next statement represents a remarkable deviation from the taken-for-granted understanding of a first-century Israelite:

> [we] know that a human being does not become righteous by works of [the] law but through faith in Jesus Christ and we believed in Christ Jesus, in order that we might be righteous through faith in Christ and not through works of the law, because no one will become righteous through works of law

> (Gal. 2.16)

In the face of solidly based claims that Israelite righteousness and the Mosaic law were inextricably connected, he proposes an alternative mode of access – from faith in Christ, not from the law. He already had a well-developed theology which we have seen in 1 Thessalonians, and now he seeks to re-work this in relation to the acquisition of righteousness. The reactive nature of his procedure is apparent.

Yet the problem of sinfulness will not so easily disappear, as he sets out in one of the most difficult verses in the letter:

> If seeking to become righteous in Christ we are also found to be sinners[*hamartōloi*], does that mean that Christ is the minister of sin? Impossible [*mē genoito*]!

> (Gal. 2.17)

The main question is whether the conditional clause (2.17a) is (a) real, that is, it rests on an actual state of affairs, the sinfulness of those who rely on Christ but not the law for righteousness, and Paul is merely denying that Christ is the agent of that sin, or (b) unreal, so that Paul, while not accepting that his converts are sinful, is intent on denying that Christ would be the agent of that sin if they were.[21] Although a full discussion of the point is not possible within the scope of this reading and some uncertainty attends my conclusion,[22] the second is probably the better interpretation in view of the overall argument, even though unreal conditions are usually expressed differently[23] and elsewhere when Paul employs the expression *mē genoito* he is rejecting a conclusion based on premises he accepts (Burton 1921: 126–127). Paul is against the notion – which was probably being actively propagated by his adversaries in Galatia as a good reason for the gentiles taking on the Mosaic law with its sophisticated ethical directions – that he and the members of his congregations are sinners. He certainly missed falling into the category of gentile sinner by his birth as an Israelite (2.15) and he has not done so by looking to Christ for righteousness. He will go on in 2.18 to note that (although he is not at present a sinner) he will make himself one if he restores the law which he had previously destroyed.[24]

Yet his position is a difficult one, for he gently intimates later, in 5.13–6.10, that there is disorder, or at least the potential for disorder, within his congregations of a sort which could have given substance to claims that the members were sinners. Part of his task in 5.13–6.10 will be to address these internal difficulties without making it clear whether they are actual or potential and without labelling them as 'sin' (hamartia), while providing a means whereby they might be addressed which offers a complete substitute for the role of the law, however ineffective it might be, to restrain sinfulness among Israelites.

Having affirmed that re-instituting the law is no answer (2.18), he moves into more interesting territory. Under the new dispensation he has gained life. He has died to the law to live for God; he has been crucified with Christ (2.19); he no longer lives, but Christ lives in him. This means that while he lives 'in the flesh' (en sarki), in the realm of human experience, he is living in the faith of the son of God who loved him and who handed himself over on his behalf (2.20). All of this constitutes a description of the new identity which he has assumed in dying to the law and coming to life in faith in Christ. Moreover, we have already seen that much of the material in Proverbs 10–15 was to the effect that the righteous person was characterised by life and blessing. From the course of his argument in Gal. 2.19–20, one might assume that Paul is seeking to make the same connection. This supposition, that life is a dimension of righteousness, is strengthened in the next line: 'I do not disregard the grace of God; for if righteousness came through law, surely Christ died in vain' (Gal. 2.21). At first sight, this is a little puzzling. Since Paul has just been describing the life which is the consequence of Christ's death of self-offering, we would expect him to say 'if life came through law, surely Christ died in vain'. His selection of 'righteousness' indicates that he sees this reality as essentially identical with life, a connection he will make explicitly at 3.11. Moreover, his insistence that this came about as a result of God's grace begins the theme of divine blessing which will loom large in the example of Abraham to which he soon proceeds (at 3.6). In both respects we are very close to the way righteousness is presented in Proverbs 10–15. Paul seems to be moving in this area of the biblical tradition (although without citing it) as he acknowledges the relationship of righteousness with life and blessing while redefining its origin as participation in the saving death of Christ.

Righteousness in Galatians 3.6–14

Paul begins the next section by reminding the Galatians that they received the Spirit and associated miraculous phenomena through proclamation of the faith and not from the works of the Mosaic law (3.1–5). At the very least, this represents a comparison indicating the extent to which Paul views righteousness as a desirable dimension of belonging to a group centred on belief in Christ. The placement of this section immediately after Paul's discussion of life in faith also suggests that he regards the experience of the Spirit as a central feature of that life; he will later note that 'we live in the Spirit' (5.25). More than this, however, Paul interprets the arrival of the Spirit as itself a feature of righteousness from faith; it is a blessing going to the very heart of what it means to be righteous. The explicit language of blessing does not appear in 3.1–5, but it becomes an explicit theme in relation to the example of Abraham which he takes up next (3.6–14).

He begins as follows, where the first word establishes the statement as referring back to vv. 1–4, while providing an introduction for the discussion to follow: 'So [*kathōs*] Abraham had faith in God and it was reckoned to him as righteousness'. This quotation from Gen. 15.6 is absolutely vital to Paul as scriptural warrant that Abraham achieved righteousness through faith and not from the law, since he was not instructed to practise circumcision until later in the biblical account (Gen. 17.9–14). Paul may well be responding to arguments from scripture in connection with Abraham which his opponents have been employing in Galatia to persuade the gentiles of the worth of their case, a possibility given further attention in Chapter 8. Nevertheless, Paul's aim is not just to join battle on this front by offering his own scriptural proof-text. He also wants to bring Abraham and his gentile converts close together and he does this in the next verse by the strongest means known to his culture – the assertion that those who rely on faith *are Abraham's sons* (3.7). They share an identity of kinship with this illustrious hero from the past. In terms of social identity theory set out in Chapter 2, this suggestion constitutes an excursion into social creativity, an attempt by a subordinate ingroup to improve its actual social location *vis-à-vis* the dominant outgroup with respect to their respective access to scarce resources and status. Paul is trying to reverse the position of the two groups on the salient dimension of Abrahamic ancestry. We may assume that such a reversal would not have been well received by Israelites who heard of it. The next verse expressly identifies righteousness and blessing:

> Scripture, foreseeing that God makes righteous [*dikaioi*] the gentiles through faith, proclaimed the gospel in advance to Abraham, 'In you all the gentiles will be blessed'.
>
> (Gal. 3.8)

The first clause recognises God as the source of all righteousness, a notion for which we have seen that there is a solid Old Testament context. The existence and identity of a righteous people depends upon the existence of a righteous God from whom righteousness derives and with respect to whom it is assessed. This was implied in Gal. 2.15 in the allusion to Ps. 143.2. The second clause in 3.8 is a quotation from Gen. 12.3b, where it appears shortly after the account of God's call to Abraham to leave his family and homeland and go off to another land (Gen. 12.1) and his promises to make Abraham a great nation (*ethnos*), to bless (*eulogein*) him, to greatly honour his name so that he will be blessed (12.2), and to bless those who bless him and to curse those who curse him (Gen. 12.3a). In this context, Gen. 12.3 records God's promise that the gentiles will share in Abraham's blessing. For this reason, Paul can also insist that his gentile converts and Abraham share an identity in relation to the fact of blessing through faith: 'Thus, those who rely on faith are blessed together with the faithful Abraham' (3.9). Paul has not yet informed us of the content of the blessing, although the progression of the argument from the earlier stress on life in faith (2.18–21) and the impact of the Spirit (3.1–4) to Abraham (3.5) implies elements which can hardly be excluded.

On the other hand, those who rely on the works of the law are under a curse (3.10, 13). This leads him to offer a scriptural proof that 'no-one becomes righteous [*dikaioutai*] through law' in the statement (from Hab. 2.4)[25] that 'the righteous person [*dikaios*] will live by faith' (3.11). Paul's point is that since scripture says that the righteous acquire life from faith, they cannot get it from law. Righteousness and life are closely linked and faith is what makes the connection. Moreover, in its context this statement confirms that Paul sees life as part of the blessing of Abraham to be enjoyed by the gentiles.

Paul concludes this section by asserting that Christ purchased us from the curse of the law by becoming a curse for our sake (3.13) for the following reasons:

in order that [*hina*] the blessing of Abraham might come upon the gentiles in Christ Jesus, in order that [*hina*] we might receive the promise of the Spirit through faith.

$$(3.14)^{26}$$

In spite of views to the contrary,[27] it is probably best to take these two clauses beginning with 'in order that' (*hina*) as alternative ways of saying the same thing, like the similar example at Gal. 4.4–5. The hitherto unspecified (although implied) blessing which the gentiles would derive from Abraham has now been narrowed down with reference to the gift of the Spirit which began this section (3.1–4). Just as Christ's crucifixion and self-sacrifice led to life (2.18–21), now his becoming accursed leads to blessing.

Later instances of righteousness language

Righteousness language occurs later in Galatians at 3.21–24 and 5.2–6. Since both passages deal more with the issue of the law rather than contributing much to the meaning of righteousness, I will omit them from present discussion, save to mention the expression 'the hope of righteousness' at Gal. 5.5. This notion imports an element of futurity into the meaning of righteousness. Yet this does not detract from its analysis as expressive of social identity, since we have seen that a group's sense of their destiny, of where they are headed, can constitute an important part of their sense of who they are. Righteousness has both a present and a future dimension; it speaks of a people who have achieved a very positive identity in the present but who know that their race is not yet run and that a bright future awaits them.

Righteousness as privileged identity

In the end, there is no sign of Luther's imputed righteousness in Galatians (the 'declaratory' or 'forensic' meaning), nor does it have an 'ethical' sense. Paul's aim in this letter regarding righteousness was to sever it from the competing Israelite outgroup where it had hitherto lodged as a most positive feature of their social identity and to claim it for his own congregations. This was no easy task. Ethical norms derived from the Mosaic law had constituted an important part of righteousness, especially in its function of signalling the ethnic separation of Israelite from sinful gentile, both now and hereafter. Without conceding that sinfulness characterised his congregations, Paul nevertheless did feel

compelled in 5.13–6.10 to say something about their internal conditions and this included instructions on behavioural norms within the
broad framework of identity construction. Yet righteousness has no role
whatever in that discussion.

Paul knew that there was a lot more to righteousness as descriptive of
Israelite identity than either ethics or divine judgement. Proverbs 10–15
had typified the righteous in many ways which had little to do with either
of these aspects by celebrating their separation from the godless in the
future and the present. Prominent among the plethora of ideas drawn
upon in these proverbs to develop this contrast were those of life and
blessing. In the *Letter of Aristeas* the interest in bringing out Israelite distinctiveness *vis-à-vis* gentiles led to righteousness also being closely tied to
this separation in a way which included, but went beyond, ethics.

To maintain that righteousness belonged with his congregations,
Paul's task was to give it adequate content while suppressing its previous
connection with nomistic ethics. The answer lay in the approach taken in
Proverbs 10–15, even though Paul never cites that part of the text. He
drew out the significance of righteousness as descriptive of a privileged
identity, as essentially equivalent to life and blessing, but with faith in the
crucified Christ as the source of that life and the experience of the Spirit
as the primary content of that blessing.

THEOLOGY

None of this is to downplay the importance of theology. I am convinced
that Paul's primary instincts and motivations were theological, not social.
I agree with E. P. Sanders that he moved from solution to plight, discovering first in the death and resurrection of Jesus Christ the reality of
salvation, especially from the pervasive sinfulness of 'the present evil age'
(Gal. 1.4) even though he himself had not been sinful (Phil. 3.6), and
then developing the implications of this for his gentile and mixed
Israelite–gentile communities throughout the diaspora.

The belief in the centrality of the death of Christ and faith in him as
the way to righteousness broke down barriers between Israelite and gentile in Paul's communities. This breaking-down was powerfully symbolised in the sharing of the one loaf and drinking from the one cup in the
Eucharist. To discontinue such a practice or to demand circumcision as
the price for its continuance inevitably meant opposing a basic incident
and effect of the salvific nature of Christ's death. Accordingly, Paul
insisted on table-fellowship as fundamental to his gospel. Here we see a
tight interpenetration of social and theological realities.

But more specifically, how can a text like Galatians, a product of such an alien culture, at least to those of us who inhabit the North Atlantic cultural zone, and dealing with particular issues, especially those of group identity, which were very much alive in Galatia but which in due course lost their significance, speak to us today? Luther's understanding of righteousness, plotting the highly individualist manner in which the sinner finds peace before God, spoke powerfully to Protestants in the sixteenth century intent on dislodging Catholic control over the media of salvation and since then has been the most widespread appropriation of this strand in Paul's religion. Luther's view still attracts followers who, like Hans Hübner, see in righteousness the core of the apostle's theology. Yet a reading like the present one, which argues for the reactive, socially contingent and group-oriented nature of righteousness in Galatians, calls for a different mode of application to our contemporary circumstances.

In Chapter 1 of this book I proposed an intercultural model for the integration of the biblical story into the lives of Christians in our con-temporary world, for moving from history to theology. Although this process can only occur within particular Christian communities, it is possible briefly to suggest how intercultural dialogue might take place. The reading of righteousness in Galatians offered here challenges us to move away (at least for a moment) from the question of the individual before God to that of the very status of modern Christian communities. Given the rampant secularism and the development of multicultural societies in the West, the inequality of wealth within and among nations, the pace of technological change, the scope of environmental degrad-ation, and the profusion of long-established religions and new religious movements, the critical question of who we, as Christians, actually are has never been more pressing.

The core of what Galatians has to say to us about righteousness is that our distinct (and illustrious) identity as a group, with all the potential for life which membership entails, is entirely dependent on Jesus Christ and the saving significance of his death. In the awkward confrontation between this aspect of early Christian culture and our own, it is the relationship of social identity and a self-sacrificing and life-giving Christ which offers the main prospect for development. For 'if righteousness came through law, surely Christ died in vain' (Gal. 2.21).

Chapter 7

Paul and the law

For Israelites in the first century, as we saw in Chapter 3, the Mosaic law played a leading role in the operation of the boundary which preserved their distinctive identity in relation to the gentiles among whom they lived. The Israelite push for the circumcision of gentile Christ-followers in Galatia stemmed from a sense of anomy – and anomaly – provoked by the breach of one aspect of this law, namely, a proscription on table-fellowship between Israelites and gentiles (in the full sense), which was under threat from the eucharistic practice of Paul's congregations. In the previous chapter I argued that Paul's opponents were parading right-eousness, meaning privileged Israelite identity, as a reward for taking on the Mosaic law and that Paul audaciously sought to redefine the notion so as to connect it exclusively with those who had faith in Christ.

All this means that the law was something into which Paul was dragged by his opponents when difficulties arose as to the question of the relationship between Israelites and gentiles in mixed communities. His interest in it was reactive, just like his interest in righteousness. Not surprisingly, the law is as absent from 1 Thessalonians as righteousness language. For this reason, the law should not be seen as central to his theology. This does not mean, however, that having taken it up as an issue Paul did not give it his most careful attention. His letter to the Galatians contains a great deal of material on the law which will occupy our attention in this chapter. There is even more discussion of the subject in Romans. In tackling it I will follow the approach already developed – by treating the law as a critical arena in which Paul struggled to establish a positive social identity for his congregations in the context of conflict with the Israelite outgroup who were naturally determined to maintain the integrity of their ethnic boundaries.

Setting out the basic data on the law in Galatians in the first section, I will discuss what Paul means by law in the second section, examine the negative picture Paul paints of it in the third and then move on to his explanation of the purpose of the law in the fourth section and its irrelevance to morality in the fifth.

THE DATA

Paul's principal concern with the law in Galatians is to state repeatedly that righteousness is not produced by law (*nomos*) or by works of law (*erga nomou*) but by faith in Christ. These passages were discussed in the previous chapter and are found at 2.15–16 (*erga nomou* – thrice), 2.21 (*nomos*), 3.11 (*nomos*) and 5.4–5 (*nomos*).Yet Paul has far more to say about the Mosaic law in this letter than simply to dismiss it as an option as far as obtaining righteousness is concerned.

He begins to develop the topic of the law further at 3.10 with the assertion that those who rely on works of law are under a curse (*katara*), coupled with a quotation from Deut. 27.26: 'Cursed [*epikataratos*] is everyone who does not remain in all things written in the book of the law to do them'.

Paul next introduces the notion that life cannot come from law, first by means of a quotation from Hab. 2.4 to illustrate that faith is the source of life: 'The righteous man will live by faith' (3.11) and then by another quotation from Lev. 18.5 to the effect that the person who has performed the requirements of the law will live by them (3.12), which is directed to showing that law is connected with faith, presumably because no one does gain life from the law.

At 3.13 Paul returns to the curse of the law to insist that Christ has ransomed us from it by becoming a curse for our sakes, which he links with a quotation from Deut. 21.23: 'Cursed is everyone who hangs upon a tree'.

Having concluded this section with mention of the blessing of Abraham and the reception of the promise of the Spirit though faith (3.14), Paul begins a new section devoted to maintaining that the promises made to Abraham and his seed were not annulled by the (Sinaitic) covenant given 430 years later and that the inheritance (*klēronomia*) derives from promise not law (3.15–18).

Gal. 3.19 marks a pronounced turning-point. Whereas hitherto Paul has brought forward a variety of negative aspects of the law, now he suddenly turns to consider what its function or purpose may have been. He asks, 'What, then, is the point of the law?', and answers the question in a very difficult and compressed way to which we will return below but which the Revised Standard Version translates as follows: 'Why then the law? It was added because of transgressions, till the offspring should come to whom the promise had been made; and it was ordained by angels through an intermediary.' The next sentence is, if anything, even more difficult: 'Now an intermediary implies more than one; but God is one' (Gal. 3.19; RSV). Is this meant to underline a strength or deficiency in the law?

In the next section (3.21–25) Paul acknowledges that the law is not against the promises (of God), yet cannot bring life (3.21). He states that scripture locked up everything under sin to pave the way for promise which comes from faith in Jesus Christ (3.22) and that before faith we were confined and guarded under law (3.23). Then, using an interesting and revealing metaphor, he rounds off these views by proposing that the law was our *paidagōgos*, the slave who looked after a boy aged from about six to sixteen (3.24), whose term of office had now come to an end with the arrival of faith (3.25).

In a related image soon after this Paul describes how during his minority an heir is under guardians and administrators, his position little better than that of a slave, until the time of his inheritance (4.1–2). Although Paul construes this as the period when we were minors, enslaved under the elements of this world, until the fullness of time when God sent out his son (4.3–4), its relevance to his perspective on the law comes out in the next verse when he specifies the purpose of Christ's mission as 'to ransom those under law, so that we might receive adoption' (4.5). Thus, the condition of those under guardians and administrators, enslaved under the elements of the world, is equivalent to being under law. The law is a form of slavery.

Freedom from slavery, previously introduced by Paul in relation to his resistance in Jerusalem to the aim of the circumcisers (2.4), is an important theme in Galatians 4, both in relation to his readers' desire to return to their previous ways (4.8–11) and as the main point of the allegory of Sarah and Hagar (4.21–31), which concludes with the exhortation: 'For freedom Christ has set us free. So stand firm and do not again put on the yoke of slavery' (5.1). The yoke mentioned is clearly that of the law.

Paul next tells them that, if they become circumcised, Christ has been of no use to them (5.2). Moreover, everyone who is circumcised is obliged to perform the whole law (5.3).

Having stressed that freedom in Christ involves slavery to one another in love and is not a licence for improper behaviour (5.13), Paul states: 'For the whole law stands fulfilled [*peplērōtai*] in one saying, "You will love your neighbour as yourself"' (5.14), citing Lev. 19.18.

Lastly, there is the striking statement at 6.2 that 'you will fulfil [*anaplērōsete*] the law of Christ [*ton nomon tou Christou*]'.

THE MEANING OF LAW IN GALATIANS

Words for law in Galatians

The usual word for law, *nomos*, occurs thirty-two times in Galatians: 2.16 (thrice), 19 (twice), 21; 3.2, 5, 10 (twice), 11, 12, 13, 17, 18, 19, 21(thrice), 23, 24; 4.4, 5, 21(twice); 5.3, 4, 14, 18, 23; 6.2, 13. Of particular importance in Galatians is the phrase 'works of the law' (*erga nomou*), appearing six times (2.16 [thrice]; 3.2, 5, 10). There is a parallel expression, 'works of the flesh' (*erga tēs sarkos*), at 5.19. Yet nowhere does Paul define what he means by *nomos*.

The reference at 3.17 to *nomos*, which came 430 years after God's promise to Abraham, must be to the commandments given to Moses on Sinai (Exodus 19–24, 34; Leviticus; Deuteronomy 5–6, 12–28).[1] Included in the Mosaic code is the requirement of circumcision (Lev. 12.3), previously imposed on Abraham (Gen.17.12–14; 21.4). This is the main meaning of the word in Galatians.

Yet the word can have a meaning wider than the Mosaic code. Thus at 4.21 *nomos* is used to denote Genesis 16–21 (the story of Abraham, Sarah and Hagar, and their sons). Elsewhere Paul cites passages from Isaiah (1 Cor. 14.21) and from the psalms and prophets (Rom. 3.10–18) as taken from the *nomos*. The word in this second sense refers to the whole of Israel's sacred tradition (see Räisänen 1986: 16) and is probably the equivalent of 'scripture' (*graphē*) at Gal. 3.22.

The one instance where *nomos* does not have an Israelite connection is at 6.2, in the remarkable expression, to which we will return in Chapter 8, (at Galatians 5–6), 'the law of the Christ'.

Whether the unwritten tradition is included is not clear. Paul never consciously distinguishes between written and oral *torah*. In 2.15–20 it seems that the table-fellowship issue is included as part of the 'works of law'; as already noted in Chapter 4, this may reflect a concern with idolatry.

The question of boundaries: 'law' and 'works of law'

In Chapter 3 I introduced as a development of the overall perspective on social identity the approach to the nature and role of boundaries in a context of ethnic interaction posited by Fredrik Barth. One aspect of Barth's views was that the cultural features which bring out ethnic distinctiveness can be divided into overt areas such as dress, language and lifestyle, and basic value orientations, the norms of morality used to assess behaviour. Anthony Cohen has offered further insights in this area by pointing out that ethnic insiders envisage the boundary in two senses, the first being the way it is perceived by outsiders (its typical or public mode) and the second being the insiders' own sense of community (the private or idiosyncratic mode). Cohen has proposed that the private mode (roughly corresponding to 'value orientations') is more important for insiders than the public mode (Barth's 'overt signals') for it involves their responding to their community in relation to its rich inner life.

These careful distinctions may be applied to the role of the law in helping to preserve Israel's ethnic distinctiveness. Israelites in the first century were aware that the ordinances of the law covered public features of lifestyle such as dietary restrictions, the observance of the sabbath and the feast days, and circumcision, which outsiders used in defining Israelite identity,[2] but also extended to value orientations which were far less visible but which Israelites themselves regarded as important aspects of their identity, as we have seen. Where we find Israelites explaining themselves to gentiles (as Josephus does in *Contra Apionem*), or purportedly doing so (as in the *Letter of Aristeas*), the concern to bring out the inner aspect, no doubt as a balance against stereotypical impressions based on overt phenomena, is very insistent. Accordingly, we would not expect a first-century Israelite to define the boundary in the external manner of an outsider.

Some of these nuances came too late, however, to assist James Dunn when he made his pioneering attempts to apply an understanding of boundaries utilising social-scientific research to the study of Galatians in 1982 and 1984.[3] Dunn argued that circumcision and the food laws functioned as identity and boundary markers both for outsiders and for Israelites themselves:

> This strong impression of Graeco-Roman authors, as to what religious practices characterise the Jews, was simply a reflection of the typical, the dominant, attitude of the Jews themselves. These identity markers identified Jewishness because they were seen by the Jews themselves as fundamental badges of covenant membership.
>
> (Dunn 1990a: 192)

Dunn posited, and continues to posit (1993: 135–137), that Paul referred only to these aspects when he used the expression 'the works of the law' (*erga nomou*). He further reasoned that Paul was not against the ethical part of the Mosaic law, which was not included under 'works of law' in this sense, and that Gal. 5.14, where Paul speaks of the whole law being fulfilled in one statement from Lev. 19.18, 'You will love your neighbour as yourself', supported his case (1990a: 200).

The first objection to this view stems from social identity theory. It is most unlikely – especially in a fiercely competitive culture such as that of the ancient Mediterranean – that one group (here comprising Greeks and Romans) would take its cue on how to regard another group from the latter's own self-understanding, rather than engaging in the usual processes of simplifying and stereotyping, often of a derogatory nature. Thus, when Josephus records at the start of *Contra Apionem* how a number of people had maliciously discredited the case he had made in his *Jewish Antiquities* for the antiquity of the Israelites, we witness a typical Mediterranean response to the claims of one group. Equally implausible is Dunn's assumption that insiders would, in effect, define themselves only with respect to 'overt signals' and not also 'value orientations' (Barth) and that they would concern themselves with the public face of the boundary to the exclusion of its private mode, which comprises all the complexities of their intragroup life and experience (Cohen). Yet Dunn's case is also difficult to sustain exegetically for a number of reasons.

First, in Galatians Paul states his thesis about righteousness coming from faith and not from law or works of law without any sense of discrimination between *erga nomou* and *nomos*, as one quickly confirms by comparing 2.16 with 2.21, and 3.10 with 3.11, or by noting the use of *nomos* with righteousness at 5.4–5.

Second, Paul is thinking about the law in its entirety. He makes this point explicitly at 3.10 ('Cursed is everyone who does not remain in all things written in the book of the law to do them') and 5.3 ('I testify again to everyone who receives circumcision that he is bound to keep the whole law'). Note that Paul says he destroyed the law (2.18) and he died to the law (2.19), not that he destroyed 'works of law', which Dunn's view requires. Paul means he has said goodbye to the whole law. For him the choice is law or Christ, not a part of the law and Christ. The enunciation of stark alternatives is a feature of competition between ingroup and outgroup over scarce resources in an agonistic culture. This fact highlights the distance Paul had moved from his ethnic traditions in the cause of establishing a form of religion which can accurately be described as sectarian in relation to Israel (Esler 1987: 89).

Third, the fulfilment of the ethical requirements of the law would have been just as important to the internal sense of boundary as some of the more public observances like food restrictions and circumcision. When Paul taxes his opponents with not keeping the law themselves in 6.13 it is more likely to be its ethical dimensions than the overt practices to which he is referring, because there is no reason to doubt their commitment to circumcision and food laws.

Last, although I will say more on this shortly, Gal. 5.14 in no way supports Dunn, nor even Räisänen, for that matter, who, although he opposes a distinction in Paul between ceremonial and moral aspects of the law, still speaks of this verse involving 'the reduction of the *torah* to the moral law' (1986: 23–28). Paul's point is that if you have love (which, of course, you get as a gift of the Spirit in the community of believers, 5.22), you do not need the law. Love, derived from the Spirit and not from the law, is being proposed as a substitute for the law.

PAUL'S CASE AGAINST THE LAW (3.10–18)

The curse of the law and death (3.10–12)

As soon as Paul begins to develop his position on the law, he does so with the blunt assertion that those who rely on it are under a curse, supported by a modified quotation from Deut. 27.26 to the effect that all those who do not adhere to everything inscribed in the book of the law are cursed (3.10).[4] Traditional exegesis of this statement seeks to determine what Paul meant by this bleak view by asking why and in what sense those who rely on law are cursed (Bruce 1982b); this tends to involve running together the bald statement in 3.10a and the alleged justification in 3.10b. Yet a social identity perspective on the matter brings other issues into prominence which may actually take us closer to Paul's concerns. Rather than immediately probing this verse for the precise sense in which it might be said to apply to the Israelites (which is still an important issue), the application of Henri Tajfel's ideas prompts us initially to enquire into its function in the ongoing struggle in Galatia between the Pauline congregations and the Israelite outgroup. This involves concentrating on 3.10a.

Paul is determined to preserve his mixed congregations of gentiles and Israelites practising shared Eucharistic table-fellowship against the blandishments of the circumcisers and the Israelite community behind them. He wants his group to resist the pressure of the circumcisers so as not to be swallowed by a powerful outgroup. One means of achieving this end is to promote the attractiveness of the ingroup to its members, as we have seen he does in the area of righteousness. Yet just as most groups do not merely engage in positive self-evaluation, but attach negative evaluations to other groups, thereby reinforcing how privileged they are in contrast to others who are assuredly not, so too does Paul seek to present Israel in the worst possible light. He must do all he can to accentuate the difference between the groups by denigrating the outgroup.

In common with many other group leaders then and since, Paul engages in stereotyping to achieve this end. His aim is to help his audience learn to perceive and interpret a complex reality in a certain simplified way. He does this by insisting that the members of the two relevant groups have the same qualities in critical areas, favourable ones in the case of the ingroup and unfavourable ones for the outgroup. Accordingly, just as he has previously affirmed that those who depend on faith are the sons of Abraham (3.7) and share his blessing (3.9), now he proceeds immediately to insist that those who rely on law are under a curse (3.10). This is an example of extreme and rigid stereotyping, of the type mentioned in Chapter 2 as flourishing in conditions, as here, where the ingroup has a limited repertoire of positive social identities and must seek fiercely to preserve them, and where their low status is regarded, at least by their leaders, as illegitimate and capable of modification. From the viewpoint of labelling theory, Paul has developed a master status for the House of Israel of a derogatory type which engulfs all other roles and labels (Malina and Neyrey 1991: 101).

We may be quite confident that Israelites would not have seen them-selves in this way; they would reject such a formulation as an exaggerated and false interpretation of their identity and its characteristic features.

Having looked at the role of Gal. 3.10a in social identity terms, we may now investigate how Paul's readers might have understood the cause and nature of the curse. The quotation from Deut. 27.26 comes from a long section in Deuteronomy in which Moses, in farewelling the Israelites, sets out a series of blessings which will result from keeping the law and curses which will ensue for those who do not (Deut. 27–30). There are explicit references to covenant in these chapters (29.8–13), and on occasion the Septuagint uses *nomos* and *diathēkē* (the common word for covenant) interchangeably (29.12). The text reaches its climax in 30.15–20 where Moses sets out the stark alternatives of life or death:

> I set before you life or death, blessing or curse. Choose life, then, so that you and your descendants may live, in the love of Yahweh your God, obeying his voice, clinging to him; for in this your life consists, and on this depends your long stay in the land which Yahweh swore to your fathers Abraham, Isaac and Jacob he would give them.
>
> (Deut. 30.20; JB)

Three factors help explain Paul's moving to this particular section of scripture for his master label that those who rely on law are cursed, factors which go beyond the mere fact that Paul could hardly just forget everything he had learned or experienced in his Israelite upbringing. First, since his opponents were urging the Galatian gentiles to accept the Mosaic law (which included circumcision, Lev. 12.3), he had a pretext to turn scripture against the Israelites, something Gal. 4.21 shows he was more than happy to do. As noted previously, the attraction of Israel was obviously so strong to at least some of the gentiles that Paul was compelled to engage with Israelite tradition; it provided the field on which much of the battle would be fought. Second, the dramatic distinction in Deuteronomy 27–30 between life and death, blessing and curse offered a close parallel from tradition for the black and white differentiation he was striving to establish between ingroup and outgroup. Its language of curse evoked a powerfully negative master status to apply to the outgroup. Third, this section of Deuteronomy (indeed, Deuteronomy as a whole) contains nothing for gentiles; in particular, they are not promised blessings or life, although they are portrayed as benefiting at Israel's expense should she be cursed. The whole thrust of Deuteronomy is particularist rather than universal: God chose Israel and set her high above the nations of the earth (Deut. 28.1) so that she would be his special and blessed people (Deut. 4.34; 7.6, 14; 14.2, for example).

This last factor went far to removing what could have been an embarrassing difficulty for Paul – that he was interpreting Deuteronomy in a very partial way. For while Paul was happy to say that the Israelites had received the curses of the Sinaitic covenant, that it was effective to this extent, he certainly did not consider that they had enjoyed the life and blessings it offered them. Nevertheless, if pressed, he could point out that Deuteronomy promised no benefits to gentiles of the sort that they were now already receiving in the Spirit-filled life of the congregations (3.1–5). The details in Genesis 15, on the other hand, fortunately gave Paul scriptural warrant to argue that their current life and blessings had their source much earlier, with Abraham (prior to the institution of circumcision), which was 430 years before Sinai (Gal. 3.17); they were promised to Abraham and realised through the Spirit for those who believed in Christ. This supported a reading of Deuteronomy along the lines that while the later Mosaic covenant had led to Israel being cursed and had not, as a matter of fact, produced blessings for Israelites, it had never even promised to do so for gentiles.

Fuelling Paul's argument from scripture was both the sheer rhetorical necessity to bring Israelite tradition to bear on his opponents and also his overwhelming personal and congregational experience of life in Christ which he mentions in Gal. 2.19–3.5. Both the social realities of his communities and his own religion drove him to theologise in particular ways from Jewish scripture and he was fortunate to have some reasonably helpful passages to bring forward.

None of this is to deny that a certain awkwardness emerges on closer examination. One obviously awkward feature is that Deuteronomy does not really support his point. Whereas Paul asserts that those *under the law* are cursed, Deuteronomy 27.26 (and the other parts of chapters 27–30) warns that those *who fail to do the law* are cursed.[5]

The most plausible view of his case is that the Israelites have not kept the law and have therefore incurred the curse.[6] This, after all, is the Deuteronomic meaning of the curse. Yet this does not necessitate that it is impossible to keep the law. Such a view is directly contradicted by Deut. 30.11–14. Non-compliance came about through the actions of human agents, not because compliance was not possible. Paul himself may have thought that it was possible to keep the law, since he later claimed that he had been blameless with regard to righteousness under the law (Phil. 3.6).[7] Nevertheless, Paul should be taken to mean that although it may have been possible to fulfil the law (for example, if you were as exceptional as he was, Gal. 1.14), as a matter of fact Israel had not kept it. After all, in Galatians itself he concedes that if he were under the law again he would be a transgressor (2.18). When Paul says in 3.12 that law is not connected with faith, but that the person who performs (the requirements of the law) will live, this can only mean that no one does actually do them, because he is convinced that life comes from faith not law (3.11). In 5.3, Paul implies the difficulty of performing the law, although not really its in-principle impossibility. Those not complying with the law include the trouble-makers in Galatia (6.13).

Once again, it is helpful to assume that Paul is arguing backwards from his experience of Christ. Since through faith in Christ gentiles had actually experienced life and blessings in the Spirit (2.19–3.9), life could not come from law. In the Mediterranean world goods such as life and blessing were finite and indivisible, as, for example, Esau bitterly discovered (Gen. 27.34–40). It is through faith that the righteous person lives (3.11). Therefore, the life and blessings available under the Mosaic law (see Deut. 5–6; 28.1–14 and 30.15–30) had not eventuated; what had resulted was curse, itself a product of non-compliance with that law. Paul's powerful experience of living for God in the faith of his redeeming Son (2.19–20), when coupled with Mediterranean notions of limited good, simply allowed of no other source of life. Yet there was scriptural legitimation for gentiles receiving blessings – in the story of the promise made to the faithful Abraham in the time before circumcision in Genesis 15.

Christ as the answer to the curse of the law (3.13–14)

Paul's next step is to introduce the death of Christ into the argument: 'Christ redeemed [*exēgorasen*] us from the curse of the law becoming a curse for our sakes, for it is written "Cursed is everyone who hangs upon a tree"' (Gal. 3.13).[8] Sometimes in the Old Testament a person may be referred to as a curse, which means that he or she is in so disastrous a state as to embody the curse which might be made against someone (Num. 5.21 and Jer. 29.18).

What does Paul mean by saying this of Christ? How is Gal. 3.13 related, moreover, to Gal. 4.4: 'God sent out his son, born of a woman, born under law, in order that he might redeem [*exagorasē*] those under law, in order that we might receive adoption'? These two statements contain the only examples of the word *exagorazein*, 'to redeem', in the Pauline corpus and seem closely related.

Within the social identity framework, Gal. 3.13 represents a statement that the ingroup has been decisively differentiated from the Israelite outgroup and that Christ has been the agent by whom this differentiation was effected.[9] That his congregations have been saved from the curse of the law is the other side of their sharing the blessings of Abraham (3.8–9) – thus, Gal. 3.14 runs on from 3.13 with a further clause which takes the reader back to this theme, 'so that the blessing of Abraham might pass to the gentiles through Christ Jesus, so that we might receive adoption'. Here, Paul emphasises that the life which is now flowing through to the gentiles is that which was offered through Abraham; it did not come from fulfilment of the Sinaitic covenant. By becoming a curse for our sakes, Christ has saved us from the curse; he has suppressed the effects of the Sinaitic curse so as to allow antecedent blessings to come into effect. By dying, he has destroyed the death which threatened from Sinai, so that he might allow us access to life promised earlier to Abraham.

But there is some lack of clarity in relation to Christ's assuming the curse. Räisänen notes with typical insight that it is not clear how the thesis of the abolition of the law is derived from the notion of a vicarious curse; if the requirement of the law is met, why should it follow that the law is rejected (1986: 59)? We can, however, pose this issue a little more concretely: any Israelite willing to entertain the possibility that Christ saved us from the Deuteronomic curse could quickly suggest that he had thereby made available the life promised in that book. Yet there was an answer to this and to Räisänen's objection. Whereas the Deuteronomic blessings extended only to Israelites, the powerful manifestations of the Spirit proved that the gentiles had already experienced life, blessing and sonship. This meant that the blessings could have no connection with the Sinaitic covenant, whereas they were in accord with the Abrahamic covenant in Genesis 15. The law of Moses is relevant only to the effect that it causes death; when that death is taken away it ceases to have any bearing on us.

Nevertheless, Gal. 3.13 does necessitate that we ask why Paul describes Christ as redeeming us from the curse by becoming a curse. In particular, is this a central Christological idea for Paul, or something he comes up with in passing as a way of loosely linking his Christology to the argument he is running – which is really aimed at providing his congregations with a positive social identity? In the latter case, we perhaps should not expect to discover too much theoretical sophistication in the concept.

Paul could speak of the redeeming effect of Christ's death, of his vicarious death on our behalf (*hyper hēmōn*), without any mention of the idea of curse or even of law. At 1 Thess. 5.10, in a context entirely removed from discussion of the Mosaic law, Paul says that Jesus Christ 'died for us [*hyper hēmōn*], so that awake or asleep we might live together with him'. There are other similar instances unrelated to any discussion of the law, for example at 2 Cor. 5.14–15, where he links sin and redemption, life and death:

we are convinced of this, that one has died on behalf of all [*hyper pantōn*]; therefore all have died. And he died on behalf of all [*hyper pantōn*], so that those who live might no longer live for themselves but for him who died on their behalf [*hyper autōn*] and was raised.

Similarly, 2 Cor. 5.21 states that God 'made him, who knew no sin, to be sin on our behalf (*hyper hēmōn*)'. At Gal. 1.4 he mentions that Jesus Christ gave himself on behalf of our sins (*hyper tōn hamartiōn hēmōn*) to rescue us from this present wicked age. Paul has a variety of expressions to denote the plight that Christ saved us from: curse or its equivalent – the law (Gal. 4.4), death and sin. There is an underlying notion of Christ's death enabling our life. Accordingly, while his broad understanding of the Cross has nothing to do with curse, one can well see why his belief that Christ's death led to our life would stimulate him to rework that belief in terms of taking on the curse in the context of an argument dealing with the baleful effects of the Mosaic law. This is especially so when the reference to the curse on someone hanging on a tree connects so easily with a death by crucifixion.[10] This is a conclusion he reaches in consequence of the particular way he was handling the argument in Galatia coming into contact with his general position on the redemptive significance of Christ's death. On the other hand, commentators who see Gal. 3.13–14 as preserving a Christological tradition derived from circles of Israelite Christ-followers[11] face the very difficult task of explaining why a group which strongly endorsed the law would refer to its effect as a curse. Richard Hays may well be right in discerning a fundamental 'story' of salvation underlying Gal. 3.13–14 (and 4.4–6), probably related to the type of story we see in Phil. 2.5–11 (1983: 85–137), but the element of curse found at 3.13–14 is best explained as an *ad hoc* modification of the story to suit the contingencies of his highly stereotyped argument, with the version at Gal. 4.4–6 being closer to the original form.

N. T. Wright has put forward an interesting proposal on the relationship of Christ and the curse of the law in Gal. 3.10–14 which, because of its very different orientation to that offered here and because it makes a substantial contribution to his overall thesis on Pauline Christology, merits consideration. Wright argues that the emphasis in Deuteronomy 27–30 falls on what happens when Israel as a whole fails to keep the law as a whole, not on what happens when individuals sin. The results of this national apostasy are exile and restoration, that is, judgement followed by mercy (not the repentance, sacrifice and atonement which accompany individual sinfulness). This pattern ends with the renewal of the covenant – by God's circumcising the hearts of his people so that they love him and keep his Torah from the heart. According to Wright, this is the new covenant theology characteristic of some groups in Second Temple 'Judaism' and Paul offers a version of it, whereby the death of Jesus on a Roman cross, which symbolised the subjugation of the people of God, brought the exile to a climax. The King of the Jews took the brunt of the exile on himself (1991: 144–148). In Wright's view Paul is 'invoking the train of thought of the last chapters of Deuteronomy' (1991: 146). Here we see a New Testament scholar construing Paul primarily in relation to how he has utilised ideas from his religious and intellectual tradition, as opposed to my approach of focusing on the social realities of his situation.

A number of initial objections can be raised against Wright's proposition: he offers no explicit evidence in the form of a statement or passage that Paul did regard Christ as 'the climax of the [Sinaitic] covenant' (which we would expect if the notion were as central as alleged); it is rather artificial to speak of an 'exile' merely because the Israelites in Palestine are living under Roman rule; and, in any event, Deuteronomy summarises the curse more in terms of death than exile (Deut. 30.15–20).

The main problem with Wright's view, however, is that it is hard to reconcile with what Paul himself says about the Sinaitic covenant. The foundation of Paul's position is that through divine mercy gentiles have experienced the Spirit (Gal. 3.1–5) in consequence of the death of Christ and therefore the law is unnecessary (Gal. 2.21); this is also essentially the view of Luke in Acts 10.44–48. In fact, Paul destroyed the law (Gal. 2.18) and died to it, so as to live for God (Gal. 2.19). Paul speaks with great enthusiasm of life in faith, of focusing on Christ, and of the reception of the Spirit (even by gentiles) (2.19–3.5), all of which are vital to the identity of his Galatian congregations. His foundational argument is from experience. We understand Paul better if we bear in mind that his religion precedes his theology. Yet in Galatians he has been forced to theologise in a particular way, by interpreting this experience in response to an Israelite tradition at the heart of the campaign being run by Israelites and Israelite Christ-followers. His overall strategy is to launch an onslaught on the central aspect of that part of Israelite scripture relied upon by his opponents, the covenant at Sinai, by stigmatising it as solely productive of a curse from which Christ liberated us, while pointing out that an older part of sacred history, recounted in Genesis 15, had foretold the blessings which would come to the gentiles. The blessings which flow to the gentiles have nothing to do with the law of Moses. The outgroup who rely on it are cursed. This pattern of argument is totally at odds with Wright's case that in Gal. 3.10–14 Paul is 'invoking the train of thought of the last chapters of Deuteronomy', in other words, that he is using the Sinaitic covenant as explained in Deuteronomy as a master template for his whole Christology. Paul does not seek to encapsulate his understanding of Christ's death in relation to a central pattern of thought from the main tradition relied on by the outgroup he is so intent upon opposing. He does precisely the opposite.[12] The same argument counts with equal strength against Bruce Longenecker's recent proposal (1996) that Paul is evoking the covenant in Gal. 2.15–21.

The validity of the promises to Abraham and the Mosaic law (3.15–18)

In Gal. 3.15 Paul begins a new section – which runs to 3.18 – in which he solidifies his case for the validity of the Abrahamic covenant in spite of the later covenant with Moses and begins to disclose new lines of argument. At 3.15 he introduces an analogy from human affairs to the effect that no one may set aside or add to a particular sort of legal instrument (which he refers to as a *diathēkē*) once it has been ratified. This is a very convenient metaphor for Paul. Not only must *diathēkē* refer to a legal document known to his readers which is immediately binding yet under which promises are made for the provision of benefits in the future, but it is also used in the Septuagint of the covenant with Abraham in Gen. 15.18. Accordingly, Paul can utilise the analogy, first, to prove that this covenant is still in effect and, second, to open up a strand of imagery which will allow him to introduce the notion of inheritance at 3.18 and to develop it later in the letter.[13]

Exactly what type of instrument Paul had in mind has proven very difficult to determine. The common suggestion of a will is unlikely since these were revocable by the testator.[14] Yet some sort of testamentary arrangement is required (rather than simply a disposition *inter vivos*),[15] since although a metaphor which depends on the action of someone who dies is a little odd in relation to the living God, Paul needs the testamentary association to be able to raise the idea of the inheritance which his Christ-followers have received.[16] Recently, Timothy Lim has proposed a type of legal instrument known from early second-century CE Palestine which seems to have been irrevocable and was capable of coming into effect immediately upon execution of the document *or* on the death of the testator.[17] A legal instrument like this would both smooth the way for Paul to introduce the notion of heirs and inheritance, yet, since it can refer to a disposition by a living donor, also soften the awkwardness of the imagery. Fortunately, it is unnecessary to reach a conclusion as to exactly what sort of document Paul had in mind since the point he makes is reasonably clear.

Rather than moving directly from the metaphor to a broad statement of its bearing on his situation, Paul introduces another connection with Christ. He has already sought to relate the covenant of Genesis 15 to the new dispensation by stating that the blessing of Abraham comes to the gentiles though Christ and that the promise made to Abraham is tied to the gift of the Spirit (3.14). Yet this connection exists essentially at the level of assertion. Now he seeks to corroborate it with scriptural proof:

> The promises were spoken[18] to Abraham and to his seed. It does not say, 'and to his seeds', as concerning many but as concerning one, 'and to his seed', which is Christ.

(3.16)

When, immediately after this, Paul returns to the analogy by concluding that since God had ratified the covenant (*diathēkē*) with Abraham, and the law which came 430 years later was not able to annul it so as to nullify its promise (3.17),[19] he has explicitly introduced Christ into the picture as the seed who, along with Abraham, was the subject of that promise.

Abraham's descendants are referred to as his seed (*sperma*) repeatedly in Genesis,[20] obviously as a collective noun, and here we have Paul audaciously interpreting the word as a reference to Christ. This type of exegesis existed in the first century CE and was later known as *peshat*, meaning 'plain', or 'open', as opposed to *derash*, meaning 'hidden' (Brewer 1992: 14). *Peshat* readings took two forms, which Brewer usefully calls nomological, which treated scripture as if it were a legal document, and ultra-literal, which 'demands the literal understanding of the words used in a text even when it is denied by the context and the plain meaning of the idioms' employed (Brewer 1992: 15). Paul's interpretation of *sperma* is of the latter form. Needless to say, Paul does not want to disenfranchise his Galatian gentiles from the promise; his aim is to interpret Christ as its primary recipient and only later to include them *via* him – through adoption as sons of God and inclusion into Christ, even so far as their also being the seed of Abraham (3.26–29).

Finally, he ends this theme by making one further point, where we find the first instance of the inheritance theme which will be prominent in the discussion to follow:[21] 'But if the inheritance [*klēronomia*] came from law, it would no longer [*ouketi*] come from promise' (3.18a). This sentence does not provide a causal explanation for 3.17,[22] but marks a development to a new, although related, issue. Paul implies such a result is impermissible because it would falsify the principle in 3.17; it would mean that the Mosaic law which arrived later had indeed caused the promise no longer (*ouketi*) to operate. For Paul 'inheritance' is a typical 'limited good' of Mediterranean culture. It exists in a finite quantity and it is indivisible, which means it can only have one source – so that if this source was the law it could no longer derive from the promise. This would entail that the Mosaic law had brought about what Paul's analogy from human legal arrangements has aimed to show is illicit, namely, the revocation by the Mosaic law of the promise to Abraham and his seed – Christ.

In his last expression of the theme he began at 3.15 Paul explicitly reminds his audience of the identity of the donor of this inheritance: 'God has graciously granted[23] it [sc. the inheritance] to Abraham through promise' (3.18b). What is the inheritance? At 3.18 Paul first introduces the theme and leaves its development until later. In Genesis it had referred to offspring and land (Gen. 15. 5, 7, 17, 18). Yet it is inappropriate to follow certain commentators in fixing on one or other attribute to which 'inheritance' might refer.[24] Although Paul is no doubt including the gift of the Spirit within the inheritance, just as he has already reinterpreted the 'promise' to refer to it, he will go on (in Gal. 3.26–4.7) to employ the notion of inheritance as a master designation for a cluster of desirable attributes attached to those who have faith in Christ.[25] Accordingly, it is an identity-descriptor which tells them who they really are.

A theological reading of the letter would probably interpret 3.15–18 as one of Paul's ways of accounting for the saving significance Christ has for those with faith in him. A social identity approach, however, while also crediting these verses with Christological significance, does so as part of a richer explanation which brings out more fully their social context. Within this perspective, Paul advances his general aim of legitimating, that is, explaining and justifying, the extremely desirable identity which comes from belonging to his groups through their close association with the illustrious Abraham and the even more illustrious Christ. He attacks one threat to that position, that the Mosaic law nullified the promises to Abraham, and further develops his positive case, the central role of Christ in linking his audience to those promises.

Gal. 3.15–18 constitute the high-water mark in Paul's critique of the law and at this point we sense him pause in the face of an obvious objection to his argument; if all this is true, why did God give us the law in the first place?

THE PURPOSE OF THE LAW

It is rather unfortunate that Paul delivers his answer to this question in the two most difficult verses in the letter, translated by the RSV as follows:

> Why then the law? It was added because of transgressions, till the offspring [*sperma*] should come to whom the promise had been made; and it was ordained by angels through an intermediary [*mesitēs*]. Now an intermediary implies more than one; but God is one.
>
> (3.19–20)

Some points are clear, however. Paul is offering an explanation for its original purpose when the law was given on Sinai, and this should be distinguished from what happened when human beings interacted with its provisions. He is building upon the case he has previously made that

Christ is the offspring of Abraham to whom the promise was made. Moreover, the word 'till' in Gal. 3.19 implies that its limited period of operation is over, an idea Paul will soon develop. The intermediary must be Moses. Now for the difficult aspects of Paul's explanation.

'Because of transgressions' (3.19a)

The expression 'because of transgressions' (*tōn parabaseōn charin*) in 3.19 has attracted much attention.[26] Before considering the two main lines of interpretation, I will begin with a basic principle of this reading – to use Galatians itself as the initial guide to understanding a particular expression.

The word used for 'transgression' in 3.19 is *parabasis*, quite common in relation to breaches of law in Greek culture of the time and also in the Septuagint (Schneider 1967). Its cognate verb is *parabainein*, 'to transgress', and there is a cognate noun, *parabatēs*, or 'transgressor'. Fortunately, Paul has already employed the word *parabatēs* earlier in the letter, when he says, 'But if I build up again those things which I tore down [sc. the law], then I prove myself a transgressor' (2.18; RSV). Presumably, Paul means a transgressor in relation to that which he tore down, that is, the law, either because he has been acting in breach of its provisions in the way he interacted with gentiles or, more probably, because he will do so in the future.[27] In short, if he takes on the law again, his conduct will stand to be condemned in relation to its ordinances; he will become a transgressor. The introduction of law into a particular context establishes a set of norms with respect to which human behaviour acquires a different character. This is an unimpeachably correct understanding of the effect of law. Thus, if a modern legislature passes an act which, for example, renders it unlawful and subject to penalty to sell packaged food with false or misleading nutritional information, companies which had previously engaged in that practice and persisted with it would thereafter discover that their behaviour had now assumed a quite different character.

There is no reason not to be guided by what Paul means by 'transgressor' in 2.18 when it comes to interpreting 'transgression' in 3.19. When he says 'the law was added because of transgressions', his earlier usage suggests that we may unfold this compressed expression as 'the law was added to establish a collection of norms in relation to which human behaviour would have an altered character, in particular to the extent that breach of those norms would incur punishment'.

Although this understanding can be readily deduced from 2.18, we could push the expression a little further to ask in addition whether the phrase also implies *a reason why* such a set of norms would have been established. I suspect that virtually anyone coming to this issue afresh, in ancient times or modern, would suggest that it was to label certain conduct as particularly reprehensible[28] and to discourage its commission.[29] Certainly it is difficult to think of the enactment of any law, in ancient times or modern, where this was not the aim of the legislator. This view has long been expressed. It can be traced back to the Patristic period[30] and is held by some modern critics such as Cosgrove (1988: 65), Dunn (1993: 189) and Thielman (1989: 74). We will soon see, moreover, how well this explanation coheres with imagery that Paul uses for the law later, of a boy's *paidagōgos* and a young heir's trustees and administrators.[31]

Those new to this field, however, may be surprised, or even shocked, to learn that a large number of Pauline commentators think that the expression means to 'produce' or 'provoke' transgression and reflects Paul's general view of the Mosaic law. This approach seems, in fact, to be the most popular one in the recent period[32] and is favoured by scholars such as Betz (1979: 165), Bruce (1982c: 175), Hong (1993: 146, 190, 194–195), Hübner (1984: 26), Lightfoot (1914: 144–145) and Räisänen (1986: 140–141). The rich variety of uses to which *charin* can be put in classical and Septuagintal Greek permits either interpretation.[33]

According to Hübner, for example, the purpose of the giving of the law was 'to make men transgress the law' (1984: 26). Most commentators who take this view consider that God intended human breach of the law deserving of punishment and wrath so as to give grace an ample field of activity, as suggested to them by Rom. 5.20–21. My reasons for rejecting this interpretation of Rom. 5.20–21 appear in the Appendix to this reading. Given this view, we might observe, Paul considered God had commanded the Israelites to worship him alone *in order that* they would serve Baal and Chemosh and so on, to honour their parents *in order that* they would shame them, not to kill *in order that* they would engage in homicide and not to commit adultery *in order that* they would do so (see Lev. 20.1–17).[34]

We will leave aside the extent to which such a notion constitutes an unacceptable affront to common sense, ancient or modern, or attributes to God so unique a perversity as a law-giver as to cause us to wonder whether 'God' is the right word to use of such an entity. The initial question is whether the view that law produces transgression is compatible with Paul's perspective as disclosed at 2.18 and the answer is 'no'. It is quite contrary to his position (and indeed to legal principle) to suppose that the introduction of a law into a given setting, which thereby identifies and attaches a different character to certain human actions (usually to prohibit them on pain of punishment), could itself produce or provoke transgression. Only human agents can *produce* transgression, when they decide to continue or begin performing certain acts in spite of the law. Paul recognises the centrality of human agency when he says 'But if I build up again those things which I tore down [sc. the law], then *I prove myself* a transgressor' (2.18 (my emphasis); RSV) and the same applies to modern examples, such as in the food labelling illustration above.

The notion that the law was meant to *provoke* transgression is equally difficult to reconcile with Paul's outlook. The idea that the law was passed to establish norms with respect to which human behaviour would be judged and punished if appropriate with the very aim of provoking (that is, of stimulating or attracting) such breaches does not occur in Galatians. It is really an idea which critics import into the text from Romans, especially 5.20–21 (see Räisänen 1986: 140–150), although in fact it is not to be found in that text either, for reasons I set out in the Appendix to this reading.

On the other hand, if we move from the original purpose of the law to what happens depending on how human beings behave under its regime, a different picture emerges. If people have been behaving wrongfully, say by misleading the public as to the nutritional value of food they are selling, and they exercise their prerogative as agents to persist in such behaviour after the passage of legislation prohibiting it, their culpability is even greater. If a law is not obeyed, those within its ambit are in an even worse position than they were before. This consideration shows that the effect of a law, however noble its intention, may be disastrous when those to whom it applies disregard its directions. This is Paul's position, as Gal. 3.22–25 (discussed below) indicates. Before the law there was sin, and since Israel did not comply with norms of behaviour established by the law – whose aim was to restrain sin – the result was that their sin became even greater. I have argued above in connection with Gal. 3.10 that Paul was of the view that Israel had not kept the law and had thereby received the curse of the law, which is death. This is also what Paul means in Rom. 5.20–21, for the reasons set out in the Appendix.

Commanded through angels by the hand of a mediator (3.19d–20)

When Paul continues in 3.19d to say that 'the law was commanded [*diatageis*] through angels, by the hand of a mediator', he seems to have in mind the origin of the Mosaic law, although the precise connotations of this statement are far from clear. Three broad options are possible (Stanton 1996: 113). First, that this is simply a way of saying God used angels to give the law to Moses; second, that angels, in particular, demonic beings with evil intention, gave the law to Moses and not God (Hübner 1984: 27–30)[35] and, third, that Paul is seeking to distance God somewhat from the giving of the law, even though the angels were his agents.

Sounding against Hübner's proposal is the evidence that angels were associated with the delivery of the law in a positive, not negative fashion. This tradition may have been stimulated by the Septuagint of Deut. 33.2, which says that 'the Lord has come from Sinai . . . and on his right hand his angels with him', although in the text the angels are not specifically associated with the giving of the law.[36] The strongest evidence for this tradition in the first century comes from Josephus, when he has Herod state 'we have learned the noblest of our doctrines and the holiest of our laws from angels sent by God' (*Jewish Antiquities*, 15.136). There is also the preface to another Israelite text, *The Life of Adam and Eve*, which is possibly from the first century CE: 'The narrative and life of Adam and Eve the first-made, revealed by God to Moses his servant when he received the tablets of the law of the covenant from the hand of the Lord, after he had been taught by the archangel Michael' (Charlesworth 1985 2: 259). *Jubilees* largely consists of the historical narrative and laws which the angel of the presence dictated to Moses for him to write down. There was also a general notion abroad in the first century that the angels were God's agents (see Philo *Som.*, 1.141–143). *Pesiqta Rabbati*, 21 (103b) speaks of angels descending together with God upon Mount Sinai, in order to give the law to Israel.

The tradition of angelic involvement in relation to the law is also reflected in the New Testament, in Heb. 2.2, in Acts 7.30 (where Stephen speaks of an angel appearing to Moses in a burning bush in a desert near Sinai), in Acts 7.38, and, the most interesting of these passages, in Acts 7.53: 'you who received the law in commandments [*eis diatageis*] of angels and did not keep it'. Here, the noun 'commandments' (*diatageis*) is cognate with the verb used of the action of the angels at Gal. 3.19 and there is also the additional allegation that Stephen's audience had not kept the law.

Yet this is not to say that belief in angels giving the law was universal in the first century. Thus, it does not figure in the account of Sinai in Pseudo-Philo (*Biblical Antiquities*, 11–13), although there is a reference to the angels 'running on ahead' amidst all the meteorological disturbances (11.5). Similarly, in the magnificent description of the giving of the law on Sinai in 4 Ezra 3.18–19, there is no mention of angels.

Of the other two possible interpretations for Gal. 3.19d, the better one is that Paul is seeking to distance God from the transmission of the law to Moses (see also Stanton 1996: 113). This is strongly suggested by the context of 3.19, since in the previous verse Paul has very emphatically stated that it was God who gave the inheritance to Abraham through promise, and this contrasts noticeably with his failure to mention God in 3.19. This is confirmed by the reference at the end of 3.19 to the mediator, although the precise point Paul wishes to make emerges somewhat more clearly at Gal. 3.20.

Verse 20 is notoriously difficult: 'A mediator is not of one, but God is one'. The simplest solution in context is to regard this as another means whereby Paul diminishes the status of the Mosaic law *vis-à-vis* the promises to Abraham. The first part of the sentence is clearer than the second. To say that a mediator is not 'of one' presumably means that he or she stands between two parties so that one has no direct dealings with the other. Social relationships in the first-century Mediterranean world often saw brokers interposed between patrons and clients (see Moxnes 1991) and Paul may have had such a pattern in mind. The second clause is more opaque. Räisänen's suggestion that usually mediators were used between parties consisting of many persons and that this could not apply to God who was One (1986: 130) runs up against the frequency with which brokers mediated between single individuals in this culture. Although it was probably Paul's intention in this clause to propose the opposite of mediation, where the parties dealt with one another face to face, as God (who is One) had done with Abraham and through him to Christ, the one seed (3.16), the second half of v. 20 can hardly be said unambiguously to reflect this meaning.

The result of this discussion of 3.19d–20 is that Paul is not suggesting anything particularly negative about the law, merely that it was not given to Israel in the direct way in which God made his promise to Abraham. Within the social identity framework being utilised in this reading, these verses constitute another way of saying that the identity and status of the ingroup is superior to that of the outgroup, even though Paul is unwilling to go too far in attacking the mechanism whereby the outgroup achieve their identity, the Mosaic law, since it did have some connection with the divine purpose. It is an important part of rhetoric not to alienate one's audience and for Paul to have denied any connection of God with the law may well have had precisely this effect on the Galatians. This issue of the place of the law in the divine plan comes up, indeed, in the very next verse.

Not contrary to promise and the law as *paidagōgos* (3.21–24)

At 3.21a, having just set out a case for the inferiority of the law in relation to the Abrahamic covenant, Paul draws back a little and asks: 'Is the law therefore contrary to the promises [of God]? Impossible!' But the concession in favour of the law is very short-lived. The next clause begins with the Greek words *ei gar* which are usually translated as 'for if,' so that what follows would supply a causal explanation for 3.21a. This is a misconception. The words *ei gar*, in line with an established Greek usage (Denniston 1934: 94), here begin a new topic in an emphatic way: 'But if law was given which was able to bring life, truly righteousness would come from law' (3.21b). That is, even granting that the Mosaic law was not contrary to the promises to Abraham, it has nevertheless not been able to bring life and therefore cannot be the source of righteousness. For the inability of the law to be a source of life Paul presumably has in mind his earlier arguments, especially in 3.10–12.

At this point Paul now begins to deploy metaphors to explain his position on the law:

3.22 But scripture confined [*synekleisen*] all things under sin, so that the promise, by faith in Jesus Christ, might be given to those who have faith.
3.23 Before the faith came we were guarded [*ephrouroumetha*], being confined [*sygkleiomenoi*] under law until the coming faith was revealed,
3.24 So that the law became our *paidagōgos*, in order that we might be justified through faith.
3.25 As the faith has come, we are no longer under a *paidagōgos*.

The first clause in v. 22, which at first sight is a rather shocking one, is further elaborated in vv. 23–25, so that we should interpret its meaning in accord with the statement in 3.23 and the imagery of the *paidagōgos* in 3.24–25. As to v. 23, it should be noted that while the expression 'we were guarded' (*ephrouroumetha*) can have a negative sense, to prevent escape, its principal sense is a positive one, to protect, to preserve from attack.[37] This meaning is confirmed by the pedagogue imagery which follows; the word should not be translated 'we were in custody'. As for

vv. 24–25, metaphors, by their very nature, evoke a range of meanings and can never simply be 'decoded' in some one-to-one fashion. Nevertheless, even metaphors convey meaning within general boundaries, so that it should be possible to get a valuable indication of Paul's understanding of the purpose of the law from this imagery. In fact, a metaphor has the potential to be far more important as a guide to Paul's thought than views dependent on the analysis of discursive language where the syntax throws up various possibilities – as it does most notably in Gal. 3.19 and Rom. 5.20–21.

There have been a number of recent attempts to explain the nature of the ancient pedagogue and relate it to this section of Galatians (Betz 1979: 177; Lull 1986; Hanson 1988). But the best treatment, because of its covering all of the ancient evidence and for the judicious nature of the analysis, is that of Norman Young (1987). Prior to his meticulous analysis of the meaning of pedagogue, many scholars saw it far too negatively.

The pedagogue was usually a household slave appointed to look after a boy twenty-four hours a day until he became a man, shortly after puberty. Very often pedagogues were old or infirm slaves who were unable to do the more productive heavy work. Their age was the basis for the frequent claim that they were sour-natured and grumpy. The pedagogue accompanied his charge everywhere, not just to school, but to theatres, gymnasia, law courts and so on. The pedagogue had two main roles. The first was to protect the boy, for example from the attentions of unwanted suitors or sadistic schoolteachers, and to prevent him getting into mischief. In this sense he was a guard, a *phrouros*. This inevitably meant imposing restrictions on the boy and pedagogues were often described as killjoys as a result. Sometimes they imposed stern physical punishment on the boys in their care. Their second role was to train and educate the boy in social etiquette and cultural mores.

Although some pedagogues were bitterly resented because of the beatings they handed out, on many other occasions there grew up strong bonds of respect and friendship between boy and pedagogue. Cicero could claim that a man's nurse and his pedagogue were the first persons he loved (*de Amicitia*, 20.74). Grateful adults often looked after the pedagogue of their youth, for example, by emancipating them. Pedagogues, therefore, had an ambiguous role, attracting ridicule and scorn on the one hand and praise and appreciation on the other. Their function was strictly temporary, only until the boy became a man. Attempts to continue the role of the pedagogue beyond this point were greatly resented.

The application of this data to Galatians immediately produces one negative result of great importance: it rules out of court the notion that the law had the purpose of producing or provoking transgression, for such ideas are completely incompatible with the function of the pedagogue, however one understands the metaphor.[38] On the other hand, perfectly compatible with the metaphor is the notion that a wayward boy who simply will not accept instruction is likely to bring the full weight of the angry pedagogue down on his head and end up in a worse condition than he would have been without one. Accordingly, as already intimated above, Gal. 3.22 means that the result of the imposition of the law in scripture, when combined with human failure to obey the law, has been to confine everything under sin in a manner worse than if there had been no law. But this is the consequence of the interaction between Israel and the Mosaic law, not the purpose for which the law was given.

In Gal 3.23–25, as Young correctly points out, there is a twofold emphasis: on the role of the pedagogue to guard and restrict, and as being strictly limited in duration. On the other hand, there is nothing particularly negative in this picture, since that was what the institution of the pedagogue was supposed to be like. They were meant to guard their charges, teach them how to behave and punish them if they went astray, and their term of office ended when the boy came of age.

Paul is not suggesting that there is anything particularly negative about the law in the use of this analogy, only that it is by definition, and of necessity, restrictive in its operation and limited as to its time of application. This interpretation accords with the meaning that I have already argued Gal. 3.19 yields as to Paul's understanding of the law. The same picture emerges at 4.1–2, where Paul uses the image of the trustees (*epitropoi*) and administrators (*oikonomoi*) who look after the affairs of an heir during his minority. Certainly, this is a period of restriction on the heir (Paul says he is in the position of a slave, 4.1), but that restriction ends when the heir comes of age in accordance with his father's instruction (4.2). On the other hand, minor heirs cannot do without trustees and administrators. They are appointed by the testator for protective purposes and with the good of the child in mind.

The main point Paul makes about the law in Gal. 3.23–4.2 is simply that it has now been superseded. It had a protective function and purpose, even though the Israelites abused the law to their own detriment so that they fell under its curse, but it now holds no sway for those who are in Christ (Gal. 3.28). The law has passed its use-by date. He will later reiterate this point at 4.31–5.2 when he exhorts his audience not to reimpose on themselves the yoke of slavery from which Christ freed them. This is all that Paul needs to say in order to generate a sufficiently negative picture of the law to ward off the approaches of the outgroup who are seeking to have his gentiles embrace it and them.

THE LAW AND LOVE

Gal. 3.21–4.2 strongly suggest that the law has no further role. What then are we to make of Gal. 5.13–14?:

> 5.13 For you were called to freedom, brothers; only not the freedom which offers an opportunity for your human nature, but that you might be slaves to one another through love [*agapē*].
> 5.14 For the whole law is fulfilled [*peplērōtai*] in the one statement, namely, 'You will love your neighbour as yourself'.

(Lev. 19.18)

Is Paul here promoting the law as a source for moral behaviour in his congregations even though he had earlier said that it was superseded? As noted earlier in this chapter, James Dunn has argued that Paul was not opposed to the ethical section of the Jewish law and that Gal. 5.14 supported his case. Heikki Räisänen speaks of this verse involving 'the reduction of the *torah* to the moral law' (1986: 23–27). I have already set out the flaws in Dunn's argument, both at the level of social theory and as a matter of exegesis, for the distinction he finds in Galatians between 'law' and 'works of law' which would be necessary for his retention of the moral aspects of the law in Gal. 5.14. One must now add to this that such a position is very difficult to maintain in view of Paul's strenuous efforts to demonstrate that the law has had its day and that it constitutes a slavery to which his gentile converts should not yoke themselves. Keeping his congregations separate from the law forms an essential element of his strategy for creating a positive group identity for them in contrast to a very negative identity attributed to the Israelite outgroup. What then does Paul mean by Gal. 5.14, especially the word *peplērōtai*?[39]

The explanation most in accord with the argument in Galatians up to this point is one which interprets Gal. 5.14 as acknowledging that the best the law can provide is love of one's neighbour (*agapē*), while insisting that such love is available within the congregations from an entirely different source – the Spirit. In fact, *agapē* is the first fruit of the Spirit (Gal. 5.22). The law and the Spirit are stark alternatives: 'If you are led by the Spirit, you are not under law' (Gal. 5.18). Paul is speaking of the replacement of the law by the Spirit, not the continuance of the ethical aspect of the law in the new dispensation in Christ.

Such an interpretation is consistent with his use of the verb *plēroō*, which is well discussed by Barclay (1988: 138–140). This word is never used for performing the law in the Septuagint, a notion for which Paul himself also uses other words.[40] Some other meaning is needed. C. F. D. Moule has suggested in an important article on 'fulfilment' in the New Testament (1967–1968) that *plēroō* refers to the consummation of the will and plan of God, as can be seen in the use of the cognate noun *plērōma* ('fulfilment') in Gal. 4.4 (Barclay 1988: 139). Barclay plausibly interprets it to designate 'the total realization of God's will in line with the eschatological fullness of time in the coming of Christ' (1988: 140).

Yet Barclay's further conclusion that 'the moral standards of the law are taken up into and fully realized in the life of the Spirit' does not necessarily follow from this view and, in fact, is in conflict with Paul's argument in Galatians. The moral standards or norms of the law, just like the rest of the law, are not 'taken up' into the new life. They have no further purpose for those who believe in Christ. On the contrary, God's plan is realised as far as the law is concerned by virtue of the fact that the best the law has to command, love of one's neighbour, is obtained by a different route – the Spirit. It is possible that Paul is alive to complaints that without the law the gentile members of his congregations would lack the moral guidance offered by the Mosaic law, but, if so, he stoutly resists giving the law any role whatever in this area. His answer is that the fulfilment, the absolute realisation, of the law is love, and love is provided by the Spirit. In this light, Gal. 5.14 is the keystone in the case for finally discarding the law as having any continuing relevance for the congregations, not an indication that its ethical provisions are in any way retained. It serves to differentiate ingroup and outgroup even further, not to blur the boundary between them.

It seems to me that this result is not affected by the use of the expression 'fulfil [*anaplērōsete*] the law of Christ' at Gal. 6.2, but I will return to this issue in Chapter 8.

Chapter 8

Freedom, the Spirit and community life (Gal. 4.21–6.10)

The subject of this last substantive chapter of my reading is Gal. 4.21–
6.10. It is not usual, however, to consider this section of the letter as
demonstrating any particular unity. In his outline of the letter on the
basis of strict rhetorical theory, for example, Betz describes 3.1–4.31 as
forming the *probatio* or statement of proof, while 5.1–6.10 constitute the
exhortation (1975, 1979), so that, given this view, the section I have
chosen awkwardly straddles two parts of the text which are quite different in function. Nevertheless, I have previously suggested that too formulaic a reading of the rhetoric in Galatians, or any other letter, is unjustified, even though it is reasonable to assume that Paul had a general
interest in using the persuasive techniques of rhetoric to achieve his ends.
Moreover, there is always a measure of artificiality in any structural
division of a Pauline letter. Similarly, although it is certainly possible to
regard 4.21–31 as a passage in which Paul seeks to reinforce his previous
argument (Bruce 1982c: 214; Dunn 1993: 243), we cannot ignore the
extent to which it paves the way for the treatment of freedom from 5.2
onward. It may, accordingly, be treated, as it is here, as a prelude to what
follows rather than as rounding off the earlier discussion.

The best course will be for me to set out the features that suggest at
least a loose shape and cohesiveness to Gal. 4.21–6.10 and to introduce
its three main subdivisions at the same time. I will scrutinise the first and
third of these in more detail later in this chapter; most of the material in
the second section (5.2–12) has been considered in connection with
topics already discussed.

My overall aim in this chapter is to build on this analysis of the
content of Gal. 4.21–6.10 by using research into Mediterranean anthropology, ethnic boundaries and social identity to investigate its connections with the rest of the letter and the distinctive way in which Paul
profiles the character of life lived in accordance with his gospel. We will

see that central to his achievement is a pervasive recourse to the oppositions of freedom versus slavery, and promise and Spirit versus flesh,
enriched with the imagery of kinship and household, to differentiate the
identity of his communities from the alternative choices on offer.

This chapter will contain four major sections: first, an overview of the
contents and structure of 4.21–6.10; second, an introduction to the two
fundamental antitheses present in this section of the letter, namely, freedom versus slavery and promise and Spirit versus flesh; and, third and
fourth, investigations of 4.21–31 and 5.13–6.10.

THE CONTENTS AND STRUCTURE OF GAL. 4.21–6.10

Gal. 4.21–5.1: the reality of freedom

Gal. 4.21 marks a new stage of the letter. Just before this, Paul has been
speaking in a discursive way about his past and present relationship with
the Galatians and their current situation (4.12–20). But at 4.21 he begins
an allegorical reading of parts of Genesis, supplemented by other Israelite traditions, directed to demonstrating that the members of his congregations are really the descendants of Sarah, that they are free, and
associated with promise and Spirit, while those who favour the
imposition of the Mosaic law are descended from Hagar, are in slavery
and are tied to the flesh. At 5.1 he utters the resounding declaration and
admonition: 'For freedom Christ has set us free. Therefore stand firm
and do not again be loaded down with the yoke of slavery'. Accordingly,
the allegory supports a case for associating freedom, a potent identity-
descriptor, with the action of Christ and those who adhere to Paul's
version of the gospel.

Gal. 5.2–12: the threat to freedom

In Gal. 5.2–12 Paul reiterates some of his earlier arguments and introduces new ideas, but now so as to reinforce the admonition in 5.1, since
circumcision will not only mean that his audience must obey the whole
law, but that they will also have cut themselves off from Christ and from
grace (5.2–4). In 5.6 he insists that in Christ Jesus the notions of circumcision and uncircumcision have become obsolete and that what matters
is faith working through love (*pistis di' agapēs energoumenē*), where the close
combination of the two realities is reminiscent of his expression 'the
breastplate of faith and love' in 1 Thess. 5.8. This is the first use of the

noun, love (*agapē*), in the letter, although the verbal form (*agapaō*) appeared in connection with the self-sacrifice of Christ at 2.20; hereafter love will be prominent in Paul's discussion of life within the community (*agapē*, 5.13, 22; *agapaō*, 5.14).

Paul continues by noting that his audience had been advancing well until someone obstructed them from the truth (5.7). Nevertheless, even though the trouble-makers might be persuasive (5.8–9), Paul is confident that his Galatians will form the right view (5.10). Paul does not preach circumcision, for if he did the stumbling-block of the cross would be removed. The circumcisers are heading for trouble (5.11–12).

Gal. 5.13–6.10: the nature of freedom in the community

At 5.13a Paul repeats his claim to the reality of freedom in a way which echoes the statement in 5.1a: 'You were called for freedom, brothers!' But now there comes a dramatic change of direction: 'Only not the freedom which is an opportunity for the flesh, but be enslaved to one another through love' (5.13b). This address to his Galatian brothers begins a section that many commentators have characterised as 'ethics'.[1] Although I will later propose an alternative framework for addressing 5.13–6.10, this passage does indeed cover material with a pronounced normative thrust (5.16–26) and also more practical advice on how members should treat one another (5.15; 6.1–6). It concludes at 6.10 with an exhortation in which Paul rounds off the subject of kinship which he began with his reference to them as brothers at 5.13: 'So then, as we have an opportune time, let us do good to everyone, but especially to the house-members [*oikeioi*] of the faith'.

What is Paul up to? What do these verses relating to internal conditions within the congregations have to do with the main problem occupying Paul's attention in Galatia, the question of whether his converts will cross the community boundaries to enter the zones of Israelite belief and practice or pagan idolatry? As we will see, many scholars have found it difficult to relate Gal. 5.13–6.10 to the rest of the letter, even though its 'ethical' parts have attracted much attention. Furthermore, how is it that having previously gone out of his way to characterise the congregations as enjoying Christ-won freedom in contrast to the state of slavery of those under the law, Paul can now interpret their freedom itself as slavery? What model of obligation does he employ to give substance to this surprising reversal?

FREEDOM VERSUS SLAVERY, PROMISE AND SPIRIT VERSUS FLESH

We must preface our more detailed enquiry into Gal. 4.21–6.10 with consideration of an important feature common to each of its three parts. In seeking to foster a pronounced differentiation between the ingroup and the Israelite and gentile outgroups, Paul develops several sets of binary oppositions in the letter to establish and legitimate the identity of his congregations. The major one is faith versus law, especially in relation to the acquisition of righteousness (already considered in Chapters 6 and 7 of this reading), but there are two others of some moment: first, that of freedom *vis-à-vis* the slavery imposed by the law and the service of idols; and, second, the antithesis between promise and the Spirit, on the one hand, and flesh on the other. While both of these latter oppositions receive their main coverage in this section of the text, Paul introduces each of them earlier.

The theme of freedom versus slavery begins with Paul's reference to the efforts of the false brothers who slipped into the Jerusalem meeting 'to spy out the freedom [*eleutheria*] which we have in Christ Jesus, so that they might enslave [*katadouloō*] us' (2.4). It continues with the metaphor of the slave (*doulos*, 4.1–2) and the reference to those 'enslaved [*dedoulōmenoi*] under the elements of this world' (4.3), both of which expressions serve to describe those who were 'under law' (4.4–5), but who have now been ransomed by the son of God (4.5–6), so that they are no longer slaves but sons and heirs (4.7). The theme next appears in connection with the status of those who were once enslaved (*edouleusate*, 4.8) to beings which are not gods and now seem willing to be enslaved (*douleuein*, 4.9) to them again.

The opposition between promise and the Spirit and flesh begins in Galatians at 3.2 when Paul asks his audience if they received the Spirit from the proclamation of the faith or from the works of the law and then immediately takes them to task for completing in the flesh (*sarki*) what they began in the Spirit (*pneumati*) (3.3). Both elements of this opposition also receive separate treatment. Paul goes to some lengths in 3.1–14 to tie the Spirit and promise closely together, with this section climaxing in the statement that through faith we receive the promise of the Spirit (3.14). As noted already, the Spirit is one of the ultimate prizes and badges of identity associated with belonging to the congregations. Since those with faith are sons, God has sent the Spirit of his Son into their hearts crying, 'Abba! Father!' (4.6). The notion of flesh, on the other hand, can have the neutral meaning of 'a human being' (as at Gal. 1.16;

2.16), but can also refer to the zone of our (generally defective) human nature as opposed to other, more desirable zones (2.20; 4.13, 14).

THE ALLEGORY OF HAGAR AND SARAH (GAL. 4.21–31)

C. K. Barrett (1982) has made a helpful contribution to explaining the function and meaning of the allegory of Hagar and Sarah in Gal. 4.21–31. Barrett's central idea is that Paul is responding to a case from Israelite scripture put against his version of the gospel in Galatia and that Gal. 4.21–31 forms one part of this response. Within this view, Paul's opponents have summoned a number of biblical passages in support of their position and Paul has been forced to meet them with scriptural arguments of his own. Thus, Barrett suggests, Paul had to rebut contentions to the effect that Gen. 15.6 referred to Abraham's faithfulness in the sense of what he did (or would do, such as offering to sacrifice Isaac)[2] rather than to the gratuitous attribution of righteousness; that only if the gentiles were circumcised could they qualify as Abraham's seed (Gen. 12.7; 13.15; 17.7; 22.18; 24.7); that those who did not observe the law were cursed (Deut. 27.26); and, most relevant to Gal. 4.21–31, that the circumcised were the descendants of Abraham's free-born wife Sarah through her son Isaac, but the gentiles were the descendants of his slave-girl Hagar through her son Ishmael. These were plausible interpretations and we have seen in Chapters 6 and 7 how hard Paul had to struggle to redirect the first two of them against his opponents.

As for the story of Hagar and Sarah, Barrett is right to note that the advocates of circumcision were giving the text of Genesis its straight-forward, literal meaning, the *peshat* of later interpretation (as more recently explained by Brewer 1992: 14). Sarah's male line were circumcised (Gen. 17.9–14) and were blessed (Gen. 17.16–19), while Hagar's were gentiles and were expelled from the family of Abraham at Sarah's instigation:

> Then she said to Abraham, 'Cast out this servant woman [*paidiskē*] and her son, for the son of this servant woman shall not inherit [*klēronomēsei*] with my son Isaac'.
>
> (Gen. 21.10)

Sarah recognises that an inheritance, like every good in Mediterranean culture, is finite and she does not want it to be divided between her son and Hagar's. Abraham is reluctant to consent to Sarah's proposal but does so on God's direction on the basis that through Isaac will his seed (*sperma*) be named (Gen. 21.11–12) and for the additional reason that Hagar's son will become a great nation (Gen. 21.13). At face value, then, the respective destinies of Sarah and Hagar sharply highlighted the benefits of being circumcised and joining the descendants of Abraham through Sarah. Given the attraction that things Israelite held for Paul's Galatian gentiles, we may fairly safely assume that those proposing circumcision would have cited such strong scriptural corroboration of their case.

It is worthwhile, however, considering these passages from the perspective of social identity theory. On the lips of Paul's rivals they represent an unambiguous attempt at stereotyping. Scripture provided powerful warrant for the differentiation of all human beings into two categories, Israelites and gentiles, the descendants, respectively, of Sarah/Isaac and Hagar/Ishmael. Not surprisingly, these stereotypes are positive for the ingroup and negative for the outgroup, especially to the extent that the inheritance – at Sarah's urging and upon God's determination – goes to the former and not the latter. As noted in Chapter 2, ethnocentrism of this sort, the pronounced enhancement of stereotypic differences, flourishes where the boundaries between groups are becoming threatened and ambiguous. The mixed table-fellowship of the Pauline congregations had produced this insecurity and the powerful assertion of ingroup/outgroup differentiation using scriptural warrant was an expected result.

But as far as Paul was concerned, sauce for the goose was sauce for the gander. For he, too, faced the problem that the boundaries of his congregations were being eroded, with the threat of some or all of his gentile converts moving across to Israel. His response was to engage in much the same process of stereotyping as his opponents. In terms of the model of intergroup comparison set out in Chapter 2, his use of the story of Sarah and Hagar constitutes an example of 'social change', the production of a positive evaluation of the ingroup in relation to a dominant or at least powerful outgroup. More particularly, he was engaged either in 'social competition', if there was a prospect of a real change in the actual state of affairs between the two groups, or in 'social creativity', if there was no such prospect. In the latter case, although he may not have been able to achieve an actual change in the social position of his congregations, he was in a position to redefine the nature of the comparison so that the story of Sarah and Hagar, which formerly had been regarded as a weakness for his congregations, now emerged as a strength. By fixing upon its hidden meaning, or *derash* (Brewer 1992: 14), which he refers to as allegory (Gal. 4.24a), Paul reinterprets it to produce the exact antithesis of the rival view, so that the gentiles are really the descendants of Sarah, while the Israelites are descended from Hagar, with the fate of each group replicating that of their biblical ancestors.

He sets out to turn the story against his opponents with great relish (Gal. 4.21). His opening gambit is very subtle: 'For it stands written that Abraham had two sons, one from a servant woman [*paidiskē*] and one from a free woman [*eleuthera*]' (4.22). Here Paul sets up a sharp contrast between Hagar and Sarah on the basis of their respective servile and free status. Yet this differentiation derives more from his need to establish a stereotyped antithesis which he can relate to the situation in Galatia than to the text of Genesis. Although Hagar is referred to in Genesis as a *paidiskē* on a number of occasions (Gen. 16.1, 2, 3, 5, 6, 8; 21.10 [twice], 12, 13), the word (a diminutive form of *pais*, meaning child) means a servant-woman without the same stress on servile status which would be conveyed by the word 'slave' (*doulē*) or by using a related verb in relation to her, neither of which are ever applied to Hagar.[3] Furthermore, while Paul's use of *eleuthera* in contrast to *paidiskē* inevitably strengthens the association of the latter with servile status, the word *eleuthera* is never used of Sarah. The contrast in Genesis is more between Sarah as wife (*gynē*, Gen. 11.29; 12.5; 16.1, 3; 17.15) and Hagar as servant (*paidiskē*), than between the former as free and the latter as servile. The clearest sign of Paul thus altering the emphasis in the biblical story comes when he quotes Gen. 21.9 in Gal. 4.29 but replaces 'my son Isaac' with 'the son of the free woman'.

Although the distinction between free and slave was certainly prominent as part of the social realities in Galatia (Gal. 3.28), Paul is concerned with the freedom and slavery which he has already begun to develop earlier in the letter, namely, the freedom associated with his gospel (2.4) and the slavery which his opponents seek to impose upon his gentile converts or which derives from worship of pagan gods (2.4; 4.1, 3, 7, 8, 9). In Gal. 4.22 Paul cleverly starts to push the Genesis story away from its natural interpretation and towards the stereotypical differentiation of ingroup and outgroup which lies at the heart of his strategy in the letter.

In v. 23 he develops this line by repeating his designations of Hagar and Sarah as servant woman and free woman respectively and by stating that Hagar's son was born 'according to flesh' (*kata sarka*) and Sarah's 'through promise' (*di' epagellias*). Although the distinction Paul draws between Ishmael and Isaac is not an unreasonable interpretation of events in Genesis, it is not explicitly made in the biblical text. Abraham's initial problem is that he is childless and that the son of one of his servant women will inherit (Gen. 15.2–3).[4] But God reassures him that this will not happen and that 'one who shall come out of you shall be your heir' (Gen. 15.4). From Abraham's perspective this divine promise (although the word 'promise' [*epagellia*] is not used here or anywhere in Genesis) was initially fulfilled with the birth of his son Ishmael to Hagar (Gen. 16.15). Nevertheless, the promise which Paul has in mind comes when God tells Abraham that he will bless Sarah and give her a son to be called Isaac with whom he will establish a covenant (Gen. 17.16–19), not with Ishmael (Gen. 17.20–21). No such specific promise, identifying by name the one who would be born, was made in relation to Ishmael. Ishmael was simply born (Gen. 16.15), 'in the ordinary course of nature' (Bruce 1982c: 217). This is the justification for Paul's distinguishing between Isaac's birth 'through promise' and Ishmael's birth 'according to flesh'. His reason for explicitly drawing a distinction not made in Genesis is to lay the foundation for connecting the Hagar and Sarah story to his picture of affairs in Galatia as he has already delineated it, with the members of his congregations being heirs of the promise made to Abraham through the gift of the Spirit (3.14; 4.6–7), while those who succumb to circumcision enter the realm of the flesh: 'Are you so foolish, that having begun in Spirit, you are now finishing in flesh [*sarx*]?' (3.3).

Although in 4.22–23 Paul carefully interprets the Genesis account in a way which admirably serves his purpose, there is nothing in these verses themselves with which his opponents in Galatia would have necessarily disagreed. The moment of divergence arrives in Gal. 4.24 with the assertion that 'these matters' (stated in 4.22–23)

> are to be interpreted allegorically [*allēgoroumena*], for these [women] are two covenants, one from Mount Sinai, giving birth into slavery, which is Hagar.
> 4.25 Now Hagar is Mount Sinai in Arabia, but it corresponds to the present day Jerusalem, for she is in slavery with her children.
> 4.26 But the Jerusalem above, which is our mother, is free.

By opting for an allegorical interpretation, Paul suggests that the true meaning of the text is not that found on its surface, but is actually a deeper or hidden one, with the word *allēgoreuō* coming from *allo* and *agoreuō*, meaning 'say something else'. This is the only time it occurs in early Christian literature (Betz 1979: 243), although allegorical interpretation was practised by Israelite authors roughly contemporary with Paul, such as Philo of Alexandria. As already noted, later rabbinic interpretation referred to non-literal biblical interpretation as *derash*. Yet the mere fact that *derash* interpretation existed in the first century CE does little to attenuate the boldness of Paul's interpretation. He is seriously maintaining that the real meaning of the Hagar and Sarah story is exactly the reverse of that maintained by the opponents. Sarah the free woman is actually aligned with his ingroup and the slave Hagar with the outgroup. The basis for his interpretation is the earlier argument that the imposition of the Mosaic law was slavery while adherence to his gospel meant freedom. Within the framework of social identity theory, we see here a fine example of an attempt to reverse the relative position of the ingroup and outgroup on a salient dimension (Tajfel and Turner 1979: 44). It is reasonable to assume that, in a conflict-ridden culture like that of the ancient Mediterranean, representatives of the Israelite outgroup who came to hear of this interpretation and the disenfranchisement from their ancestry which it involved would have angrily rejected it.

Paul does, however, seek to offer scriptural support for his audacious exegesis in the form of a verbatim quotation from Isa. 54.1, where the reference to a barren woman justifies a link to the barren Sarah, a type of Israelite interpretation known from the first century and referred to as *gezerah shavah*, a comparison of similar words (Barrett 1982: 164):

> For it is written,
> 'Rejoice, O barren one who does not bear;
> break forth and shout, you who are not in travail;
> for the children of the desolate one are many more
> than the children of her that is married'.
>
> (Gal. 4.27; RSV)

Even though this verse was useful in summoning forth a vision of the success of the mission among the gentiles previously mentioned by Paul (Gal. 2.7–9), it is unclear that it is 'highly appropriate' (Dunn 1993: 255). Once a connection is granted to Sarah, it could just as easily be cited by Paul's opponents; it provides no help at all in establishing a connection between Sarah and Paul's congregations rather than with the rival gospel on offer in Galatia. Moreover, the quotation is inapt in relation to Sarah since Isaiah is celebrating a woman who lacks a husband and in the Genesis story that is the position of Hagar, not Sarah.

In the next verse Paul expressly connects his audience with the descendants of Sarah: 'But you, brothers, are children of promise, like Isaac' (4.28). Once again, he depends on the fact that he has previously established their status as heirs of the promise to create a link with Isaac who was also the child of a promise. Paul is invoking the positive social identity which will flow from his congregations' identification with Isaac (in a manner consonant with Tajfel's theory), rather than doing much to strengthen the scriptural case he is making. His next step, however, is even less convincing exegetically:

> 4.29 But just as in those days he who was born according to flesh persecuted him born according to Spirit, so it is also the case now.
> 4.30 But what does scripture say? 'Drive out the servant woman and her son; for the son of the servant woman will not inherit with the son of the free woman.'

In Gal. 4.29 Paul alters the terms of comparison somewhat by speaking of Isaac as born according to Spirit, rather than the phrase 'according to promise' which we might have expected in view of the flesh/promise contrast which has figured in the allegory up to this point. Again, he is able to take this step because of the relationship he has previously established between Spirit and promise, especially in 3.14. In relation to Gal. 4.29, however, one looks in vain in the Old Testament for any indication that Ishmael persecuted Isaac, although there are statements in subsequent rabbinic tradition that he did, apparently based on a hostile reading of the statement at Gen. 21.9 that Sarah saw Ishmael playing (the Septuagint adds, 'with Isaac'). In fact, it was Sarah who had been the persecutor, initially afflicting Hagar to such an extent when she was pregnant with Ishmael that she fled to the wilderness (Gen. 16.6–7) and ultimately persuading Abraham to drive Hagar and her son away for good (Gen. 21.10–14). But Paul's interpretation of Ishmael as persecutor allowed him to make a very pointed connection with his own situation, which to his view was characterised by various types of Judaic persecution (Gal. 1.13, 23; 5.11; 6.12).

Paul's response to the persecution in v. 30, quoting Gen. 21.10 with the alteration noted previously whereby 'the son of the free woman' replaces 'my son Isaac' so as to foreground the slave/free dichotomy not obvious in the source, evidences yet again his interest in bringing about the exact reverse of what his audience have hitherto been told. Whereas those urging circumcision are seeking to exclude (*ekkleisai*, 4.17) those who will not accept circumcision, just as in the past Peter and the Israelite Christ-followers in Antioch barred the gentiles from table-fellowship, so now Paul informs his readers that the tables will be turned on his opponents and they will not inherit. In a world of limited and indivisible goods, only one group can come into the inheritance and it will comprise those who stick to Paul's gospel.[5]

Paul concludes this section of the letter as follows:

> Therefore, brothers, we are not children of the servant woman but of

the free woman. For freedom Christ has set us free. Therefore stand firm and do not again be loaded down with the yoke of slavery.

(Gal.4.31–5.1)

By means of his reinterpretation of the story of Hagar and Sarah, Paul has furthered his aim of establishing a very positive identity for his congregations which ties them ever more closely to freedom, promise and Spirit, while the outgroup are consigned to slavery and flesh. By this means, should the members of his congregations ask, 'Who are we?', they are enabled to reply with a repertoire of most attractive group designations which differentiate them from an outgroup which is negatively characterised as experiencing the wretched antithesis of these features. Within the theory of social identity, Paul's achievement emerges as a pervasive and effective exercise in social stereotyping taking a particular profile from its context in Mediterranean culture.

LIFE IN THE HOUSEHOLD OF FAITH: GAL. 5.13–6.10[6]

Existing approaches to the puzzle of Gal. 5.13–6.10

The very existence of 5.13–6.10 in Galatians has long been regarded by New Testament critics as posing a real conundrum for understanding the letter. Put simply, the issue has been posed like this: why, in a letter which deals mainly with a problem originating in the external environment, the pressure on the members to be circumcised and become Israelites, does Paul now focus his attention on an issue internal to his congregations, the qualities, values and behaviour which should characterise the lives of the Christ-followers, especially in their dealings with one another? More specifically, does not Paul, having previously attacked the relevance of the law for the attainment of righteousness, now virtually contradict himself by the establishment of a different form of nomism?

There is a wide range of positions on this question, with commentators falling into two camps, those who think that 5.13–6.10 is not well integrated into the letter as a whole, on the one hand, and those who consider it is, on the other. The scholar most sensitive to the difficulties of relating 5.13–6.10 is John O'Neill, who regards the passage as a later interpolation (1972). Dibelius argued that the passage was by Paul but was poorly integrated into the overall argument to the extent that it did not represent the apostle's own ethics but rather an early Christian tradition of moral exhortation (1934: 238–239; 1976; 1–11). Burton regarded it as an apologetic appendix aimed at reassuring those who might be misled into thinking that Paul's opposition to the law meant the end of all restraints on human wickedness (1921: 290). Another approach, represented by Lütgert (1919) and Ropes (1929), was to suggest that Paul actually had two distinct problems to deal with in Galatia, legalists who advocated the imposition of the Mosaic law, who are answered in the bulk of the letter, and spiritualistic radicals whose freedom from the law had led to the looseness which flows from anti-nomism.

Those who consider that 5.13–6.10 is integrated into the letter as a whole also encompass a variety of positions. Schmithals (1972) argued that Paul's opponents in Galatia were Israelite gnostics who advocated circumcision but were libertines in the area of morality. Betz (1979: 8–9, 195–196, 273–274) has proposed that one factor attracting the Galatians to the law was the strictures it placed on immoral behaviour and that once Paul had disposed of the law he needed to come up with some other means of dealing with immorality. Howard (1979: 11–14) sees Paul continuing his attack on the law in this passage since he has his sights set precisely on the condition of being under flesh which is the product of subjection to the law (cf. Gal. 3.3). Barclay has argued that Paul actually faced a dual crisis in Galatia which encompassed the distinct though inseparable issues of identity and behaviour and that Paul was forced to address both of them through his treatment of the law-free gospel and the moral life; within this view, those who are led by the Spirit actually fulfil the law (1988: 73). Although Barclay's approach, especially through his interest in identity, is the closest among current scholarship to the position I will outline below, the social-scientific theories I employ and the distinctive exegetical results I reach lead to a different interpretation.

Group boundaries and internal conditions

From an anthropological perspective, the controversy in Pauline scholarship concerning how Paul could discuss in the one text both a problem relating to the external boundaries of his congregations, that is, the relationship of the membership with the Israelite *ethnos*, and their internal life and characteristics is misconceived. Anthropological research suggests that there is a close relationship between the position of a group with respect to outsiders and its internal conditions. The status of individuals who have recently crossed a boundary to join a group which exists in an uneasy relationship with other competing groups in the local environment is often awkward and troubled and this is likely to be reflected in tensions among the membership, such as those with which Paul is concerned in Gal. 5.13–6.10. The relationship between the outer limits of community and its inner dynamics has been admirably described by Anthony Cohen, professor of social anthropology at Edinburgh University. Inspired by Arnold van Gennep's explanation of ritual as a three-stage process involving the separation from an original group or status, an in-between or 'liminal' phase and a reaggregation into a new group or status (1960), Cohen casts doubt on the idea that the confusion characteristic of liminality, the troubling sense of being 'betwixt and between', terminates as soon as one becomes reaggregated:

> Transformations of status, like crossing geopolitical borders, require a process of readjustment, of rethinking . . . They require a reformulation of self which is more fundamental than admission to items of lore, or being loaded with new rights and obligations. The difficulties inherent in such self-adjustment may vary according to the nature of frontiers which are crossed; but our experience of politics and travel should also alert us to the deceptively innocuous character of crossing between supposedly proximate statuses or cultures . .
> Having crossed a boundary, we have to think ourselves into our transformed identity which is far more subtle, far more individualised than its predication on status.
>
> (Cohen 1993: 10, also see Cohen 1994: 128)

Within this perspective, not only is it mistaken to draw a sharp distinction between the outer and the inner aspects of community, at least where its origins lie in the recent past, but also the incorporation of members depends more upon their developing a distinctive identity than on simply acquiring a new status or a different set of ethical norms, even though these latter factors are conditions precedent to the process of transformation. Such an insight offers a way of examining the material in Gal. 5.13–6.10, which includes the significance of the status acquired by crossing the boundaries into the Pauline congregations, and has room for the notion of ethical norms, but incorporated as aspects of a much larger reality called identity. Moreover, this stress on identity dovetails with the treatment of social identity developed by social psychologists like Henri Tajfel which has been employed extensively already in this reading and which offers a detailed model for the creation of identity in situations of intergroup conflict. On the other hand, the fact that existing Pauline scholarship largely treats the passage under the rubric of 'ethics' or 'paraenesis' indicates the limitations placed upon biblical exegesis by

the use of agendas drawn from theology or moral philosophy in preference to more inclusive approaches available from the social sciences.
The discussion of social identity theory in Chapter 2 and its application with help from Fredrik Barth's analysis of the nature of boundary
creation in an ethnic context in Chapter 3 will be presupposed and
utilised in the discussion of Gal. 5.13–6.10 which follows. Before proceeding to this, however, it is necessary to establish a context in both
Mediterranean culture and in some specific Graeco-Roman authors for
a theme of great importance in this section of the text, that of family
honour,[7] since I will propose that Paul employs imagery of family and
household in this passage as a way of giving substance to the distinct
identity with which he wants to characterise the members of his congregations. There is a steadily growing literature on family life in the ancient
Mediterranean,[8] while the context, nature and dynamics of early Christian families are considered in an important collection of essays recently
edited by Halvor Moxnes (1997a).

Family honour in Mediterranean culture

An anthropological perspective

The centrality of honour as the primary social value in the Mediterranean region has already figured in the argument elsewhere in this
reading. It is equally fundamental to gaining some notion of what first-
century Galatians would have understood by 'family' and 'household'. If
we do not consciously make the effort to understand this, we run the risk
of anachronistically and ethnocentrically imposing modern North
Atlantic notions of family onto the ancient data, a problem insufficiently
appreciated by many critics writing on early Christian families.[9] The best
model of Mediterranean culture is that of Bruce Malina (1993) and this
will be utilised in what follows, supplemented with specific data from
Graeco-Roman literature.[10]

Honour means a claim to worth made by an individual or group
together with the public acknowledgment of the truth of that claim.
Honour resides in proper behaviour or demeanour in public. It is either
ascribed, such as through noble birth or by being attached to positions of
eminence in family, village, association, city or nation, or may also be
acquired, through the process of challenge-and-response, which was
considered in some detail in Chapter 5 in connection with Paul's dealings with the community in Jerusalem. As a rule, challenges are not
issued to one's kin, since the shame attendant on such an affront to the

cohesion and hence honour of the family of which the challenger is a member would more than outweigh any honour gained by the exchange.

However it is obtained, honour can be lost, being replaced with shame. Since this is a limited good society, with only a finite amount of honour in any situation, an accretion of honour to one person means the public shaming of his (or, very rarely, her)[11] rival. The fact that honour can be bestowed or taken away in virtually any form of social interaction is the main reason why this was (and is) such a fiercely agonistic culture. Those who are unsuccessful in social contests tend to develop an extremely negative attitude towards the winners, quite outside the experience of those of us situated in the North Atlantic cultural zone, which is manifested in envy (*phthonos*; *invidia*) and the evil eye, a power to injure discharged by someone envious of another. This aspect of Malina's model has been well amplified by John H. Elliott (1988, 1990b, 1991, 1992, 1994). The pattern appears clearly in 1 Sam. 18.6–11 when the women praise the performance of David as slayer of foes in comparison with Saul's efforts, so that the king responds – in the expected way – with envy, manifested in the evil eye, and a desire for revenge.

We have seen earlier in this reading that Mediterranean society is far more group-oriented than North Atlantic cultures or their ex-colonial offshoots. Personal development and fulfilment, and the achievement of an honorable position in society, are closely tied to belonging to certain groups, rather than to the exercise of individual aspirations. The most important group of all is the family. The notion of family honour is one of the most important and pervasive features of Mediterranean culture. While fierce competition for honour may be the order of the day outside the family, within its ranks everyone is expected to work to maintain its collective honour. Malina explains it as follows

> Honor is always presumed to exist within one's own family of blood, that is among all those one has as blood relatives. Outside that circle all persons are presumed to be dishonorable, guilty, if you will, unless proved otherwise. It is with all these others that one must play the game, engage in the contest, put one's honor and one's family honor on the line.
>
> (Malina 1993: 38)

In consequence of this state of affairs, honour gained, or shame suffered, by one member accrues to the family as a whole. If a son acts violently or extravagantly in public, or a father is disobeyed by a family member, or a daughter seduced before marriage, the whole family will be dishonoured. The need to preserve the collective honour of the family means that anything which interferes with the presentation of a united front to a highly critical public will be a cause of shame. Yet even in the Mediterranean family conflicts occur and we need to assess how they might be viewed. Malina helpfully distinguishes three degrees of events whereby individuals or groups might be dishonoured:

1 the gross dishonour occasioned by murder, kidnap or adultery, which must be repaid by vengeance since the complete restoration of the previous situation is impossible;
2 significant attacks on honour which yet allow of some revocation, as by the restitution of stolen items or an apology for a verbal insult;
3 everyday social interactions which simply require a manageable response, as with a return dinner invitation extended to someone who has previously been one's host.

If we apply these categories to the family, it is clear that the first type of dishonour will be viewed as sacrilegious. Murder of a father is not just homicide but patricide, of a brother, fratricide, and such acts are thought to constitute an assault on the very structure of reality (Malina 1993: 46–47). But even events of the second type, such as where brothers are publicly in contest in sport or politics or trade, will have a heavy impact on family honour.

Greek and Roman examples of family honour and dishonour

There is no shortage of emic data which could be summoned to illustrate the usefulness of this model in the ancient Graeco-Roman world. To keep the discussion within a reasonable compass, however, I will refer briefly to three texts, the *Seven Against Thebes* by Aeschylus, the *Adelphoe* by Terence, and the treatise *On Brotherly Love (Peri Philadelphias)* by Plutarch.

Aeschylus' *Seven Against Thebes*, first performed in Athens in 467 BCE, reflects dissension between brothers corresponding to the first type of dishonour, since it culminates in mutual fratricide. Eteocles and Polyneices are the two sons of the now dead Oedipus. They are in serious dispute, for Eteocles has seized power in Thebes for himself and this has induced Polyneices to gather six other champions and an army to attack the city. At one point, one of these other champions rebukes Polyneices for seeking to destroy his father's city and his native gods in a way which richly reveals how sensitive he is to the disorder inherent in brother seeking to supplant brother (580–589). The horror of one brother killing another is the subject of an exchange between Eteocles and the chorus (690–720) and when the brothers have killed one another the chorus comments:

When men die by a kinsman's hand,
When brother is murdered by brother,
And the dust of the earth drinks in
The crimson blood that blackens and dries,
Who then can provide cleansing?
Who can wash it away?
O house, whose guilty agonies,
The old vintage and the new, mingle together!
              (*Seven Against Thebes* 735–742; ET by Vellacott 1961: 110)

Our second text, Terence's *Adelphoe*, was first performed in Rome in 160 BCE, although based on an original by Menander written a century earlier. Its successful adaptation for a Roman audience indicates that the stock morals and other cultural features upon which it draws were common across large stretches of the Mediterranean area. The plot, too complicated to be summarised here, revolves around two elderly brothers, the town-dwelling and easy-going Demea (*senex lepidus*) and the rustic and strict Micio (*senex durus*), and their sons, Ctesipho and Aeschines, who cause their fathers a great deal of trouble, each in the pursuit of the women upon whom their hearts are set. In the end, both the young men are united with their women, but the issue of family honour is prominent in the comic processes which lead to that result. Demea comes across almost as a mouthpiece for the importance of family honour in the Malina model. Although his views are comically subverted throughout the play, they triumph in the end. Demea and others continually complain or assert that the actions of Aeschines, including an apparent kidnap, are a cause of shame to the family (*pudor*: 84, 457–459, 485, 489, 504) or even comprise *grievously* shameful acts (*flagitia*: 100–112, 407–409). A slave in the family of a pregnant woman who has seemingly been abandoned by Aeschines gives voice to the view that all of the members (himself included) have suffered disgrace (*infamia*) as a result (303). The extent to which the actions of some family members can bring a whole family into disrepute is one of the cultural themes expressed in the play. It represents abundant proof of the usefulness of Malina's model for both Greece and Rome.

Plutarch's *Peri Philadelphias* was written in the first century CE and is a compilation of much stock morality from both Greece and Rome on how brothers should treat one another. Plutarch is concerned with the fact that in his day brotherly hatred is actually more common than brotherly love (478c) and sets out to offer careful advice on how and why such love might be fostered.

Although Plutarch does not treat at length the idea central to Malina's treatment that brotherly love should be encouraged in order to preserve family honour, it is occasionally mentioned and may be argued to underlie the discussion. The importance of family honour appears, for example, when Plutarch quotes Sophocles to the effect that the relationship between brothers 'is yoked in honour's bonds not forged by man' (*aidous achalkeutoisin ezeuktai pedais*: 482a; ET by Helmbold 1939: 269), and when he notes that strife between brothers is like disharmony among the limbs of an animal which lead to its most shameful end (479a). Similarly, honour is owed by children to parents (479d) and by brother to brother (479f). Many statements in *Peri Philadelphias* have a direct bearing on Galatians and these will be mentioned later where relevant. The broader subject of brotherhood in Plutarch and Paul has recently been helpfully considered by Reidar Aasgaard (Moxnes 1997a: 166–182).

A reading of Gal. 5.13–6.10

I have already observed in Chapter 6 that the language of righteousness plays no part in Paul's presentation of life in the community in 5.13–6.10, which we are now about to consider. This is an indication of the dangers that righteousness posed for him by reason of its origins in, and natural connections with, the Mosaic law – against the imposition of which Paul so desired to defend his congregations. We have seen in Chapter 6 how Paul separates righteousness from its Israelite home to establish it as a way of describing the identity of those who had faith in Jesus Christ. And yet this left the question of how life within the congregations might be ordered; in particular, how might their identity be further developed in ways which would suggest normative behaviour of a sort appropriate to the new dispensation? Paul gives us his answer to this problem in Gal. 5.13–6.10.

Gal. 5.13–15

Paul's statement at 5.13a comes as no surprise, 'You were called for freedom, brothers!', since one of his main aims in the allegory of Hagar and Sarah was to prove that his congregations had an identity characterised by the freedom – associated with promise and Spirit – which derives from Sarah in contrast to the slavery – associated with flesh – which issues from Hagar. He had encapsulated this message in 5.1: 'For freedom Christ has set us free. Therefore stand firm and do not again be loaded down with the yoke of slavery'. But the remainder of 5.13 is quite remarkable: 'Only not the freedom which is an opportunity for the flesh, but be enslaved to one another through love'. While at a general level Paul is delivering the paradoxical message that freedom actually involves a form of slavery, a number of factors related to the position of this statement in its context make it even more provocative and arresting.

First of all, we now learn something we have hitherto not had any cause to suspect, namely, that there are two types of freedom, typically stereotyped as absolutely good and absolutely bad. Whereas when Paul was speaking of freedom in its capacity to distinguish his congregations from the Israelite alternative, such a qualification was unnecessary, the dual nature of freedom now becomes a very live issue as far as intragroup existence is concerned.

Second, the dark side of freedom at this level is so stamped by its connection with the flesh, even though in Gal. 4.21–5.1 this forms one of the set of realities which represent the stark antithesis of freedom in the context of intergroup comparison. Paul is shocking his audience with the suggestion that if they abuse the freedom which, *inter alia*, serves to distinguish them from the dominant outgroup, they actually risk subjecting themselves to one of the worst features which characterise those outsiders – their immersion in the flesh. Paul is not saying that the Mosaic law and the flesh are exactly coincident; rather, he suggests that the law ensnares its adherents in the wider reality of the flesh which also encompasses theological and social distortions outside the House of Israel. Thus, when he comes in a moment (5.16–26) to set out two contrasting modes of existence and behaviour, the flesh will serve to designate the pole to be avoided and one of the elements of the flesh itemised will be idolatry, a characteristic of pagans not Israelites. Generally speaking, Paul's acknowledgment of the potential for freedom to be abused in this way illustrates Anthony Cohen's insight that the process of boundary crossing is not easily effected and that the experience of liminality, of being betwixt and between, may persist for some time. Merely joining a community differentiated by freedom is not the end of the story, since we need to work ourselves into our transformed identity and to Paul's mind that involves recognising the rival possibilities which freedom offers and choosing the good over the bad.

The third remarkable factor in 5.13b is the way in which Paul describes the desirable sort of freedom, as mutual slavery through love (*di' agapēs*). Once again, although he has previously presented slavery as a condition which at the level of intergroup differentiation and boundary delineation characterises the outgroups, he now employs the same word in connection with conditions within the congregations. Sharpening the paradox, moreover, is the fact that the notion of mutual slavery, of being enslaved to one another, is a very odd one, since the institution elsewhere presupposed a strongly hierarchical and unequal status where the slave was totally in the power of his or her master. Thus Paul boldly employs the concept while at the same time subverting one of its central aspects. Nor should we forget that he mentioned *agapē* only a little earlier as the means whereby faith becomes active (5.6).

A significant feature of Gal. 5.13 as a whole merits close attention. While the verse presents *in nuce* the contents of 5.13–6.10, the description of his addressees as brothers (*adelphoi*) constitutes the first in a sequence of explicit and implicit fictive kinship references in the passage which will culminate in 'the house-members of the faith' at 6.10. Prior to 5.13, Paul has been concerned to introduce a large amount of family imagery in order to establish a particular type of identity for his congregations in relation to outgroups. Thus, there are six instances of *adelphoi* (which can be translated – somewhat archaically – as 'brethren' to bring out the inclusion of women in the congregations implied at 3.28) in relation to the believers in Galatia before 5.13. In addition, they experience God as Father (1.1, 3, 4). This horizontal relationship as fictive siblings is reinforced by a rich array of material connected with their shared sonship to various 'fathers'. They are all sons of God through faith in Christ Jesus (3.26) and through Him they have become God's adopted sons (4.1–7), vividly expressed in 4.6: 'Because you are sons, God has sent out the Spirit of his Son into your hearts crying "Abba", that is "Father"'.

But also, through Christ, the seed of Abraham (3.16), they are sons (3.7) and seed of Abraham (3.29) and children of the promise made to Sarah (4.21–31), who is their mother (4.31). Lastly, they are Paul's own 'children' (4.19–20). All of this imagery making them members of one family plays upon the role of that institution as the most significant in Mediterranean culture and the most important contributor to social identity. Yet, as we have just seen, mere membership of a family, which Tajfel categorises as the 'cognitive' component of group-belonging, was not the end of the story. Ancient Mediterranean people also needed their family to be an honourable one, so that they could have a very positive regard for it (the evaluative dimension), and be confident they gained honour by membership, in contrast to other families on the local scene who were negatively perceived (the emotional dimension). This meant that members had to work together harmoniously, since intrafamilial dissension was regarded as seriously besmirching family honour, as we have just seen in relation to certain Greek and Roman texts. Just as in

5.13 Paul advances from treating freedom solely as an identity-descriptor to raise the antithetical forces it represents as far as intracommunity experience is concerned, so too does he begin to consider the character of life within the congregation. Brothers should not be free towards one another in the way of the flesh, but should be mutually enslaved to one another in *agapē*, with the latter part reinforcing the domestic context since most slaves worked within families in domestic settings (Bartchy 1992: 68). He is advocating a reciprocal love relationship among the members. Earlier in his career, Paul had identified the notion of loving one another (*to agapan allēllous*) with brotherly love (*philadelphia*) as if the point needed no further explanation (1 Thess. 4.9).

I have already considered the meaning in 5.14 in Chapter 7, concluding that to say the whole law is fulfilled in one saying, 'You will love your neighbour as yourself', did not mean that the ethical part of the Mosaic law was still relevant for the congregations, but that through love, which was the first gift of the Spirit (5.22), law-free Christ-followers had access by a different route to the best which the law could provide. Nevertheless, the collocation of vv. 13 and 14 does suggest that his gentile converts were facing claims in Galatia that the law of Moses offered a collection of ethical norms to guide and regulate behaviour. Paul needs to counter this argument by establishing an alternative path to the moral life, although he does so within and as an aspect of his overall concern with identity.

Gal. 5.15 has much the same shock value as Luke's sudden reference to strife within the early Jerusalem church in Acts 6.1: 'But if you bite and devour one another take heed that you are not consumed by one another'. This is the first intimation we have had of disorder internal to the congregations, which Paul equates with the savagery of wild animals. Some commentators are loath to reach the view that Paul is describing actual conduct in the congregations, especially since his language here is typical of diatribal style (Betz 1979: 276–277; Dunn 1993: 293). While the danger may only be a potential one, the argument from style is not strong, since if Paul was faced with dissension of this type it would have been quite natural for him to use diatribal language to stigmatise it. On the other hand, Anthony Cohen's argument about the persistence of liminality among persons once they have crossed a boundary to join a new group raises the prospect that the members of the congregations had not yet internalised the values expected of them and continued to treat one another in the fiercely competitive way typical of unrelated persons in this culture. We should expect the process of acquiring a new identity to be a very difficult one. Gal. 5.15 is really a generalised summary of the works of the flesh listed in 5.19–21 which, as we shall soon observe, are inimical to intracommunity life and lead to forfeiture of the Kingdom of God, as Paul had previously warned them (5.21), and it would be odd indeed if the Galatian congregations were not experiencing at least some of these pathologies; exactly this, in fact, is suggested at 6.1. Accordingly, we are probably on firmer ground if we see 5.15 as reflecting actual not just potential behaviour. In a context where Paul is writing to communities of whom he has received the disturbing news that they are transferring their allegiance to a different gospel (1.6–7), the abrupt transition to internal strife at 5.15 reads rather like his dispirited response to another element in the situation in Galatia, another feature of the exigence of this communication. At the same time, the nature of his remark has a connection to the issue of kinship raised in 5.13, because of the striking contrast between the ideal in that verse and the reality expressed at Gal. 5.15. Plutarch raises the hostility of wild animals towards one another in search of food as an example of the behaviour which brothers should avoid (*Peri Philadelphias*, 486b). While the actions criticised in 5.15 no doubt represent the world of the flesh, they also illustrate precisely the opposite of the behaviour which family members should manifest towards one another.

Nevertheless, Paul has to be careful, and his success in this regard is reflected in the views of critics who see only potential wrongdoing in this section. For Paul is suitably reticent about directly accusing the Galatians of any specific wrongs, probably because this would come dangerously close to an admission of 'sinfulness' (*hamartia*) in the congregations which, as we argued earlier (in Chapter 6 of this reading), he disavowed at 2.17.

Perhaps, indeed, the advocates of circumcision were actually pointing to internal conflict as a good reason for taking on the Mosaic law, with its extensive set of moral norms. If so, Paul does recognise that the law contains ethical norms, even if they have proved ineffective in stemming sin, while insisting both that his congregations have access to love, the fulfilment of the law, via an entirely different route, the Spirit, and that the trouble-makers do not keep the law anyway (6.13).

Gal. 5.16–26

In Gal. 5.16 Paul further develops the contrast between the possibilities inherent in freedom, which he introduced in 5.13: 'But I say, walk by the Spirit and you will certainly not carry out [*telesēte*]¹² the desire of the flesh'. He adds in 5.17 that the Spirit and the flesh are locked in continual conflict, with the result that 'you cannot do what you want'. Paul will go on in 5.19–23 to set out in detail two lists of antithetically opposed features, one of which relates to the conflict-ridden behaviour between unrelated males in this culture and the other to a family operating in peace and amity. It is worth noting that, in context, the lists are related to the two sons of Abraham mentioned at 4.21–31, Isaac and Ishmael, who represent absolute opposites.

Although in 5.13 the flesh was opposed to freedom and not the Spirit, since Paul has just closely intertwined freedom and the Spirit in the allegory of Hagar and Sarah (4.21–31), we are justified in regarding the treatment of this antithesis in 5.16–26, beginning at 5.16, as an expansion of the theme announced in 5.13. At the same time, Paul introduces a number of echoes of the earlier thread of the rhetoric. The most significant one is to 3.3: 'Are you so stupid that having begun in Spirit [*enarxanemoi pneumati*] you are now being completed in flesh [*sarki epiteleisthe*]?' The same juxtaposition of Spirit and flesh is strengthened by the fact that a form of the verb *teleō* (finish, complete) is used at 3.3 and 5.16 in relation to the flesh. As already noted, the realm of the flesh is seen as including but going beyond subjection to the Mosaic law, since it also embraces idolatry (5.20). Nevertheless, that Paul does have the Judaic law in mind emerges unambiguously in 5.18, 'If you are led by Spirit, you are not under law', and also in 5.19, where the phrase 'the works of the flesh' is an ironic parallel to 'the works of the law', which he attacked earlier in the letter (2.16; 3.2, 5 and 10).

What are these 'works of the flesh'? The list is an intriguing one (5.19–21):

1 sexual misconduct (*porneia*)
2 impurity (*akatharsia*; see Hauck 1966a)
3 licentiousness, wanton violence, insolence (*aselgeia*; see LSJ 255)
4 idolatry
5 sorcery (*pharmakeia*)
6 hostilities (*echthrai*; see Foerster 1964), often long-standing ones between individuals (as at Luke 23.12)
7 actual conflict, quarrelling (*eris*)
8 jealousy (*zēlos*), meaning the attitude of stoutly maintaining control over some good in one's possession against any threats to it[13]
9 outbursts of rage (*thymoi*), which indicate loss of the Mediterranean virtue of self-control (see Pilch and Malina 1993: 53–55)
10 selfish manipulation (*eritheiai*; see Büchsel 1964)
11 dissensions (*dichostasiai*; see Schlier 1964b)

12 factions (*haireseis*; see Schlier 1964a), that is, rival groups within the congregation
13 outbreaks of envy (*phthonoi*), meaning the begrudging of another some singular good which can even lead to an activation of the evil eye at the possessor of the good (Pilch and Malina 1993: 55–59)
14 instances of drunkenness (*methai*)
15 drunken revels, even through the streets (*kōmoi*)
16 things similar to these.

Paul had previously issued a warning, which he now repeats, that those who engage in these practices would not inherit the Kingdom of God, which is a reference to the ultimate destiny of those who are in Christ (5.21).

The striking feature of the list is that nine of the fifteen works of the flesh mentioned by name (nos 5–13 inclusive) are forms of behaviour which have the tendency to tear the community apart, either because they entail one member being pitted against one or more other members, or one faction within the congregation coming into conflict with another. They represent specific instances of the savagely competitive conduct about which Paul warned his audience in 5.15. Although he does not explicitly make the point in 5.19–21, it follows from our previous discussion that these activities are completely at odds with what was expected to characterise family life, where siblings especially were expected to work together to maintain the harmony of the family and to preserve its respected position in the local setting. The other categories concern sexual misconduct (1, 2 and 3, although the last item can refer to violent insult), idolatry (4) and drunkenness and extravagant dining habits (14 and 15). To assess how alien this list is to our own experience, we need only imagine the list of 'works of the flesh' which would be produced on request by Christians from a modern, North Atlantic culture.

From our previous discussion in this reading, we are able to locate the activities pathological for group existence, which Paul condemns, as typical features of a culture in which all goods, including honour, were thought to exist in very limited amounts and where unrelated males competed against one another in every social arena to gain those goods at the expense of someone else. When these are added to idolatry, sexual immorality and riotous drunkenness we have a portrait, or rather a stereotype, of the world of the flesh which should have been left behind when his addressees joined the congregations. It is a world which includes both pagans and Israelites, since it is part of his overall strategy in the letter, and in 5.16–26 in particular, to bring Israel and its law under this same general rubric of the flesh. His audience must keep themselves on the right side of the boundaries that separate them from this world.

Within the social identity perspective explained previously, Paul's point is that these negative features characterise the identity of the outgroups in which the members of his congregations should have no part. All of them are the opposite of the type of freedom which involves mutual enslavement in love, which is a critical identity-descriptor for his converts. Paul begins to tell the Galatians who and what they must be by setting out what they must not do. However, the full extent to which he adopts the tactic mentioned in Chapter 2, of asserting that the true values are the antithesis of those of the outgroups, comes in 5.22–23, when he lists the fruits of the Spirit: love, joy, peace, forbearance, kindness, goodness, faith, humility and, finally, the great virtue of Greek ethics (Betz 1979: 288), self-control, adding, 'there is no law against things such as these' (5.22–23).

The 'fruits' of 5.22–23 evoke the proper identity of the congregations in Christ. In Chapter 2 I argued that within a framework focusing on identity, ethical norms did have a critical role, but for maintaining and enhancing group identity, rather than as distinctive from it. By telling group members how to act generally or in new and ambiguous situations, norms form one part of the larger ensemble of social processes whereby they learn who they are. It is clear that ethical norms are only one aspect of the identity Paul is seeking to fashion with respect to the features listed in 5.22–23, both from their function in the broad contrast between the Spirit and the flesh as diametrically opposed categories differentiating rival groups and because of the inclusion of joy and peace in the list. Joy and peace are not ethical norms but badges of identity.

The final remark in 5.23, 'there is no law against things such as these', is probably a response to an argument being run by his opponents in Galatia that the Mosaic law was able to counter the sort of nastiness listed in 5.19–21. Paul replies to the effect that if they enjoy and manifest the fruits of the Spirit, they will have nothing to do with the works of the flesh, and the law will have no relevance to their lives. This is corroborated by the following verse: 'Those who are of Christ have crucified the flesh with its sufferings and desires' (5.24), which is somewhat reminiscent of 2.21b, with its insistence on the effectiveness of Christ's death rather than the law, although there in relation to the attainment of righteousness, a concept which has no place whatever in 5.13–6.10.

In Gal. 5.25 Paul urges his readers not only to live, but also to 'keep in line' (*stoichein*),[14] by Spirit. This expression encapsulates the need to act as a group, that is, in a manner conducive to the harmonious life of the community. On the other hand, the admonition in 5.26, 'Let us not engage in empty boasting [*kenodoxoi*], challenging [*prokaloumenoi*] one another, envying [*phthonountes*] one another', constitutes a crystallisation of the outlook of Mediterranean man which Paul sees as the antithesis to the proper identity of the congregations. Typical unrelated males in this culture were ever alert to engage in the social pattern of challenge-and-response to win the contests of honour which resulted, they habitually envied others who were fortunate in various ways, and they were prone to raising claims to honour where they were not justified.[15] In criticising this behaviour, Paul is asking his readers/listeners to adopt the type of conduct appropriate among family members who did not engage in honour contests with one another, nor envy their achievements, since the glory of one was shed on all. As noted above, the proper course for *adelphoi* was to defend their family's honour and it was scandalous if they fell out among themselves. Plutarch comes close to this view in *Peri Philadelphias* when he describes the need for brothers to do everything possible to avoid becoming envious of one another (485). He even says that if brothers find it impossible not to envy, they should at least try to discharge the evil eye (*to baskanon*) which results at people outside the family,[16] like the politicians who divert sedition at home by wars abroad (485e). And Paul himself later expressed a view very similar to this in Rom. 12.10 (see Moxnes 1995): 'Be affectionate toward one another in brotherly love [*philadelphia*]; rate one another more highly in honour [*timē*]'.

Gal. 6.1–10

Paul proceeds to explicit family imagery at Gal. 6.1, with the reference to brothers in that verse beginning a sub-section which contains other allusions to the realities of kinship and concludes with the 'house-members of the faith' at 6.10. In 6.1–6 he advises on ways of encouraging ethically appropriate behaviour, but as an aspect of a larger concern for the maintenance of group identity. His opening recommendation is to bring erring members into line by peer pressure, which is not surprising given that this is a standard method in a group-oriented culture for having wayward members conform, that is, to act in accordance with group norms and thereby reflect group identity and honour:

> Brothers, if someone is detected in a transgression, you who are people of Spirit [*pneumatikoi*] restore such a person in the spirit of gentleness, looking to yourself lest you also should be tempted.

Although it is possible that *pneumatikoi* was a group self-designation in Galatia (Betz 1979: 297),[17] more probably it is an *ad hoc* expression used here by Paul to relate their identity as those who have received the Spirit (3.3) with the spirit of gentleness (one of the fruits of the Spirit, 5.23) to be shown in restoring their fellow. It should be noted that mention of the Spirit evokes the notion of kinship through its connection with descent from Abraham in 3.14 and 4.21–31. Paul offers advice essentially based on the way brother should correct brother, since apart from the general familial context here, gentleness is the mode one adopts in dealing with the members of one's family or household. As Hauck and Schulz observe, 'it is fitting to show mildness to one's own people, one's *oikeioi*' (1968: 646). Plutarch, moreover, advises that brothers should seek to correct brothers frankly, pointing out their sins of commission and omission, but with care and concern (*Peri Philadelphias*, 483a–b).

Paul next exhorts them to share one another's burdens, so that they will fulfil 'the law of Christ [*nomon tou Christou*]' (6.2). The first part of this verse, given its proximity to the mention of brothers in 6.1 and the fact that families were the most common site for mutual co-operation in this culture, further contributes to a sense of group identity derived from the family. Plutarch considered that brothers had a good relationship with one another if they had in common their father's property, friends and slaves (*Peri Philadelphias*, 478c).

The reference to 'the law of Christ' in the second part of Gal. 6.2 is one of the boldest expressions in the letter. This is the only occasion out of thirty when *nomos* does not refer to the Mosaic law or to Israelite tradition. The law of Christ does not mean, as Barclay suggests (1988: 134), the Mosaic law redefined by Jesus, since this view is based on a failure to appreciate that Gal. 5.13 envisages the total substitution of the law with an alternative path to *agapē*. Nor does it mean a body of ethical tradition derived from the historical Jesus (Dodd 1968), since this plays no part in Galatians and is excluded by Paul's derivation of moral behaviour from the Spirit.[18] Rather, Paul uses the phrase as a striking metaphor for the way in which love, the first fruit of the Spirit, becomes the guiding force in the life of those who are in Christ. As noted in Chapter 2, one form of the process of social creativity, in which a group seeks to improve its social identity by redefining elements in its comparative situation, is to assert that the true positive values, the desirable group norms, are the very antithesis of those espoused by the dominant group. In this light, the 'law of Christ' represents Paul's most daring inversion of the position of the Israelite outgroup and the final nail hammered into his argument that the Mosaic law is quite irrelevant in the new dispensation. Suggesting that the members of his congregations also have a law further serves in his ascription to them of a fictive ethnic identity. Not only do they have Abraham as an ancestor, they also have their own equivalent to the law, albeit only metaphorically.

In Gal. 6.3 Paul rehearses the Mediterranean wisdom that it is foolish to claim honour for oneself without foundation, a condition referred to as *kenodoxos* at 5.26. Yet in 6.4 he argues against a practice which characterised unrelated males in the prevailing culture:

> Let each person examine his own practice, and then he will have a foundation for a making a claim to honour[19] in relation to himself, and not in relation to someone else.

Paul asks his audience to eschew their habit of measuring themselves against others – so as to maximise their stake of honour – and to draw public attention to their successes. In other words, Paul is suggesting that they act as family members towards one another, with whom it would be shameful to engage in tussles over honour. Verse 5 ('For each will bear his own load') has a similar point; they should remember that they each have their own responsibilities and get on with them, rather than continually comparing their performance with that of others. Plutarch comes close to this in *Peri Philadelphias*, when he advises brothers who cannot eliminate envious comparison with one another to at least choose separate fields of activity (486d).

In Gal. 6.6 Paul recommends that a person being instructed in the word share all that he has with his teacher, and although it is difficult to determine the precise significance of this saying he presumably means that ministers of the word deserve to be supported, even though he rarely made such claims for himself. In certain philosophical circles, such as the Pythagoreans, there was a saying to the effect of 'all things in common', and this outlook was sometimes seen as modelled on family life.[20] Accordingly, this constitutes another link with family life.

Verses 7–9 mark a brief change of direction away from details of right conduct to an expression of what is ultimately at stake, eternal life:

> Do not be deceived. God is not treated with contempt. For one will reap whatever one sows. For whoever sows into one's flesh will reap corruption out of the flesh. But whoever sows into the Spirit will reap eternal life from the Spirit. Let us not tire of doing good, if we do not grow faint in the proper season we will bring in the harvest.

The position is predicated upon the basic dichotomy between flesh and the Spirit announced at 5.16 and subsequently expanded, while the reference to eternal life is similar to the warning about the possibility of not inheriting the Kingdom of God set out at 5.21. Paul's understanding of God is a Mediterranean one. God values his honour, which he manifests in the gifts he has lavished on human beings through his Son and the Spirit, and those who abuse those gifts, by following the flesh and not the Spirit, reprehensibly hold him in contempt and will pay the price. It is not enough to belong to the congregations, 'to live by Spirit' (5.25a), one must also manifest the fruits of the Spirit, 'keep in line by Spirit' (5.25b). Love, *agapē*, is the first of the fruits (5.22), the means whereby faith comes into operation (5.6). Paul is open to the possibility that members of his congregations will ultimately fail to attain eternal life, to inherit the Kingdom of God, because they abandon the Spirit and revert to the realms of the flesh. He draws a very direct link between actions by members of the congregations and their ultimate responsibility for them, either in reward or punishment, which is rather at odds with a Lutheran reading of Galatians. Even here, however, the eschatological issue is closely tied to that of group identity. In general, as I proposed in Chapters 2 and 6, a sense of where we are heading is very important in our sense of who we are. Any complete self-description by Paul's converts would necessarily include statements of the form, 'We are people aiming to inherit the Kingdom of God and to attain eternal life'.

At last we reach Gal. 6.10: 'So then, as we have an opportune time, let us do good to everyone, especially to the house-members [*oikeioi*] of the faith'. Paul initially advocates doing good to everyone, which must include all people whether they are inside or outside the congregations. Betz comments that this indicates that Paul's ethics are more universal than those of Plutarch, who is interested in the duties of family members towards one another (1978: 255). Although a similar Pauline interest in doing good to outsiders appears in Rom. 12.14–21, it is hard to know how much emphasis Paul placed on this obligation given his preoccupation with life inside the communities and the heavily negative stereotypes he applies to all those outside. Certainly at 5.14 Paul seems to interpret 'neighbour' as a member of the congregations. In any event, our interest here lies in the last part of the verse, which makes explicit a theme which has been present although largely implicit since 5.13, that the Galatian converts are members of the one *oikos*, a household, comprising relatives and, perhaps, slaves, and that this reality should determine how they treat one another. The household represents the most natural metaphor to express the unique identity of the Galatian believers in Christ when it comes to their living in accordance with the love which the Spirit brings. That they should behave towards one another as members of the one family is a central feature of an identity which is characterised earlier in the letter, as far as outsiders were concerned, as rooted in kinship with God and Abraham. It is worth noting that Halvor Moxnes has recently reached conclusions similar to these with respect to Romans 12, which he suggests speaks of a new community in which one does not pursue one's personal honour but, instead, acts towards other members like brothers (1995).

It is possible that in Galatia, as elsewhere in the early movement (Esler 1996c), there was a link between domestic architecture and the identity based on fictive kinship which Paul was seeking to promote, given that the congregations probably met in houses owned and still used as such by some of the members. Important research into architectural forms used by early Christ-followers, especially the house, has recently been undertaken by L. M. White (1990) and Blue (1994). The use of members' houses, still functioning as such, for meetings of the congregations may even have differentiated them from local groups of Israelites if the latter group had begun to assemble in buildings which no longer doubled as the houses of members.[21]

Epilogue: the intercultural promise of Galatians

The phrase 'culture shock' was coined by the anthropologist K. Oberg in the late 1950s to describe the distress experienced by a sojourner in another culture as a result of being cut loose from the familiar signs and symbols of social interaction. It included features such as (a) the strain due to the effort required to make necessary psychological adjustments; (b) confusion over roles, values, feelings and self-identity; (c) surprise and unease at local cultural features; (d) a sense of impotence at not being able to cope with the new environment; (e) a sense of loss in relation to the friends, status and possessions enjoyed in the home culture; and (f) feelings of rejection by members of the new culture.[1] Classic candidates for culture shock include volunteers abroad, exchange students and international business men and women. A related phenomenon, 're-entry shock', is often experienced when those who have become thoroughly acculturated abroad return home (N. J. Adler 1981).

Yet we do not need to sojourn outside our own country to discover culture shock or to undergo a cross-cultural experience, as we see in cases such as parolees from prison, high-school students starting a university degree, or even recent divorcees or those who have changed their career (P. S. Adler 1975: 13). Similarly, those who seek thoroughly to immerse themselves in the strange culture of the first-century Mediterranean world and, for present purposes, in that part of it represented by Paul's letter to the Galatians, are likely to encounter something very like culture shock. Plainly, the fact that the experience is a literary one involving an imaginative translocation to Paul's time and place without any hope of dialogue with the foreigners in question will attenuate the force of the experience. Nevertheless, while this means that the last two of the six features of culture shock listed above have no place in the process, the first four do have a role to play, especially for those imbued with the robust individualism of northern Europe and North America and who have previously read the Bible in that perspective.

Many people who experience culture shock survive the stresses it places on their personalities, although cases of the unhappy emigrants who after a few years give up and return home shows that others do not. There have been many approaches to charting the patterns of adaptation to a new cultural environment, with the literature describing the U-curve, the W-curve and the inverted U-curve (Furnham and Bochner 1986: 49–50).

Adler has usefully interpreted adjusting to culture shock as a transitional process featuring a number of stages: first, *initial contact*, marked by the excitement and euphoria of fresh experience; second, *disintegration*, when the sojourner becomes confused and anxious over his or her role on the local scene and ability to relate successfully with others; third, *reintegration*, involving a strong rejection of the host culture linked to actively seeking connections with the original culture; fourth, *autonomy*, when the newcomer is now acquiring skills of personal flexibility shown in social competence and the ability to act without cultural cues and props from the home culture; and, fifth, *independence*, when the individual can fully accept and benefit from cultural differences and similarities and is capable of giving as well as eliciting high levels of trust and sensitivity, while being open to having preconceptions, assumptions, values and attitudes challenged (P. S. Adler 1975: 16–18).

All of these stages, which begin with an encounter with another culture and culminate in an encounter with self, are possible in the process of opening ourselves to Galatians as the powerful product of both first-century Mediterranean culture and the early counter-culture of Paul's congregations. The following statement by P. S. Adler is readily applicable to such a reading of the letter, with the exception that it applies as much to communities as to individuals:

> the transitional experience is a set of intensive and evocative situations in which the individual perceives and experiences other people in a distinctly new manner and, as a consequence, experiences new facets and dimensions of existence.
>
> (P. S. Adler 1975: 18)

Those who make the transition progress from a monocultural to an intercultural frame of reference and enjoy the growth and development of personality in a number of dimensions:

> In the encounter with another culture, the individual gains new

experiential knowledge by coming to understand the roots of his or her own ethnocentrism and by gaining new perspectives and outlooks on the nature of culture . . . Paradoxically, the more one is capable of experiencing new and different dimensions of human diversity, the more one learns of oneself.

(ibid. 1975: 22)

Other writers have commented to similar effect. Intercultural persons mediate between different social systems, by selecting, combining and synthesising various features without loss of their cultural core, which is like travelling on two or more passports, providing links across cultures while aware of the strengths and weaknesses of each (Smith and Bond 1993: 201–202). They are capable of 'introducing, translating, representing and reconciling the respective societies to each other' (Furnham and Bochner 1986: 31). Applied to Galatians, this approach raises the prospect that modern readers who allow themselves to be shaped by Paul's communication in the full force of its cultural otherness may become capable of mediating between it and their own modern cultures in a similar way.

As noted in Chapter 1 of this reading, it is impossible to be prescriptive as to the type of intercultural perspectives which will flow from in-depth exposure to Galatians, or other New Testament texts, both because the experience of encountering another culture affects everyone differently and because the appropriate locus for the process of enrichment which will result is a community and not the heart and mind of the individual.

Nevertheless, it is possible to chart certain broad areas where the cultural difference between us and our first-century ancestors in faith is so great that we would expect them to provoke both culture shock and the various stages of the transitional process which follow. The major such area is the ensemble of features which characterise a group-oriented society which Paul both takes for granted, develops and in some ways subverts.[2]

Whereas first-century Mediterraneans found meaning in belonging to stable and largely immobile groups, especially the family, and in representing their views and interests, we have been socialised to regard ourselves as individualists, committed to striking out on our own so as to essay new endeavours and to live in new places. Whereas they sought to align themselves with group expectations, we value independence and autonomy. Whereas they saw fulfilment in terms of honourable conformity to group norms and actions on behalf of the group, we aim for the satisfaction of personal aims and values, for individual self-realisation. Whereas they saw kinship as God-given, sacred and central to human agency, we view it as important but less significant unless elaborated in terms of friendship or economic co-dependence. Whereas for them religion was embedded in kinship and politics and, in Israel at least, concerned with the maintenance of a moral order, we treat religion as a free-standing institution largely concerned with the plight and values of individuals and having an ambiguous relationship with the political and social realms.

The extent to which Paul brings group-oriented cultural attitudes such as these to bear on the creation of a distinctive and positively valued social identity for his Galatian congregations has been a central theme of this reading. The high points of this enterprise came in his efforts to create a relationship of fictive kinship for his audience by demonstrating that they were the true sons of Abraham and, indeed, the sons of God (Galatians 3–4) and by proffering a properly functioning family as the model for life within his congregations (Galatians 5–6).

Since this mode of contextualising the 'truth of the gospel' cannot strike those of us who inhabit a North Atlantic cultural zone as anything other than remote from our own notions of taken-for-granted reality, it is likely to stimulate the various stages of the transitional process which can flow from exposure to the shock of another culture.

The intercultural promise of Galatians lies in the extent to which we will be able to mediate between the strange dimensions of Paul's world and vision of life in Christ and our own situation, with all its challenges, its hopes and disappointments as a new millennium dawns. The recent movement to formulate ethics in vital connection with the character of a particular community (Hauerwas 1981)[3] has done much to pave the way for an intercultural mediation between Paul's understanding of the identity of his congregations and contemporary forms of community.

For all this, we must remember that although the first-century people whose voices we have striven to hear, understand and honour are somehow awkward strangers, they are, like the distant cousin who arrives on our doorstep from another country, also in some sense kin. In spite of their contextualising the gospel in a setting which is not ours, they tell us things which still go to the heart of who we say we are or want to be. Reading Galatians in this way is like clambering down through deep bush on a rainy night to the illuminated house in the valley below, only to find upon entry that we have come home.

At the same time, however, none of this constitutes a warrant for envisaging Christianity as a religion of the ghetto. Even in so strongly a group-oriented text as Galatians Paul himself acknowledges that believers must do good to all, not just the house-members of the faith (6.10). This concern with the world beyond the community, however seriously Paul intended it in the 50s of the first century, has been repeatedly taken up by the tradition and cannot be repudiated. Yet while identity in Christ which embodies the values in Gal. 5.22–23 has much the same potential to serve as an inspiration for others as it did in the first few centuries of the Church, the modes of engagement of faith in Christ with contemporary cultures will continue to vary widely. But whatever mode we employ, immersion in the distant yet familiar Pauline version of identity in Christ holds the capacity to enrich such engagement interculturally.

Paul is not concerned in Galatians with working out his understanding of faith in Jesus Christ in a way comparable to the procedures of systematic theology, let alone with offering a defence of Christian truth-claims. Rather he is intent on legitimating, that is, explaining and justifying, a particular type of largely domestic religion tied to kinship patterns and local politics and having a strong emphasis on normative behaviour which finds its source in the Spirit, who is poured out on those who believe. He does this above all by generating a sense of the glorious identity enjoyed by the members of his congregations. The heart of this identity persists today for all those who, in their entirely different contexts, acknowledge the same Messiah as Paul and those to whom he wrote.

Appendix: Paul's attitude to the law in Rom. 5.20–21

Rom. 5.20–21 are critical in the discussion of Paul's understanding of the Mosaic law, yet they contain syntactical ambiguities which have rendered their interpretation controversial. The following translation sets out the possibilities:

> 5.20 Law slipped in [*pareisēlthen*], so that it might increase/increased [*pleonasē*] wrongdoing,
> (or: so that [*hina*] wrongdoing [*paraptōma*] might increase/increased [*pleonasē*]
> But where sin [*hamartia*] increased [*epleonasen*], grace abounded,
> 5.21 so that [*hina*] just as [*hōsper*] sin reigned in death, so [*houtōs*] also grace might reign/reigns through righteousness unto eternal life through Jesus Christ our Lord.

I will begin with some issues less central to the controversy.

The verb 'slipped in' (*pareisēlthen*), literally 'came in beside', is fairly uncommon in classical Greek. Polybius uses it three times, once of people who 'slipped in as friends' and then captured the city (1.7.3), and on two other occasions of people who gained access to a city with the help of people living within (1.8.4 and 2.55.3). It occurs a few times in Plutarch's *Moralia*, 596a (of fugitives who had slipped into a city and were lying concealed), 964c, 980b, etc. (see *Index Verborum Plutarcheus*). Lucian uses it of entering a house by stealth at midnight (*Dial. Meret.*, 12.3). Although it can designate effecting an entrance in a biological or medical context, it often refers to gaining entrance by stealth. The only other place where Paul uses the verb is Gal. 2.4, in connection with the false brothers who slipped into (or 'infiltrated') the Jerusalem meeting to spy out the freedom of Paul's gentile converts and to enslave them (sc. under the law). Accordingly, it carries the connotation of someone or something (such as the law in the present case) which initially seems benign but which reveals itself as vicious in due course.[1]

The word *paraptōma* derives from the verb *parapiptō* which means 'to fall aside', 'to err', 'to go astray'. In the LXX it means a culpable mistake or sin, a disruption of a person's relationship to God through his or her own mistake. It therefore has a wider meaning than *parabasis* which means the contravention of a promulgated ordinance. Rom. 5.20 suggests that *paraptōma* was in the world before the law, just as was sin (*hamartia*) – with which it is synonymous – as we learn from Rom. 5.13 (Michaelis 1968).

If we turn to the controversial aspects of these verses, the first concerns whether 'increases' (*pleonasē*) is transitive, with its subject the law, that is 'so that it [sc. the law] might increase/increased transgression', thereby directly linking law and transgression, or intransitive, that is, 'so that transgression might increase/increased', thus weakening the connection between them. Scholars who believe Paul meant that law produced or provoked transgression,[2] and many versions,[3] interpret it as transitive. Yet this is clearly the less likely alternative. The word is usually intransitive in Paul and in the New Testament at large.[4] Moroever, the fact that it is clearly intransitive in 5.20b, which parallels 5.20a, strongly suggests that it is also intransitive in 5.20a.

The word *hina* in each of the verses is difficult. Normally *hina* expresses purpose and this is the usual meaning bestowed on it by versions and commentators. Yet it can also express *result*, that is, have a consecutive force. It is interesting to note that in antiquity John Chrysostom thought *hina* expressed result in Rom. 5.20–21 (MPG: 60, 478). It is unfortunate that so many critics either do not consider this possibility or dismiss it.[5]

Moule notes that 'the Semitic mind' was unwilling to draw a sharp dividing line between purpose and consequence, with the result that *hina* plus the subjunctive does not always have its most common function of expressing purpose, but result. He cites a number of examples, some from Paul (Gen. 22.14; Luke 9.45; Gal. 5.17; 1 Thess. 5.4; 1 John 1.9). Yet he expressly declines to interpret the use of this construction at Rom. 5.20–21 and 6.1 in this way, although the fact that he mentions these examples suggests that the issue is obviously a live one with respect to them and, moreover, he gives no reason for his view (Moule 1959: 142–143).[6]

It is difficult to see anything in v. 20 which allows one decisively to adjudicate between a purpose or result meaning for *hina*. It is significant that the second half of the verse contains a statement of fact relating to the past, 'where sin increased', in which the same verb is used, although now in the aorist tense of an event in the past, as was used with *hina* in the subjunctive mood in the first part, and the word sin (*hamartia*) in 5.20b is synonymous with 'wrongdoing' (*paraptōma*) in 5.20a. Normally, however, the circumstance that the main clause of a sentence speaks of the precise contents of a preceding *hina* clause as an accomplished fact in the past would not necessarily decide the issue since that could follow from a clause expressing purpose as well as result. In the present case, however, the events of the main clause are more than usually related to those of the *hina* clause by use of the words 'but where' at the start of 5.20b, so that the main clause looks back more definitively to the accomplishment of facts in the past than would otherwise be the case. This may offer a reason, although hardly a compelling one, for favouring a consecutive over a final meaning for the *hina* clause in 5.20a.

The position is clearer, however, in 5.21. *Hina* in 5.21 begins a clause dependent on the statement in 5.20b that 'where sin increased, grace abounded' which looks on the abundance of grace as an accomplished fact. Since the first half of the *hina* clause parallels that of the principal clause, with 'just as [*hōsper*] sin ruled by death' in the aorist indicative mood amplifying 'where sin increased', it is more natural to interpret the second element in the *hina* clause as matching the second part of the principal clause to express result and not purpose: 'so also grace reigns' (not 'might reign'). Käsemann reached a similar view to this, for although he regarded the *hina* in 5.20 as final he thought the instance in 5.21 was consecutive, 'since 21a and 21b are parallel' (1980: 158).

The fact that a consecutive meaning clearly makes better sense of the *hina* in 5.21 necessitates that we consider whether this does not also push the previous *hina* in the same direction, given the parallels in meaning set up in vv. 20 and 21. Thus, the increase in sin in 5.20 is paralleled by the reign of sin in 5.21 and the abounding of grace in 5.20 is paralleled by the reigning of grace in 5.21. It is submitted that these parallels tend to indicate that 5.20 should also be taken to describe the result of sin increasing under the law, rather than suggesting that sin was the purpose of the law.[7]

Even if this view is not accepted, however, it is submitted that since the syntax of 5.20–21 certainly has nothing on the face of it which indicates purpose rather than result, the latter alternative is much more easily reconciled with Paul's attitude to the law in Galatians than to the extra-ordinary and counter-intuitive idea that God gave the law to promote rather than to restrain sin.

To conclude, Rom. 5.20–21 does not express the view that the law produced or provoked transgression and is better interpreted as speaking of transgression and sin as the result of the law coming onto the scene (when coupled with the failure of human agents to observe its provisions).

This interpretation is consistent with the understanding I have concluded is to be found in Galatians. The law was given by God for the good purpose of identifying particularly heinous types of immorality and restraining their commission under threat of punishment. The law initially looked benign, yet its consequences were not (thus it 'slipped in', 5.20a). The Israelites did not adhere to its ordinances and thereby brought down the curse upon their heads. The way they interacted with the law meant that by their breaches they put themselves into a more sinful position than they had been in before. The result was (*hina*) that 'transgression increased' (5.20a) and 'sin reigned in death' (5.21a). Yet 'grace abounded' (5.21b) and 'reigns through righteousness unto life eternal through Jesus Christ our Lord' (5.21b).

Notes

1 READING GALATIANS

1 I briefly discuss the possibilities as to the destination and date of composition of the letter at the beginning of Chapter 2 of this reading of Galatians.

2 Cited in Plato, *Cratylus* 402a.

3 Plato, *Cratylus* 439c and *Theaetetus* 182c refer to this idea. Plato sometimes cites the saying in the form *panta chōrei*, as at *Cratylus* 402a.

4 I speak of the situation especially in the USA, Great Britain, the Nordic countries, Australasia and South Africa. In Germany, however, New Testament scholarship, with some notable exceptions including Gerd Theissen and Wolfgang Stegemann, has signally failed to move on much from the issues which agitated discussion in the 1950s and 1960s. To many outsiders, the great German New Testament tradition, which led the field in innovations from the 1830s to the 1960s, has become distressingly bogged down in previous agendas. This may be the explanation for the declining citation of German New Testament scholarship in the English-speaking world.

5 For an admirable introduction to social-scientific criticism, see Elliott 1993.

6 This seems a more useful way to proceed than that of Burton Mack, who, in a book largely on Mark, only informs his reader at the very end (1988: 351–376) of the detailed basis for his foundational and extraordinarily negative view of the evangelist as the creator of a myth of an innocent yet crucified Jesus which, in the hands of the powerful, has been (it is alleged) extremely dangerous ever since, even in the manner in which the USA has developed (ibid.: 369–374).

7 I do not discount the possibility that the authors envisaged that their communications would be received by persons later than them in time, but I do insist that they had no way of knowing what these persons would be like and certainly made no allowance for possible differences. Nor am I here assuming that every New Testament text was written for a particular community, or an ensemble of communities of a particular type (as Galatians was in any event), although I continue to believe that such was the case, in spite of recent proposals (which seem to me to rest on a mistaken understanding of first-century social realities) that the gospels at least were directed at a general Christian audience in the first century, as argued by Richard Bauckham and others (Bauckham 1997, critiqued in Esler 1998).

8 See Georgi 1987: 347–348. In the New Testament the word *Christianos* only occurs at Acts 11.26 and 26.28, and 1 Pet. 4.16, and not as a self-designation.

9 For an excellent treatment of *Christianos*, see Elliott 1997. This material will appear as a note in his forthcoming Anchor Bible Commentary on 1 Peter, Garden City, NY: Doubleday and Co., Inc.

10 I do not suggest that dropping the use of 'Jew', 'Jewish' and 'Christian' is the only solution to the problem I have outlined, simply that it is one possible way of keeping at the forefront of our analysis the dangers of unconsciously construing ancient data in the light of modern understandings and social categorisations. For interesting explorations of some of the issues at stake here, also see Pilch 1993, 1996 and 1997.

11 For details, see Fisher 1978; Fiske 1990; Miller and Steinberg 1975; and Watzlawick, Beavin and Jackson 1967.

12 For an excellent introduction to the field of intercultural communication, see Gudykunst and Kim 1992.

13 On these four influences, see Gudykunst and Kim 1992: 31–38.

14 See Malina 1993 (the revised edition of a seminal book first published in 1981 in the USA and in 1983 in the UK); Esler 1994: 19–36; and Pilch and Malina 1993. On the use of models and modelling generally, see Elliott 1993: 36–59; and Esler 1987: 6–12 and 1995a: 4–8.

15 For an orientation to this subject, see Stowers 1986; J. L. White 1986; and Malherbe 1988.

16 This work was wrongly attributed to Cicero.

17 Butts 1986 is a translation and commentary of the *Progymnasmata* of Aelius Theon. For the Greek remains of Aphthonius and Hermogenes, see Rabe 1995: 73–170, 171–447. For English translations, see Nadeau 1952 (Aphthonius) and Baldwin 1928 (Hermogenes). For Menander Rhetor, see Russell and Wilson 1981.

18 Important ancient texts on rhetoric include Plato's *Gorgias* and *Phaedrus*, Aristotle's *Rhetoric*, Isocrates' *Against the Sophists*, the *Rhetorica ad Herennium*, Cicero's *de Oratore*, Quintilian's *Institutes* and the *Progymnasmata* of Aelius Theon.

19 Pogoloff (1992: 23–26) warns of the need not to confuse old and new rhetoric, even if they are 'intertwined' in any particular reading.

20 He identified the five key elements as the *exordium* in 1.6–11, the *narratio* in 1.12–2.14, the *propositio* in 2.15–2.21, the *probatio* in 3.1–4.31 and the *exhortatio* in 5.1–6.10.

21 I do not seek to suggest that in his 1994 book, or in his important 1997 volume (which came too late for consideration in this reading), Watson eschews all interest in the historical realities of the first century CE. My problem with his approach is that he devalues the significance of the particular historical circumstances which provided the various contexts for the New Testament texts when they first appeared.

22 This point is well made by McDonald in relation to the position of Brevard Childs (1995: 306).

23 For an introduction to the postmodernist analysis of modernity, see Lyotard 1984. For a recognition of the postmodern challenge to biblical studies, see Fiorenza 1989; F. Watson 1994: 79–106; and, most notably, the Bible and Culture Collective 1995: 2–15.

24 This characteristic of the postmodernist enterprise is encapsulated in the

story about the anthropologist of this persuasion who was addressed by a member of a pre-industrial tribe he was investigating like this: 'I'm sick of talking about you; let's talk about me.'

25 It is ironic in view of their sensitivity to the way some interpretative strategies are kept in place that the ten members of this group find no room in their volume for a discussion of social-scientific interpretation, in spite of its flourishing status (see Elliott 1993).

26 For the sort of critical realism I have in mind, see Barbour 1976: 172–176.

2 SOCIAL IDENTITY AND THE EPISTLE TO THE GALATIANS

1 The Romans called the Celts, whom they had encountered in invasions of Italy early in their history, the *Galli*, and the Greeks referred to these same people as *Keltoi* and later *Keltai*.

2 For the details and maps of the Celtic conquest and settlement, see S. Mitchell 1993: 42–58.

3 As noted in the text, there were parts of the province of Galatia further north than the old Celtic area.

4 I am indebted to Murphy-O'Connor (1996: 161) for this argument.

5 In Gal. 1.18 and 2.1 Paul deals with previous visits and in Rom. 15.22–33 he speaks of his proposed journey to Jerusalem with the collection.

6 The five visits in Acts occur at 9.26–27; 12.25; 15.1–29; 18.22 and 21.15.

7 See Bruce 1969–1970 and Hemer 1989: 278.

8 As some, such as Hemer (1989: 278), suggest.

9 See S. Mitchell 1993: 108.

10 That he dictated the bulk of the letter to a scribe emerges at Gal. 6.11.

11 For some of the rare exceptions, scholars who do take the social dimension seriously, see Pilch 1983 (the first attempt to use anthropology in reading Galatians and Romans), Neyrey 1990 and Witherington 1997.

12 I am grateful to Dr James Good, of the Psychology Department of the University of Durham, for first alerting me to the importance of Tajfel in understanding group dynamics.

13 The paper was 'Social Identity, Group Conflict and the Matthean Beatitudes: A New Reading of Matt. 5:3–12', delivered at a plenary session of the British New Testament Conference in Nottingham on 16 September 1994.

14 Initially Tajfel referred to his theory as 'social categorisation', but later came to favour the description 'social identity', as can be seen in his 1986 article co-written with former Bristol fellow-worker John C. Turner.

15 In addition to established classics in this field such as Worsley 1957 and Burridge 1969, also see Steinbauer 1979 and the magisterial contributions of Trompf 1991, 1994.

16 In a letter dated 1 October 1997 in response to this chapter, Peter Robinson, the Professor of Social Psychology at Bristol (the chair which Tajfel held), has made the significant suggestion that even these aspects which Hogg and Adams regard as aspects of personal identity are actually features of social identity. He favours restricting personal identity to characteristics such as

cheerfulness and intelligence, that is, quantitative differ
individuals.
17 Examples include Houlden 1973; Schrage 1988; Marxsen 1~~~, ~~~ ~~~,~
1996.
18 For similar sentiments, see Plutarch's *Old Men In Public Affairs*, 787d; and
Josephus, *Vita*, 122–123. I am indebted to Jerome H. Neyrey for these references to Philo, Plutarch and Josephus, from his extensive collection of emic
data relating to prominent features of Mediterranean culture.

3 CONTEXT AND RHETORIC IN GALATIANS

1 Although the extant rhetorical treatises were written by Greek or Roman
authors, the success of the processes of Hellenisation meant that a Jewish
author like Josephus was very familiar with rhetorical technique. The way in
which he applies encomiastic techniques in his autobiography – *Vita* – has
been well explained by Jerome H. Neyrey (1994).
2 Lyons (1985) is a useful discussion of the nature of ancient autobiography in
relation to Paul, although (as we will see) not convincing in all respects.
3 It seems to me quite unprofitable to argue, as some do, over whether the
narratio begins at 1.12 or 1.13.
4 Hester was attracted to the idea, albeit with some reservations (1984: 223).
5 See Hester (1991), who now wishes to characterise Galatians as a speech of
blame, having previously favoured the judicial option (1984)!
6 See Malina 1993: 28–62 for his latest formulation of this theme.
7 1428a, 1432b–1433b, 1437a–b, 1439b, 1440a, 1442b and 1443a–b.
8 See the references in Cousin 1936: 124.
9 For this feature see Rom. 1.8–14; 1 Cor. 1.4–9; Phil. 1.3–11; 1 Thess. 1.2–10;
Phlm 4–7.
10 I have discussed this passage in similar terms in Esler 1994: 55–57.
11 See Lyons 1985: 78; Jewett 1970–1971: 198; and Murphy-O'Connor 1996:
193.
12 See Stark 1996: 6, and the literature he cites.
13 Josephus, *Antiquities*, 12.148–153. The settlements are to be dated to the
period 212–205/4 BCE, see Trebilco 1991: 5.
14 I have greatly profited in this section from discussions with Professor Nigel
Rapport of the Social Anthropology department of the University of
St Andrews, but responsibility for the views expressed here rests with me and
not him.
15 This point has been noted by Mark Brett in the introduction to a recent
collection entitled *Ethnicity and the Bible* (1996b: 13–14).
16 My earlier discussions of this topic can be found in Esler 1994: 52–69 and
1996a.
17 I have used a similar diagram in Esler 1997a: 129.
18 For accounts of how sectarian theory can be employed in New Testament
interpretation, see Esler 1987: 46–53; Holmberg 1990: 77–117; and Elliott
1995.

4 THE PROBLEM WITH MIXED TABLE-FELLOWSHIP

1 In his *Aegyptiaca*, cited in Diodorus Siculus, *Bibliotheca Historica*, 40.3.4.

2 These views of Apollonius from his *de Iudaeis* are referred to in Josephus, *Contra Apionem*, 2.148 and 258.

3 'Et quoniam metu contagionis pulsos se ab Aegypto meminerant, ne eadem causa invisi apud incolas forent, caverunt, ne cum peregrinis conviverent; quod ex causa factum paulatim in disciplinam religionemque convertit' (Since they [sc. the *Iudaei*] remembered that they had been driven from Egypt because of fear of infection, they took care not to live with foreigners. This rule, adopted for that particular cause, became in time a matter of religious discipline), *Historicae Philippae*, Book 36, cited in Justin's *Epitome*, 1.15.

4 It is used in the Septuagint of profane, probably idolatrous objects placed on the altar of the Temple in the time of Antiochus IV Epiphanes (2 Macc. 6.5), of swine's flesh which pious Israelites were forced to eat during this time (2 Macc. 7.1), of blasphemous (and perhaps idolatrous) words uttered by the gentiles at Israelite soldiers (2 Macc. 10.34) and on gentile lips, of 'impious' *Ioudaioi* (3 Macc. 5.20).

5 I suggested that Judith may have bathed each evening before eating her own food because she had become ritually defiled by contact with gentiles (Esler 1987: 81) and that the *Jubilees* passage was interesting as the prohibition was explicitly related not to what gentiles ate but to the pollution which attached to their actions (ibid.: 83).

6 For my critical review of Hill's attractively iconoclastic work (1992), see Esler 1995b. Hill's book is based on an Oxford D.Phil. thesis supervised by Sanders.

7 Sanders' 1990a essay has made a favourable impression on a number of commentators, such as Wright 1992: 238–241; Barclay 1996b: 292; and Nanos 1996: 56–57. For one view sympathetic to my 1987 position, see Matson's (1996) accomplished study of the household conversion narratives in Acts.

8 For a view rather similar to that of Sanders, see Nanos (1996: 348–351), who, however, argues that the problem concerned Peter's eating with the gentiles without observing important status distinctions, especially that between righteous gentiles and proselytes.

9 Dunn has now adopted a different view, perhaps in response to Sanders' criticism. He considers that the problem was that Peter and the other Israelite believers were sharing table-fellowship with gentile believers on less clearly defined Israelite terms, not only welcoming gentiles to their table, 'but accepting invitations to Gentile tables without asking too many questions [cf. 1 Cor. 10.27], though presumably on the assumption that the Gentile believers would have been mindful of the basic food rules', so that James' people were shocked by their laxity (1993: 121).

10 'Since Dunn had taken the view that "the dominant tendency within Judaism" was to avoid social intercourse with Gentiles as much as possible, Esler's criticism shows that he took an extreme stand: they avoided it altogether. Dunn, proposed Esler, was wrong to think that "table-fellowship occurred between Jews and Gentiles in the first century CE." ' Sanders 1990a: 176.

11 The fact that I was offering this as an explanation for the separate issue of the phenomenon of the ban was clear from the start of my treatment: 'But there also developed another reason for avoiding table-fellowship with Gentiles: namely, the fact that they were ritually impure' (1987: 85). Peter's statement in Acts 10.28 strongly suggests there might be something in this explanation, yet although Sanders does mention this passage (1990a: 188, fn. 20) he does not deal with this point. Moreover, his statement that 'when they met sympathetic Gentiles – I mean, sympathetic to Judaism – we may be confident that Jews in general made them feel welcome' (1990a: 184) runs up against a hard rock in Acts 11.3.

12 See Plato, *Symposium*, 176a: 'After this, he said, when Socrates had reclined and dined [*deipnein*] with the rest, they offered libations [*spondai*], sang a chant to the god and attended to the other customary matters appropriate before the drinking.' The whole process between meal and the start of drinking went like this. First there was a libation of unmixed wine to the *daimōn*; second, the servants cleared away the tables and brought in more water for hand-washing; third, wreaths were distributed among the guests; fourth, libations were poured out to (a) Zeus Olympios and the Olympian gods, (b) to the Heroes, and (c) to Zeus Soter; and, fifth, a hymn was sung (Bury 1909: 15).

13 See the excellent discussion and references in Corley 1993: 25–28.

14 I am reliant for most of the details in this paragraph on Murray 1996a.

15 Epictetus, Fragment 17 (Loeb). I am reliant on Gooch 1993: 43 for this quotation.

16 This reference undercuts Segal's emphatic statement, 'there is no law in rabbinic literature that prevents a Jew from eating with a gentile' (1990: 231). In any event, there was always the possibility of the application of certain general rules, such as the biblical ones prohibiting idolatry, in a wide range of contexts.

17 For the substance of a possible Samaritan blessing, I am indebted to Rabbi Apple, of the Great Synagogue, Sydney, Australia.

18 He does not mention it in his 1990a essay, nor in Sanders 1990b or 1992.

19 Hill's discussion of the classical sources (1992: 118–119) underestimates their significance.

5 PAUL, JERUSALEM AND ANTIOCH

1 That the revelation *concerned* Jesus Christ and was not *from him* (the other meaning possible in the Greek) emerges in v. 15, where God is specified as the revealer.

2 At 1.16 Christ is the object of the verb, while at 1.23 the object is 'the faith' in an absolute sense.

3 Paul's use of the expression 'among the gentiles' at 1.16 and 2.2 means that he was to be active in the diaspora; it does not mean that he would not also seek to make Israelites believers in Jesus Christ (contra Betz 1979: 72). Paul's problem originates in his insistence that the communities comprise gentiles and Israelites sharing Eucharistic table-fellowship.

4 For discussion, see Elliott 1990a and 1995; Esler 1987: 46–53 and 1994: 13–17; and Holmberg 1990: 77–117.

5 John H. Elliott prefers to refer to the movement from 'faction' to 'sect' and has now elaborated a sophisticated set of indicia for sectarianism in early Christianity (1995).

6 Exceptions to the general disinclination to offer anything more than a brief mention of this subject include M. Smith 1967 (this essay deals with why Paul himself was persecuted – for libertinism in relation to the law – but the same case can be made for the earlier period); Hultgren 1976; and Hengel 1991: 79–84.

7 See the careful discussion and references in Dunn 1993: 278–280.

8 The verb *historēsai* means more than just visit, since it usually covers the sense of obtaining information. But it certainly does not imply that Paul saw himself as in any way subordinate to Peter – see Dunn 1993: 73–74. God, not any human being, was the source of Paul's understanding of the gospel. But there is no reason as to why on this occasion he could not have learned interesting things about Jesus from Peter.

9 John Knox wrongly assumed that Gal. 1.22 meant Paul had never been in Judea before and therefore could not have persecuted the church there (1989: 22); this formed an important plank in his Pauline chronology. But this view falters on the syntax Paul employs, since the point of the periphrastic imperfect, 'I was being unknown by sight', is to express the duration of the activity of the verb (Moule 1959: 17). That this is Paul's point is confirmed beyond doubt when he uses exactly the same construction in the next verse: 'Only they [sc. the Judean churches] were hearing [i.e. throughout the duration of this period] that "The person once persecuting us is now preaching the faith which he tried to destroy"'. For a rejection of Knox's view without reference to this syntactic point, see Hultgren 1976: 106.

10 'Thus a man drinks to you at dinner when you have had your fill. Do not yield or force yourself to comply, but set the cup down. Another again invites you to play at dice over the wine: do not yield or let his scoffing daunt you, but . . . confess in your turn that you are a great coward indeed and too faint-hearted to risk disgrace . . . ' (Plutarch, *Peri Dysōpias*, 530f; ET by De Lacy and Einarson 1959: 59).

11 For details of this argument, see Esler 1995c: 295.

12 But it is certainly not an impossible view, as one can see from the interesting case put by Mark Nanos in a paper entitled 'Intruding "Spies" and "Pseudo" Brethren: The Intra-Jewish Context of "those of repute" in Jerusalem (Gal. 2.1–10)', delivered at the SNTS conference in Birmingham in August 1997. My case here would not require any fundamental change even if Nanos were right.

13 For the text of Gaius, with translation and admirable comments, see de Zulueta 1946.

14 '*Unde inter absentes quoque talia negotia contrahuntur*', Gaius, *Institutes*, 136.

15 The other three types were sale, hire and mandate.

16 1 Macc. 6.58; 11.50, 62, 66; 13.45, 50; 2 Macc. 4.34; 11.26; 12.11; 13.22; 14.19.

17 Rom. 15.26; 1 Cor. 1.9; 10.16 (twice); 2 Cor. 6.14; 8.4; 9.13; 13.13; Gal. 2.9; Phil. 1.5; 2.1; 3.10; Phlm 6.

18 In Josephus, *Jewish Antiquities*, 18.326–331, the expression 'giving right hands' also occurs in a military context and an oath is taken as well.
19 Rom. 1.19; 9.1; 1 Cor. 15.31; 2 Cor. 1.23; 11.23; Phil. 1.8; 1 Thess. 2.5, 10.
20 Deut. 7.24; 9.2; 11.25; 2 Chron. 13.7. Also cf. very similar expressions at Josh. 1.5 and 23.9, although in these cases another phrase is substituted for *kata prosōpon*.
21 Rom. 15.25–27; 1 Cor. 16.1–4; 2 Cor. 8–9.
22 The only other instance of *spoudazein* in Paul means 'to be eager', see 1 Thess. 2.17, and this is its most common meaning elsewhere in the New Testament: see Eph. 4.3; 2 Tim. 2.15; Heb. 4.11; 2 Pet. 1.10, 15; 3.14. The related adjective *spoudaios* means 'eager' or 'earnest' in Paul, not 'quick' (2 Cor. 8.17 and 22), and the related adverb *spoudaiōs* means 'eagerly' not 'quickly' (Phil. 2.28), even though both words are used with the other meaning. The alternative view is that he *hastened* to effect the collection. For this meaning of the verb see 2 Tim. 4.9, and also probable examples at 2 Tim. 4.21 and Tit. 3.12.
23 That gatherings of the whole community in Antioch were still possible flows from the fact of Paul's saying that he rebuked Peter 'in front of everyone'.
24 See Dunn 1993: 129–131. Mark Nanos, however, has recognised that the issue in Paul's accusation was one of circumcision (1996: 337–371).
25 For further discussion, see Esler 1994: 57–62.
26 Dunn notes that 'by that time Peter had ceased "living like a Gentile"' and considers that the charge that Peter lives like a gentile and not a *Ioudaios* echoes what James' messengers said to him (1993: 128).
27 For the opposite view, see Nanos 1996: 358.

6 RIGHTEOUSNESS AS PRIVILEGED IDENTITY

1 Even the notion that the judgement mentioned in Ps. 143.2 is the final or 'eschatological' one, although common (see Betz 1979: 118), is unsustainable, since the psalmist, beset by his enemies, is there simply beseeching God not to condemn him but to come to his aid – and soon (cf. v. 7).
2 It is hard to see why he would be so bent on denying that righteousness came from law unless this formed a central plank in the case he opposed; as noted in Chapter 3 of this reading, in ancient rhetoric such a strategy constituted anticipation.
3 It referred to the former as *zakkai* ('pure', the adjective is not in the OT) and the latter as *hayyab* ('guilty', also not in the OT) (Falk 1972: 107, citing *m. Sanhedrin* 3.7 and 5.5).
4 This emerges with crystal clarity at Deut. 25.1 (LXX), where *dikaioō* and *dikaios* must extend to both criminal and civil cases: 'And if there should be a dispute between people and they should come forward to judgement, they [sc. the judges] should judge, and they should find in favour of [*dikaioō*] the righteous party [*dikaios*] and condemn the wicked.'
5 I assume that Gal. 2.16 may just possibly contain a muted reference to the last days, as may 5.5.
6 This is the first explicit reference to the saving significance of Jesus' death, although it passes unmentioned by Tuckett in his 1992 discussion of atonement in the *ABD*.

7 See Rom. 5.1–5; 1 Thess. 5.8; Col. 1.4–5; Eph. 4.2–5; Heb. 6.10–12; 10.22–24; 1 Pet. 1.21–22.

8 These words are discussed by Procksch 1964.

9 As has been done by Neyrey in connection with various parts of the Pauline corpus (1990).

10 Although *dikaiōma* nearly always means either 'statute' (translating *hoq*) or 'commandment' (translating *mishpat*) and to that extent may certainly be said to have a 'legislative' or 'judicial' sense, this meaning should not automatically be read onto the other words in the field. In the areas of the LXX where *dikaios* is most common (such as in certain Psalms and Proverbs, to be discussed later in the text of this chapter), *dikaiōma* does not appear. There is also little intersection in the uses of *dikaiōma* and *dikaiosunē*, except that we find *dikaiōma* and *dikaiosynē* (together with one case of *dikaios* in relation to God, v. 138) in Psalm 119 (Psalm 118 LXX), a text which accounts for nearly one-sixth of all examples of *dikaiōma* and which is massively preoccupied with adherence to God's laws. We should not let the collocation of God's commandments and God's righteousness in a psalm of this type – whose very subject is the law – push our interpretation of *dikaiosynē* too strongly in a legislative or judicial direction. This is not to say, however, that there is no connection between *dikaiosynē* and adhering to the divine ordinances. It is worth noting, lastly, that eleven of the thirteen references to *dikaiosynē* in Psalm 119 are to the *dikaiosynē* of God, with the exceptions occurring at vv. 121 and 138. The God of righteousness commands righteousness (v. 138) which the person faithful to him practises (v. 121).

11 Goodspeed has noted how lexicographers have oddly ignored this sense of *dikaioō* in the middle voice (1954: 87).

12 See also Lagrange 1931: 124. This is the expression used by Judah, who is on the verge of burning Tamar to death because she has played the prostitute and borne a child, when he has been shown himself to be the father. The word *dedikaiōtai* is middle not passive in voice; there is no adjudication in mind by anyone. It translates the qal of *tsâdaq*. Put precisely, Tamar has acted more in accordance with the prevailing conventions governing social relationships, especially those relating to family honour, than he has. This means that *dikaioō* is an appropriate word to describe acceptable conduct within the honour–shame code operating in this culture. Perhaps a better translation is 'she has acted more honourably than I'. Ziesler has 'she has fulfilled the community obligations better than I have' (1972: 43). This is fairly good, although probably too general. Quite erroneous is the translation (of the Hebrew underlying expression) 'The law is on Tamar's side', as suggested by J. J. Scullion (1992: 726).

13 See the probable allusions to Siracides at 1 Cor. 2.9 (Sir. 1.10), 1 Thess. 4.6 (Sir. 5.3), Rom. 2.6 (Sir. 16.14), 1 Cor. 6.12 (Sir. 37.28), 2 Cor. 7.10 (Sir. 38.18) and Gal. 3.8 (Sir. 44.21).

14 Of the 350 examples of *dikaiosynē* in the LXX, there are 82 (or 23 per cent) in the Psalms and 33 (or 9 per cent) in Proverbs. Even more noteworthy is *dikaios*; of the 375 examples of this word, fully 52 (or 14 per cent) are found in the Psalms and 102 (or 27 per cent) in Proverbs.

15 The fact that there is first-century evidence in Josephus (*Contra Apionem*, 1.8)

for the authority of these biblical books as containing instruction on how to conduct one's life gives added weight to this proposal.

16 Schrenk: 'If in the rest of the Greek world a man is *dikaios* who satisfies ordinary legal norms, fulfilling his civic duties in the most general sense, here the *dikaios* is the man who fulfils his duties towards God and the theocratic society, meeting God's claim in this relationship. It is as he satisfies the demand of God that he has right on his side and therefore a righteous cause before God' (1964: 185).

17 Ziesler considers that instances of *saddiq* (the Hebrew word translated in the Septuagint as *dikaios*) in Proverbs 'are used as the opposite of a word for "wickedness, evil, wicked" or as general words for doing what is right in God's eyes, being faithful to him, not in some "spiritual" sense, but in the conduct of life and society' (1972: 24–25).

18 There are some 225 instances of *asebēs* in the Septuagint, of which there are 89 in Proverbs (about 40 per cent of the total), and of these 45 appear in Proverbs 10–15 (or some 20 per cent of the Septuagint total). There are 35 examples in Job and 19 in the Psalms.

19 As suggested by my colleague Professor Richard Bauckham, in response to an earlier version of this chapter.

20 This is so whether the plural is an epistolary one (referring only to himself, as I have argued in Esler 1995c: 310) or includes any other Israelites, such as Peter or those in his Galatian audience.

21 Here my translation interprets *ara* at the beginning of 2.17b as an interrogative particle (accented with a circumflex) since *mē genoito* is elsewhere in Paul preceded by a question, not a statement (Rom. 3.3f, 5f, 31; 6.2, 15; 7.7, 13; 9.14; 11.1, 11; 1 Cor. 6.15; Gal. 3.21), even though *ara* in this sense is not used elsewhere in Paul.

22 See the discussion in Lightfoot 1914: 116–117; Burton 1921: 124–130; Lagrange 1926: 48–51; Betz 1979: 119–120; Bruce 1982c: 140–141; and Dunn 1993: 141–142.

23 By *ean* with the subjunctive, not by *ei* with the indicative as here.

24 The words *ei gar* at the start of 2.18 do not link this verse causally with v. 17 but constitute an example of the emphatic use of *ei gar* (Denniston 1934: 89–95), rarely mentioned by commentators but which is used five times in Galatians (2.18, 21; 3.18, 21; 6.3), virtually with adversative force; *ei gar* may be translated 'but if'. I will discuss 2.18 more fully in Chapter 7 of this reading.

25 The original in the LXX has a quite different meaning: 'The righteous one will live by my [God's] faithfulness'.

26 It is also possible to read these two clauses as expressing result, not purpose.

27 See Betz 1979: 152. Although there is a reasonably good textual tradition for reading 'blessing' rather than 'promise' in 3.14b, 'promise' is the better-attested (and more difficult) reading and should be retained.

7 PAUL AND THE LAW

1 The figure of 430 years is probably based on the statement in Exod. 12.40 that the Israelites dwelt in Egypt for this period.

2 See the attitudes to Israelites expressed by Greeks and Romans in Stern

1974–1980; Juvenal is particularly revealing, although allowance must be made for his satirical exaggeration.

3 For his use of Mary Douglas and Hans Mol, see his paper delivered at the SNTS Conference in Basle in August 1984; Dunn 1990a: 216–225. Also see Dunn 1990a: 101–196, which represents an earlier expression of his views (from 1982) without recourse to such explicit social-scientific perspectives.

4 The LXX of Deut. 27.26 has: 'Cursed is every human being who does not remain in all the words of this law to keep them. And all the people shall say, "So be it."'

5 For the curses which are provoked by non-compliance with the law, see Lev. 26.14–43; Deut. 27.26 and Deut. 28.15–68 (covering breach of the whole law, whereas Deut. 27.11–25 covers curses for breach of individual laws).

6 The idea that Paul means keeping the law is wrong (see Bruce 1982b) is inconsistent with 3.10 and 3.12, let alone 3.19–20 (discussed later in the text of this chapter). Cranfield's suggestion that Paul was attacking legalistic adherence to the law has been subjected to a devastating critique by Räisänen 1986: 43–44.

7 It is possible that this is an exaggerated claim made as his past life grew fainter in his memory, or that 'blameless' covers the situation where he had sinned but repented.

8 The scripture cited is from Deut. 21.23, where the clause begins, however, 'Cursed by God is'.

9 I agree with Heikki Räisänen that the 'us' in 3.13 includes gentiles as well as Israelites (1986: 19). This is not necessarily because Paul considered gentiles to be already under the curse of the law (Räisänen 1986: 20), but because those whom he is addressing are contemplating taking on the law and thereby falling under its curse. For Christ to redeem Israelites and gentiles from the curse means to provide to all an alternative path to life.

10 Räisänen notices this connection (1986: 60). His view that Paul wanted to make a point about the manner of Christ's death seems to me unnecessary, however, when the relationship between hanging on a tree and curse simply presented Paul with a convenient pretext to link Christ and curse, just as he elsewhere highlighted death and sin as that from which Christ's death redeemed us.

11 Such as Dahl (1977: 171) and Hays (1983: 90).

12 Heikki Räisänen has also found difficulty with Wright's placing the covenant at the centre of Pauline theology (1994).

13 Perhaps less helpful for Paul was the fact that *diathēkē* is also regularly used of the covenant with Abraham in Genesis 17 and with Moses in the Sinaitic traditions in Exodus, Leviticus, Numbers and Deuteronomy, both of which involved circumcision.

14 For revocability of wills under Roman law, see Nicholas 1962: 234–270, and for the position under Greek law, see Betz 1979: 155.

15 There is support in the Greek world for the use of *diathēkē* in relation to dispositions *inter vivos*, although the testamentary use is more common (Behm 1964: 124–125).

16 Bammel has argued for the Israelite institution *mattenat bari* which permitted someone contemplating death to make an irrevocable testament (Bammel 1959–1960).

17 Lim suggests that Paul had in mind an instrument of the type mentioned in a
   papyrus dated 128 CE from the Babatha archive, containing remains from the
   Bar Kokhba period. This is a deed of a gift from a father to his daughter of
   certain property in En-gedi, half the gift to be effective from the date of the
   instrument and half from the date of the donor's death, with the whole to be
   registered with the public authorities at any time to be nominated by the
   donee. The document contains a separate Aramaic statement that the father
   has given the property to his daughter and the signatures of six witnesses
   appear on it. The text uses the verb *diatithēmi*, cognate with *diathēkē*, of the
   disposition and the editor even detects *diathēkē* in the text, although this is
   uncertain (Lim 1997: 58–65). This type of arrangement may have been
   widely known in the ancient Mediterranean but other evidence for it has
   simply not survived.
18 'Were spoken' is the so-called 'divine passive'. God is the speaker.
19 It is interesting that there is a modern legal principle (very close to that
   enunciated by Paul) in the area of determining priorities between rival
   claimants to property, *qui prior est tempore potior est iure* ('the person first in time
   takes precedence').
20 Gen. 12.7; 13.15, 16 (twice), 17; 15.5, 13, 18; 17.7 (twice), 8, 9, 10, 12, 19;
   22.17, 18 and 24.7.
21 See Gal. 3.18 (inheritance – *klēronomia*), 3.29 and 4.1 (heir – *klēronomos*), and
   4.30 and 5.21 (inherit – *klēronomeō*).
22 This is assumed by many translations and commentaries on the basis of the
   Greek words *ei gar* at its start, which are usually translated 'For if', see the
   RSV and NRSV for this translation, while Betz (1979: 154) has the similar
   'Hence, if'. In fact, this is the so-called emphatic use of *ei gar* (Denniston
   1934: 89–95), rarely mentioned by commentators but which is used five
   times in Galatians (2.18, 21; 3.18, 21; 6.3), virtually with adversative force.
   NEB and JB fudge the issue by translating *ei gar* as 'If'.
23 The perfect tense in 'has graciously granted' is the 'allegorical perfect',
   denoting the continuance into the present of the effects of a past act
   recorded in the scripture.
24 Thus Matera suggests the inheritance is the promised Spirit (1992: 127).
25 Betz reasonably suggests from a more traditional perspective that the
   inheritance includes 'all the benefits of God's work of salvation' (1979: 159).
26 For a good discussion of the possibilities in existing scholarship, see Räisänen
   1986: 140–141.
27 Lambrecht has recently argued that Paul means a transgressor with respect
   to the will of God as clearly revealed in Christ (1991, 1996: 63–66), not with
   respect to the Mosaic law. The ease with which the Mosaic law fits into 2.18
   and into the relationship of that verse with 2.17 (which I set out in the
   previous chapter) contrasts markedly with the subtlety of the argument
   Lambrecht must develop to sustain his proposal. Furthermore, there are
   problems with the way in which he rules out existing explanations of the
   sense in which Paul would show himself a transgressor (1996: 64–65). Nevertheless, Lambrecht concedes that Pauline usage (the *parabainein* words in
   Paul always referring to a breach of the law – Rom. 2.23, 25, 27; 4.15;
   Gal. 3.19 – or to something closely analogous – Rom. 5.14) and the context
   in Galatians necessitate some kind of legal concept (1996: 64). Thus, even if

he were correct the broad point I wish to draw from 2.18 – that Paul has in mind a norm which identifies and punishes certain behaviour if human beings choose to disregard it – is essentially unaffected.

28 In modern legal interpretation this is described as the 'mischief' which the law was enacted to address.

29 There is ancient Israelite support for this view. Consider the following from *Jubilees*, 30.21: 'All of these words I have written for you, and I have commanded you to speak to the children of Israel that they might not commit sin or transgress the ordinances or break the covenant which was ordained for them so that they might do it and be written down as friends' (Charlesworth 1985, vol. 1: 113–114).

30 Chrysostom described the law as teaching, training and hindering transgression (*Patrologia Graeca*, 61.654).

31 Even Räisänen, who does not favour this view, concedes that 'the image of *paidagōgos* (3.24) suggests rather the notion of preventing transgressions' (1986: 145, fn. 84).

32 As suggested by Thielman 1989: 74.

33 Bruce goes uncharacteristically astray here, with his blunt '*charin* expresses purpose not antecedent cause' (1982c: 175) falling foul of the numerous instances of the word with a causal sense, such as at 3 Kings 14.16a, Sir. 29.7; 31.12; 35.2; 1 Macc. 3.29; 6.24, 59; 11.11; 13.6; and 1 John 3.12.

34 Hübner at least avoided the consequences of this view by distinguishing, in a convoluted and unconvincing way (see later in the text of this chapter), between God's intention for the law, its immanent intention and the alleged evil intention of the wicked angels whom he considers gave the law (1984: 30).

35 A less extreme version of this idea is offered by Schweitzer (1931: 70–71), who suggests that the law meant dominion by angels not by God.

36 Although Betz (1979: 169) suggests that the presence of angels is assumed.

37 The positive sense emerges elsewhere in Paul at Phil. 4.7. At 2 Cor. 11.32, the word means to prevent someone (sc. Paul) from making an exit. See Dunn 1993: 197–198.

38 Räisänen concedes in a footnote (1986: 145) that 'the image of the *paidagōgos* (3.24) suggests rather the notion of preventing transgressions', rather than increasing them, but unfortunately fails to give the metaphor the full weight it deserves.

39 In Rom. 13.8–10, which is very similar to Gal. 5.14, Paul says that 'the person who loves [*agapōn*] the other has fulfilled [*peplērōken*] the law', that the other commandments are summed up (*anakephalaioutai*) in the love command of Lev. 10.17 and that 'love [*agapē*] is the fulfilment [*plērōma*] of the law'.

40 Barclay (1988: 139) cites *phylassō* ('keep') and *poieō* and *prassō* (both meaning 'do', 'perform').

8 FREEDOM, THE SPIRIT AND COMMUNITY LIFE (GAL. 4.21–6.10)

1 See Barrett 1985: 53–90; Barclay 1988; and Hays 1996: 16–59, as examples.
2 Barrett does not put the opponents' case in quite the way it is stated in the parentheses, but see Dunn 1993: 161. This interpretation of Gen. 15.6 occurs at James 2.20–23.
3 This is the case in spite of the fact that two verbs with the root *doul-* are used in Gen. 15.13 and 14 of the slavery which Abraham foretells lies in store for his descendants.
4 Abraham may have in mind something like the practice mentioned in fifteenth-century BCE texts from Nuzi, east of the Tigris – von Rad 1972: 183–184. Also cf. the accounts of Rachel and Bilhah, and Leah and Zilpah, in Gen. 30.3–13.
5 It matters not to this interpretation whether Paul is actually urging his addressees to expel the trouble-makers (see Hansen 1989: 145–146), which seems to me the more probable view, as most in keeping with the depth of animosity Paul displays towards his opponents in the letter and the general tendency in Mediterranean culture to fall heavily on one's enemies, or, as Barrett suggests, that the imperative to drive out Hagar and her son is rather the command of God to his angelic agents and reflects what the fate of each party is to be (1982: 165).
6 While the detail of the argument in this section is based on two essays I have previously published which focus on various aspects of Gal. 5.13–6.10 (Esler 1996a, 1997), I have completely rewritten and integrated this earlier material, in most cases abbreviating but in others amplifying the discussion, as well as bringing all of it into line with my overall understanding of the letter as set out in this reading.
7 For a more detailed treatment of the material in this section, see Esler 1997: 122–128.
8 As examples, see Pomeroy 1975; Hallett 1984; Bradley 1991; Rawson 1986; Joubert 1995; Guijarro 1997; and Lassen 1997.
9 See, for example, Deming 1995 and Barton 1994, critically reviewed on this point by Esler 1996b and Moxnes 1997b. For an approach which does pay proper respect to the Mediterranean context of early Christian families, see the important essay by Moxnes 1997a: 13–41 (also cf. 1–9).
10 For richly instructive examples of interpretation alive to the nature of family life in Mediterranean culture, see Duling 1995; Love 1995; Neyrey 1995; and Rohrbaugh 1995.
11 Most of the ancient examples of challenge-and-response concern men, who are in the public limelight. But the pattern is occasionally represented by women, as when a man has two wives, or one wife and another woman, and only one of the women has a child or becomes pregnant, resulting in an enhancement of her honour over that of the other woman; see Hagar and Sarah in Genesis 16, and Hannah and Peninnah in 1 Samuel 1.
12 In the Greek, the words translated as 'you will certainly not carry out' are in a form (*ou mē* plus the subjunctive) which constitutes a very emphatic way of negativing a future possibility.

13 For the critical but little appreciated distinction between jealousy and envy in the ancient world, see Pilch and Malina 1993: 55–59, 185–188.

14 The verb *stoichein* does not just mean 'to walk' but 'to be one of a series' (like a soldier in a rank), 'to agree', see Delling 1971. The expression 'to keep in line' captures these nuances.

15 Boasting itself is not problematic in the Mediterranean, if not done to excess. Any honourable man or family will seek to draw the attention of the public to his or their honour. But boasting without a foundation exposes one to ridicule.

16 This statement is also interesting evidence for the fact that a much lower standard of morality was owed to outsiders, who were fair game for deception and assault.

17 It is quite unlikely to refer to a sub-group within the congregations, as Barrett suggests (1985: 79), since that would entail legitimating the tendency to form factions which he earlier decried (5.20).

18 The phrase '*ennomos Christou*' occurs at 1 Cor. 9.21. For a useful discussion of existing views on '*nomos tou Christou*', see Matera 1992: 218–221.

19 'Foundation for making a claim to honour' is my translation of *kauchēma*, which, as Lightfoot notes, 'is the matter of *kauchēsis*' (1914: 217), although 'boast' carries a negative connotation for us that it did not have in antiquity and is best omitted from translations.

20 As it clearly is in a provision of the Hippocratic Oath, see Betz 1979: 305.

21 For my detailed argument on this point, see Esler 1997: 134–138.

EPILOGUE: THE INTERCULTURAL PROMISE OF GALATIANS

1 See Oberg 1960 for the original formulation of this idea. More recent discussions of a flourishing topic include P. S. Adler 1975; Furnham and Bochner 1982, 1986; and Smith and Bond 1993.

2 Many of these have been admirably tabulated against their modern 'equivalents' by Malina and Neyrey 1996: 227–231.

3 This research has largely revolved around renewed interest in Aristotelian ethics; for a powerful application of Aristotle to the field of business ethics, see Solomon 1993.

APPENDIX: PAUL'S ATTITUDE TO THE LAW IN ROM. 5.20–21

1 There are useful discussions of classical instances of this word in Thielman 1989: 100–101 and Hofius 1996: 200.

2 A transitive meaning is assumed without discussion of the alternative by Thielman 1989: 101; Ziesler 1989: 152; Dunn 1988: 285–286.

3 For example, RSV and NEB.

4 Elsewhere in Paul it is intransitive in 2 Cor. 4.15 and 8.15 (with an accusative of respect) and Phil. 4.17, and transitive at 1 Thess. 3.12. The other New Testament instances are also intransitive: 2 Thess. 1.3 and 2 Pet. 1.8.

5 Hofius has recently asserted that 'Die Konjunktion *hina* hat finalen Sinn und nicht etwa konsekutiven' (the conjunction *hina* has a final and not really a consecutive sense) and rejected Chrysostom's view to the contrary (1996: 201 fn. 229), though without venturing any reason as to why his modern interpretation of a point like this should be superior to that of someone from the ancient period who actually spoke the language.

6 The instance of *hina* in Rom. 6.1 should be treated separately from those in 5.20–21; with the verb in the main clause in the subjunctive mood, *hina* clearly begins a final clause.

7 It is surprising that in spite of the importance of the issue commentators often fail to mention the possibility of the *hina* cl uses in Rom. 5.20–21 expressing result and not purpose – so Dunn 1988: ?85–288 and 298–300; Ziesler 1989: 152–153.

References

Aasgaard, Reidar (1997) 'Brotherhood in Plutarch and Paul: Its Role and Character', in Moxnes ed. 1997a: 166–182.

Adler, N. J. (1981) 'Re-Entry: Managing Cross-Cultural Transitions', *Group and Organisation Studies* 6: 341–356.

Adler, Peter S. (1975) 'The Transitional Experience: An Alternative View of Culture Shock', *The Journal of Humanistic Psychology* 15: 13–23.

Allport, Floyd (1924) *Social Psychology*. Boston, MA: Houghton Mifflin.

Anderson, H. George, Murphy, T. Austin and Burgess, Joseph A. eds (1985) *Justification by Faith: Lutherans and Catholics in Dialogue VII*. Minneapolis, MN: Augsburg Publishing House.

Anderson, R. Dean, Jr. (1996) *Ancient Rhetorical Theory and Paul*, in Contributions to Biblical Exegesis and Theology, 18. Kampen: Kok Pharos.

Aune, David E. (1987) *The New Testament in its Literary Environment*. Library of Early Christianity. Ed. Wayne A. Meeks. No. 8. Philadelphia, PA: The Westminster Press.

Baldwin, C. S. (1928) *Medieval Rhetoric and Poetic*. New York: Macmillan Publishing Co.

Bammel, Ernst (1959–1960) 'Gottes DIATHĒKĒ (Gal. III.15–17) und das jüdische Rechtsdenken', *NTS* 6: 313–319.

Barbour, Ian G. (1976) *Myths, Models and Paradigms: A Comparative Study in Science and Religion*. New York *et alibi*: Harper and Row.

Barclay, John M. G. (1988) *Obeying the Truth: A Study of Paul's Ethics in Galatians*. Edinburgh: T. and T. Clark.

—— (1995) 'Deviance and Apostasy: Some Applications of Deviance Theory to First-Century Judaism and Christianity', in Esler ed. 1995a: 114–127.

—— (1996a) *Jews in the Mediterranean Diaspora: From Alexander to Trajan (323 BCE–117 CE)*. Edinburgh: T. and T. Clark.

—— (1996b) '"Do We Undermine the Law?": A Study of Romans 14.1–15.6', in Dunn ed. 1996: 287–308.

Barker, Margaret (1987) *The Older Testament: The Survival of Themes from the Ancient Royal Cult in Sectarian Judaism and Early Christianity*. London: SPCK.

—— (1992) *The Great Angel: A Study of Israel's Second God*. London: SPCK.

Barrett, C. K. (1982) 'The Allegory of Abraham, Sarah, and Hagar in the Argument of Galatians', in his *Essays on Paul*. London: SPCK, 154–170.

—— (1985) *Freedom and Obligation: A Study of the Epistle to the Galatians*. London: SPCK.

Bartchy, S. Scott (1992) 'Slavery (New Testament)', *ABD* 6: 65–73.

Barth, Fredrik ed. (1969) *Ethnic Groups and Boundaries: The Social Organization of Culture Difference*. Boston: Little, Brown and Company.

Barton, Stephen C. (1994) *Discipleship and Family Ties in Mark and Matthew*. SNTS Monograph Series 80. Cambridge: Cambridge University Press.

Bauckham, Richard (1996) 'Why Did Paul Go to Arabia?' Unpublished lecture delivered in St Mary's College, the University of St Andrews.

—— ed. (1997) *The Gospels for All Christians*. Grand Rapids, MI and Edinburgh: William B. Eerdmans and T. and T. Clark.

Behm, Johannes (1964) 'diathēkē', *TDNT* 2: 106–134.

Berger, Peter and Luckmann, Thomas (1984 [1966]) *The Social Construction of Reality: A Treatise in the Sociology of Knowledge*. London: Pelican.

Bergquist, Birgitta (1990) 'Sympotic Space: A Functional Aspect of Greek Dining Rooms', in Murray ed. 1990: 37–65.

Best, Ernest (1972) *The First and Second Epistles to the Thessalonians*. London: Adam and Charles Black.

Betz, Hans Dieter (1975) 'The Literary Composition and Function of Paul's Letter to the Galatians', *NTS* 21: 353–379.

—— ed. (1978) *Plutarch's Ethical Writings and Early Christian Literature*. Leiden: E. J. Brill.

—— (1979) *Galatians: A Commentary on Paul's Letter to the Churches in Galatia*. Hermeneia Commentary. Philadelphia, PA: Fortress Press.

Bible and Culture Collective (1995) *The Postmodern Bible*. New Haven and London: Yale University Press.

Bitzer, L. F. (1968) 'The Rhetorical Situation', *Philosophy and Rhetoric* 1: 1–14.

Blue, Bradley (1994) 'Acts and the House Church', in Gill and Gempf eds 1994: 119–222.

Bourdieu, Pierre (1965) 'The Sentiment of Honour in Kabyle Society', in Peristiany ed. 1965: 191–241.

Bradley, Keith R. (1991) *Discovering the Roman Family: Studies in Roman Social History*. Oxford: Oxford University Press.

Brett, Mark G. ed. (1996a) *Ethnicity and the Bible*. Leiden: E. J. Brill.

—— (1996b) 'Interpreting Ethnicity: Method, Hermeneutics, Ethics', in Brett ed. 1996a: 3–22.

Brewer, David Instone (1992) *Techniques and Assumptions in Jewish Exegesis before 70 CE*. Tübingen: J. C. B. Mohr (Paul Siebeck).

Brown, Rupert (1988) *Group Processes: Dynamics Within and Between Groups*. Oxford: Basil Blackwell.

Bruce, F. F. (1969–1970) 'North or South Galatians?', *BJRL* 52: 243–266.

—— (1982a) *1 and 2 Thessalonians*. Word Biblical Commentary. Vol. 45. Waco, Texas: Word Books.

—— (1982b) 'The Curse of the Law', in Hooker and Wilson eds 1982: 27–36.

—— (1982c) *The Epistle of Paul to the Galatians: A Commentary on the Greek Text*. The New International Greek Testament Commentary. Exeter: The Paternoster Press.

Büchsel, Friedrich (1964) 'eritheia', *TDNT* 2: 660–661.

Bultmann, Rudolf (1952) *Theology of the New Testament*. Vol. 1. London: SCM Press.

—— (1964) 'Dikaiosynē tou Theou', *JBL* 83: 12–16.

Burkert, Walter (1985) *Greek Religion: Archaic and Classical*. ET by John Raffan. Oxford: Basil Blackwell.

Burridge, Kenelm (1969) *New Heaven New Earth: A Study of Millenarian Activities*. Oxford: Basil Blackwell.

Burton, Ernest de Witt (1921) *A Critical and Exegetical Commentary on the Epistle to the Galatians*. Edinburgh: T. and T. Clark.

Bury, R. G. (1909) *The Symposium of Plato: Edited, with Critical Notes and Commentary*. Cambridge: W. Heffer and Sons.

Butts, James R. (1986) *The Progymnasmata of Theon. A New Text with Translation and Commentary*. Ph.D. dissertation, Claremont Graduate School.

Campbell, J. K. (1964) *Honour, Family and Patronage: A Study of Institutions and Moral Values in a Greek Mountain Community*. New York: Oxford University Press.

Carcopino, Jerome (1941) *Daily Life in Ancient Rome: The People and the City at the Height of the Empire*. Edited by Henry T. Rowell. Translated from the French by E. O. Lorimer. London: George Routledge and Sons Ltd.

Charlesworth, James H. ed. (1985) *The Old Testament Pseudepigrapha*. Vols 1 and 2. London: Darton, Longman and Todd.

Cohen, Anthony P. (1989) *The Symbolic Construction of Community*. London and New York: Routledge.

—— (1993) 'Boundaries of Consciousness, Consciousness of Boundaries'. Plenary paper delivered at the conference on The Anthropology of Ethnicity: A Critical View, The University of Amsterdam, 15–18 December.

—— (1994) *Self Consciousness: An Alternative Anthropology of Identity*. London and New York: Routledge.

Corley, Kathleen E. (1993) *Private Women: Public Meals: Social Conflict in the Synoptic Tradition*. Peabody, MA: Hendrickson.

Cosgrove, Charles H. (1988) *The Cross and the Spirit: A Study in the Argument and Theology of Galatians*. Macon, GA: Mercer University Press.

Cousin, Jean (1936) *Études sur Quintilien. Tome II. Vocabulaire Grec de la Terminologie Rhétorique dans l'Institution Oratoire*. Paris: Boivin and Co.

Dahl, Nils Alstrup (1964) 'The Doctrine of Justification: Its Social Function and Implications', in Dahl 1977: 95–120.

—— (1977) *Studies in Paul. Theology for the Early Christian Mission*. Minneapolis, MN: Augsburg.

Darr, John A. (1992) *On Character Building: The Reader and the Rhetoric of Characterization in Luke–Acts*. Literary Currents in Biblical Interpretation. Louisville, KY: Westminster/John Knox Press.

Davies, W. D. (1977–1978) 'Paul and the People of Israel', *NTS* 24: 4–39.

De Lacy, Phillip H. and Einarson, Benedict (1959) *Plutarch Moralia*. Vol. 7. Loeb edition. Cambridge, MA and London: Harvard University Press.

Delling, Gerhard (1971) 'stoicheō', *TDNT* 7: 666–669.

Deming, Will (1995) *Paul on Marriage and Celibacy: The Hellenistic Background of 1 Corinthians 7*. SNTS Monograph Series 83. Cambridge: Cambridge University Press.

Denniston, J. D. (1934) *The Greek Particles*. Second edition. Oxford: The Clarendon Press.

Dibelius, Martin (1934) *From Tradition to Gospel*. ET by Bertram Lee Woolf. London: Nicholson and Watson.

—— (1976) *A Commentary on the Epistle of James*. Revised by H. Greeven. Hermeneia Commentary. ET by Michael A. Williams. Philadelphia, PA: Fortress.

Diels, Hermann (1935) *Die Fragmente Der Vorsokratiker: Griechisch und Deutsch*. Fifth edition edited by Walther Kranz. Vol. 2. Berlin: Weidmannsche.

Dillenberger, John (1961) *Martin Luther: Selections from His Writings*. New York: Doubleday.

Dodd, C. H. (1968) 'Ennomos Christou', in his *More New Testament Studies*. Grand Rapids: Eerdmans, 341–366.

Duling, Dennis C. (1995) 'The Matthean Brotherhood and Marginal Scribal Leadership', in Esler ed. 1995a: 159–182.

Dunn, James D. G. (1983) 'The Incident at Antioch (Gal. 2:11–18)', *JSNT* 18: 3–57. Reprinted with an addendum in Dunn 1990a: 129–182.

—— (1988) *Romans 1–8*. Word Biblical Commentary. Vol. 38a. Dallas, Texas: Word Books.

—— (1990a) *Jesus, Paul and the Law: Studies in Mark and Galatians*. London: SPCK.

—— (1990b) 'The New Perspective on Paul', in Dunn 1990a: 183–206.

—— (1993) *The Epistle to the Galatians*. Black's New Testament Commentary. Peabody, MA: Hendrickson.

—— ed. (1996) *Paul and the Mosaic Law: The Third Durham–Tübingen Research Symposium on Earliest Christianity and Judaism (Durham, September 1994)*. WUNT 89. Tübingen: J. C. B. Mohr (Paul Siebeck).

Eagleton, Terry (1983) *Literary Theory: An Introduction*. Oxford: Basil Blackwell.

Eller, J. D. and Coughlan, R. M. (1993) 'The Poverty of Primordialism: The Demystification of Ethnic Attachments', *Ethnic and Racial Studies* 16: 185–202.

Elliott, John H. (1988) 'The Fear of the Leer: The Evil Eye from the Bible to L'il Abner', *Forum* 4: 77–85.

—— (1990a) *A Home for the Homeless: A Sociological Exegesis of 1 Peter, its Situation and Strategy*. Revised edition. Philadelphia, PA: Fortress.

—— (1990b) 'Paul, Galatians, and the Evil Eye', *CurrTM* 17: 262–273.

—— (1991) 'The Evil Eye in the First Testament: The Ecology and Culture of a Pervasive Belief', in David Jobling et al., eds 1991 *The Bible and the Politics of Exegesis: Essays in Honor of Norman K. Gottwald on His Sixty-Fifth Birthday*. Cleveland, Ohio: Pilgrim Press, 147–159.

—— (1992) 'Matthew 20:1–15: A Parable of Invidious Comparison and Evil Eye Accusation', *BTB* 22: 52–65.

—— (1993) *Social Scientific Criticism of the New Testament: An Introduction*. London: SPCK.

—— (1994) 'The Evil Eye and the Sermon on the Mount: Contours of a Pervasive Belief in Social Scientific Perspective', *Biblical Interpretation* 2: 51–84.

—— (1995) 'The Jewish Messianic Movement: From Faction to Sect', in Esler ed. 1995a: 75–95.

—— (1997) 'Jesus Wasn't a Christian: Historical, Social and Theological Implications of the Disparaging Label Christianos and Other Nomenclature'. Paper delivered to the Context Group in Portland, Oregon, in March 1997.

Esler, Philip F. (1987) *Community and Gospel in Luke–Acts: The Social and Political*

Motivations of Lucan Theology. SNTSMS 57. Cambridge: Cambridge University Press.

—— (1994) *The First Christians in their Social Worlds: Social-Scientific Approaches to New Testament Interpretation.* London and New York: Routledge.

—— ed. (1995a) *Modelling Early Christianity: Social-Scientific Studies of the New Testament in its Context.* London and New York: Routledge.

—— (1995b) Review of Hill 1992, in *Biblical Interpretation* 3: 119–123.

—— (1995c) 'Making and Breaking an Agreement Mediterranean Style: A New Reading of Galatians 2.1–14', *Biblical Interpretation* 3: 285–314.

—— (1996a) 'Group Boundaries and Intergroup Conflict in Galatians: A New Reading of Gal. 5:13–6:10', in Brett ed. 1996a: 215–240.

—— (1996b) Review of Deming 1995, in *The Expository Times* 107: 184.

—— (1996c) ' "House Members of the Faith": Domestic Architecture and Early Christian Identity', *Cosmos* 12: 223–239.

—— (1997) 'Family Imagery and Christian Identity in Gal. 5.13–6.10', in Halvor Moxnes ed. 1997a *Constructing Early Christian Families: Family as Social Reality and Metaphor.* London and New York: Routledge, 121–149.

Falk, Ze'ev W. (1972) *Introduction to the Jewish Law of the Second Commonwealth.* Leiden: E. J. Brill.

Fiorenza, E. Schüssler (1987) 'Rhetorical Situation and Historical Reconstruction in 1 Corinthians', *NTS* 33: 386–403.

—— (1989) 'Biblical Interpretation and Critical Commitment', *Studia Theologika: Scandinavian Journal of Theology* 43: 5–18.

—— (1998) 'Community and Gospel in Early Christianity: A Response to Richard Bauckham's Gospels for All Christians', *SJT* Volume 51, forthcoming.

Fisher, B. A. (1978) *Perspectives on Human Communication.* New York: Macmillan.

Fiske, John (1990) *Introduction to Communication Studies.* London and New York: Routledge.

Fitzmyer, Joseph A. (1982) 'The Biblical Basis of Justification by Faith: Comments on the Essay of Professor Reumann', in Reumann 1982: 193–227.

Foerster, Werner (1964) 'echthra', *TDNT* 2: 815.

Forster, E. S. (1924) *Rhetorica ad Alexandrum,* in W. D. Ross ed. 1924 *The Works of Aristotle Translated into English under the Editorship of W. D. Ross.* Oxford: The Clarendon Press (not paginated).

Furnham, Adrian and Bochner, Stephen (1982) 'Social Difficulty in a Foreign Culture: An Empirical Analysis of Culture Shock', in Stephen Bochner ed. 1982 *Cultures in Conflict: Studies in Cross-Cultural Interaction.* Oxford *et alibi*: Pergamon Press, 161–198.

—— (1986) *Culture Shock: Psychological Reactions to Unfamiliar Environments.* London and New York: Routledge.

Gadamer, H.-G. (1984) *Truth and Method.* New York: Crossroad.

Gaventa, Beverly Roberts (1986) 'Galatians 1 and 2: Autobiography as Paradigm', *NovT* 28: 309–326.

Geertz, Clifford (1973) 'The Integrative Revolution: Primordial Sentiments and Civil Politic in the New States', in his *The Interpretation of Cultures.* New York: Basic Books, 255–310.

Georgi, Dieter (1987) *The Opponents of Paul in Second Corinthians.* Edinburgh: T. and T. Clark.

Gerbner, G. (1956) 'Toward a General Model of Communication', *Audio Visual Communication Review* 4: 171–199.

Gill, David W. J. and Gempf, Conrad eds (1994) *The Book of Acts in its First-Century Setting. Vol. 2. The Book of Acts in its Graeco-Roman Setting.* Grand Rapids, MI and Carlisle: William B. Eerdmans Publishing Co./The Paternoster Press.

Gooch, Peter D. (1993) *Dangerous Food: 1 Corinthians 8–10 in its Context.* Studies in Judaism and Christianity 5. Waterloo, Ontario: Wilfred Laurier University Press.

Goodspeed, E. J. (1954) 'Some Greek Notes', *JBL* 73: 86–91.

Grant, Robert M. with Tracy, David (1984) *A Short History of the Interpretation of the Bible.* London: SCM Press Ltd.

Gudykunst, William B. and Kim, Young Yun (1992) *Communicating with Strangers: An Approach to Intercultural Communication.* Second edition. New York *et alibi*: McGraw-Hill.

Guijarro, Santiago (1997) 'The Family in First-Century Palestine', in Moxnes ed. 1997a: 42–65.

Gurevich, Aaron (1995) *The Origins of European Individualism.* ET from the Russian by Katharine Judelson. Oxford: Blackwell.

Hadas, Moses (1951) *Aristeas to Philocrates (Letter of Aristeas).* New York: Harper and Brothers.

Hall, Robert G. (1987) 'The Rhetorical Outline for Galatians: A Reconsideration', *JBL* 106: 277–287.

—— (1991) 'Historical Inference and Rhetorical Effect: Another Look at Galatians 1 and 2', in Watson ed. 1991: 308–320.

Hallett, Judith P. (1984) *Fathers and Daughters in Roman Society: Women and the Elite Family.* Princeton, NJ: Princeton University Press.

Halliday, Michael A. K. (1978) *Language as Social Semiotic: The Social Interpretation of Language and Meaning.* Baltimore, MD: University Park Press.

Hansen, G. Walter (1989) *Abraham in Galatians: Epistolary and Rhetorical Contexts.* Sheffield: JSOT Press.

Hanson, A. T. (1988) 'The Origin of Paul's Use of *Paidagogos* for the Law', *JSNT* 34: 71–76.

Hauck, Friedrich (1966a) 'akathartos, akatharsia', *TDNT* 3: 427–429.

—— (1966b) 'koinos', etc., *TDNT* 3: 789–809.

Hauck, Friedrich and Schulz, Siegfried (1968) 'praus, prautēs', *TDNT* 6: 645–651.

Hauerwas, Stanley (1981) *A Community of Character: Toward a Constructive Christian Ethic.* Notre Dame, IN: University of Notre Dame Press.

Havener, Ivan (1981) 'The Pre-Pauline Christological Credal Formulae of 1 Thessalonians', in Kent Harold Richards ed. 1981 *Society of Biblical Literature 1981 Seminar Papers.* Chico, CA: Society of Biblical Literature, 105–128.

Hayman, Peter (1991) 'Monotheism – A Misused Word in Jewish Studies?', *JJS* 42: 1–15.

Hays, Richard B. (1983) *The Faith of Jesus Christ: An Investigation of the Narrative Substructure of Galatians 3:1–4:11.* SBLDS 56. Chico, CA: Scholars Press.

—— (1996) *The Moral Vision of the New Testament: A Contemporary Introduction to New Testament Ethics.* Edinburgh: T. and T. Clark.

Helmbold, W. C. (1939) *Plutarch's Moralia.* Vol. 6 (of 14). Loeb Classical Library. London and Cambridge, MA: William Heinemann Ltd/Harvard University Press.

Hemer, Colin J. (1989) *The Book of Acts in its Hellenistic Setting*. Edited by Conrad H. Gempf. Tübingen: J. C. B. Mohr (Paul Siebeck).

Hengel, Martin, in collaboration with Deines, Roland (1991) *The Pre-Christian Paul*. London: SCM Press and Trinity Press International.

Hester, James D. (1984) 'The Rhetorical Structure of Galatians 1.11–2.14', *JBL* 103: 223–233.

—— (1991) 'Placing the Blame: The Presence of Epideictic in Galatians 1 and 2', in D. F. Watson ed. 1991: 281–307.

Hill, Craig C. (1992) *Hellenists and Hebrews: Reappraising Division Within the Earliest Church*. Minneapolis, MN: Fortress Press.

Hinkle, Steve and Brown, Rupert (1990) 'Intergroup Comparisons and Social Identity: Some Links and Lacunae', in Dominic Abrams and Michael A. Hogg eds 1990 *Social Identity Theory: Constructive and Critical Approaches*. New York *et alibi*: Harvester Wheatsheaf, 48–70.

Hirsch, E. D. Jr (1976) *The Aims of Interpretation*. Chicago: University of Chicago Press.

—— (1982) 'The Politics of Theories of Interpretation', *Critical Inquiry* 9: 235–247.

Hobbs, Raymond (1995) 'The Language of Warfare in the New Testament', in Esler ed. 1995a: 259–273.

Hofius, Otfried (1996) 'Die Adam-Christus-Antithese und das Gesetz: Erwägungen zu Röm 5. 12–21', in Dunn ed. 1996: 165–206.

Hofstede, Geert (1980) *Culture's Consequences: International Differences in Work-Related Values*. Beverly Hills, CA: Sage Publications.

—— (1994) *Cultures and Organizations: Software of the Mind: Intercultural Cooperation and its Importance for Survival*. London: HarperCollins.

Hogg, Michael A. and Abrams, Dominic (1988) *Social Identifications: A Social Psychology of Intergroup Relations and Group Processes*. London and New York: Routledge.

Holmberg, Bengt (1978) *Paul and Power: The Structure of Authority in the Primitive Church as Reflected in the Pauline Epistles*. Lund: Studentlitteratur.

—— (1990) *Sociology and the New Testament: An Appraisal*. Minneapolis, MN: Fortress Press.

Hong, In-Gyu (1993) *The Law in Galatians. JSNT* Supplementary Series 81. Sheffield: JSOT Press.

Hooker, Morna D. (1990a) *From Adam to Christ: Essays on Paul*. Cambridge *et alibi*: Cambridge University Press.

—— (1990b) 'Paul and "Covenantal Nomism"', in Hooker 1990a: 155–164. First published in Hooker and Wilson eds. 1982: 47–56.

Hooker, Morna D. and Wilson, Stephen G. eds (1982) *Paul and Paulinism: Essays in Honour of C. K. Barrett*. London: SPCK.

Horbury, William and Noy, David (1992) *Jewish Inscriptions of Graeco-Roman Egypt: With an Index of the Jewish Inscriptions of Egypt and Cyrenaica*. Cambridge: Cambridge University Press.

Horner, Winnifred Bryan ed. (1983) *The Present State of Scholarship in Historical and Contemporary Rhetoric*. Columbia: University of Missouri Press.

Horrell, David (1995) 'The Development of Theological Ideology in Pauline Christianity: A Structuration Theory Perspective', in Esler ed. 1995a: 224–236.

Houlden, J. L. (1973) *Ethics and the New Testament*. London and Oxford: Mowbrays.

Howard, George (1979) *Paul: Crisis in Galatia: A Study in Early Christian Theology*. Cambridge: Cambridge University Press.

Hübner, Hans (1984) *Law in Paul's Thought*. ET of 1978 German original. Edinburgh: T. and T. Clark.

Hultgren, Arland J. (1976) 'Paul's Pre-Christian Persecutions of the Church: Their Purpose, Locale, and Nature', *JBL* 95: 97–111.

Hurtado, Larry W. (1988) *One God One Lord: Early Christian Devotion and Ancient Jewish Monotheism*. London: SCM Press Ltd.

Jefferson, Ann and Robey, David (1986) *Modern Literary Theory: A Comparative Introduction*. Second edition. London: B. T. Batsford Ltd.

Jenkins, Richard (1996) *Social Identity: Key Ideas*. London and New York: Routledge.

Jewett, Robert (1970–1971) 'The Agitators and the Galatian Congregation', *NTS* 17: 213–226.

Joubert, Stephan J. (1995) 'Managing the Household: Paul as *Paterfamilias* in the Christian Household Group in Corinth', in Esler ed. 1995a: 213–223.

Käsemann, Ernst (1969a) *New Testament Questions of Today*. London: SCM Press.

—— (1969b) 'The "Righteousness of God" in Paul', in Käsemann 1969a: 168–183.

—— (1980) *Commentary on Romans*. Grand Rapids, MI: William B. Eerdmans Publishing Company.

Kelly, J. N. D. (1977) *Early Christian Doctrines*. Fifth edition. London: Adam and Charles Black.

Kennedy, George A. (1963) *The Art of Persuasion in Greece*. Princeton: Princeton University Press.

—— (1980) *The Art of Rhetoric in the Roman World*. Princeton: Princeton University Press.

—— (1984) *New Testament Interpretation through Rhetorical Criticism*. London: Chapel Hill.

Kinneavy, James L. (1983) 'Contemporary Rhetoric', in Horner ed. 1983: 167–170.

—— (1987) *The Greek Rhetorical Origins of Christian Faith: An Enquiry*. Oxford: Oxford University Press.

Kirk, G. S. and Raven, J. E. (1971) *The Presocratic Philosophers*. Cambridge: Cambridge University Press.

Knox, John (1989) *Chapters in a Life of Paul*. Revised by the author and edited and introduced by Douglas R. A. Hare. London: SCM Press Ltd.

Kümmel, Werner Georg (1929) *Römer 7 und die Bekehrung des Paulus*. Leipzig: Hinrichs'sche.

Lagrange, M. J. (1926) *Saint Paul: Épître aux Galates*. Paris: Gabalda.

—— (1931) *Saint Paul: Épître aux Romains*. Paris: Gabalda.

Lambrecht, Jan (1991) 'Transgressor by Nullifying God's Grace: A Study of Galatians 2.18–21', *Biblica* 72: 217–236.

—— (1996) 'Paul's Reasoning in Galatians 2.11–21', in Dunn ed. 1996: 53–74.

Lassen, Eva Marie (1997) 'The Roman Family: Ideal and Metaphor', in Moxnes ed. 1997a: 103–120.

Levick, Barbara (1967) *Roman Colonies in Southern Asia Minor*. Oxford: The Clarendon Press.

Lightfoot, J. B. (1914) *Saint Paul's Epistle to the Galatians: A Revised Text with Introduction, Notes, and Dissertations*. London: Macmillan and Co.

Lim, Timothy (1997) *Holy Scripture in the Qumran Commentaries and Pauline Letters*. Oxford: The Clarendon Press.

Lindbeck, George A. (1984) *The Nature of Doctrine: Religion and Theology in a Post-liberal Age*. London: SPCK.

Lissarrague, François (1990) 'Around the Krater: An Aspect of Banquet Imagery', in Murray ed. 1990: 196–209.

Longenecker, Bruce W. (1996) 'Defining the Faithful Character of the Covenant Community: Galatians 2.15–21 and Beyond: A Response to Jan Lambrecht', in Dunn ed. 1996: 75–97.

Love, Stuart L. (1995) 'Women and Men at Hellenistic Symposia Meals in Luke', in Esler ed. 1995a: 198–210.

Lull, D. J. (1986) 'The Law was our Pedagogue: A Study in Galatians 3.19–25', *JBL* 105: 481–498.

Lütgert, W. (1919) *Gesetz und Geist. Eine Untersuchung zur Vorgeschichte des Galaterbriefes*. Gütersloh: Bertelsman.

Lyons, George (1985) *Pauline Autobiography: Toward a New Understanding*. SBLDS 73. Atlanta, GA: Scholars Press.

Lyotard, J.-F. (1984) *The Postmodern Condition*. Manchester: Manchester University Press.

McDonald, Lee M. (1995) *The Formation of the Christian Biblical Canon*. Revised and expanded version. Peabody, MA: Hendrickson.

Mack, Burton L. (1988) *A Myth of Innocence: Mark and Christian Origins*. Philadelphia, PA: Fortress Press.

McKane, William (1970) *Proverbs: A New Approach*. Old Testament Library. London: SCM Press Ltd.

McKnight, Scot (1991) *A Light Among the Gentiles: Jewish Missionary Activity in the Second Temple Period*. Minneapolis, MN: Fortress Press.

Malherbe, A. J. (1970) 'Gentle as a Nurse: The Cynic Background of 1 Thess. 2', *NovT* 12: 203–217. Reprinted in Malherbe 1989: 35–48.

—— (1988) *Ancient Epistolary Theorists*. SBLSBS 19. Missoula, MY: Scholars Press.

—— (1989) *Paul and the Popular Philosophers*. Minneapolis, MN: Fortress Press.

Malina, Bruce J. (1993) *The New Testament World: Insights from Cultural Anthropology*. Revised edition. Louisville, KY: Westminster/John Knox.

—— (1996) 'Reading Theory Perspectives', in his *The Social World of Jesus and the Gospels*. London and New York: Routledge, 3–31.

Malina, Bruce J. and Neyrey, Jerome H. (1991) 'Conflict in Luke–Acts: Labelling and Deviance Theory', in Neyrey ed. 1991: 97–122.

—— (1996) *Portraits of Paul: An Archaeology of Ancient Personality*. Louisville, KY: Westminster/John Knox Press.

Marrou, H. I. (1956) *A History of Education in Antiquity*. ET by George Lamb. New York: Sheed and Ward.

Marshall, I. Howard (1982) 'Pauline Theology in the Thessalonian Correspondence', in Hooker and Wilson eds 1982: 173–183.

Martyn, J. Louis (1986) 'A Law-Observant Mission to Gentiles: The Background of Galatians', *SJT* 38: 307–324.

Marxsen, Willi (1993) *New Testament Foundations for Christian Ethics*. ET by O. C. Dean. Philadelphia, PA: Fortress.

Matera, Frank J. (1992) *Galatians*. Sacra Pagina 9. Collegeville, MN: The Liturgical Press.

Matson, David Lertis (1996) *Household Conversion Narratives in Acts: Pattern and Interpretation*. *JSNT* Supplementary Series 123. Sheffield: Sheffield Academic Press.

Michaelis, Wilhelm (1968) 'parapiptō, paraptōma', *TDNT* 6: 170–172.

Miller, G. and Steinberg, M. (1975) *Between People*. Chicago, IL: Science Research Associates.

Mitchell, Margaret M. M. (1991) *Paul and the Rhetoric of Reconciliation: An Exegetical Investigation of the Language and Composition of 1 Corinthians*. Hermeneutische Untersuchungen zur Theologie 28. Tübingen: J. C. B. Mohr (Paul Siebeck).

Mitchell, Stephen (1993) *Anatolia: Land, Men, Gods in Asia Minor. Vol. I. The Celts in Anatolia and the Impact of Roman Rule*. Oxford: The Clarendon Press.

Moore, George Foot (1921) 'Christian Writers on Judaism', *HTR* 14: 197–254.

—— (1927) *Judaism in the First Centuries of the Christian Era. The Age of the Tannaim*. 3 vols. Cambridge, MA: Harvard University Press.

Morgan, Robert ed. (1989) *The Religion of the Incarnation: Anglican Essays in Commemoration of Lux Mundi*. Bristol: Bristol Classical Press.

Morgan, Robert with Barton, John (1988) *Biblical Interpretation*. Oxford: Oxford University Press.

Moule, C. F. D. (1959) *An Idiom Book of New Testament Greek*. Second edition. Cambridge *et alibi*: Cambridge University Press.

—— (1967–1968) 'Fulfilment Words in the New Testament: Use and Abuse', *NTS* 14: 293–320.

Moxnes, Halvor (1991) 'Patron–Client Relations and the New Community in Luke–Acts', in Neyrey ed. 1991: 241–268.

—— (1995) 'The Quest for Honor and the Unity of the Community in Romans 12 and in the Orations of Dio Chrysostom', in T. Engberg-Pedersen ed. 1995 *Paul in His Hellenistic Context*. Edinburgh: T. and T. Clark, 216–229.

—— ed. (1997a) *Constructing Early Christian Families: Family as Social Reality and Metaphor*. London and New York: Routledge.

—— (1997b) Review of Barton 1994, in *Biblical Interpretation* 5: 212–214.

Murphy-O'Connor OP, Jerome (1996) *Paul: A Critical Life*. Oxford: The Clarendon Press.

Murray, Oswyn ed. (1990) *Sympotica: A Symposium on the Symposion*. Oxford: The Clarendon Press.

—— (1996a) '*Convivium*', *OCD*: 387.

—— (1996b) '*Symposion*', *OCD*: 1461.

Nadeau, Ray (1952) 'The Progymnasmata of Aphthonius in Translation', *Speech Monographs* 19: 264–285.

Nanos, Mark D. (1996) *The Mystery of Romans: The Jewish Context of Paul's Letter*. Minneapolis, MN: Fortress Press.

—— (1997) 'Intruding "Spies" and "Pseudo" Brethren: The Intra-Jewish Context of "those of repute" in Jerusalem (Gal. 2.1–10)'. Delivered at the SNTS conference in Birmingham in August 1997.

Neyrey, Jerome H. (1990) *Paul in Other Worlds: A Cultural Reading of His Letters*. Louisville: Westminster/John Knox.

—— ed. (1991) *The Social World of Luke–Acts: Models for Interpretation*. Peabody, MA: Hendrickson.

—— (1994) 'Josephus' Vita and the Encomium: A Native Model of Personality', *JSJ* 25: 177–206.

—— (1995) 'Loss of Wealth, Loss of Family and Loss of Honour: The Cultural Context of the Original Makarisms in Q', in Esler ed. 1995a: 139–158.

Nicholas, Barry (1962) *An Introduction to Roman Law*. Oxford: The Clarendon Press.

Oberg, K. (1960) 'Culture Shock: Adjustment to New Cultural Environments', *Practical Anthropology* 7: 177–182.

O'Neill, J. C. (1972) *The Recovery of Paul's Letter to the Galatians*. London: SPCK.

Overman, J. Andrew (1990) *Matthew's Gospel and Formative Judaism: The Social World of the Matthean Community*. Minneapolis, MN: Fortress Press.

Pelletier, André (1962) *Lettre d'Aristée à Philocrate. Introduction, Texte Critique, Traduction et Notes, Index Complet des Mots Grecs*. Sources Chrétiennes 89. Paris: Les Éditions du Cerf.

Perelman, Chaim and Olbrechts-Tyteca, Lucie (1969) *The New Rhetoric: A Treatise on Argumentation*. Notre Dame: University of Notre Dame Press. (First published in French in 1958.)

Peristiany, J. G. ed. (1965) *Honour and Shame: The Values of Mediterranean Society*. London: Weidenfeld and Nicolson.

Peristiany, J. G. and Pitt-Rivers, J. eds (1992) *Honour and Grace in Anthropology*. Cambridge: Cambridge University Press.

Pilch, John J. (1983) *Galatians and Romans*. Collegeville Bible Commentary. Vol. 6. Collegeville, MN: The Liturgical Press.

—— (1993) 'Jews or Judeans: A Translation Challenge', *Modern Liturgy* 20:19.

—— (1996) 'Jews and Christians: Anachronisms in Bible Translation', *Professional Approaches for Christian Educators* 25:18–25.

—— (1997) 'Are There Jews and Christians in the Bible?' *Hervormde Teologiese Studies* 53:1–7.

Pilch, John J. and Malina, Bruce J. eds (1993) *Biblical Social Values and Their Meanings: A Handbook*. Peabody, MA: Hendrickson.

Pitt-Rivers, Julian (1965) 'Honour and Social Status', in Peristiany ed. 1965: 19–77.

Pogoloff, Stephen Mark (1992) *Logos and Sophia: The Rhetorical Situation of 1 Corinthians*. SBLDS 134. Atlanta, GA: Scholars Press.

Pomeroy, Sarah B. (1975) *Goddesses, Whores, Wives and Slaves: Women in Classical Antiquity*. New York: Schocken Books.

Porton, Gary G. (1988) *Goyim: Gentiles and Israelites in Mishnah-Tosefta*. Atlanta, GA: Scholars Press.

Procksch, Otto (1964) 'hagios, hagiazō, hagiasmos, hagiotēs, hagiōsunē', *TDNT* 1: 88–115.

Przybylski, Benno (1980) *Righteousness in Matthew and His World of Thought*. Cambridge: Cambridge University Press.

Rabe, Hugo ed. (1995 [1931]) *Prolegomenon Sylloge: Accedit Maximi Libellus de Obiectionibus Insolubilibus. Rhetores Graeci*. Vol. 14. Stuttgart and Leipzig: Teubner.

Rad, Gerhard von (1972) *Genesis: A Commentary*. Revised edition. London: SCM Press Ltd.

Räisänen, Heikki (1986) *Paul and the Law*. Philadelphia, PA: Fortress Press.

—— (1994) Review of Wright 1991, in *SJT* 47: 117–119.

Ramsay, William Mitchell (1922) 'Studies in the Roman Province of Galatia. III. Imperial Government of the Province Galatia', *JRS* 12: 147–186.

Rapport, Nigel J. (1993) *Diverse Worldviews in an English Village*. Edinburgh: Edinburgh University Press.

Rawson, Beryl ed. (1986) *The Family in Ancient Rome: New Perspectives*. Ithaca, NY: Cornell University Press.

Reed, Jeffrey T. (1994) 'The Use of Rhetorical Conventions in Graeco-Roman Letter Writing'. Paper presented at the British New Testament Conference, Nottingham, September 1994.

Rensberger, David (1988) *Overcoming the World: Politics and Community in the Gospel of John*. London: SPCK.

Reumann, John (1982) *'Righteousness' in the New Testament: 'Justification' in the United States Lutheran–Roman Catholic Dialogue*. Philadelphia and New York: Fortress and Paulist.

—— (1992) 'Righteousness', *ABD* 5: 745–772.

Robbins, Vernon K. (1995) 'Social-Scientific Criticism and Literary Studies: Prospects for Cooperation in Biblical Studies', in Esler ed. 1995a: 274–289.

—— (1996) *The Tapestry of Early Christian Discourse: Rhetoric, Society and Ideology*. London and New York: Routledge.

Roberts, R. H. and Good, J. M. M. eds (1993) *The Recovery of Rhetoric: Persuasive Discourse and Disciplinarity in the Human Sciences*. Charlottesville and London: University Press of Virginia.

Roberts, W. Rhys (1924) *Rhetorica*, in W. D. Ross ed. 1924 *The Works of Aristotle Translated into English under the Editorship of W. D. Ross*. Oxford: The Clarendon Press (not paginated).

Robinson, Peter ed. (1996) *Social Groups and Identities: Developing the Legacy of Henri Tajfel*. Oxford: Butterworth Heinemann.

Rohrbaugh, Richard L. (1995) 'Legitimating Sonship – A Test of Honour: A Social-Scientific Study of Luke 4.1–30', in Esler ed. 1995a: 183–197.

Ropes, J. H. (1929) *The Singular Problem of the Epistle to the Galatians*. Cambridge, MA: Harvard University Press.

Rüegg, Walter (1993) 'Rhetoric and Anti-Rhetoric in the Nineteenth- and Twentieth-Century Human Sciences in Germany', in Roberts and Good eds 1993: 87–100.

Russell, D. A. and Wilson, N. G. (1981) *Menander Rhetor*. New York: Oxford University Press.

Sampley, J. Paul (1980) *Pauline Partnership in Christ: Christian Community and Commitment in the Light of Roman Law*. Philadelphia, PA: Fortress Press.

Sanders, E. P. (1977) *Paul and Palestinian Judaism*. Philadelphia, PA: Fortress Press.

—— (1983) *Paul, the Law and the Jewish People*. Philadelphia, PA: Fortress Press.

—— (1990a) 'Jewish Association with Gentiles and Galatians 2.11–14', in Robert T. Fortna and Beverly R. Gaventa eds 1990 *The Conversation Continues: Studies in Paul and John in Honour of J. Louis Martyn*. Nashville: Abingdon Press, 170–188.

—— (1990b) *Jewish Law from Jesus to the Mishnah: Five Studies*. London and Philadelphia: SCM Press/Trinity Press International.

—— (1992) *Judaism: Practice and Belief 63 BCE–66 CE*. London and Philadelphia: SCM Press/Trinity Press International.

Saussure, Ferdinand de (1974) (1st edition 1915) *Course in General Linguistics*. London: Fontana.

Schlier, Heinrich (1964a) 'hairesis', *TDNT* 1: 180–185.

—— (1964b) 'dichostasia', *TDNT* 1: 514.

Schmithals, W. (1972) *Paul and the Gnostics*. ET by J. E. Steely. Nashville: Abingdon Press.

Schneemelcher, Wilhelm (1991) *New Testament Apocrypha. I. Gospels and Related Writings*. Revised edition. ET edited by R. McL. Wilson. Cambridge and Louisville, KY: James Clarke and Co and Westminster/John Knox Press.

Schneider, Johannes (1967) 'parabainō' etc., *TDNT* 5: 736–744.

Schrage, Wolfgang (1988) *The Ethics of the New Testament*. ET by David E. Green. Philadelphia, PA: Fortress.

Schrenk, G. (1964) 'dikē, dikaios, dikaiosynē' etc., *TDNT* 2: 178–225.

Schweitzer, Albert (1931) *The Mysticism of Paul the Apostle*. ET by William Montgomery. London: A. and C. Black, Ltd.

Scullard, Howard H. (1961) *A History of the Roman World from 753 to 146 BC*. 3rd edition. London: Methuen and Co Ltd.

Scullion, J. J. (1992) 'Righteousness (Old Testament)', *ABD* 5: 724–736.

Segal, Alan F. (1990) *Paul the Convert: The Apostolate and Apostasy of Saul the Pharisee*. New Haven and London: Yale University Press.

Shannon, C. and Weaver, W. (1949) *The Mathematical Theory of Communication*. Champaign, Illinois: University of Illinois Press.

Sherif, M. (1966) *Group Conflict and Cooperation: Their Social Psychology*. London: Routledge and Kegan Paul.

Shils, E. (1957) 'Primordial, Personal, Sacred, and Civil Ties', *British Journal of Sociology* 8: 130–145.

Shutt, R. J. H. (1985) '*Letter of Aristeas*: A New Translation and Introduction', in Charlesworth ed. 1985. Vol. 2: 7–34.

Smit, Joop (1989) 'The Letter of Paul to the Galatians: A Deliberative Speech', *NTS* 35: 1–26.

Smith, Morton (1967) 'The Reason for the Persecution of Paul and the Obscurity of Acts', in E. E. Urbach, R. J. Zwi Werblowski and Chaim Wirszubski eds 1967 *Studies on Mysticism and Religion, Presented to Gershom G. Scholem on his Seventieth Birthday by Pupils, Colleagues, and Friends*. Jerusalem: Magnes Press, 261–268.

Smith, Peter B. and Bond, Michael Harris (1993) *Social Psychology Across Cultures: Analysis and Perspectives*. New York *et alibi*: Harvester Wheatsheaf.

Snaith, H. N. (1944) *The Distinctive Ideas of the Old Testament*. London: The Epworth Press.

Solomon, Robert C. (1993) *Ethics and Character: Cooperation and Integrity in Business*. The Ruffin Series in Business Ethics. New York and Oxford: Oxford University Press.

Stanton, Graham (1996) 'The Law of Moses and the Law of Christ – Galatians 3.1–6.2', in Dunn ed. 1996: 99–116.

Stark, Rodney (1996) *The Rise of Christianity: A Sociologist Reconsiders History*. Princeton, NJ: Princeton University Press.

Steinbauer, Friedrich (1979) *Melanesian Cargo Cults: New Salvation Movements in the South Pacific*. ET by Max Wohlhill. Brisbane: Queensland University Press.

Stendahl, Krister (1963) 'The Apostle Paul and the Introspective Conscience of the West', *HTR* 56: 199–215. Reprinted in Stendahl 1977: 78–96.

—— (1977) *Paul Among Jews and Gentiles*. London: SCM Press. (First published in the USA by Fortress in 1976.)

Stern, Menahem (1974–1980) *Greek and Latin Authors on Jews and Judaism*. Two volumes. Jerusalem: The Israel Academy of Sciences and Humanities.

Stowers, Stanley K. (1986) *Letter Writing in Greco-Roman Antiquity*. Library of Early Christianity. Ed. Wayne A. Meeks. Philadelphia, PA: The Westminster Press.

Tajfel, Henri (1972) 'La catégorisation sociale', in S. Moscovici ed. 1972 *Introduction à la Psychologie Sociale*. Vol. 1. Paris: Larousse, 272–302.

—— (1978) *Differentiation between Social Groups: Studies in the Social Psychology of Intergroup Relations*. London *et alibi*: Academic Press.

—— (1981) 'Social Stereotypes and Social Groups', in John C. Turner and Howard Giles eds 1981 *Intergroup Behaviour*. Oxford: The Clarendon Press, 144–167.

Tajfel, Henri and Turner, J. C. (1979) 'An Integrative Theory of Intergroup Conflict', in W. G. Austin and S. Worchel eds 1979 *The Social Psychology of Intergroup Relations*. Monterey, CA: Brooks-Cole, 33–47.

—— (1986) 'The Social Identity Theory of Intergroup Conflict', in S. Worchel and W. G. Austin eds (1986) *Psychology of Intergroup Relations*. Chicago, IL: Nelson-Hall, 7–24.

Taylor, Charles (1989) *The Sources of the Self: The Making of Modern Identity*. Cambridge: Cambridge University Press.

Taylor, G. A. (1966) 'The Function of *Pistis Christou* in Galatians', *JBL* 85: 58–76.

Thielman, Frank (1989) *From Plight to Solution: A Jewish Framework for Understanding Paul's View of the Law in Galatians and Romans*. *NovT* Supplementary Series 61. Leiden: E. J. Brill.

Tigay, Jeffrey H. (1986) *You Shall Have No Other Gods: Israelite Religion in the Light of Hebrew Inscriptions*. Atlanta, GA: Scholars Press.

Tomson, Peter J. (1990) *Paul and the Jewish Law: Halakha in the Letters of the Apostle to the Gentiles*. *Compendium Rerum Iudaicarum ad Novum Testamentum. Section III. Jewish Traditions in Early Christian Literature*. Volume 1. Assen/Maastricht and Minneapolis: Van Orcum and Fortress Press.

Trebilco, Paul R. (1991) *Jewish Communities in Asia Minor*. SNTSMS 69. Cambridge: Cambridge University Press.

Triandis, H. C. (1989) 'The Self and Social Behaviour in Different Cultural Contexts', *Psychological Review* 96: 506–520.

Triandis, H. C., Bontempo, R., Villareal, M.J., Asai, M. and Lucca, N. (1988) 'Individualism and Collectivism: Cross-Cultural Perspectives on Self-Group Relationships', *Journal of Personality and Social Psychology* 54: 323–338.

Trompf, Gary W. (1991) *Melanesian Religion*. Cambridge: Cambridge University Press.

—— (1994) *Payback: The Logic of Reciprocity in Melanesian Religions*. Cambridge: Cambridge University Press.

Tuckett, Christopher (1992) 'Atonement in the NT', *ABD* 1: 518–522.

Tyson, Joseph B. (1968) 'Paul's Opponents in Galatia', *NovT* 10: 241–254.

Uprichard, R. E. H. (1979) 'Person and Work of Christ in 1 Thessalonians', *Irish Biblical Studies* 1: 19–27.

Van Gennep, Arnold (1960) *The Rites of Passage*. ET by Monika B. Vizedom and Gabrielle L. Caffee. Chicago, IL: University of Chicago Press.

Vatz, Richard E. (1973) 'The Myth of the Rhetorical Situation', *Philosophy and Rhetoric* 6: 154–161.

Vellacott, Philip (1961) *Aeschylus: Prometheus Bound, The Suppliants, Seven Against Thebes and The Persians*. London: Penguin Books.

Verseput, D. J. (1993) 'Paul's Gentile Mission and the Jewish Christian Community: A Study of the Narrative in Galatians 1 and 2', *NTS* 39: 36–58.

Vickers, Brian (1993) 'The Recovery of Rhetoric: Petrarch, Erasmus, Perelman', in Roberts and Good eds 1993: 25–48.

Vogels, Henricius Iosephus ed. (1969) *Ambrosiastri Qui Dicitur Commentarius in Epistulas Paulinas. Pars Tertia. In Epistulas ad Galatas etc*. Vindobonae: Hoelder-Pichler-Tempsky.

Vouga, François (1988) 'Zur rhetorischen Gattung des Galaterbriefes', *ZNW* 79: 291–292.

Wallman, Sandra ed. (1992) *Contemporary Futures: Perspectives from Social Anthropology*. ASA Monographs 30. London and New York: Routledge.

Watson, Duane F. ed. (1991) *Persuasive Artistry: Studies in Rhetoric in Honor of George A. Kennedy*. Sheffield: JSOT Press.

Watson, Francis (1994) *Text, Church and World: Biblical Interpretation in Theological Perspective*. Edinburgh: T. and T. Clark.

—— (1997) *Text and Truth: Redefining Biblical Theology*. Edinburgh: T. and T. Clark.

Watson, Nigel M. (1960) 'Some Observations on the Use of DIKAIOŌ in the Septuagint', *JBL* 79: 255–266.

Watzlawick, P., Beavin, J. and Jackson, D. (1967) *The Pragmatics of Human Communication*. New York: Norton.

Weiser, Artur (1962) *The Psalms: A Commentary*. ET by Herbert Hartwell from fifth revised German edition. London: SCM Press Ltd.

Westerholm, Stephen (1988) *Israel's Law and the Church's Faith: Paul and His Recent Interpreters*. Grand Rapids, MI: William B. Eerdmans Publishing Company.

White, J. L. (1986) *Light from Ancient Letters*. Philadelphia, PA: Fortress.

White, L. M. (1990) *Building God's House in the Roman World. Architectural Adaptation among Pagans, Jews, and Christians*. The ASOR Library of Biblical and Near Eastern Archaeology. Baltimore and London: Johns Hopkins.

Wilckens, Ulrich (1972) 'hypokrinomai' etc., *TDNT* 8: 559–571.

Witherington III, Ben (1997) *Grappling with Grace in Galatia: A Socio-Rhetorical Commentary on Galatians*. Edinburgh: T. and T. Clark.

Wittgenstein, Ludwig (1967) *Philosophical Investigations*. ET by G. E. M. Anscombe. Oxford: Blackwell.

Worsley, Peter (1957) *The Trumpet Shall Sound: A Study of 'Cargo' Cults in Melanesia*. London: MacGibbon and Kee Ltd.

Wrede, W. (1907) *Paul*. ET by Edward Lummis. London: Philip Green.

Wright, N. T. (1991) *The Climax of the Covenant: Christ and the Law in Pauline Theology*. Edinburgh: T. and T. Clark.

—— (1992) *The New Testament and the People of God*. London: SPCK.

—— (1994) 'Gospel and Theology in Galatians', in L. Ann Jervis and Peter Richardson eds (1994) *Gospel in Paul: Studies On Corinthians, Galatians and Romans for Richard N. Longenecker*. Sheffield: Sheffield Academic Press, 222–239.

Yamba, C. Bawa (1992) 'Going There and Getting There: The Future as a Legitimating Charter for Life in the Present', in Wallman ed. 1992: 109–123.

Young, Norman H. (1987) 'Paidagogos: The Social Setting of a Pauline Metaphor', *NovT* 29: 150–176.

Young, Robert (1996) *Intercultural Communication: Pragmatics, Genealogy, Deconstruction*. Clevedon, Philadelphia and Adelaide: Multilingual Matters Ltd.

Ziesler, J. A. (1972) *The Meaning of Righteousness in Paul*. Cambridge: Cambridge University Press.

—— (1989) *Paul's Letter to the Romans*. London and Philadelphia, PA: SCM Press/Trinity Press International.

Zulueta, F. de (1946) *The Institutes of Gaius: Text with Critical Notes and Translation*. 2 vols. Oxford: The Clarendon Press.

Index of Ancient Sources

Index of Modern Authors